Cotton Dust

Controlling an Occupational Health Hazard

Cotton Dust

Controlling an Occupational Health Hazard

Joseph G. Montalvo, Jr., EDITOR
United States Department of Agriculture
Southern Regional Research Center

Based on a symposium sponsored by
the ACS Division of
Chemical Health and Safety
at the 181st Meeting of
the American Chemical Society,
Atlanta, Georgia,
March 29–April 3, 1981.

ACS SYMPOSIUM SERIES **189**

AMERICAN CHEMICAL SOCIETY
WASHINGTON, D. C. 1982

Library of Congress Cataloging in Publication Data

Cotton dust.
(ACS symposium series, ISSN 0097-6156; 189)

Includes bibliographies and index.

1. Cotton manufacture—Hygienic aspects—Congresses. 2. Byssinosis—Congresses. 3. Cotton manufacture—Dust control—Congresses.
I. Montalvo, Joseph G., 1937– . II. American Chemical Society. Division of Chemical Health and Safety. III. Series.

RC965.C77C67 363.1'196772 82-6857
ISBN 0-8412-0716-X AACR2 ACSMC8 189 1-341
1982

PRINTED IN THE UNITED STATES OF AMERICA

FOREWORD

The ACS SYMPOSIUM SERIES was founded in 1974 to provide a medium for publishing symposia quickly in book form. The format of the Series parallels that of the continuing ADVANCES IN CHEMISTRY SERIES except that in order to save time the papers are not typeset but are reproduced as they are submitted by the authors in camera-ready form. Papers are reviewed under the supervision of the Editors with the assistance of the Series Advisory Board and are selected to maintain the integrity of the symposia; however, verbatim reproductions of previously published papers are not accepted. Both reviews and reports of research are acceptable since symposia may embrace both types of presentation.

CONTENTS

PREFACE

COTTON DUST IN THE WORKPLACE is a major problem facing the cotton and textile industry. Workers breathing cotton dust may develop byssinosis, a disease that resembles chronic bronchitis and, in its later stages, emphysema. The agent believed to cause the disease is not actually cotton but microscopic foreign matter in the cotton that is released when bales are processed in the mills.

The industry, union, and government are interested in controlling cotton dust in the occupational environment. An OSHA standard is currently in effect limiting the allowable dust concentration in the textile mills and in certain allied industries. One way to reduce dust levels is through enclosed machinery and air filters. Such improvements are costly, however, and even as the mills modernize and reduce dust concentrations, problems concerning byssinosis remain unsolved. Questions concerning compensation for workers who contracted the disease before mills began to reduce dust levels, how smoking affects susceptibility, and what are the causative agent(s) remain unanswered.

Alternative short- and long-term solutions to the problem have been proposed. Washing cotton is a short-term means for reducing the hazard. Apparently the byssinogenic agent can be washed from cotton, but the fiber is rendered somewhat difficult to process into yarn. Long-range approaches to the problem are chemical treatment of raw cotton and prevention of initial contamination at pre-textile mill stages of operation, particularly ginning.

Byssinosis is characterized clinically by shortness of breath, cough, and chest tightness on the first day a worker returns to work after time off (the "Monday-morning" syndrome). The acute byssinotic response has been documented, but the prevalence of chronic respiratory effects in the current population of cotton textile workers is still being debated. The pathogenesis, etiology, and mechanisms of the disease are not readily understood. Bioassay techniques and the use of models closely akin to byssinosis should eventually lead to understanding the disease. A host of byssinogenic agents ranging from chemical species in plant parts such as leaf and bract to microorganisms and microbial products have been suggested. Continued research will undoubtedly provide the ultimate solution to the byssinosis problem.

This book is based on a symposium designed to assess the current perspective and future directions of research to regulate, control, measure, and solve the problem of cotton dust in the workplace. Specific topics discussed include the OSHA standard and court-related decisions, lint cleaning and dust in gins, washing cotton, dust generation in textile mills, measuring dust in the workplace, byssinosis mechanisms, epidemiology, and causative agent analysis. In this volume as in the symposium, the proceedings represent an attempt to present the scope and a balanced view of the occupational hazard due to cotton dust, and they are arranged into four sections: (1) OSHA standard, (2) engineering controls and measurements, (3) etiology and epidemiology, and (4) analysis.

I wish to acknowledge the contributions of the authors and reviewers. I would also like to thank the ACS Division of Chemical Health and Safety for the invitation to organize the symposium, and the Southern Regional Research Center, Agricultural Research Service, USDA, for the support of my participation in this activity.

JOSEPH G. MONTALVO, JR.
Southern Regional Research Center
New Orleans, La.

January 27, 1982

OSHA STANDARD

1

A Historical Perspective on Cotton Dust in the United States Textile Industry

JOHN G. TRITSCH

American Textile Manufacturers Institute, Inc., Washington, D.C. 20036

The American Textile Industry involvement with cotton dust as a workplace hazard began over ten years ago with industry studies to determine whether the industry had such an illness problem. Then followed major dust removal and ventillation efforts. The industry developed a work practices and medical surveillance program which was presented to OSHA. The Labor Department conducted lengthy hearings on numerous standard proposals for controlling cotton dust exposures resulting in the 1978 promulgation of the present OSHA standard. Industry doubts about need for that standard, its feasibility and its capability of solving the dust illness problem coupled with disagreement with claimed cotton dust illness dimensions led to challenge in the courts. Industry belief in ability of medical surveillance and administrative practices in support to reduce greatly or just about eliminate future byssinosis cases. Problems exist with diagnosis of cotton dust illness which complicate compensation awards. Causative agent arrives at the mill in the bale of cotton and industry supports aggressive research efforts to identify cause and seek its removal.

Prior to enactment of the Occupations Safety and Health Act in 1970, the U.S. textile industry had barely become aware of worker problems with cotton dust. There had been a limited awareness abroad in a few countries whose textile operations were older, well established and with visible and obvious high levels of dust featuring their operations. U.S. mill working environments improved considerably with the general advent of industrial air conditioning in the 1950's and the closing of the mills to the outside accompanied by improved air cleaning techniques. Both of these general activities accelerated in the 1960's and 1970's. Few people in the U.S. government or in industry had even heard of the word, "byssinosis", a term used to describe the ailment of sufferers of cotton dust problems.

0097-6156/82/0189-0003$06.00/0

Industry Actions

Late in the 1960's, speculation about raw cotton dust respiratory problems in the U.S. mills was raised in medical journals stimulating investigation by the textile industry. The industry employed the Industrial Health Foundation, an affiliate of the Melon Institute in Pittsburgh, to study the question in 1969. The study covered some twenty companies in four states and no other study either before or since that time covered so many companies(1). The results clearly indicated that there were some individuals who did suffer some adverse affects when exposed to cotton dust and the government was informed of these findings.

The industry then sought to find out what there was about cotton dust that created the problem. The search involved researchers at the Industrial Health Foundation, the Medical University of South Carolina, Tulane University and other institutions. Even staff members of the American Textile Manufacturers Institute became involved. It is unfortunate, but true, that identification of the cause or causes of byssinosis so far continues to elude all research efforts, including those of government, textile industry and cotton producers. Recognizing that the causative agent comes to textile mills in the bales of cotton received from growers, industry representatives, in cooperation with growers and others concerned with cotton, cannot overemphasize how important it is for the Department of Agriculture to expand and accelerate its research programs designed to identify and seek removal of the causative agents(2).

In further recognition of industry responsibilities, efforts were made through the American Textile Manufacturers Institute to develop a set of work practices for industry-wide application to diminish the exposure of individual employees to cotton dust hazards. The comprehensive and stringent series of work practices developed were consolidated into a printed booklet in 1973(3). This publication was distributed widely through the industry. In addition, an industry delegation called on the Secretary of Labor, urging that the recommended practices be established immediately as a mandatory OSHA standard(4). This was not done.

Related in part to these work practices developments, the mills also instituted medical surveillance programs designed to identify those few individuals with a cotton dust sensitivity so that they might be considered for assignment outside the yarn processing areas(3).

On still another front, the industry stepped up its installation of dust cleaning equipment. Expenditures for such installations amounted to hundreds of millions of dollars(5). All these efforts were done by the industry internally and without government help. It may be said without hesitation that the U.S. textile industry today is the most modern, safest and cleanest of any textile industry in the world.

Proposed Standard

While OSHA never accepted the work practices program proposed by the industry as a standard, the Agency issued a proposed rule in December 1976 to replace the original 1 milligram per cubic meter total dust standard for regulating cotton dust exposure(6). The proposal would have set a standard maximum allowable cotton dust level at 0.2 milligrams per cubic meter. During the hearings held in the months of April and May of 1977, numerous ATMI representatives participated. The industry and these witnesses proposed a standard maximum dust levels set at 0.5 milligrams (1.0 for weaving and slashing) backed up with the medical surveillance and work practices programs developed by the industry (5). OSHA again ignored industry recommendations.

New Standard

The Federal Register for June 23, 1978, publicized the OSHA promulgation of the final rule to go into effect September of that year(7). The three level standard of 0.2 milligrams per cubic meter for opening through yarn manufacture, 0.75 milligrams per cutic meter for weaving and slashing and 0.5 milligrams per cubic meter for other operations represented only a minor variation from the 1976 proposal. The industry could not live with what appeared as an insurmountable and infeasible burden. When its request for reconsideration was rejected by the Agency, the industry had no choice but to appeal to the courts.

Court Appeals

Court action was instigated by the industry in the U.S. Court of Appeals for the Fourth Circuit(8). Meanwhile, AFL-CIO also entered suit against the Department of Labor in the Court of Appeals for the District of Columbia Circuit, claiming that the final rule was too lax(9). All court actions eventually were consolidated in one case in the D.C. Circuit Court of Appeals (10).

A stay of the standard was granted effective October 12, 1978, temporarily reinstituting the 10. milligrams per cubic meter of total cotton dust as the sole standard. The industry submitted oral arguments in eloquent briefs emphasizing the infeasibility of the standard, questioning its need and doubting its potential effectiveness, all to no avail. On September 24, 1979, the Court's decision upheld the OSHA standard(11). In a series of orders on January 11, 1980, the court rejected requests for a re-hearing and set in motion the machinery for OSHA to make the standard effective March 27, 1980.

On March 4, 1980, attorneys for ATMI and related petitioners filed a petition with the Supreme Court for a writ of certiorari requesting a review of the action of the D.C. Circuit Court concerning the dust standard. This is the last avenue of relief available through the judicial system. The industry position raised four points: 1) There's a conflict among the circuits as to the showing OSHA must make to establish that its standards are economically feasible. 2) There's a conflict among the circuits whether OSHA must demonstrate the existence of a reasonable relationship between the cost of the standard and the benefits expected from it and as to whether OSHA must demonstrate a reasonable necessity for the standard. 3) This case presents the important question as to the proper role of the reviewing court under the substantial evidence standard of review. 4) The wage guarantee provision concerning respirators exceeds OSHA's statutory authority. In October the Supreme Court accepted the petition for review but declined to include point 3 on evidentiary standards(12).

Briefs and replies were submitted by both sides and oral arguments were heard on January 21, 1981. Shortly after the oral arguments were heard an issue raised by one justice on the relationship of the Supreme Court benzene decision to cotton dust was given treatment in supplementary briefs by all concerned. We are now awaiting the court's decision.

Compliance and Defects in the Standard

Meanwhile, the Agency has been administering enforcement of the standard since March 27, 1980(13). Textile mills have been attempting to meet the various transitional steps required by the standard under the watchful eyes of the OSHA regional administrators and state OSHA plan administrators. This enforcement experience has revealed shortcomings in the standard difficult, if not impossible, to enforce. These defects are itemized briefly below in two basic categories.

First of all, the standard is oriented excessively to exacting specifications rather than performance. Nowhere is this more evident than in the requirements for the measurement of dust levels and exposures and instrumentation to accomplish these measurements. The methods of compliance with the permissable exposure levels offer employers little in the way of options. Even such mundane matters as the signs to be posted, the keeping of records and the education and training of employees are tightly specified. Exacting respirator requirements make reconciliation with sensitive employee relations difficult if not impossible.

The other major category covers requirements defective in a technical or technological sense. Selection of the permissible exposure limits in some cases goes beyond current technological capabilities. In this sense, the standard has been technology forcing. The standard includes within its coverage some operations where cotton dust exposure does not pose a significant risk to employees in those areas. The medical surveillance section even calls for the physician's report to include information that assumes a knowledge of the individual patient for beyond any need related to carrying out the cotton dust standard provisions. Lastly, and perhaps most significant of all, there is no provision for action levels or limits of application of the standard so that the standard has no clear beginning or end.

In closing, permit me to observe that the industry doubts that the cotton dust standard developed by OSHA with its all-encompassing provisions is the answer to a problem that has been grossly exaggerated. The standard has many defects and sooner or later the Agency must engage in supplementary rulemaking to rectify many of them. In view of the fact that the component of cotton dust causing the byssinosis problems comes to the mills already in the cotton bale, research efforts to isolate and remove the causative agent offer the best chance for ultimate solution. This underlines the importance of meetings like this one featuring the exchange of research information. Whatever the outcome, the U.S. textile industry will be certain to perform as a good citizen and to meet its obligations to provide a safe and healthful working place for its employees.

(Since this paper was prepared, two events have occured which are certain to have significant impact on the cotton dust standard. On March 27, 1981, the Department of Labor began rulemaking procedures to give the standard regulatory reconsideration. On June 17, 1981, the Supreme Court rendered its decision upholding the standard as promulgated by OSHA).

Literature Cited

1. Braun, D.C.; Jurgiel, J.A.; Tume, Jiri. "Report on Cotton Dust Research"; Industrial Health Foundation, Inc.: Pittsburgh, Penn., 1971, 1972 and 1973.
2. G.S. Buck, Jr. to William E. Reid; Communication: Jan. 14, 1974.
3. Safety and Health Committee "Work Practices Standard for Raw Cotton Dust"; American Textile Manufacturers Institute: Charlotte, N.C., 1973.
4. Donald Comer to Peter J. Brennan; Communication: Nov. 27, 1973
5. Department of Labor; OSHA Cotton Dust Proceedings Docket No. H-052, 1977.
6. Federal Register, 41, 56498-527.
7. Federal Register, 43, 27350-463.

8. U.S. Court of Appeals 4th Cir. No. 78-1979 ATMI vs Dr. Eula Bingham, Peitition filed June 19, 1978.
9. U.S. Court of Appeals D.C. Cir. No. 78-1562 AFL-CIO vs Ray Marshall, Petition filed June 19, 1978.
10. U.S. Court of Appeals D.C. Cir. No. 78-1562 AFL-CIO vs Ray Marshall Consolidation Ordered Oct. 3, 1978.
11. U.S. Court of Appeals No. 78-1562 AFL-CIO vs Ray Marshall Decided Oct. 24, 1978.
12. Supreme Court of U.S. No. 79-1429 ATMI vs Ray Marshall Petition granted Oct. 6, 1980.
13. Federal Register, 45, 12416-7.

RECEIVED January 20, 1982.

ENGINEERING CONTROLS AND MEASUREMENTS

2

Technology For Pre-Textile Cotton Cleaning

WILLIAM F. LALOR

Cotton Incorporated, Raleigh, NC 27612

When cotton bolls open, the production phase is over and the processing phase begins. At boll opening, the fiber is virtually free of visible foreign matter. Like many natural products, cotton becomes contaminated during the preharvest and harvest periods and has to be cleaned during the processing phase before marketing. This paper is a review of how cotton becomes contaminated, nature of the foreign matter found in cotton, and importance of clean cotton with respect to textile performance of the fiber. Strategies to prevent contamination of cotton during harvesting will be examined. Currently used cleaning techniques will be reviewed and current research to clean cotton will be discussed briefly.

Regulations promulgated by OSHA (1) to limit the amount of cotton dust to which textile workers are exposed, constitute the principal new aspect of cotton cleaning in the 1980s. It should be emphasized, however, that even though high dust levels in mills are associated with high foreign matter levels in lint (2), it is unlikely that any gin-applied cleaning measure will alone permit full compliance with current OSHA standards (3). This leaves researchers with the conclusion that compliance with the OSHA standards will likely be the result of applying several proven dust-control measures during fiber processing (4). Furthermore, a recent publication by Fischer, Morey, and Sasser (5) presents data showing a very poor relationship between visual trash rating of fiber samples and the presence of gram-negative organisms--a possible causative agent of byssinosis. Lint cleaning per se is not therefore likely to solve health problems arising out of cotton-dust exposure but lint cleaning will

0097-6156/82/0189-0011$6.00/0

nevertheless play a prominent roll in the preparation of cotton for markets of the 1980s and beyond.

Trash Constituents

Morey, Sasser, Bethea, and Kopetzky (6) examined and classified the plant parts in Shirley analyzer waste from six raw cottons that had been processed through the model card room at North Carolina State University. Bract, leaf, weeds, veins and endocarp were the major plant parts present. Bract and leaf constituted up to 52 percent of the foreign matter in the cottons they examined. There was evidence that using gin lint cleaners reduced the total trash content but increased the proportion of bract relative to other foreign-matter particles remaining in the fiber.

The leaf-like material in other samples examined was 58 percent bract, 22 percent cotton leaf and 20 percent weed leaf (7). Morey calculated that a bale of cotton could contain the equivalent of up to 50,000 bracts, depending on grade. At harvest time, about three million bracts were found on the plants that would yield harvested material for one bale. The bract removal efficiency of commerical harvesting and ginning is therefore extremely high. Leaflike trash, especially the bract, was shown to be easily subdivided into particles less than 10 microns in size by processing in a laboratory mill (8). Equipment in gins and in textile mills can be expected to produce the same grinding effect. Particles less than 15 microns in size are the target of cotton-dust regulations applicable to areas where cotton is being processed. Preventing processing equipment from creating respirable-size particles from big particles is, therefore, very important.

Preventing Contamination

Because mechanical cleaning of fiber almost always results in some fiber damage, prevention of contamination by foreign matter is preferable to using machines subsequently to remove the contaminants. Preventive cultural practices are therefore of great importance because they have a bearing on the leaf content of harvested material. Approximately one-fourth of the smaller trash particles sifted from Shirley-analyzer waste was found to be monootyledonous and dicotyledonous weed parts (7, 8, 9). Leaf particles are very difficult to remove from the fiber especially if they are from hairy leaves--the leaf hairs become entangled with the cotton fibers. Bract particles are hairy, and they become entangled with fiber for the same reason.

Apart from workplace-related problems like cotton dust, the presence of grass, bark, sand, seeds and seed parts in lint causes grade reduction and associated reductions in the market value of the fiber (10). For instance, unbleachable grass-seed glumes have been found as a disfigurement in finished fabric. The presence of grass causes deterioration in yarn qualitly and an increase in ends down during spinning (11).

Because of the importance of weed parts as a trash component, weed and grass control during the production phase is extremely important. It may be concluded (12) that if there is grass in the field, there is likely to be grass in the fiber. Broad-leaf-weed and grass control in the field provide, therefore, the first effective opportunity available to reduce the foreign matter content of ginned fiber.

The design of production systems for cotton is being re-examined at this time with the objective of ensuring maximum productivity. System-related factors can play important roles in determining the cleanness of cotton. Wanjura and Baker (13) found that row spacing affects the stick content of stripper-harvested cotton--stick content was lower for narrower rows. Varietal characteristics have also been shown to be important. Morey, Sasser, Bethea, and Kopetzky (6) showed that varieties, harvesting methods and ginning procedures affect the type and amount of trash in lint cotton. Some varieties are hairy and lint becomes entangled in leaf hairs, greatly increasing the difficulty of separating the fiber from foreign matter. Openboll types tend to have more small particles entrained in the fiber than do the more storm-proof types which have less-open bolls (14). Because bract content of the foreign matter seems so important, the development of caducous-bract cotton types is receiving particular attention (15).

Irrigation is a factor in cultural practices that are used in the Southwest and West. Irrigation is beginning to be used in other areas. Because irrigated crops tend to have higher moisture content than non-irrigated crops, the foreign matter content of fiber could be affected. Cleaning efficiency is reduced when moisture contents of seed cotton and fiber are elevated during ginning and cleaning (see later). Whether the crop is irrigated or rain grown is also important in determining the preharvest preparation that leads to lowest trash content in ginned lint.

Profit is the motivation for cotton production. Production practices will therefore be responses to market conditions. The extent to which there are premiums for clean cotton and for cotton that is unlikely to produce a lot of dust will determine the production and harvesting practices used. Price will also affect the amount of processing to which the cotton will be submitted before shipment to mills.

Because of cost/profit relationships, for example, harvesting methods vary with cultural practices. About 30 percent of the U. S. cotton crop is stripper-harvested. In Texas, more than 80 percent of the cotton is stripper-harvested because of crop culture, low harvesting cost, and high harvesting capacity associated with strippers.

Large differences in the amount of harvested material required to yield a bale of fiber constitute the main difference between the two harvesting methods. During spindle-picking, about 680 kg of harvested material are gathered to produce one 218-kg bale of fiber. Most of the burs, pendücles and stem material are left on the plant. This method of harvesting is the more commonly used in the irrigated west and in the rainbelt areas of the south and southeast.

Harvesting by means of strippers is practiced mainly in West Texas and the adjoining areas of Oklahoma and New Mexico. This method has also gained great importance in the Coastal Bend area of Texas. Because a stripper harvester (whether a finger stripper or a brush stripper) removes almost all vegetative material from the plant (except for the central stem and major branches), about 1100 kg of harvested material are brought to the gin to yield one 218-kg bale of lint. The lint therefore is approximately one-third of the harvested material in spindle-picked cotton and can be as little as one-fifth in stripper-harvested cotton.

Because of the cost advantages of stripper harvesting, its use is likely to increase. In Mississippi, approximately 25 percent of the total cotton-production cost was attributable to spindle-picker harvesting in 1979 (16). Cost advantages in favor of stripper harvesting and the cultural system that accompanies it are estimated to range from eleven to eighteen cents per kilo of lint (17). The extent of the likely spread of stripper harvesting will depend upon the success achieved by plant breeders and agronomists in developing plant types and cultural systems appropriate for stripper harvesting.

Transplanting cultural practices and harvesting methods from one geographic area to another is not always successful. It is for this reason that there are many reports of stripper-harvested cotton having more trash, more neps, more mill waste and more dust than cotton from the same fields harvested with a spindle picker. When used in the appropriate production system, however, stripper harvesting is an acceptable strategy. The work by Kirk, Corley, Kummer, Brashears, Hudspeth, Laird, and Baker (18-22) should be carefully reviewed in studying applicability of stripper-harvesting techniques to the rain belt areas.

Regardless of harvesting method, skillful management of the crop during the harvest season is essential to keep foreign matter content at a minimum. Using seed cotton storage is one way for farmers to avail themselves of the very best harvesting conditions. Harvesting when the crop is ready is extremely important. The harvesting-ginning system should be such that no producer feels the need to harvest the crop under compromising circumstances in order to gain a place in the queue at the gin.

High moisture content is the single biggest problem that arises because of improper harvesting. Cocke (23) concluded that cotton harvested at high moisture content was extremely difficult to clean and was put at a permanent disadvantage by having been harvested damp. This disadvantage could not be eliminated by use of gin dryers. Dampness at harvest results from rain, or from humidity from dew, or from moisture content of green material harvested with the fiber. The skillful use of preharvest chemicals can reduce green-material content dramatically. Freezing also causes plant tissues to dry out. Unusually dry plants become brittle, however, and lead to other cleaning problems (24, 25).

Some stripper harvesters are equipped with onboard cleaners that have cleaning effectiveness of up to 50 percent. Their cleaning effectiveness depends, however, on machine adjustment and on other factors not yet identified. In one test, big differences in cleaning performance have been shown to exist between identical harvesters operating under identical field conditions (26). This study is continuing and should lead to improved stripper-mounted cleaner performance.

In summary, good management and the application of existing technology to harvesting and handling prior to ginning are the keys to ensuring that the ginning process is given every opportunity to produce the highest quality lint possible.

Ginning

Ginning per se is the process of removing the fiber from the seed. The force required to remove an individual fiber from a seed depends on the variety. Interspecific differences exist also--the lint on pima cotton has lower attachment strength relative to fiber strength than do the upland types examined by Moore and Griffin (27). This characteristic makes pima cotton well suited to roller ginning, which is a method of ginning particularly appropriate for preserving the extra-long-staple fiber properties of pima cottons.

Virtually all of the upland cotton in the United States is ginned by saw gins. In saw ginning, the fibers are engaged by the teeth of the saw and pulled between closely-spaced ribs. The seed is too big to pass between the ribs, and the fiber is consequently pulled from the seed. This is clearly a point at which fiber damage could take place. The graph in Figure 1 (27) shows the relationship between moisture content and the forces required to detach the fiber from the seed and to break the fiber. The height difference between the two curves is the margin of safety between the force that must be applied to detach the fiber and the force that would result in breaking the fiber. This margin of safety can be seen to diminish as moisture content decreases. In the discussions that follow, reference will be made to the desirability of obtaining the optimum drying effect. One factor in the concept of "optimum drying" is that of retaining the greatest margin of safety possible between fiber breakage force and fiber separation force.

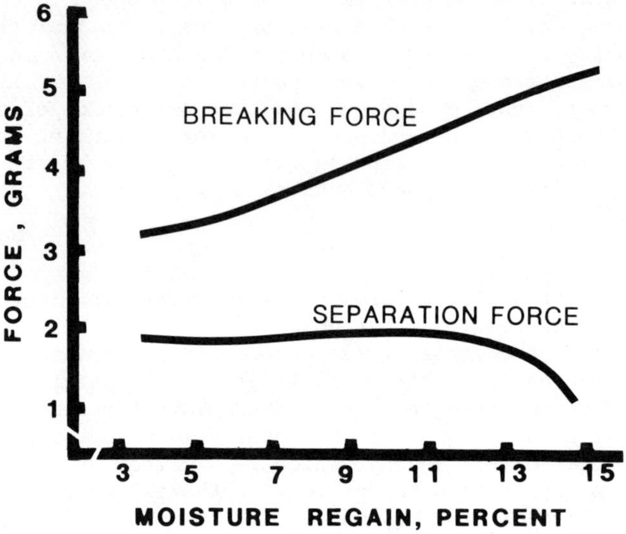

Figure 1. Graphs of relationships between fiber strength (upper), strength of fiber attachment to seed (lower) and percentage moisture regain (dry basis) after partial drying (27).

Cleaning in the Gin

Cleaning elements precede and follow the actual ginning or fiber-seed-separation process. Cleaning before ginning is referred to as seed-cotton cleaning or "overhead cleaning". Lint cleaners follow the gin stands in arrangements that vary from one manufacturer to another.

Overhead Cleaning. A dryer is usually the first item on the seed-cotton side. One effect of a dryer is to increase the cleaning efficiency of cleaners. The dryer, though not a cleaner, is regarded as essential to the proper operation of cleaners. Dryers are discussed in more detail in the lint-cleaner section.

Cylinder cleaners are an important type of seed-cotton cleaner. They remove small trash (16, 28) and operate by scrubbing seed-cotton against a grid-bar grate (inclined cleaner) or by the interaction of an upper and lower set of cylinders (impact cleaner). Cylinder cleaners are well described in the Cotton Ginners Handbook (29).

Cleaners that use a sling-off principle are also found in overhead equipment. In these, saw-wrapped cylinders rotate in relation to grid bars so that the seed cotton is dragged past the grid bars to a doffing brush, but heavy foreign matter is thrown out between the grid bars by the action of centrifugal force. Speed of the cylinders, cylinder-to-grid clearance and grid-to-grid distance are factors having an important bearing on cleaning efficiency. Some seed cotton is usually slung off with the unwanted foreign matter, and this causes the need for a reclaiming cylinder. The extracted (slung-off) material is fed onto the reclaimer cylinder, which is similar in construction to the primary cylinder. The action of this cylinder is to retrieve seed cotton by engaging it with the saw teeth and by slinging off the foreign matter. Kirk's work (20) shows the nature of the reclaiming action and shows that considerable amounts of foreign matter are returned to the mainstream. The conclusion that there must be ways to improve these cleaners is inescapable. Studies now being conducted by Baker seek such improvements (22).

The cleaning efficienty of a stick machine can be over 60 percent but might be less at high feed rates (30). Cleaning efficiencies of up to 90 percent have been observed for the entire seed-cotton cleaning system. Good overhead cleaning was found to reduce the amount of lint cleaning needed to get acceptable results. Two stages of cylinder cleaning are approximately equivalent to one lint cleaner (28). Specific combinations of overhead cleaning equipment vary with the application and, to the extent that recommendations about optimum combinations are possible, they will be found in the Cotton Ginners Handbook (29). Adequate seed-cotton cleaning is important because by avoiding the need to use excessive lint-cleaning stages, fiber damage is also avoided.

Reductions in bur and stick content of stripper-harvested cotton before actual ginning are important for two reasons. First, gins can operate at higher hourly output than when trash content is not substantially reduced. Second, bark-contaminated samples are easier to avoid if most sticks have been removed before entering the gin stand. Under some circumstances, however, extreme brittleness of the sticks can permit them to be broken by cleaners (even though they are mostly removed) and this could lead to increased bark (31). This situation likely relates to timeliness of application of pre-harvest chemicals and to other factors that affect brittleness of the plants.

Ginning rate per hour and the percentage of theoretical ginning rate attained are cost-related factors of importance to ginners. Power and labor costs, for example, are approximately inversely proportional to ginning rate. To gain hourly capacity, ginners sometimes dry cotton more than is desirable (see Figure 1), and the cleaning equipment is sometimes overloaded and thus operated at lower efficiency. Part of the reason for hurried ginning stems from the need for rapid harvesting--about 65 percent of the crop can arrive at some gins in a 20-day period. Any harvesting system that avoids the need for very rapid ginning, would be conducive to more effective cleaning. A harvesting system that includes seed-cotton storage is thus desirable.

Lint Cleaning. Lint cleaning follows ginning and has a marked effect on fiber quality as reflected by classer's grade and also by spinning performance. Fiber damage often occurs during lint cleaning, especially if lint moisture is low--below five to six percent. Trash removal by mill carding, for example, is more effective and causes less fiber damage than does trash removal by lint cleaners. A lint cleaner, however, sometimes operates at about 1120 kg/hr per meter of cleaning-cylinder width wheras a card operates at about 30 kg/m/hr. This striking difference between mill and gin processing rates characterizes the operational dissimilarities between these two phases of operation.

Mangialardi (32) studied the relationship between lint-cleaner efficiency and lint-cleaner loading. He found that a thin batt, combined with a high combing ratio, resulted in good lint grades and (often) in highest revenue per unit of material harvested. (Combing ratio is the speed of the lint cleaner saw relative to the speed of the cotton batt being fed onto the saw by the feed-roll-feed-plate assembly.)

The damage occurring during gin lint cleaning consists of fiber breakage (increased short-fiber percentage) and nep formation. Neps are entanglements of fiber that disfigure yarn and fabric. Lint that has not been through a saw-type lint cleaner has been found to have fewer card-web neps and a better length uniformity than cleaned cotton. Provided trash content is not high enough to lead to poor yarn quality and to manufacturing defects, the minimum amount of lint cleaning at gins and mills results in the best yarn. Spinning production rates have been found to parallel fiber quality (25). Increased lint-cleaner saw speed breaks fiber and causes neps (32), thus reducing spinning productivities. Reduced feed rates lead to an increase in lint cleaner efficiency and to improved grades without sacrificing fiber length or producing neps. This means higher spinning productivity.

Dust levels in card rooms have been shown to be reduced by use of successive lint-cleaning stages (33). Most gins (65 percent) have two lint cleaners in series and some (19 percent) had three stages in 1978 (34). Up to three stages of lint cleaning caused continued dust reduction (35, 36) and use of dryers in conjunction with cleaners enhanced their effect (33). At very low moisture, however, fiber damage is significant. An increase of 30 percent in fiber shorter than 12.5 mm was observed when lint moisture was 3.0 percent rather than 5.7 percent at cleaning time.

The factors affecting lint cleaner performance are of interest to gin designers and to gin managers. They have therefore been intensively studied (10, 32, 37). The relationship of cleaning efficiency to combing ratio for several feed rates is shown in Figure 2. Cleaning efficiencies above 70 percent can be achieved by feeding the batts at high combing ratios and high cylinder speeds. Unfortunately these conditions cause high lint wastage, reduced staple length and increased nep content (32). Combing ratios above 30 are difficult to justify in gins (37) but can be used to advantage in mills where feed rate per hour is low.

Grid-bar-to-saw clearance was also found to be important (37). A wide clearance gave poor cleaning while the improved cleaning achieved at narrow clearance was accompanied by fiber loss. The optimum clearance is about 1 mm. Cleaning efficiency also depends on trash content of the entering fiber. The first lint cleaner stage might operate at 35 percent efficiency while the second would operate at 25 percent efficiency in a commerical gin.

Air-jet cleaners are also used in cotton gins. These cleaners separate trash by forcing a rapid change in direction on a fast moving lint stream and allowing the heavy particles of trash to exit through a slit. Their cleaning efficiency is not as high as that of saw-type cleaners, and they do not cause significant reduction in card-room dust levels (36). Air-jet cleaners are valued for their gentle treatment of fiber, hence their widespread use in pima-cotton gins.

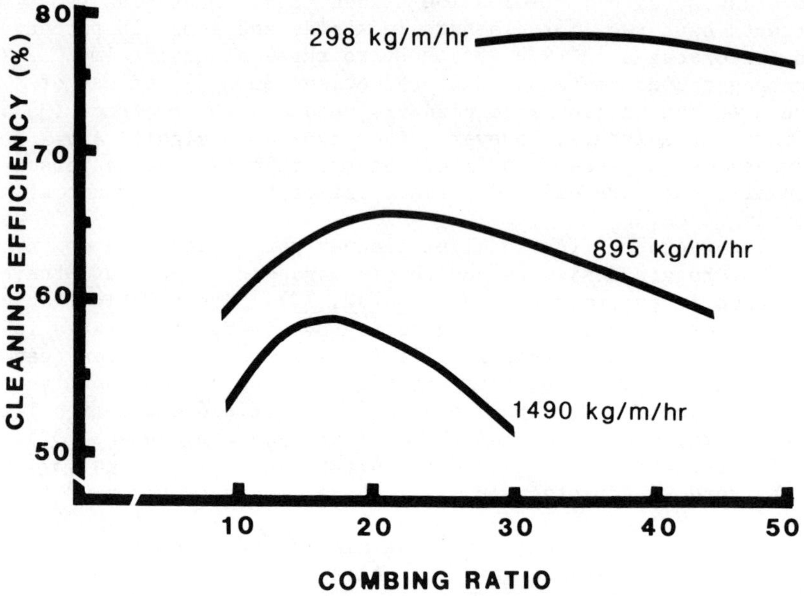

Figure 2. Relationship between cleaning efficiency and combing ratio for three feed rates with constant saw speed (adapted from (37)).

Economic Aspects

Economic considerations play an important role in influencing the amount of cleaning to which cotton is submitted. The ideal situation, from the grower's viewpoint, would be where the results to be achieved by cleaning could be specified to produce maximum revenue. Process control in gins is, however, not yet sufficiently accurate to permit ginning to a specification with respect to either moisture content or trash content of the baled lint. Both factors affect marketable weight per hectare of crop raised. The other factor affecting marketable weight is the fiber loss which occurs at every cleaning operation.

Seed-cotton loss in overhead cleaning equipment can range from 0.2 percent upward (28) but should not be over 1.0 percent. The amount of overhead cleaning machinery needed depends on the trash content of incoming seed cotton. Stripper-harvested cotton with over 30 percent trash can benefit from three extractor stages in addition to the two cylinder stages normally used. Some cotton gins use five stages of cylinder cleaning. The system should, however, have the flexibility to bypass unneeded cleaning stages.

Lint cleaners cause fiber loss--up to six percent has been reported (28). Each additional stage of lint cleaning causes more loss of fiber. Lint cleaners cause reduced value by shortening staple length. Seed-cotton cleaning was not observed to shorten staple (15) or cause neps. For cleaning to be profitable, the increased fiber value because of cleaning should be higher than the losses caused by reduced marketable weight.

The economic aspects of lint cleaners have been examined (38, 39). In some cases, lint cleaning could be inadvisable from an economic standpoint. On the other hand, up to three stages could be appropriate when cotton is very dirty. Some lint cleaning is almost always desirable, but market premiums and discounts for each grade are the determining influence. Mangialardi (38) worked out a decision-aiding system to help growers and ginners make the best choices. One of the big difficulties arises from lint loss during cleaning. The results of an experiment comparing conventional grid bars with notched grid bars in lint cleaners show potential for increasing revenue by about five percent as a result of reducing lint-cleaner waste (39).

Improper use of dryers to enhance cleaning can result in shorter staple because of fiber breakage and in lower marketable weight because of excessive moisture loss (40). Conclusions and recommendations for optimum dryer operation are as follows:

- Overdrying reduces spinning performance.
- Cotton of moisture content seven percent or less should not be dried.

- Cotton of moisture content eight percent or more should be dried.
- Dryers in cotton gins have an important effect on cleaning efficiency of lint cleaners and on dust generation in mills (33).

Because of the importance of lint cleaning and of the way in which lint cleaning and fiber performance are affected by drying, accurate moisture control is important (40, 41). Moisture-control techniques now used in cotton gins are unsatisfactory. The theoretical aspects have been examined and approaches to fiber moisture control have been suggested (42, 43, 44, 45). Research programs now in progress are attempting to bring the benefits of modern electronic technology to bear on the problem.

Management Aspects

Management aspects of harvesting and ginning play a big role in decisions about how machines are operated. Mangialardi (32) pointed out that reduced ginning rate led to better cleaning, improved grades and higher crop value without shortening fiber or causing neps. Griffin reached similar conclusions (41). But ginning rate is a management issue related to the need to reduce power and labor costs and to the need to keep the gin queue as short as possible when all the community's harvesters are operating. Appropriate maintenance and supervision is often lacking during rush periods and, for reasons already alluded to in previous paragraphs, fiber quality can suffer. Seed-cotton storage is a recent technology improvement that permits scheduling of gin operations in a manner to permit greatest control of resources. It gives maximum opportunity for quality control in the ginning operation.

Current Developments

Direct improvement of the lint-cleaning process is likely to result from several efforts now underway. The USDA Ginning Research Laboratories, the Texas Agricultural Experiment Station, Cotton Incorporated and private corporations are engaged in this endeavor. The broad objective of these studies is to find a more effective lint cleaner that does not damage fiber. Apart from the need to control airborne dust for OSHA standards, there is a need to reduce rotor deposits in open-end spinning. There is also a need to compensate for inabilitly of high-speed modern cards to clean fiber as thoroughly as cards operating slower, and there is a need to improve the trade-off point between the desirable and undesirble effects of lint cleaners.

Cleaning-related studies going on at the locations mentioned above include development of moisture-sensing and dryer-control instrumentation and of trash-measuring instruments for use as control-system components in gins. Success in both these areas would result in a cotton ginner's abilitly to exert quality control where it is needed--at the gin. Under the present system, it can take more than a week for grade information to reach the gin. By then it is too late for use as an input to process control. The ideal control system would use feed-forward and feed-back loops to specify the drying effort required and the number and severity of lint cleanings to be used. This would also permit rapid supply of information to cotton growers so that harvesting-system strategies could be altered in response to the end-product quality. Griffin and colleagues at the U.S. Cotton Ginning Research Laboratory at Stoneville, Mississippi are investigating the behavior of unusually strong strains of cotton as they undergo repeated lint cleanings. This is a logical way of trying to exploit the properties that genetics can impart to cotton varieties. High strength fiber might sustain more lint cleaning than normal fiber. Hybrid cotton types show promise of fitting into this category.

Economic and management studies are being conducted under sponsorship of Cotton Incorporated at Texas Tech University. These studies seek to identify ways in which the processing and handling system can be streamlined, with added value to the cotton growers' product and added profit for textile mills. The textile scene has changed during recent decades (Table I) and

TABLE I
Changes in Textile Processing Rates

Process	1960	1980
Carding (kg/hr)	3.6-5.5	82
Drawing (m/min)	60-120	600
Roving Spindle Speed (r/m)	500-900	1800
Ring Spinning (m/min)	3.5-5.0	7.0
Weaving (picks/min)	120-200	600
Open-end-spinning (m/min)	---	46

full compensation to adapt cotton to these changes has not been accomplished. Better cleaning is needed, better fiber properties are needed and cotton-bale lots with even-running, predictable properties are needed. Table II (46) shows how technology has changed over the past three decades to accomplish the cleaning needed. This is the period during which the mechanical harvesting of cotton grew from almost zero percent to one hundred percent in the U. S.

TABLE II

Foreign-matter Percentage in Three Grades of Cotton

Year	Grade		
	M(31)	SLM(41)	LM(51)
1947	4.6	5.5	7.8
1952	3.3	4.8	6.8
1958	2.3	3.4	4.7
1962	2.0	2.7	4.3
1967	2.2	3.0	4.6
1972	2.1	2.8	3.9
1977	2.4	3.1	4.2
1980[a]	2.3	3.0	4.1

[a]Data for 1980 (unpublished), by private communication with Bobby E. Phillips, Cotton Division, USDA, AMS, Memphis, Tennessee.

The technology with which cotton is now processed between the field and the mill was developed before the energy crisis, before OSHA, before EPA, before wage-and-hour laws, before open-end-spinning, before electronic data processing and before economical seed-cotton storage. That is to say that it predates factors that cause the need for advances, but it also predates the technology that will eventually lead to advances that permit cotton to meet the needs of the modern textile trade.

Literature Cited

1. Federal Register 1978, 43, 27355.
2. Cocke, J. B.; Bragg, C. W.; Kirk, I. W. Marketing Research Report No. 1064, USDA, ARS: Washington, D. C., 1977.
3. Griffin, A. C.; Bargeron,J. D., III. Marketing Research Report No. 1110, USDA, SEA: Washington, D. C., 1980.
4. Claassen, D. J., Jr.; Basil, A., Jr. Text. Res. J. 1981, 51, 101-5.
5. Fischer, J.J.; Morey, P. R.; Sasser, P. E. Text. Res. J. 1980, 50, 735-9.
6. Morey, P.R.; Sasser, P. E.; Bethea, R. M.; Kopetzky, M. T. Am. Ind. Hygiene Assn. J. 1976, 407-12.
7. Morey, P. R. Departmental Report, Texas Tech Univ., Dept. of Bio. Sci., Lubbock, TX, 1980.
8. Morey, P. R. Proceedings of the National Cotton Council, Third Special Session on Cotton Dust Research 1979, p 2.
9. Morey, P. R.; Bethea, R. M.; Wakelyn, P. J.; Kirk, I. W. Am. Ind. Hygiene Assn. J. 1976, 321-8.

10. Mangialardi, G. J., Jr. Text. Res. J. 1979, 49, 476-80.
11. Bargeron, J. D., III; personal communication, 1981.
12. Mangialardi, G. J., Jr. ARS-S-94, USDA, ARS: Washington, D. C., 1976.
13. Wanjura, D. F.; Baker, R. V. Production Research Report No. 160, USDA, ARS: Washington, D. C., 1975.
14. Brashears, A. D.; Ulich, W. L. ASAE, Paper No. 79-3088, 1979.
15. Muramoto, H.; Sherman, R.; Ledbetter, C. Proceedings of the National Cotton Council, Fifth Cotton Dust Research Conference 1981, p 23.
16. Smith,l L. A.; Dumas, W. J. ASAE, Paper No. 80-1047, 1980.
17. Kirk, I. W.; Carter, L. M.; Bragg, C. K.; Curley, R. G.; McCutcheon, O. D. Marketing Research Report No. 1118, USDA, ARS: Washington, D. C., 1981.
18. Kirk, I. W.; Corley, T. E.; Kummer, F. A. Trans. ASAE 1970, 13, 171-6.
19. Kirk, I. W.; Brashears, A. D.; Hudspeth, E. B., Jr. Trans. ASAE 1972, 15, 1024-7.
20. Kirk, I. W.; Hudspeth, E. B., Jr.; Brashears, A. D. Trans. ASAE 1973, 16, 446-9.
21. Laird, W.; Baker, R. V. ARS S-3, USDA, ARS: Washington, D. C., 1973.
22. Baker, R. V.; Laird, J. W. ASAE, Paper No. 81-3060, 1981.
23. Cocke, J. B. Production Research Report No. 157, USDA, ARS: Washington, D. C., 1974.
24. Wanjura, D. F.; Baker, R. V.; Hudspeth, E. B. ASAE, Paper No. 78-3028, 1978.
25. Bargeron, J. D., III; Garner, W. E.; Baker, R. V. Marketing Research Report No. 1095, USDA, SEA: Washington, D. C., 1978.
26. Wilkes, L. H.; Jones, J. K. ASAE, Paper No. 80-1048, 1980.
27. Moore, V. P.; Griffin, C., Jr. ARS 42-105, USDA, ARS: Washington, D. C., 1964.
28. Baker, R. V.; Columbus, E.P.; Laird, J. W. Technical Bulletin No. 1540, USDA, ARS: Washington, D. C., 1977.
29. Cotton Ginners Handbook, USDA, ARS, Agricultural Handbook No. 503: Washington, D. C., 1977.
30. Baker, E. C.; Boving, P. A.; Laird, J. W. ASAE, Paper No. 80-3557, 1980.
31. Wanjura, D. F.; Baker, R. V. Trans. ASAE 1979, 22, 273-8, 282.
32. Mangialardi, G. J., Jr. Production Research Report No. 175, USDA, SEA: Washington, D. C., 1978.
33. Cocke, J. B.; Kirk, I. W.; Wesley, R. A. Marketing Research Report No. 1066, USDA, ARS: Washington, D. C., 1977.
34. Cotton Gin Equipment, USDA, AMS, Cotton Division: Memphis, TN, 1978.
35. Sasser, P. E.; Jones, J. K.; Slater, G. A. Agro-Industrial Report 1976, 3 (3), Cotton Incorporated: Raleigh, NC.

36. Griffin, A. C., Jr.; Bargeron, J. D., III. Marketing Research Report No. 1110, USDA, ARS: Washington, D. C., 1980.
37. Baker, R. V. The Cotton Ginners' Journal and Yearbook 1977, 45, 5-12.
38. Mangialardi, G.J., Jr. ASAE, Paper No. 80-3073, 1980.
39. Leonard, C. G.; Wright, T.E.; Hughs, S. E. ASAE, Paper No. 80-3072, 1980.
40. Childers, R. E.; Baker, R. V. Trans. ASAE 1978, 21, 379-84.
41. Griffin, A. C., Jr. Cotton Ginners' Journal and Yearbook 1977, 45, 25-9.
42. Mangialardi, G. J., Jr.; Griffin, C. "Fiber Moisture Lint Cleaning and Lint Quality"; University of Missouri, Extension Division, Columbia, MO, 1967.
43. Mangialardi, G. J., Jr.; Griffin, C. Marketing Research Report No. 708, USDA, ARS: Washington, D. C., 1965.
44. Gillum, M. N.; LaFerney, P. E.; Mullikin, R. A. Marketing Research Report No. 967, USDA, ARS: Washington, D. C., 1972.
45. Mangialardi, G. J., Jr.; Griffin, A. C., Jr. Trans. ASAE 1977, 20, 979-84.
46. Phillips, B. E. "1976 Color and Trash Survey - Upland Cotton"; USDA, AMS, CD: Memphis, TN, 1977, p 17.

RECEIVED January 20, 1982.

3

Dust in Cotton Gins: An Overview

A. C. GRIFFIN, JR. and E. P. COLUMBUS

U.S. Cotton Ginning Laboratory, Stoneville, MS 38776

The results of studies and surveys of air-borne dust conducted in cotton ginneries in the U.S. within the last decade are summarized. Gin dust levels in the major U.S. production areas were found to be in the same range for similarly harvested cotton. Gins processing machine-stripped cotton had higher dust levels than those handling spindle-picked cotton, and roller gins were dustier than saw gins. The location of a gin in relation to its dust and trash collecting equipment outside the gin was of major importance in the occurrence of dust in gins, and the dust content of ambient air outside gins also had a major impact on dust levels within gins. Particulate size, concentration and chemical constituent data are also reported.

The criteria document (1) for a recommended standard for occupational exposure to cotton dust defines cotton dust as dust generated into the atmosphere as a result of the processing of cotton fibers combined with any naturally occurring materials such as stems, leaves, bracts, and inorganic matter which may have accumulated on the cotton fibers during the growing or harvesting period.

Our interest in cotton dust has three aspects. One has to do with the physical effects of cotton dust on the processing performance of cotton in spinning mills. Excessive amounts of cotton dust may cause machinery stoppages and thereby add to product manufacturing costs. The second aspect concerns the health of workers in cotton spinning mills and cotton gins; and the third aspect is that of gin emissions into the ambient atmosphere. The recent U.S. Environmental Protection Agency (EPA) report (2) listing cotton gins as one of the seven primary sources of atmospheric arsenic gives an added sense of urgency to the need for careful study of the situation. This report relates to the health of gin employees and is a general summary of our knowledge of dust in and around cotton gins.

There were 2,332 active gins in the U.S. in 1979 (3). These gins with a typical employment of 9 persons per shift, ginned 14,161,000 bales of cotton. These bales may be subdivided by cotton type into about 14,061,000 bales of Upland cotton and 100,000 bales of American Pima cotton. The Upland cottons have shorter, weaker, and higher micronaire fiber than the Pima cottons, and are ginned on gins using the saw-and-rib principle whereas the Pimas are ginned on roller gins that create fewer fiber neps. The method of harvesting cotton offers another interesting way of categorizing the crop; harvesting by spindle-pickers accounted for 62 percent of the crop with stripper-harvesting accounting for 37 percent of the crop. The methods of harvest and ginning will be important as the dust and its composition data are presented.

Dust Levels in Ambient Atmosphere

Our first cotton dust measurements were made in 1967 when one of the authors of this paper measured the ambient dust concentrations downwind from three Mississippi cotton gins (4). The results of this study showed that uncontrollable variations in wind direction and velocity during sampling adversely affected the reliability of the measurements and made the data difficult to analyze. It was also found that the airborne dust burden by winds from unpaved approach roads and cotton-trailer parking areas often overshadowed that emitted by the gins. It soon became apparent that the principal impact of gins in Mississippi on ambient air quality was principally that of a nuisance. Improved cyclone collectors and filters were developed and used in gins to eliminate all but the finest of particulates released by cotton during gin processing (5, 6, 7, 8, 9).

Durrenberger (10, 11) in 1973 studied airborne particulates at varying distances from gins in Texas. He developed a prediction equation for estimating the dust concentration in air downwind from gins. The equation was based on ginning rate, foreign matter content of the cotton as harvested, and took into account the amount of emission control equipment in use at the gin. His study showed that the heavier particulates released into the atmosphere fell to earth near the gin but that the finer particles were transported several hundred meters.

Dust Levels in Cotton Gins

Airborne dust concentrations inside Midsouth and Texas gins were measured by Wesley (12, 13) in 1972, 1973 and 1974 and are summarized in Table I. The gins did not have the same hourly

TABLE I

Representative Dust Levels at Three Locations Within Commercial Cotton Gins in Arkansas, Mississippi, and Texas[a]

Gin			Harvest method		Respirable Dust, mg/m^3			Total Dust, mg/m^3		
					Console	Lint cleaner	Press	Console	Lint cleaner	Press
1	1972	Miss	Spindle	High	0.33	0.84	0.94	ns[b]	ns	ns
				Low	0.20	0.50	0.14	ns	ns	ns
2	1972	Miss	Spindle	High	0.76	0.53	0.92	ns	ns	ns
				Low	0.07	0.32	0.08	ns	ns	ns
3	1973	Miss	Spindle	High	0.59	1.13	0.51	2.66	3.75	2.49
				Low	0.13	0.49	0.23	0.45	0.47	0.23
4	1973	Miss	Spindle	High	0.98	1.07	0.97	2.29	3.39	3.49
				Low	0.37	0.44	0.15	0.49	0.27	0.24
5	1974	TX	Stripper	High	3.78	3.41	5.02	4.93	9.28	6.09
				Low	1.82	2.04	1.98	1.48	0.97	2.58
6	1974	TX	Stripper	High	3.67	ns	2.53	3.83	ns	2.99
				Low	1.54	ns	1.21	0.77	ns	0.62
7	1974	Ark	Spindle	High	1.02	0.83	0.50	1.90	1.28	1.23
				Low	0.45	0.72	0.30	0.41	0.80	0.29
8	1974	Ark	Spindle	High	0.97	0.49	0.43	2.79	1.94	0.96
				Low	0.66	0.43	0.32	0.34	0.45	0.26

[a] From Wesley (12).
[b] ns = not sampled.

processing capacity, and the cottons ginned were dissimilar in variety, production history, and method of harvest. The data listed represent high's and low's for individual measurements. Levels of both total dust as measured using a high-volume air sampler and respirable dust as measured using a large vertical eleutriator are reported for three distinct areas within the same gin. When the Mississippi gins are considered as a group, the lint cleaner area generally had the highest dust level, while the baling press and console areas had approximately the same dust concentration. The console area of the Arkansas gins generally had the highest dust level, and the press area the lowest. The Texas gins handling stripper-harvested cotton were dustier than the Mississippi and Arkansas gins handling spindle-picked cotton. The lowest levels found in the stripper-cotton gins were higher than the highest dust levels in the gins processing spindle-picked cotton. These data point out that the dust level varies with location inside gin plants as well as the method used to harvest the cotton.

Hughes (14) studied dust levels in a California gin in 1978. He found widely varying dust levels at both the baling press and gin stand areas that were roughly in the same range as in Wesley's Mississippi study, Table II.

Kirk, Leonard, and Brown (15) did an excellent study of dust in New Mexico gins in 1973. They examined roller gins as well as saw gins and found that air in the gin stand area was dustier than air near the baling press in both kinds of gins. They also found that roller gins processing Pima cotton were considerably more dusty than gins processing Acala (upland) spindle-picked cotton, Table II.

A new gin for ginning spindle-picked cotton was constructed in the Mississippi Delta in 1977. The layout of the machinery, doors, and waste collecting system was designed to reduce worker and community exposure to airborne dust by optimizing functional area locations with respect to the prevailing winds from the southwest and northwest. Dust levels were measured in this gin (16) during the peak of the ginning period in 1979, and were found to be:

Ambient upwind, respirable dust	0.053 mg/m^3
Ambient downwind, respirable dust	0.791 mg/m^3
Inside the gin, respirable dust at	
Gin stands	0.282 mg/m^3
Lint cleaners	0.354 mg/m^3
Baling press	0.289 mg/m^3
Inside the gin, total dust at	
Gin stands	0.500 mg/m^3
Lint cleaners	0.801 mg/m^3
Baling press	0.481 mg/m^3

TABLE II
Airborne Dust Concentrations in Commercial Gins in Four Geographic Areas and in New Mexico From Two Types of Gins

State	Year	Gin type	Harvest method	Location in gin		Dust concentration mg/m³ Respirable	Total
California[a]	1978	Saw	Spindle	Press-	High	1.184	1.926
					Low	0.397	0.646
				Gin stands	High	1.639	2.234
					Low	0.347	0.552
Texas[b]	1974	Saw	Stripper	Press	High	4.16	ns[d]
					Low	1.87	ns
				Gin stands	High	3.02	ns
					Low	2.60	ns
MS Delta[b]	1975	Saw	Spindle	Press	High	1.02	ns
					Low	0.07	ns
				Gin stands	High	0.92	ns
					Low	0.15	ns
New Mexico[c]	1973	Saw	Spindle	Press	Avg	0.56	1.02
				Stand	Avg	0.90	1.93
New Mexico[c]	1973	Roller	Spindle	Press	Avg	1.75	4.05
				Stand	Avg	2.85	6.51

[a]See Literature Cited (14).
[b]See Literature Cited (13).
[c]See Literature Cited (15).
[d]ns = not sampled.

These data, when compared to data from the other gins fall within the high and low values reported for older gins, handling similar types of cotton. Thus, the low values reported in this paper appear to be the result of ginning relatively clean cottons or from cotton ginned when ambient wind direction was favorable, or both, rather than resulting from an intentional machinery layout pattern.

In summary, dust levels in ginneries may cluster about a central value, but actual values are highly dependent upon the natural, and usually uncontrollable, production and harvesting situation that exists at the time.

Composition of Gin Dust

As cotton is brought under the unloading suction telescopes at a gin, one may observe in the load of seed cotton foreign material such as leaf parts; unopened whole bolls; boll fragments; pieces of field weeds, grasses, and vines; soil particles; and sometimes insect residues and evidence of fungal/bacterial infection. Fragments of these materials are carried over into the baled lint in spite of gin efforts to remove them. There are several opportunities in the ginning system for particles of these materials to be released into the atmosphere along with fugitive fibers. Morey's (17) statement that cotton dusts emitted during opening, cleaning,and carding of raw cottons in textile mills should be relatively rich in bract, leaf and weed microparticulate applies equally well to dust in gins.

In his analysis of parts of mature cotton plants, Brown (18) reported constituents in roots, stem, leaves, bolls, seed and lint. In Table III, I have listed his values for leaves and lint which are among the principle components of unginned cotton. These data do not show the presence of crop protection or harvest aid chemicals.

Wesley and Wall (19) collected and analyzed airborne dust samples collected from three areas within five Mississippi gins in 1975. The general composition of their samples are summarized in Table IV. These data show the dust to be about 30 percent cellulosic, the remainder being soil and other materials. The quantitative elemental analysis of their samples is detailed in Table V. Although the percentages are different, the constituents in these samples of gin dust are very similar to those listed by Brown (18) in whole plant parts. None of the data presented have identified residues from insecticides or harvest aid chemicals. This may be because they were not specifically sought.

TABLE III
Chemical Analysis of Leaf and Lint Parts of Mature Cotton Plants[a]
(percent dry basis)

Constituent	Leaf	Lint
Nitrogen	2.25	0.18
Phosphoric acid	0.48	0.09
Potash	1.09	0.59
Lime	5.28	0.70
Magnesia	0.94	0.14
Iron oxide	0.43	0.16
Soda	0.66	0.07
Sulphuric acid	1.05	0.09
Silica	1.70	0.07
Ash	12.55	1.25
Protein	14.06	1.12
Fiber	8.71	87.02
Fat	8.49	0.61
Carbohydrates	56.19	10.00

[a]After Brown (18).

Table IV
Chemical Separation of Cotton Dust Collected in Mississippi Gins, Crop of 1975[a]

Material	Composition (percent)
Ash	32.9
Protein	11.8
Moisture	3.4
Water soluble component	12.6
Alcohol soluble component	1.7
Noncellulose organic	24.7
Cellulose	30.5
Residual inorganic	27.1

[a]After Wesley and Wall (19).

TABLE V
Quantitative Elemental Analysis by X-ray Fluorescence of Cotton Dust Collected in Mississippi Gins, Crop of 1975[a]

Element	Percentage	Element	Percentage
Si	7.69	S	0.32
K	1.82	Cl	0.16
Al	1.46	Cu	0.08
Ca	1.15	Ti	0.05
Mg	1.04	Zn	0.05
P	0.52	Mn	0.01
Fe	0.49		

[a]After Wesley and Wall (19).

As pointed out earlier, all U.S. cotton in commercial production is now harvested by machines. The application of harvest-aid chemicals to cause the plants to shed their leaves (defoliation) or to kill and dry the plant (desiccation) are common practices in many areas. Chlorates and organic phosphates are popular defoliant materials and arsenic acid is commonly used as a desiccant.

Paganini (20) in 1966 found arsenic in the air near cotton gins in Texas in concentrations of 0.01-141 ug/m^3 at distances of 150 to 8000 feet from the gin. Schacht and LePori (21) reported on chemical properties of cotton gin waste from six gins in Texas in 1977. They included gins handling only desiccated stripper-harvested and non-desiccated spindle-harvested cotton. They observed a striking difference in arsenic levels in gin wastes from the two areas; the As level from the desiccated cottons was 0.02%, but was only 0.001% from the non-desiccated cottons (Table VI).

TABLE VI
Mean Values for Chemical Composition of Ginning Wastes at Six Texas Gins, Crop of 1977[a]

Item	Composition, percent
Volatile[b]	85
Carbon	42
Hydrogen	5.4
Nitrogen	1.4
Sulfur	1.7
Oxygen and error	34.5
Arsenic - in areas using arsenical desiccants	0.02
Arsenic - in areas not using arsenical desiccants	0.001

[a]After Schacht and LePori (21).

[b]Heated 7 minutes at 950°C.

Although arsenic was not initially reported in the samples studied by Wesley and Wall, re-examination of one of the samples did show it to be present. The cotton from which this sample came probably had not been desiccated; the arsenic could have had its orgin in the soil from earlier days or as fiber residue from chemical pest control during the present cotton-growing season.

Present Status and Outlook

We are presently readjusting our research program at the U.S. Cotton Ginning Laboratory at Stoneville, MS, to take advantage of newly developed rapid response instrumentation for measuring airborne dust concentrations, as well as the cotton dust analyzer described by Baker (22). We are expanding cooperative relationships with other USDA-ARS research units to obtain chemical and biological analyses heretofore unavailable to us. We expect to continue our efforts to reduce airborne dusts in the vicinity of cotton gins, and to identify and quantify not only the elements present, but also identify residues from growth regulators, pesticides and herbicides as well as desiccants and defoliants. This work will include analyses of materials remaining on the fibers being baled for commercial use.

Literature Cited

1. HEW Publication No. (NIOSH) 1974, 75 (118), 1.
2. Suta, B.E. SRI International, Menlo Park, CA, 1980, 1.
3. USDA ESCE 1980, (84).
4. U.S. Cotton Ginning Laboratory, USDA-SEA-ARS, Stoneville, MS Annual Report for FY 1967 and 1968.
5. Alberson, D.M.; Baker, R.V. USDA ARS 42-103, 1964.
6. Anderson, J.D.; Baker, R.V. USDA ARS-S-150, 1976.
7. Baker, R.V.; Parnell, C.B., Jr. USDA ARS 42-192, 1971.
8. McCaskill, O.L.; Wesley, R.A. USDA ARS-S-144, 1976.
9. Wesley, R.A.; McCaskill, O.L.; Columbus, E.P. USDA ARS 42-167, 1970.
10. Durrenberger, C. Texas Air Control Board Report. 1974.
11. Durrenberger, C.J. Texas Air Control Board. 1975
12. Wesley, R. A. The Cotton Ginners' Journal and Yearbook 1975, 43 (1), 51-53.
13. Wesley, R. A. Cotton Dust Proceedings 1977, 21-24.
14. Hughs, S. E.; Urquhart, N.S.; Smith, D.W. Am. Soc. of Agr. Engr. Winter Meeting 1979, 79 (3553), 24.
15. Kirk, I.W.; Leonard, C.G.; Brown, D.F. Trans. of the ASAE 1977, 20 (5), 962-68.
16. Hicks, M.; Nevins, P. Environ. Control, Inc. Draft report, 1980.
17. Morey, P.R. Special Session of Beltwide Cotton Production Research Conference 1977, p 4-6.
18. Brown, H.B. "Cotton"; McGraw-Hill Book Co. New York, p 220.
19. Wesley, R.A.; Wall, J.H. Am. Ind. Hyg. Assoc. J. 1978, 39, 962-69.
20. Paganini, O. Texas State Dep. of Health, Austin, TX. 1965.
21. Schacht, O.B.; LePori, W.A. The Cotton Ginners' Journal and Yearbook 1980, 48 (1), 27-36.
22. Baker, R.V. ACS Symposium on OSHA Cotton Dust Standards, March 29-30, 1981, Atlanta, GA.

RECEIVED December 15, 1981.

Washing Methods for Cotton

Effects on Fiber, Processing Qualities, and Dust Generation

HENRY H. PERKINS, JR. and JOSEPH B. COCKE

U.S. Department of Agriculture, Agricultural Research Service,
Cotton Quality Research Station, Clemson, SC 29631

Thoroughly washed cotton generates less dust in processing and is biologically less active than unwashed cotton and has been exempted from the OSHA cotton dust standard. Cottons washed under different conditions of time, temperature, detergency, and fiber finish were evaluated for effects on noncellulosic constituents, fiber properties, dust generation, and processing and yarn qualities. The more severe washing treatments adversely affected fiber properties and caused removal of large percentages of the natural waxes. The milder washing treatments did not affect fiber properties and left the natural waxes intact. All washing treatments reduced dust levels generated in processing. The effects of washing on processing and yarn qualities were variable and generally somewhat adverse, but the yarns produced were of acceptable commercial quality.

Washed cotton is biologically less active and generates less dust in processing than unwashed cotton (1). Thoroughly washed cotton has been exempted from coverage by the OSHA cotton dust standard (2). The washing conditions specified in the dust standard are vague and include statements such as: (1) "Washed cotton means cotton which has been thoroughly washed in hot water and is known in the cotton trade as purified or dyed," and (2) "The washing process can be as simple as the water washing of baled cotton with wetting agent as described by Merchant et al. (1), or as elaborate as bleaching and purifying processes commonly practiced in the health products industry".

The wash conditions described by Merchant are 30 minutes at the boil at pH 12. Any conditions less severe than this require verification for effectiveness. The conditions mentioned in the standard are more severe than are either economically or technically acceptable to the textile industry. Research is active to determine whether economically and technically feasible washing conditions less severe than those stated can be effective in purifying cotton to an acceptable level of biological activity and dust generation potential.

If acceptable washing conditions can be achieved, then processing washed cotton may be a realistic long term method for dealing with the dust standard and for insuring worker safety and health, for at least some segments of the textile industry.

Both independently and in conjunction with Cotton Incorporated and industry, USDA has conducted laboratory, pilot-scale, and production-scale washing trials to determine the effects of washing on: (1) the levels of noncellulosic constituents removed from the cotton, (2) fiber properties, (3) dust levels, and (4) processing quality. Some results have been reported previously (3). The washing methods and significant findings are described and summarized in this report and represent our understanding of the current state-of-the-art of cotton washing.

Cotton has been washed by different processes or methods as follows:

- Laboratory
- Rayon washing line, rain pan wetting of a batt of cotton - pilot-scale.
- Batch process - production kiers.
- Wool scouring process - cotton submerged.

Laboratory Washing Conditions

Fifty g cotton samples were washed with vigorous stirring for 5 minutes in a 0.1% solution of a nonionic wetting agent at 38°, 60°, 80°, and 100°C. Water-to-fiber ratio was 50/1. Each sample was rinsed in two changes of water at the same temperature as the wash and air-dried. Contents of reducing sugars, wax (as determined by 1,1,1-trichloroethane extraction), and ethyl alcohol-extractables were determined for the washed cottons and the unwashed control (4). Reducing sugar content decreased from 0.31% for the unwashed cotton to 0.02% for all washing treatments. As washing temperature increased, the level of wax remaining on the fiber steadily decreased from 0.5% for the control to less than 0.2% for the cottons washed at 100°C (Figure 1). The mechanical action and enhanced emulsification conditions created by the stirring apparently were partly responsible for the decreases in wax content, because in other washing trials involving high temperatures but minimal mechanical action, decreases in wax content were not large.

The level of alcohol-extractables remaining on the fiber also decreased as washing temperature increased (Figure 2). However, the quantity of material removed at the lowest wash temperature was significant and did not increase markedly with increases in wash temperature. Apparently, little would be gained in using the higher temperatures to remove these types of extractables.

Washing temperatures above 60°C tended to lower fiber length

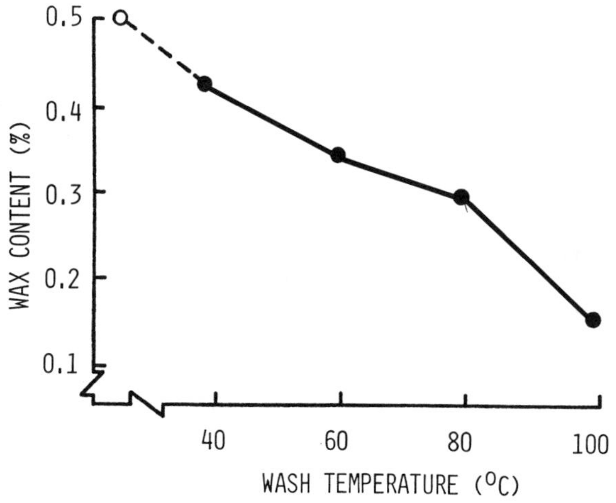

Figure 1. Plot of wax content vs. wash temperature. Laboratory washing conditions. Key: ○ *unwashed;* ●, *washed.*

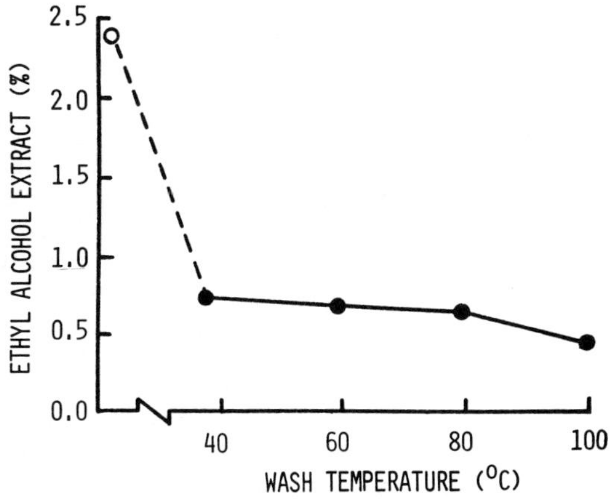

Figure 2. Plot of ethyl alcohol content vs. wash temperature. Laboratory washing conditions. Key: ○, *unwashed;* ●, *washed.*

qualities (Table I). As shown by length-array tests, both the upper quartile and mean lengths were shortened, and short-fiber contents were increased by the 80° and 100°C washes. Similar trends in length characteristics of washed cotton were reported by Sasser in 1979 (5).

Under the washing conditions of this laboratory experiment -- 5 min with a wetting agent and agitation -- temperatures above 60°C appear to offer little benefit in removing extraneous materials and, moreover, may cause fiber damage. Similar results on the effects of temperature on removing solvent and water soluble materials from cotton have been reported by Ross, et al. (6). They concluded that temperatures above 60°C did not remove significant additional quantities of these extractables from cotton.

Table I
Effects of Washing Temperatures on Fiber Length Characteristics(3)

Wash Temperature[a] (°C)	Upper Quartile Length (mm)	Mean Length (mm)	Short Fibers (%)
Unwashed	31.5	24.9	10
38	31.5	25.4	9
60	31.5	25.1	11
80	31.0	24.4	12
100	30.0	23.4	14

[a]Washed 5 minutes with wetting agent and agitation.

Commercial Batch Washing Conditions

About 900 kg per lot of cotton was washed batch-wise by a commercial firm at 45°, 60°, and 80°C for 20 minutes. No wetting agent or washing aid was used. After washing, the fibers were rinsed for 15 minutes with water at 30°C, centrifuged and dried at 55-65°C to a moisture content of 6%. No finish was applied to any of the cottons. Wax content was not affected by any of the washing treatments and remained at a level of about 0.55% (Figure 3). The level of alcohol-extractables was reduced significantly by the washing treatments, but washing temperature had no effect on the amount of material removed (Figure 4). The levels of water-extractables remaining on the cottons were determined in a 6-h Soxhlet extraction with boiling distilled water. Water-extractables were reduced significantly by all washing treatments and, like the level of alcohol-extractables, to about the same extent regardless of washing temperature (Figure 5). The level of water-extractables was reduced from 2.6% for the unwashed control to about 0.3% for all the washed cottons.

Fiber properties of the unwashed and washed cottons were similar, as determined by standard methods (Table II).

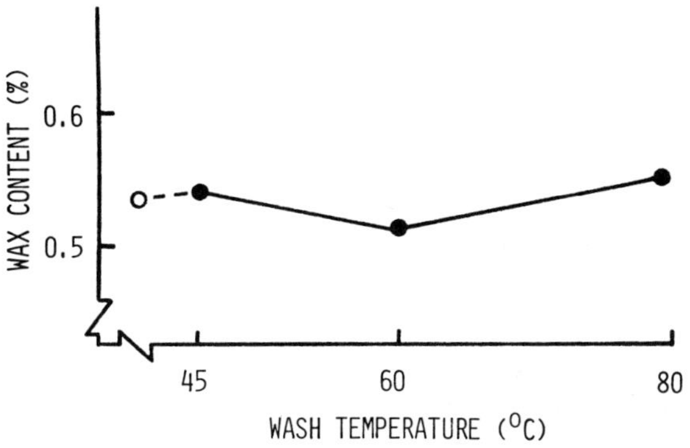

Figure 3. Plot of wax content vs. wash temperature. Commercial batch washing conditions. Key: ○, unwashed; ●, washed.

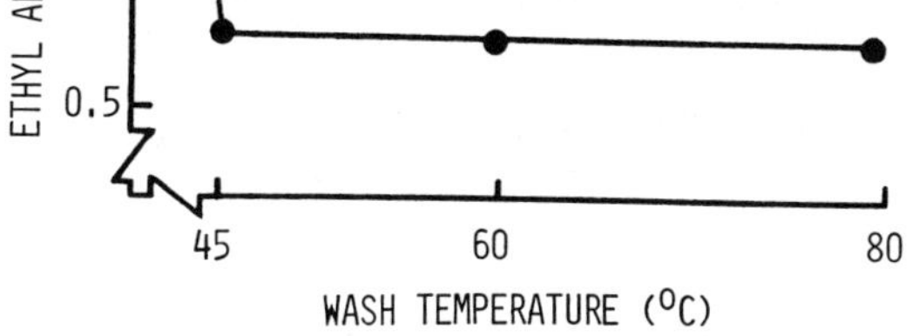

Figure 4. Plot of ethyl alcohol content vs. wash temperature. Commercial batch washing conditions. Key: ○, unwashed; ●, washed.

Table II
Fiber Properties of Cottons Washed by Batch Process[a] (3)

Treatment	Micronaire Units	Fibrograph 2.5% Span Length (mm)	Fibrograph Uniformity Ratio	Strength, 3.175 mm gage (kN m/kg)
Unwashed	4.6	29.5	50	218
Washed 45°C	4.6	29.5	49	220
Washed 60°C	4.6	29.7	49	220
Washed 80°C	4.5	29.5	50	232

[a]Measurements made on finisher drawing sliver.

Both washed and unwashed cottons were processed through a blender feeder, a No. 12 horizontal opener, and a two-beater picker and made into picker laps. The carding was conducted in our model cardroom at 18.2 kg/h, and dust levels were determined by use of vertical elutriators. The cottons were spun into 19.7 mg/m yarn of 38.2 twist factor at 13000 rpm spindle speed in a 4536 spindle-hour test.

Generally, the processing and yarn qualities of the unwashed cotton were better than those of the washed cottons (Table III). However, from a practical standpoint the differences were not great. The differences of greatest practical significance concerned factors that affect yarn appearance, and these factors were clearly superior for the unwashed cotton.

Table III
Processing Qualities of Cottons Washed by Batch Process[a] (3)

Treatment	Card Web Neps per 645 cm^2	EDMSH[b]	Yarn-Break Factor (Units)	Yarn Neps per 914.4m	Yarn CV (%)	Yarn Appearance (Index)
Unwashed	11a	27a	1891a	737a	21.8a	111a
Washed 45°C	14a	39a	1981a	1208b	22.6b	104ab
Washed 60°C	14a	56b	1748b	1425c	23.8c	105ab
Washed 80°C	15a	35a	1862ab	1294b	22.7b	100b

[a]Means in a column not having a letter in common are significantly different at the 5% level.
[b]Ends down per thousand spindle hours.

Dust level generated during carding was reduced by about 70% as a result of washing but was little affected by washing temperature(Figure 6). These results strongly indicate that washing under relatively mild conditions effectively reduces dust levels and removes soluble constituents that may be related to byssinosis.

Continuous Washing on a Pilot Scale Rayon Wash Line

Washing experiments have been conducted on a pilot-scale rayon washing line that employs the rain-pan technique of gravity-flow wetting. In this system, precision-drilled, stainless-steel pans are used to "rain" measured quantities of solutions onto a batt of cotton. The batt is conveyed by a perforated stainless-

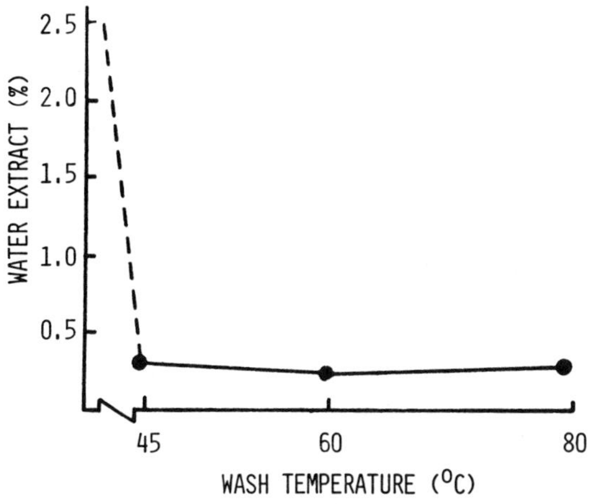

Figure 5. Plot of water extract vs. wash temperature. Commercial batch washing conditions. Key: ○, unwashed; ●, washed.

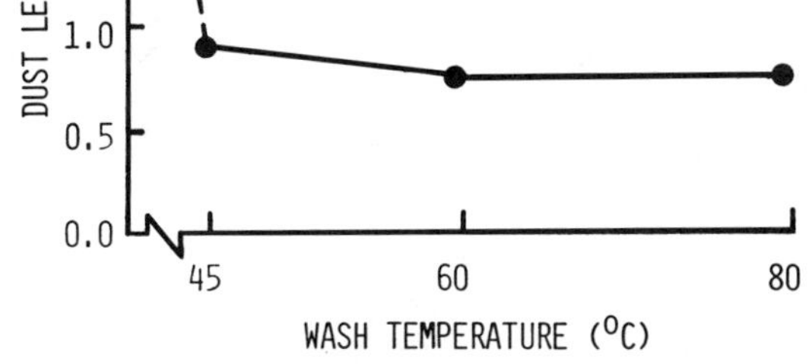

Figure 6. Plot of dust level vs. wash temperature. Commercial batch washing conditions. Key: ○, unwashed; ●, washed.

steel belt that lies approximately 12 inches below the pans. The batt is squeezed at intervals along the wash track to enhance the wetting by removing trapped air and minimizing channeling of solutions. Cotton will hold 10 to 15 times its weight of water and the squeezing aids transport of water and solubilized materials. The early pans contain the wetting agent, the middle pans contain either water or water plus finish for rinsing, and the final pans contain water plus finish for additional rinsing and finish application. The solutions from the wetting and water rinses are not reused and go to the drain. The final rinse containing the finish is recirculated and reused and is replaced each 12-16 hours. For all rayon washing experiments, the cotton was prepared for washing by processing it through opening with minimum cleaning and making 25-cm-wide picker laps.

In the first experiment, about 1600 kg of Mississippi cotton was washed. The laps were fed in composites of four to give a total weight of 2.64 kg/m^2. This is a relatively heavy batt as compared with one of about 1.02 kg/m^2, the weight suggested as optimum by Winch in 1979 (7). The batt was completely composited before reaching the first rain pan. Solution temperatures in all rain pans were 68^oC. Concentration of the anionic wetting agent contained in the first four pans was 0.2%. The last five pans contained finish at a concentration level to give about 0.7% finish on the dry weight of cotton. These five pans served the dual purpose of rinsing and finish application. Dwell time on the wash line was about 3½ minutes. The final squeeze reduced moisture content of the cotton batt to about 60%. The compact batt was broken up by a spiked beater as it entered the dryer. The drying unit consisted of 3 sections of tunnel dryers that were independently controlled for temperature. Drying temperatures were maintained mostly at 70^oC, 50^oC, and 60^oC in the 3 sections, respectively.

The temperature in the middle section was varied from 40^oC - 70^oC as required to maintain a final cotton moisture content of 3-4%. The total water-to-fiber ratio was 55/1 for this experiment and represents a minimum for wetting under these conditions. Water distribution was 50% in the washing section and 50% in the rinsing, finishing section. Production rate was 60 lbs/hr. A small quantity of cotton was washed under the same conditions but was rinsed without the finish.

Levels of extractables in the unwashed, washed with finish, and washed without finish stocks were determined. Finish level as determined by ethyl alcohol extraction was 0.7%. Washing did not reduce wax content but did significantly reduce ethyl-alcohol and boiling-water extractables (Table IV). Dust level generated in carding was reduced about 50% by the washing treatment and was about the same whether or not the finish has been applied. Fiber properties were not affected by the washing treatments. (Table V).

The washed cottons and the unwashed control cotton were made into 19.7 mg/m yarn under the same processing conditions used for

Table IV
Effects of Washing on Cotton-Extractables and Dust Levels -- Rayon Wash Line, First Experiment (3)

	Cotton Treatment		
Property	Unwashed	Washed Plus Finish	Washed, No Finish
Wax Content (%)	0.65	----	0.64
Ethyl Alcohol Extract (%)	1.94	1.86	1.16
Boiling Water Extract (%)	2.22	1.28	0.73
Dust level (mg/m^3)	1.51	0.82	0.73

the batch-washed cottons. Yarn processing and quality results were not statistically analyzed for lack of replication in one of the washing treatments. These results indicate, however, that the performance of the unwashed cotton was generally superior to that of the washed cottons (Table VI). The excessive neps and increased levels of end breakage in spinning were the most serious defects. We recalled, however, that the washed cottons were processed twice through the opening line -- the first time to form picker laps for the washing treatments, and a second time for the normal processing sequence.

Table V
Fiber Properties of Cottons Washed on Rayon Wash Line, First Experiment[a] (3)

		Fibrograph		Strength,
Treatment	Micronaire Units	2.5% Span Length (mm)	Uniformity Ratio	3.175 mm gage (kN.m/kg)
Unwashed	3.6	29.5	40	24.6
Washed, plus Finish	3.7	29.2	42	23.9
Washed, no Finish	3.7	29.5	42	23.8

[a]Measurements made on raw stock.

Table VI
Processing Qualities of Cottons Washed on Rayon Wash Line, First Experiment (3)

Treatment	Card Web Neps per 645 cm^2	EDMSH[a]	Yarn Break Factor (Units)	Yarn Neps per 914.4 m	Yarn CV (%)	Yarn Appearance (Index)
Unwashed	35	21	1889	1376	23.9	66
Washed, Plus Finish	86	58	1819	2335	25.8	61
Washed, No Finish	104	40	1817	2422	25.2	60

[a]Ends down per thousand spindle hours.

To evaluate the independent effects of the double processing on the cotton, we processed two lots of unwashed cotton into picker laps. Half of the laps were processed a second time through the opening line before carding. The cottons were made into 14.8 mg/m yarn of 37.2 twist factor. Even though this test was not replicated, the results shown in Table VII indicate that to a significant extent the double processing adversely affected the processing quality of the cotton.

Table VII
Processing Qualities of Single- and Double-Processed Unwashed Cottons(3)

Treatment	Card Web Neps per 645 cm^2	EDMSH[a]	Yarn Break Factor (Units)	Yarn Neps per 914.4 m	Yarn CV (%)	Yarn Appearance (Index)
Unwashed	35	41	1799	1960	25.1	63
Unwashed, Double Processed	78	66	1789	2534	26.1	60

[a]Ends down per thousand spindle hours.

No direct comparison could be made between the yarn properties of the double processed unwashed cotton and the washed cotton because of the differences in yarn sizes. However, the neps in card web could be compared directly: 78/645 cm^2 for the double processed unwashed cotton and averaged 95/645 cm^2 for the washed cottons. Indications are that eliminating the extra opening and cleaning steps in the washing operation would significantly improve the quality. Additionally, the washed cotton that did not contain finish was judged superior in processing quality to the washed cotton that contained finish. We feel that the level of finish was too high, considering the fact that the relatively mild washing conditions did not lower the natural wax content of the cotton. The combination of natural waxes and high finish level apparently had an adverse effect on fiber cohesion and drafting properties.

In a second experiment on the pilot scale rayon system, about 1100 kg per lot of cotton from Mississippi, Texas, and California were washed. Washing conditions including bath temperatures of 68°C were essentially identical to the first experiment on the rayon line with the following exceptions. Instead of completely compositing the batt before the first rain pan, the four laps were wet individually with wetting solution before compositing. This accelerated the wetting of the lower regions of the batt and also helped prevent channeling. Wetting was accomplished in the first 5 pans, water rinsing in the next 2, and rinsing plus finishing in the final 4. Finish concentration was controlled to give about 0.4% finish on dry fiber weight. The total water-to-fiber ratio was 50/1. Water distribution was 40% in the wetting section, 20% in the rinsing section, and 40% in the rinsing plus finishing section. Final squeeze roll pressure was increased to reduce moisture content of the batt to about 57% as it entered the dryer. Dryer temperatures were 90°C, 65°-85°C, and 60°C for the three sections, respectively. Production rate was 80 lbs/hr. A small quantity of each cotton was washed that did not contain finish.

The Mississippi cotton was much more difficult to wet out than either the California or Texas cottons. This is apparently related to the nature of noncellulosic constituents on the fiber surfaces. The Mississippi cotton was a mature, low noncellulose content cotton, whereas, both the California and Texas cottons had high noncellulose contents. The ratio of wax content to total noncellulosics was much higher for the Mississippi cotton than for either the California or Texas cottons. The surface of the Mississippi cotton is thus more hydrophobic and resists wetting. Levels of extractables and dust levels are summarized in Table VIII.

Table VIII
Levels of Extractables and Dust for Mississippi, California, and Texas Cottons
Rayon Wash Line, Second Experiment

Cotton	Finish Level %	Wax[a] Content (%)	Reduction in Wax (%)	Ethyl Alcohol[b] Extractables (%)	Card Room[b] Dust Level (mg/m^3)
Miss. Unwashed	----	0.46	----	1.20	1.38
Miss. Washed	0.38	0.38	17	0.64	0.59
Calif. Unwashed	----	0.62	----	2.72	0.58
Calif. Washed	0.35	0.51	18	0.93	0.38
Texas Unwashed	----	0.61	----	2.26	1.07
Texas Washed	0.41	0.57	7	0.88	0.59

[a]For the washed stock, the samples without finish were tested.
[b]For the washed stock, the samples with finish were tested.

Finish levels were near the target value of 0.4% and were about one-half that of the cotton from the first rayon wash line experiment. The wax contents of the cottons were lowered only slightly by the washing treatment, whereas, ethyl-alcohol extractables were lowered considerably as was expected. The final level of alcohol-extractables is related to the original level--the higher the initial level, the higher the percentage reduction.

Fiber length, length uniformity, and strength of the cottons were not affected by the washing treatments (Table IX). These results agree with those from previous trials in which moderate washing temperatures (below 70°C) were employed.

All cottons were carded at 13.6 kg/hr. The Mississippi and California cottons were processed into both 14.8 mg/m yarn of 37.2 twist factor and 19.7 mg/m yarn of 38.3 twist factor at several spindle speeds. The Texas cotton was made into 19.7 mg/m yarn of 38.3 twist factor at 12500 rpm spindle speed.

The only significant difficulty in processing occured at carding where static electricity caused the web to behave erratically. The static was controlled by carding the cotton with a static bar in place under the web just as it exited the crush rolls. Processing and yarn quality results for the 3 cottons made into 19.7 mg/m yarns at 13000 rpm spindle speed are shown in Table X. Spinning quality results for the Mississippi and California cottons that were made into 14.8 mg/m yarn are shown in Table XI.

Table IX
Fiber Properties of Mississippi, California, and Texas Cottons -- Rayon Wash Line, Second Experiment

Cotton	2.5% Span length (mm)	Uniformity ratio	Strength (g/tex)
Mississippi Unwashed	28.4	45	23.9
Mississippi Washed	28.2	46	23.7
California Unwashed	28.7	45	30.2
California Washed	29.2	47	30.4
Texas Unwashed	26.2	44	23.8
Texas Washed	26.4	45	23.7

Table X
Processing Quality, 19.7 mg/m Yarn -- Rayon Wash Line
Second Experiment

Cotton	Card Web neps per 645 cm^2	EDMSH[a]	Yarn Break Factor Units	Yarn Neps per 914.4 m	Yarn CV (%)
Mississippi Unwashed	10	23	1888	1009	22.6
Mississippi Washed	16	93	1818	1201	23.3
California Unwashed	57	12	2371	1622	22.6
California Washed	75	16	2157	1848	23.0
Texas Unwashed	33	28	1830	1217	23.7
Texas Washed	58	81	1759	1533	24.3

[a]Ends down per thousand spindle hours.

Card web neps were higher for the washed than for the unwashed cotton for each of the cottons. However, the effects of the washing treatment were overshadowed by other characteristics of the cotton that affect neps. Nep levels were much higher for the California and Texas cottons than for the Mississippi cotton. Nep level in the unwashed Mississippi cotton was much lower than that of either the unwashed California or washed Texas cottons. However, increased neppiness of carded washed cotton must be considered a liability. All washed cottons were successfully processed into yarn under commercially acceptable conditions. However, spinning and yarn qualities were generally somewhat poorer for the washed cotton than for the corresponding unwashed cotton for both yarn sizes. Differences between unwashed and washed cottons were less pronounced for the strong California cottons than for the other two cottons.

Table XI
Spinning Quality, 14.8 mg/m Yarn -- Rayon Wash Line, Second Experiment

Cotton	Spindle speed (rpm)	EDMSH[a]	Yarn Break Factor Units	Yarn Neps per 914.4 m	Yarn CV (%)
Mississippi Unwashed	12000	52	1730	1472	23.5
Mississippi Unwashed	10000	20	1822	1524	23.7
Mississippi Washed	10000	53	1549	1753	24.5
California Unwashed	13000	42	2113	2025	24.0
California Unwashed	12000	16	2205	2350	24.5
California Washed	12000	31	2079	2638	24.9

[a]Ends down per thousand spindle hours.

Continuous Washing on a Pilot Scale Wool Scouring Line

Mississippi cotton, identical to that used in the second rayon experiment, was washed on a pilot scale wool scouring line. In this system, the cotton is submerged in an infinite volume of solution and is conveyed by reciprocating rakes and water movement created by pumping the solution squeezed from the cotton back to the entry end of the bowl. The line is a 4-bowl train with squeeze rolls at the outlet of each bowl. The first bowl contained 0.1% of an anionic wetting agent, the next two bowls contained plain water, and the fourth bowl contained water plus finish. The water in the third bowl was overflowed more or less continuously to assure a clean rinse before the cotton entered the finish bath. Make up wetting and finish solutions were added to bowl 1 and bowl 4, respectively, as required to maintain volume. No other additions of water were made and the final water-to-fiber ratio was estimated as less than 10/1. All bath temperatures were 68°C. Moisture content of the cotton entering the dryer was about 40%. Cottons were dried in a single section tunnel dryer at a temperature of about 120°C. Multiple passes through the dryer were required to dry the cottons to moisture content of about 5%. A small amount of cotton was washed that did not receive finish.

Finish level was 0.25% on dry fiber weight. Results of extractions showed that levels of wax content and alcohol extractables of the cottons containing no finish were no different from those of the same cottons washed on the rayon line. Fiber length, length uniformity, and strength were not affected by the washing treatment and were also identical to those of the same cottons washed on the rayon line.

This cotton was carded at 13.6 kg/hr and processed into 14.8 mg/m yarn of 37.2 twist factor at 10000 rpm spindle speed. Ends down per thousand spindle hours was 40 as compared to 56 for the same cotton washed on the rayon line. Yarn appearance characteristics were also slightly better for the wool scoured cotton. These findings have been substantiated by results of additional washing experiments on the wool scouring system in which spinning quality evaluations have been made. Phases of these latter experiments are still in progress and complete results will be published elsewhere. One reason for the improved processing quality of the wool scoured cotton over that of the cotton washed on the rayon line is that the stock for washing does not have to be double-processed through the opening-picking line. For the wool scouring system, raw stock was fed directly to the first bowl in the wash line, whereas, for the rayon line, the cotton was processed into picker laps for feeding to the washing line.

Summary

Results of laboratory, pilot-scale, and production-scale washing experiments indicate that relatively mild washing conditions remove significant quantities of the water- and alcohol-soluble materials from cotton. Use of temperatures above 70°C does not significantly increase the amount extracted. The natural cotton waxes are left intact by the mild washing conditions. Vigorous washing conditions employing agitation and high temperatures lower the natural waxes and adversely affect fiber length characteristics. Depending on the initial dust level and the nature of the cotton, dust levels generated in carding are lowered 35 to 70% even by the mild washing conditions. These findings agree generally with those of Ross et al. (5).

Washing cotton tends to lower its processing and yarn qualities. A similar finding was reported by Gibbs et al. (8). However, cottons washed batchwise and without a finish were little different from unwashed cottons. Cottons washed on the rayon wash line were double-processed through the opening-picking line and this accentuated differences between the washed and unwashed cottons. Cottons washed under identical conditions of temperature and detergency on a wool scouring line exhibited somewhat better processing and yarn qualities than similar cottons washed on the rayon line. This is due primarily to absence of double-processing of the stock. Indications are that better prewash preparations to avoid double-processing and application of a carefully selected finish at a low level to alleviate static electricity and to complement the natural cotton waxes would lead to improved processing performances of washed cotton. Static electricity at carding was the most serious processing difficulty encountered and that was controlled by using a static bar under the web. Better control of finish at low, uniform application levels will minimize this problem.

On the rayon washing system, a minimum water-to-fiber ratio for the batt weights used was about 55/1. The Mississippi cotton was much more difficult to wet out than either the California or Texas cottons. The Mississippi cotton, compared with the California and Texas cotton, was a low noncellulose cotton and had a more hydrophobic surface. Thus, the wettability and, consequently, the washing efficiency of cotton is related to and dependent upon the surface characteristics of the cotton. Configuration of the materials on the fiber surface are related to variety, area of growth, environmental conditions, method and time of harvest, storage conditions, and other factors.

Wetting of cotton on the wool scouring system is potentially more efficient than that of the rayon system because the volume of water initially encountered by each tuft of cotton on the wool system is essentially infinite. However, the wash water on the wool scouring system is reused, whereas, it is not on the rayon system. Therefore, consideration must be given to establishing the loading of the wash water on the wool scouring system that can be tolerated and still have adequate washing of cotton. In the initial experiments, loadings equivalent to total water-to-fiber ratios varying from less than 10/1 to greater than 60/1 have been employed. More work is required to determine optimum water ratios on the wool scouring system.

The general characteristics exhibited by washed cottons are as follows:

- Lower dust levels
- Lower levels of extractables
- Static problems at carding
- Higher levels of card web neps
- Poorer yarn quality

The first two of these are positive and the last three are negative. The negative problems are being attacked in an ongoing research program and indications are that improvements can be made. Research is also underway to (1) optimize finishes to control static and facilitate drafting and (2) optimize yarn manufacturing configuration to accommodate washed cotton.

Literature Cited

1. Merchant, J.A.; Lumsden, J.C.; Kilburn, K.H.; Germino, V.H.; Hamilton, J.D.; Lynn, W.S.; Byrd, B.; Baucom, D. Brit. J. Indust. Med. 1973, 30, 237-47.
2. Federal Register 1978, 27350-418.
3. Perkins, Henry H., Jr. Textile Res. J. 1981, 51, 123-27.
4. Perkins, H.H., Jr. Textile Ind. 1971, 135(3), 49-64.
5. Sasser, P.E. Textile Res. J. 1980, 50, 61-63.
6. Ross, S.E.; Gibbs, A.H.; Trexler, J.E.; Riser, W. H. Textile Res. J. 1981, 51, 128-135.
7. Winch, A. R. Textile Res. J. 1980, 50, 64-73.
8. Gibbs, A.H.; McKenna, F.P.; Riser, W.H.; Rogers, W.B., Jr. Ross, S.E. Textile Res. J. 1981, 51, 135-141.

RECEIVED February 11, 1982.

5

Measurement of Dust-Release Potential of Cotton

ROY V. BAKER

U.S. Department of Agriculture, Agricultural Research Service, Southern Plains Cotton Research Laboratory, Lubbock, TX 79401

Measurable quantities of cotton dust were extracted from small cotton lint samples by means of high-velocity air jets. Dust removed in this manner was sized by a wire-mesh screen that restricted the flow of particles larger than the openings in the screen. Particles smaller than the openings in the screen were collected for gravimetric analysis. The weight of dust extracted by this technique represented an estimate of the dust-release potential of raw cotton lint. Equipment was designed, constructed, and evaluated for extracting dust particles smaller than 100, 50, and 17 micrometers from 20-gram, ginned lint-cotton samples. The development of experimental equipment and the operating procedures for preparing lint samples and for extracting, sizing, and collecting particulates are discussed. Representative dust level measurements for three cotton cultivars and for three particle sizes are presented.

Respirable dust escaping from cotton during processing becomes airborne and lowers the quality of the working atmosphere in a textile mill. This problem is currently a source of considerable concern in the textile industry. The amount of dust escaping from cotton during processing is influenced by many factors, including the dust-release potential of the cotton being processed (1). Experimental-card-room testing procedures have been developed in recent years for determining the dust-release potential of various types of cotton (2). These procedures, although reliable, are time consuming and require relatively large amounts of cotton for testing. A method by which dust-release potential could be determined more rapidly and with only small cotton samples would be extremely useful to the research community and might benefit textile mills in selecting cotton for their manufacturing needs.

Background

Anderson and Baker (3) demonstrated the feasibility of removing measurable quantities of cotton dust from small (10-g) lint samples by means of high-velocity air jets. Dust removed by this technique was conveyed by air through a sizing screen containing 100- x 100-micrometer openings. Dust smaller than the openings in the screen was collected on a glass-fiber filter for gravimetric analysis. These principles were used to develop a prototype cotton-dust analyzer for measuring the dust-release potential of lint cotton. (4).

The cotton-dust analyzer was used to measure the dust-release potential of cotton that had been subjected to various harvesting and cleaning treatments. Results of the measurements were compared with corresponding measurements with a vertical elutriator in an experimental card room. Generally, the cotton-dust analyzer detected significant differences in the dust-release potential of lint, and the differences were similar to the differences in card room dust levels as measured by the vertical elutriator. However, linear correlation analysis of the two measurement techniques produced a relatively low coefficient of determination (r^2=69%). These studies indicated that the cotton-dust analyzer was a potentially useful tool for studying the effects of various mechanical treatments on the dust-release potential of a given cotton. However, whether the cotton-dust analyzer would accurately measure the dust-release potential of cotton from a broad range of growth and production conditions was not determined.

The prototype cotton-dust analyzer used in the initial study was designed to measure dust smaller than 100 μm, whereas a vertical elutriator in a card room measures only the dust that is smaller than about 15 μm. Differences in particle size distributions of dust from various types of cotton would likely affect the relationship between the two dust measurements. Therefore, we deemed it necessary to investigate the use of sizing screens with smaller openings; i.e., openings whose size approximated the maximum size of particles collected by a vertical elutriator. The purpose of this report is to describe additional modifications to the cotton-dust analyzer and to present data on the performance of the machine when 17-, 50-, and 100-μm sizing screens were used.

Machine Modifications

A new model of the cotton-dust analyzer was constructed to overcome some of the shortcomings of the prototype. It was more compact and easier to operate than the original machine. The sizing-screen arrangement in the new model was more accessible than in the original machine to facilitate the evaluation of various screen sizes. It was also equipped with an air regulator to maintain a constant air pressure on the spray bar for improved airflow characteristics. Also, a high-efficiency particulate air filter (HEPA) was used for improved filtering of the air introduced into the analyzer by the high-pressure fan. Figures 1 and 2 illustrate the essential components of the new model of the cotton-dust analyzer.

The air jet spray bar consisted of 6.4-mm copper tubing that contained 17 openings of 1.6-mm diameter spaced at 9.5 mm along its axis. The spray bar was positioned 2.2 cm above the lint batt and was moved back and forth by a small roller chain powered by an electric reversing drive. This arrangement produced a spray bar movement across the entire batt surface once every 8 s. Air from an 827-kPa conventional compressed-air source was preconditioned before delivery to the spray bar by a combination prefilter/water trap and a secondary air filter rated at 0.01 micrometer. An adjustable air regulator in the compressed-air line maintained a constant pressure on the spray bar.

Lint specimens were contained between two wire-mesh screens. The top screen was 10 x 10 mesh (per cm) and held lint batts in place during processing. The bottom screen served as a sizing screen by collecting particles larger than the screen's openings and allowing smaller particles to move downward to the glass-fiber collecting filter. Another 10 x 10 mesh screen (per cm) below the sizing screen was used to support the glass-fiber filter.

A high-pressure fan directly under the glass-fiber filter provided sufficient airflow to convey dislodged dust from the lint batts through the sizing screen to the collection filter. Room air, induced into the top of the cotton-dust analyzer by the fan, passed through the HEPA filter, lint batt, screens, and collection filter before entering the fan. The air was then exhausted back to the room through a port near the botton of the machine enclosure. The fan had an operating capacity of 0.03 m^3/s against a static pressure of 5 kPa.

An aluminum enclosure housed the working components of the cotton-dust analyzer. The upper section of the enclosure, which was hinged to the lower section, contained the HEPA filter, the spray bar assembly, and the top, hold-down screen for the lint batt. The botton section housed the sizing screen, filter support, fan, and the electrical and pneumatic controls. The entire enclosure was 60 cm wide, 46 cm deep, and 72 cm tall.

Figure 3 is a schematic of the electrical control system. The electrical system provides power for the operation of the fan motor, the gear motor and magnetic clutches in the reversing drive, the timer motor, and the air solenoid valve. The manually initiated timer was adjustable for processing times up to 15 min.

Operating Procedures

Collection Filters. The cotton-dust analyzer requires 20.3-cm x 25.4-cm glass-fiber filters for collection of dust particles. These filters are binder-free and specially designed for gravimetric analysis of air pollutants. The filters are rated at 99.9%

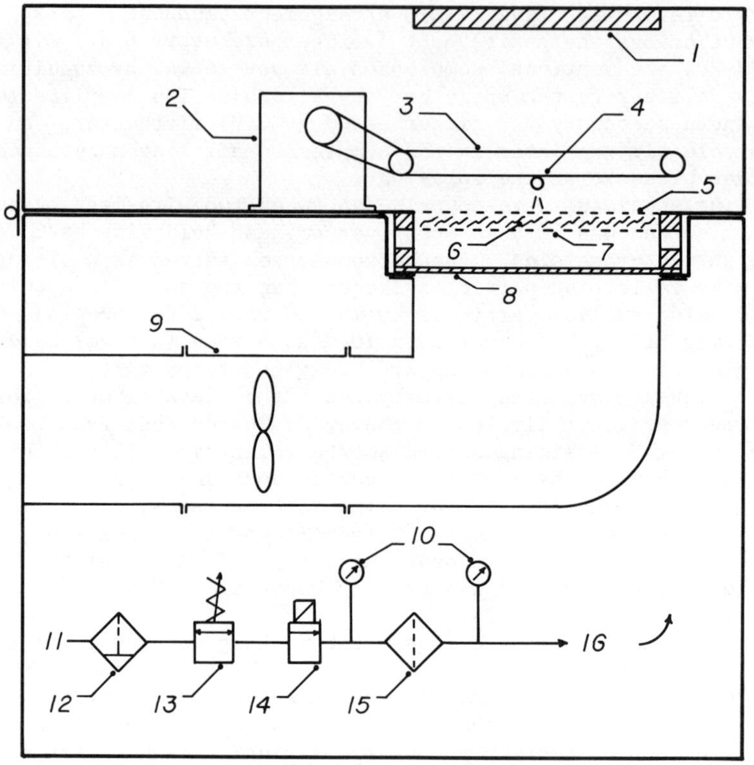

Figure 1. Schematic of cotton dust analyzer. 1, high efficiency particulate air filter; 2, reversing drive; 3, chain drive; 4, spray bar; 5, top screen; 6, lint batt; 7, sizing screen; 8, glass fiber filter; 9, high-pressure fan; 10, pressure gages; 11, compressed-air entrance; 12, prefilter/watertrap; 13, air-pressure regulator; 14, solenoid valve; 15, secondary air filter; 16, hose to spray bar.

Figure 2. Cotton dust analyzer showing top holding screen, sizing screen, and front control panel.

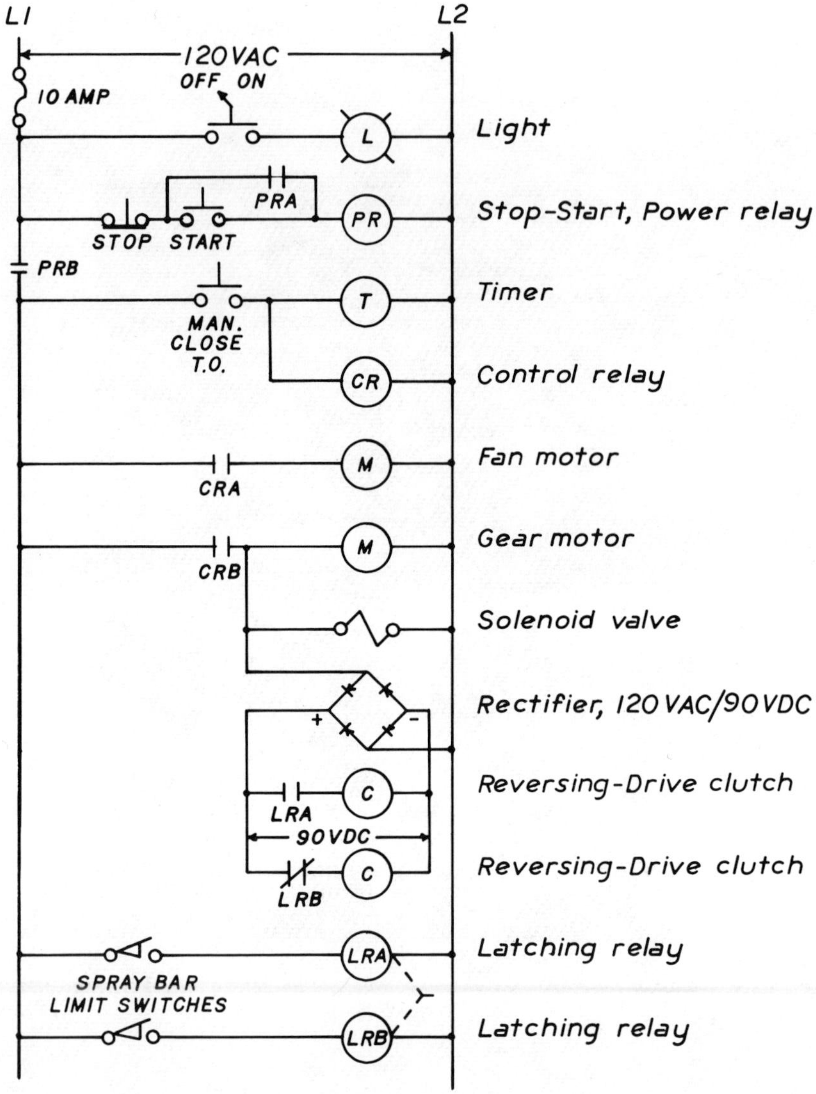

Figure 3. Schematic of electrical circuit for cotton dust analyzer.

efficiency (0.3 μm) by the Dioctyl Phtahlate Penetration (DOP) test.

Since the weight of dust collected by the filters is normally within the 5- to 15-mg range, we deemed it necessary to weigh the filters to the nearest 0.01 mg. An analytical balance equipped with an extra-large weighing pan was used for this purpose. The balance was in an environmental chamber that was maintained at a constant air temperature of 20°C and at a relative humidity of 60%. Filters were weighed in groups of 20 after an 8-h conditioning period in the environmental chamber. One of the 20 filters was a control filter that was not exposed to cotton dust. This filter was handled in exactly the same manner as the other filters and was processed in the cotton-dust analyzer without cotton. The difference between the initial and final weights of the control filter was used to correct the weights of the other 19 filters.

The specific weighing procedures were as follows:

1. The 20 filters were conditioned at least 8 h at 20°C and 60% relative humidity.

2. Then they were weighed to the nearest 0.01 mg and placed in dust-proof enclosure.

3. After the filters were exposed in the cotton-dust analyzer, they were conditioned for at least 8 h then reweighed to the nearest 0.01 mg.

4. From the control filter weights, the correction factor was determined and applied to the weights of dust collected by the remaining 19 filters.

Batt Preparation. In ititial trials of the new model of the cotton-dust analyzer, we used batt preparation techniques similar to those reported by Anderson and Baker (3). Generally, these techniques involved the use of a fiber blender to construct a thin, uniform batt of lint weighing 10 g. The 20.3- x 53.3-cm batt was then divided into three equal sized of specimens weighing about 3.33 g each. The three specimens were then processed in rotation; one glass-fiber filter was used to collect the dust from all three specimens. With a 17-μm sizing screen in the cotton dust analyzer, this procedure yielded dust weights of less than 5 mg. We considered these dust weights to be too small for accurate measurements of dust potential. Therefore, larger lint samples should be used to obtain sufficient yields of dust when the 17-μm sizing screen is used.

Two approaches were evaluated for increasing the size of the lint samples. In one approach, we simply used six speciments of 3.33 g each to comprise a 20-g lint sample. In the other approach, we doubled the thickness and weight of the specimens and used three specimens of 6.67 g each. We found that the cotton-dust analyzer technique was sensitive to variations in the thickness and weight of the batt. Doubling the batt weight and thickness reduced by about 50% the amount of dust extracted from a 20-g lint sample. Therefore, we decided to use six specimens of 3.33 g each in our analyses. Generally, these six specimens produced dust yields of 10 to 15 mg per 20-g lint sample.

Based on these evaluations we formulated the following batt-preparation procedures:

1. Hand feed 10 g of lint into the fiber blender as smoothly and uniformly as possible.
2. Remove the lint batt from the card cloth cylinder of the blender with a straight, heavy-gage wire rod without breaking or stretching the batt.
3. Lay the batt on a flat, clean surface and fold each end over about one-third of the batt length to form a three-layer batt of approximately 20 x 16 cm.
4. Feed the folded batt back through the blender with one of the 16-cm edges leading.
5. Remove the finished batt from the card cloth cylinder as in step 2.
6. Cut the batt into thirds to form three specimens of 3.33 g each.
7. Repeat steps 1 through 6 to obtain three more specimens from the same sample of lint. The six specimens formed by the above procedures will comprise a single, 20-g lint sample for exposure in the cotton-dust analyzer.

Analyzer Operation. Operating procedures for the new model of the cotton-dust analyzer were similar to those used for the original model, but with two exceptions. For the new model we reduced the specimen processing time and increased the air pressure on the spray bar. These changes allowed us to process a complete cotton sample (six specimens) in 18 min. and to obtain acceptable dust yields. After investigating several spray bar pressure levels, we selected 517 kPa as our standard operating pressure. This pressure level produced near-maximum dust yields and was near the maximum operating capability of our machine and its compressed air source. The 517-kPa operating pressure produced an airflow of about 0.03 m^3/s through the spray bar jets.

The following procedures were used to operate the new model of the cotton-dust analyzer:

1. A clean, preweighed filter was placed on lowermost screen surface.
2. The sizing screen was placed on top of the filter.
3. One lint specimen was placed on top of the sizing screen.
4. The upper lid of machine was closed and latched.
5. The timer was set for 3 min. and operation begun.
6. The air-pressure gage was checked. A 517-kPa reading was maintained by adjusting air-pressure regulator inside cabinet.
7. After 3 minutes exposure, the specimen was removed and another was inserted. This procedure was continued until all six specimens had been processed.

8. The sizing screen and exposed filter were removed and the filter was placed in a dust-tight enclosure.

9. The sizing screen was cleaned with compressed air to remove any material lodged on its upper surface in preparation for testing next sample.

Sizing Screen Evaluations

Lint samples from three cotton sources were analyzed by the use of 17-, 50-, and 100-μm sizing screens. All three cottons were commercial stripper varieties produced in the Lubbock, Texas, area during the 1979 growing season. Cottons 1 and 2 were stripper harvested in early December of 1979, and cotton 3 was stripper harvested in mid-January of 1980. All cotton was processed through a conventional ginning system designed for stripper cotton. Lint samples from each cotton source were evaluated in a randomized complete block experiment consisting of the three screen sizes and four replications. Significant differences between dust means for the three screen sizes were determined by Duncan's Multiple Range Test. The results of these measurements are presented in Table I.

There were no significant differences between the weight of dust sized with the 17- and 50-μm screens for any of the three test cottons. However, the 100-μm screen produce significantly higher dust weights for two of the cottons. These results indicated that particle size distribution of dust varied among the three cottons and suggested that the 17-μm screen would probably produce dust weights more representative of vertical elutriator measurements than would the other two screen sizes. Analysis of variance indicated that dust levels also differed significantly among cottons sized by the three screen sizes. This analysis showed that cotton 3 produced significantly higher 17- and 50-μm dust levels than either of the other two test cottons and a significantly higher 100-μm dust level than cotton 2. Whether these differences in dust levels of the cottons were due to varietal effects or to the different harvest dates could not be determined in this experiment. The pooled error mean squares from the analyses of variance for the 17-, 50-, and 100-μm screens were 0.53, 4.61, and 4.37, respectively--indicating that the 17-μm screen produced the most consistent dust-level measurement.

Additional measurements were made with the 17-μm sizing screen to obtain more information on the variability of our measurement techniques. Eight lint samples from a single source of cotton were analyzed by the procedures outlined previously. The dust levels obtained in this test were 11.7, 12.1, 13.5, 11.8, 10.8, 11.2, 10.9, and 9.7 mg, respectively, per 20 g of lint. The mean and standard deviation of these measurements were 11.5 and 1.1, respectively. The estimated standard error of the mean was 0.42, and the interval from 10.5 to 12.5 represented a 95% confidence interval for the lot mean.

Table I. Effect of Opening Size in Sizing Screen on Dust Content of Three Cotton Cultivars, mg/20 g Lint.

Rep. no.	Sizing screen opening size, μm		
	17	50	100
		COTTON 1	
1	11.1	10.4	13.7
2	9.6	10.9	16.3
3	10.4	10.2	14.0
4	10.7	11.0	19.4
AVG	10.5a[a]	10.6a	15.9c
		COTTON 2	
1	13.1	16.2	13.2
2	11.6	9.6	10.9
3	10.2	8.5	10.5
4	10.8	10.7	9.0
AVG	11.4a	11.3a	10.9a
		COTTON 3	
1	15.5	14.3	18.4
2	14.2	14.9	17.8
3	14.7	14.2	17.2
4	15.7	16.8	19.3
AVG	15.0b	15.1b	18.2c

[a]Means followed by different letters are significantly different at the 0.05 level.

Operational Performance

The new model of the cotton-dust analyzer has been used to measure the dust content of approximately 200 additional lint samples obtained from various gin and mill cleaning studies conducted during 1980. The results of these analyses have been or will be presented in other research reports and will not be disucussed here. However, the experience we gained during the processing of these samples provided us with an impression of the operational performance of the cotton-dust analyzer. We found that the operation of the analyzer was relatively easy and troublefree. Based on these experiences, we estimate that a laboratory technician could weigh and process 15 to 20 lint samples in an 8-h work shift. The handling, conditioning and weighing of the collection filters is the most critical operation for the success of the cotton dust analyzer technique.

Additional tests are underway to more accurately determine relationships between data from the cotton-dust analyzer and data on card-room dust levels as measured with a vertical elutriator. At present, the information available as a basis for comparing the two dust-measurement techniques is limited. The comparisons shown in Figure 4 were based on several analyses of samples from six cotton lots. Although limited in scope, the data indicate the likelihood that the correlation between the two measurement techniques will be reasonably good.

Summary

A redesigned cotton-dust analyzer equipped with a 17-μm sizing screen and operated at 517-kPa spray bar pressure was used to measure the dust content of 20-g lint cotton samples. High-velocity air jets were used in the analyzer for release of dust from specially prepared batts of lint. The dust was then sized by a 17-μm screen and collected on a glass-fiber filter for gravimetric analysis. Operating procedures for handling and weighing the filters, preparing the lint batts, and operating the analyzer were developed. The equipment and techniques developed in this study comprise a laboratory method for estimating the dust-release potential of raw lint cotton.

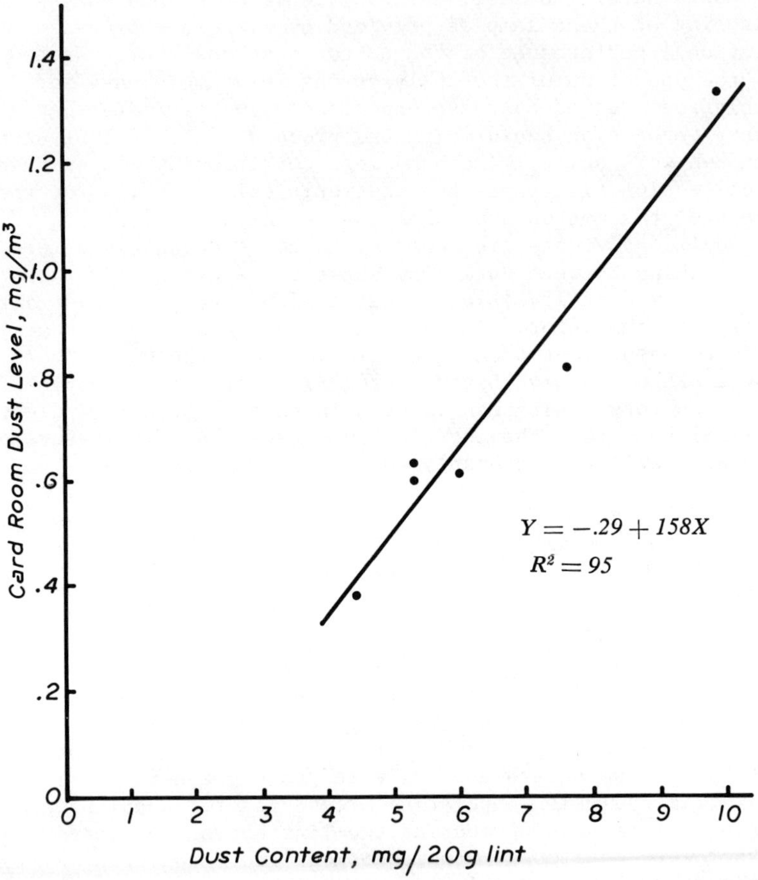

Figure 4. Card room dust levels vs. dust content measurements by a cotton dust analyzer (17-μm sizing screen).

Literature Cited

1. Cocke, J. B.; Wesley, R. A.; Kirk, I. W. USDA Market Res. Rep. 1977, No. MRR 1065, p 1-16.
2. Cocke, J. B.; Hatcher, J. D. Trans ASAE 1975, 18, 1006-10.
3. Anderson, J. D; Baker, R. V. Trans. ASAE 1979, 22, 918, 925.
4. Anderson, J. D.; Baker, R. V. U.S. Patent 1979, 4, 154,111.

RECEIVED December 15, 1981.

6

Cotton Trash and Dust Contents and Airborne Dust Concentration

Feasibility of Predicting by Nondestructive Light Reflectance

JOSEPH G. MONTALVO, JR., MARIE-ALICE ROUSSELLE, and ALBERT BARIL, JR.

Southern Regional Research Center, New Orleans, LA 70179

TERRY A. WATKINS

University of New Orleans, Lakefront, New Orleans, LA 70148

In situ content of trash and dust and airborne dust generated by mechanical processing in grade representative-randomly selected raw cottons correlated significantly with nondestructive testing by visible light reflectance. The linear correlation coefficient of particulate content (y) on ln (1/reflectance) (x) was: trash (nonlint), -0.969; dust (dry assay), -0.977; dust (wet assay), -0.989; trash plus dust (dry), -0.970; trash plus dust (wet), -0.997; airborne dust, -0.930. Variation of dust-trash contents in the cottons was also investigated. Dust content increased with trash content. The ratio of dust to trash content decreased with increase in the trash value and approached a constant value at the higher trash levels.

OSHA has determined that worker exposure to cotton dust presents a significant health hazard commonly referred to as byssinosis (1). This respiratory disease is characterized by shortness of breath, cough, and chest tightness. Permissible exposure limits have been established for selected processes in the cotton industry: 200 $\mu g/m^3$ or less in yarn manufacturing, 750 $\mu g/m^3$ or less in slashing and weaving, and 500 $\mu g/m^3$ or less elsewhere in the cotton industry. An urgent need exists for innovative approaches to monitoring and controlling cotton dust.

Monitoring dust and trash concentrations in cotton by a simple, rapid, on-line process analyzer with feedback control could provide ginners an incentive to produce cleaner cotton and thus improved marketability of the commodity. Based on the dust and trash in the baled cotton, it may also be possible to predict airborne dust levels in textile milling. Bales could be automatically blended to minimize mean dust level in the workplace. (In

0097-6156/82/0189-0067$06.00/0

this paper dust is defined as foreign particles with diameter generally $\leq$ 17 μm and trash is defined as foreign particles with diameter > 17 μm.)

Several advances in instrumentation have provided tools to evaluate trash in cotton. The cotton colorimeter (2) selects cotton for grade standards and as a reference in classification. Taylor (3) measured cotton trash using near infrared reflectance. Kasdan (4) developed a prototype instrument for grading cotton according to trash and color. Lyons and Barker (5) correlated trash surface area with trash content grade. No single instrument, however, has been developed with combined capabilities for nondestructive estimation of in situ concentrations of dust and trash in cotton and the dust-release potential of cotton during mill processing.

This paper presents a feasibility study of visible light reflectance as a tool to predict in situ concentration of dust and trash in baled cotton and the airborne dust released in mechanical processing. Mathematical relationships between dust and trash levels in the cottons were also investigated.

Selection of visible light reflectance as a candidate nondestructive test method was based on results from probing experiments. It was observed that as cotton was mechanically cleaned, its visible light reflectance increased. Conversely, addition of trace amounts of particulate (trash and dust) to extensively cleaned cotton resulted in a decrease in visible light reflectance. Finally, it was noted that off-colored cotton was rendered whiter with repetitive mechanical cleaning.

Theoretical

Visible light reflectance from incident white light on raw cotton may include signal contributions from fiber, and the dust and trash on the fiber surfaces. Then the reflectance is a function depending on fiber, dust, and trash.

Changes in reflectance due to changes in fiber might be due to fiber color, fineness, maturity or other similar aspect. We will assume, however, that the changes in reflectance due to these factors are negligible. Thus the reflectance will depend only on dust and trash.

Changes in relectance values due to changes in dust and trash may depend on particle source (bract, leaf, etc.), diameter, or other factors in addition to concentration. Again we make a simplifying assumption that reflectance (R) depends only on the concentrations of dust (D) and trash (T) in cotton. Thus we may write

$$R = R(D,T) \qquad (1)$$

and consider the nature of the relationship expressed in Equation 1.

If one assumes that there is a functional relationship between dust and trash concentrations, say

$$D = f(T) \tag{2}$$

then it follows, by substituting Equation 2 into 1 and solving for T, that there is some function g with

$$T = g(R). \tag{3}$$

Similarly, upon substituting Equation 3 into 2, one obtains

$$D = h(R). \tag{4}$$

By similar assumptions, Equations 1 and 2 may be rewritten to show there is a

$$AD = i(R) \tag{5}$$

functional relationship between the concentration of airborne dust (AD) and R.

Kubelka-Munh theory (6) shows that R varies non-linearly with the concentration of an absorber, and Norris (7) has suggested that the logarithm (1/R) varies linearly with the concentration of an absorber. These results suggest that Equations 3 and 4 may be rewritten such that

$$T = a_i + b_i \ln (1/R) \tag{6}$$

and

$$D = a_i + b_i \ln (1/R) \tag{7}$$

$$AD = a_i + b_i \ln (1/R). \tag{8}$$

where a_i is the intercept and b_i is the slope of the equation.

Eliminating R in Equations 6 and 7 shows that if this is a correct model then the relationship between T and D is linear, and hence, Equation 2 may be rewritten as

$$D = a_i + b_i T. \tag{9}$$

It now follows from Equations 6,7, and 9 that

$$D + T = a_i + b_i \ln (1/R) \tag{10}$$

and

$$D/T = a_i + b_i/T. \tag{11}$$

As a final comment with regard to Equations 6, 7, and 8, we observe that if R is scaled 0-100, but values of R are in fact contained in an interval C-100, where C is not near zero, (say $C > 25$) then there is a strong linear relationship between R and ln $(\overline{1}/R)$. This suggests that the model given by Equations 6, 7, and 8 may not be a significant improvement over that obtained by assuming that T and D are each linearly related to R (i.e. by replacing ln (1/R) in Equations 6, 7, and 8 with R).

We should also note that Equation 9 is valid so long as D and T are linearly related to some function of R (not necessarily ln (1/R). Thus, if ln (1/R) in Equations 6 and 7, is replaced by R, Equation 9 continues to be valid.

Materials, Methods, and Protocols

Instrumentation. Light reflectance in the visible range was measured with a Model 610 Photovolt Reflectance Meter using white incident light. The instrumentation developed by Anderson and Baker (8) was utilized to measure dust in cotton by dry assay. In brief, compressed air is forced through a thin layer of cotton to detach the dust from the fiber and to transport the suspended material out of the fiber mass so that it can be collected on a filter.

A 100 watt ultrasonic bath was used to detach dust from the fiber by wet assay. A Shirley Analyzer (9) was used to remove trash from cotton. In brief, the analyzer contains two rotating cyclinders with saw teeth to mechanically remove the trash from cotton. The Continuous Aerosol Monitoring (CAM) analyzer developed by ppm, Inc. (10) was used to measure airborne dust.

Cotton Samples. The six cottons utilized in this feasibility study included one representative bale from each of the major grade divisions as determined by the United States Department of Agriculture-Agricultural Marketing Service (USDA-AMS) Classers. Designated grades are tabulated in Table I; the color group for each grade was 1(white). Each grade representative cotton was selected at random by the AMS from that produced in the following geographical regions: far west (1 sample), southwest (2 samples), southcentral (1 sample),southeast (1 sample), and unknown (1 sample). Selection of one bale per major grade reflects trash content range in cotton. Each bale was blended and a 50 lb bulk sample randomly taken from each of the blended bales.

Procedures. The light reflectance instrument was turned on 30 min prior to initiating reflectance observations. The sensitivity switch was set in the low position. The combination visible light emitter-reflectance detector was positioned vertically; the active end of the detector faced upward. The sample cup was a glass cylindrical cuvette with optically flat bottom. A constant mass of 165 g (brass slug) was placed on top

TABLE I

Cotton Source and Particulate Burdens

Grade	Source	Trash Content(%)	Dust Content (%)		Dust(%)/Trash(%)		Airborne Dust(%)
			Dry assay	Wet assay	Dry	Wet	
Strict Middling(SM)	Montgomery Ala.	0.0756	0.0643	0.106	0.850	1.400	0.075
Middling(M)	Austin, Tex.	0.365	0.0874	0.215	0.240	0.590	0.097
Strict Low Middling(SLM)	Unknown	0.407	0.109	0.226	0.270	0.560	0.064
Low Middling(LM)	Macon, Ga.	1.907	0.153	0.314	0.080	0.160	0.150
Strict Good Ordinary(SGO)	Corpus Christi, Tex.	2.020	0.170	0.368	0.080	0.180	0.196
Good Ordinary (GO)	Fresno, Calif.	3.298	0.241	0.649	0.070	0.200	-[a]
Average Value		1.345	0.137	0.314	0.100	0.230	0.116
Pooled standard deviation(%)			0.0115	0.0272			
Coefficient of variation(%)			8.5	8.7			

[a]Run invalid

of the cotton tuft in the cuvette to hold the fiber tightly against the optically flat bottom. Cotton tufts (about 0.5 g) were plucked at random from each of the six bulk samples. A tuft was placed in the cuvette, weighted down with the brass slug, and the cuvette placed over the center of the detector. Preliminary reflectance observations indicated which two cottons gave the lowest and highest reflectance values. The scale expansion switch was turned on and the instrument calibrated at 90% and 30% reflectance using the high and low reflectance tufts, respectively. A tuft from one of the six cottons was (a) randomly selected, (b) reflectance recorded, (c) tuft discarded, and (d) the instrument recalibrated. The a-b-c-d protocol was repeated until three observations were taken per sample. Slight differences in glass optical reflectance were negated by using only three cups to make the measurements, two calibration and one sample cuvette.

Two hundred g of cotton was randomly taken from each of the six bulk samples to measure trash content. Each was weighed to two decimal places then mechanically cleaned in a Shirley analyzer (9). After completing the first processing stage in the analyzer, the cleaned lint was recleaned seven additional times to completely remove visible trash. The trash box residue was recovered and entrained lint removed from it with the aid of forceps, hand cards, and sonic sieves. The remaining nonlint trash was weighed and its content in cotton computed in percentage units.

The wet assay technique to measure dust in cotton was a modification of the method described by Thibodeaux (11). A 400-mg tuft of cotton, randomly selected from a bulk sample, was subjected to multiple ultrasonic washings in methanol. Clean methanol (200 ml) was used for each of three 5-min washings. The combined methanol washings were filtered through a 17 μm sizing screen (the screen was identical for both wet and dry assay procedures) and collected on a 0.5 μm filter. Increase in filter weight provided the measure of dust content (%) in cotton by wet assay.

The dry assay method to measure dust in cotton was described by Anderson and Baker (8). A fiber blending wheel was used to prepare a relatively thin rectangular shaped batt. Twenty g of cotton was randomly taken from a bulk sample. Six 3 1/3 g batts were prepared from each cotton, for a total of 20g. Each batt was placed in a specially constructed box, air at 75 psi was forced through the passive batt, then through a 17 μm sizing screen, and the dust collected on a 0.5 μm glass fiber filter. Dust collection continued for 3 min. Five additional batts were then processed. The total increase in filter weight reflected the dust concentration (%) in cotton by dry assay. Actual room conditions for dry assay were 58% relative humidity and 78°F.

Airborne dust measurements were performed by Dr. F. Shofner of ppm, Inc. (10). Approximately 100 to 300 mg preweighed samples of hand-formed sliver were fed into the opening beater of a commercial open-end spinning head. Air flow transported the individualized fibers and airborne dust through a transport tube. The dust ($\leq$ 15 μm) was electro-optically weighed during a 2 1/2 min. sampling period. Each sample was passed four times through the system and the airborne dust contents summed to provide a measure of total airborne dust(%) released by repetitive mechanical processing.

Data Processing and Statistics. Linear, power, and exponential lines were fitted to the dust, trash, and reflectance data by standard regression methods.

Results and Discussion

Cotton Grade and Source. It should be noted that the six grade representative-randomly selected cottons were produced in different states (Table I). Variety planted, harvesting, ginning technique, and commodity grade are characteristic of each area. All of these factors may influence cotton particulate concentrations and visible light reflectance properties. Thus, using cottons with the natural range of variables for this feasibility study should add credence to the observed trends in the data.

Particulate Burdens and Refectance Data. Table I gives the particulate concentrations. Percentage trash reported in Table I reflects nonlint trash only. These trash values are not positively biased by the lint entrainment associated with the so-called Shirley analyzer visible trash concentrations (9). Only one trash observation was taken per sample because of the excessive amount of time required to manually separate lint from nonlint.

Coefficient of variation for dust (dry assay) and dust (wet assay) was 8.5 and 8.7%, respectively. The range of trash contents is about 50 compared to about four for dust content. As explained by Montalvo (12), differences in dust content by the dry and wet assay methods are a result of a geometry effect associated with the former technique and the variation of adhesion force of dust on cotton with environment. Only one airborne dust measurement was taken on five of the six cottons. The run was declared invalid on the remaining sample.

Table II summarizes the visible light reflectance results. Results for each observation (j) on each sample (i) are included in the table. The j observations for the ith sample were averaged (i•); the coefficient of variation was 4.5%. The variance in light reflectance results is about half that observed with dust content measurements.

Particulate-Reflectance Functions. Regression parameters for particulate-reflectance relationships are shown in Table III.

TABLE II

Visible Light Reflectance Results

Grade	Light Reflectance(%) j=1	j=2	j=3	i·
SM	88.0	93.9	90.2	90.7 ± 3.0 (std. dev.)
M	82.9	81.3	86.3	83.5 ± 1.6
SLM	80.0	80.1	84.0	81.4 ± 2.3
LM	61.7	59.7	63.0	61.5 ± 1.7
SGO	51.9	65.2	59.9	59.0 ± 6.7
GO	32.3	32.1	32.2	32.2 ± 0.1
Mean Reflectance				68.1
Pooled standard deviation				3.1
Coefficient of variation(%)				4.5

TABLE III

Linear Regression Parameters of Particulate-Reflectance Relationships

Regression (y=particulate)	Correlation Corefficient (r)	Coefficient of determination (r^2,%)	intercept (a_i)	slope (b_i)
x=ln(1/reflectance)				
Trash	0.969	93.9	15.54	3.406
Dust(dry)	0.977	95.5	0.8237	0.1647
Dust(wet)	0.989	97.9	2.345	0.4877
Trash plus Dust(dry)	0.970	94.1	16.38	3.575
Trash plus Dust(wet)	0.997	95.4	17.77	3.867
Airborne Dust	0.930	86.5	1.260	0.2656
x=reflectance				
Trash	-0.993	98.6	5.307	-0.0582
Dust(dry)	-0.994	98.8	-.3387	-0.00296
Dust(wet)	-0.981	96.2	0.8921	-0.00851
Trash plus Dust(dry)	-0.994	98.8	5.646	-0.0612
Trash plus Dust(wet)	-0.997	99.4	6.198	-0.0667
Airborne Dust	-0.919	84.4	0.3877	-0.00361

For comparison purposes, regression parameters were computed for the model defined by Equations 6, 7, 8, and 10 and the model obtained by replacing ln (1/R) in those equations by R. The dependent variable (y) is particulate concentration because it is desired to predict particulate content from reflectance values. Data from Tables I and II were also fitted to exponential and power functions where the independent variable (x) was reflectance but the fits were found to be inferior to that of the linear relationship.

Figure 1 and 2 demonstrate the linear relationship of trash and dust content (wet assay) to both ln (1/reflectance) and reflectance. The coefficient of determination (r^2) is the percentage of total variation explained by the regression. For example, percentage of unexplained variation (i.e. 1.4% for y = trash content and 3.8% for y = dust content (wet assay) with x = reflectance) is indicative of a significant relationship between particulate content in cotton and ln R. A small unexplained variation was observed for all of the trash and dust content functions in Table III. Airborne dust unexplained variation, however, was poorer; precision of the measurement for the five cottons investigated was not reported.

Dust content (dry assay) in the cottons, and a measure of total particulate content, arbitrarily defined here as the sum of the dust (wet assay) and trash content, were computed from the regression relationships using the mean reflectance values given in Table II. Calculated particulate contents were plotted against the observed values in Table I and are shown in Figures 3 and 4. These two graphs indicate that the regression lines predict the particulate content of the six cottons very well.

Particulate Functions. Table IV summarizes the regression results from exploring linear relationships between dust and trash levels in cotton. Exponential and power relationships were considered but the fits were found inferior to the linear case. The unexplained variation ranging from 1% to 9% suggest that a model leading to Equation 7 and 9 may indeed be an appropriate choice.

Dust content increased with increase in trash content. A presentation of the dust (dry assay) linear relationship is shown in Figure 5. Dust/trash content was also linearly regressed on x = reciprocal of trash content (Figure 6). The curves illustrated in Figures 5 and 6 are the first documentation of actual dust-nonlint trash trends in raw cotton. Note in Figure 6 that with increasing trash content, the dust/trash ratio approaches a constant, the intercept a_i of Equation 9.

Conclusions and Recommendations. This study encompassed the particulate content range found in the major commercial grades of raw cotton. Changes in visible light reflectance between the grades exceeded within-grade variances. *In situ* contents of dust

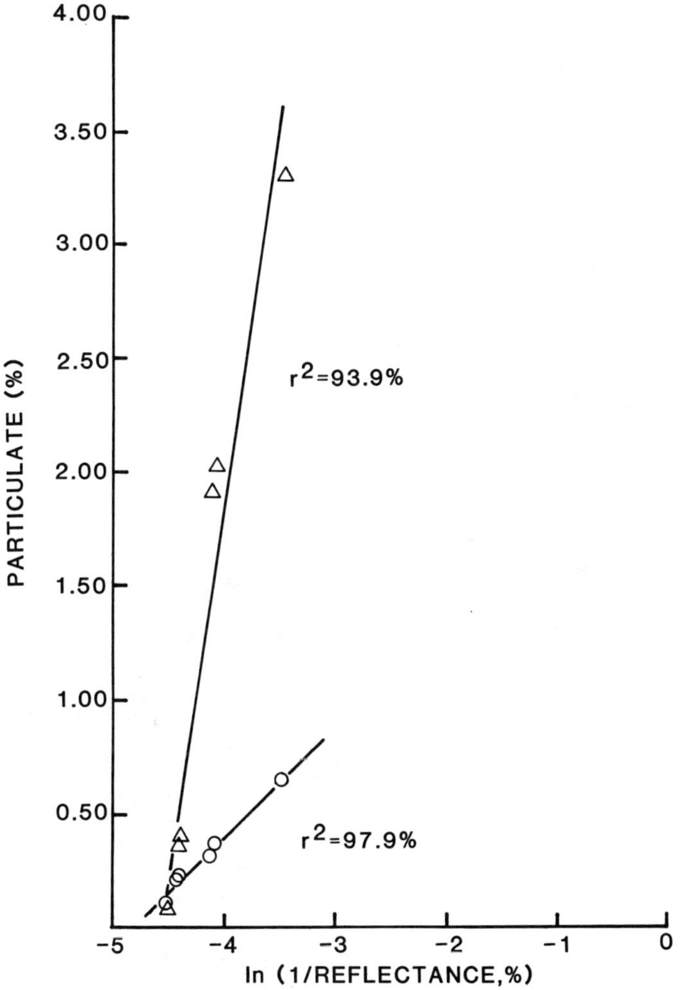

Figure 1. Correlation of particulate with ln(1/light reflectance). Key: △, trash; ○, dust, wet assay.

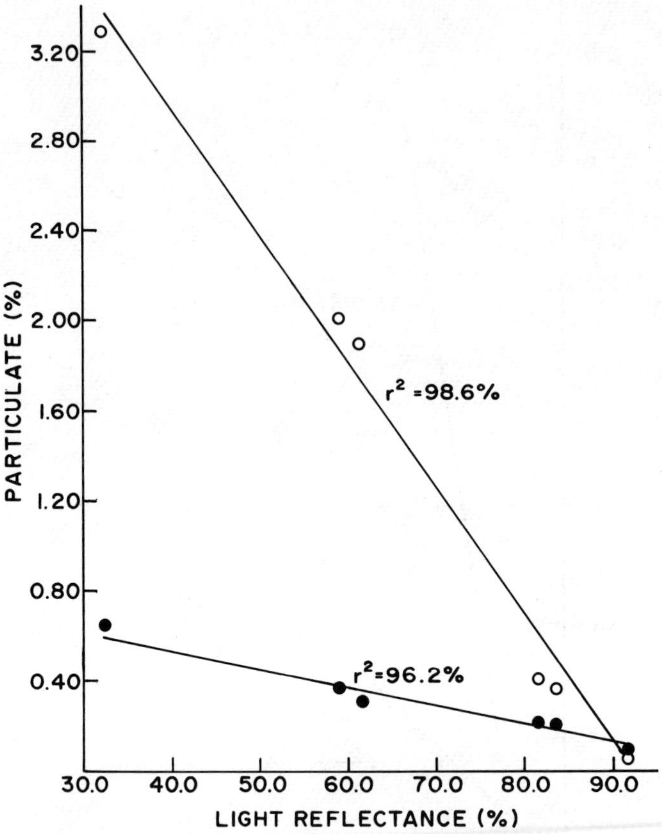

Figure 2. Correlation of particulate with light reflectance. Key: ○, trash; ●, dust, wet assay.

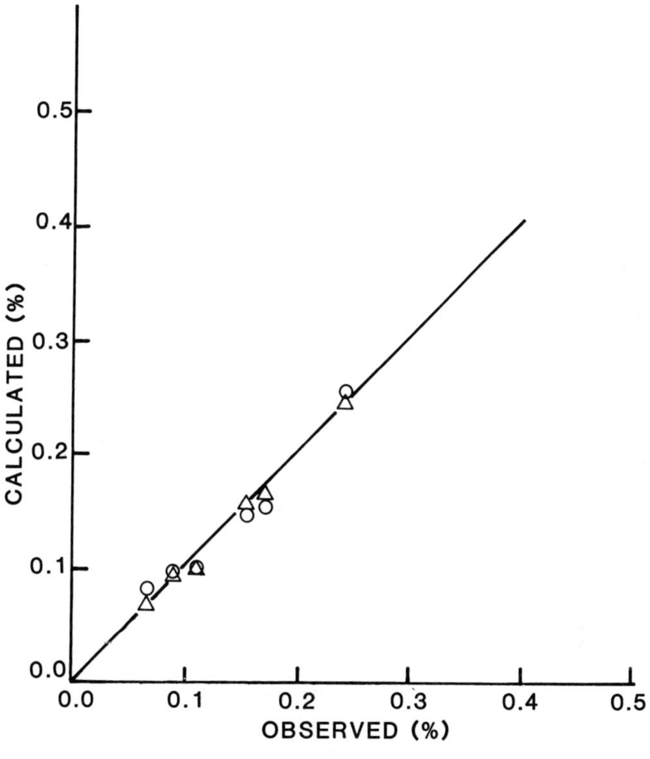

Figure 3. Dust content (dry), calculated vs. observed. Key: ——, theoretical slope (1:1); △, calculated vs. observed (from linear regression on reflectance); and ○, calculated vs. observed (from linear regression on ln(1/R)).

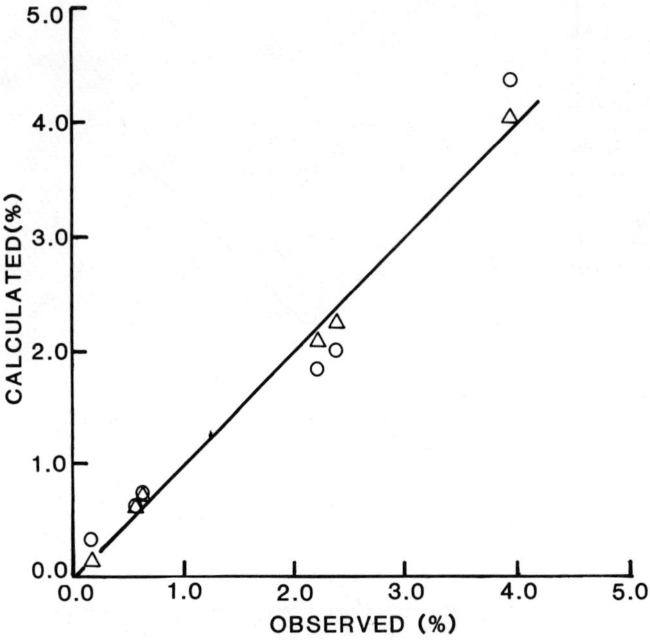

Figure 4. Dust plus trash content, calculated vs. observed. Key: ——, theoretical slope (1:1); △, calculated vs. observed (from linear regression on reflectance); and ○, calculated vs. observed (from linear regression on ln(1/R)).

TABLE IV

Linear Regression Parameters of Particulate Relationships

Regression y	Regression x	Correlation Corefficient (r)	Coefficient of determination (r^2,%)	intercept (a)	slope (a)
Dust(dry)	Trash	0.985	97.0	0.0702	0.0499
Dust(wet)	Trash	0.954	91.0	0.1228	0.1414
Dust(dry)/Trash	1/Trash	0.995	99.0	0.0678	0.0589
Dust(wet)/Trash	1/Trash	0.978	95.6	0.2080	0.9033

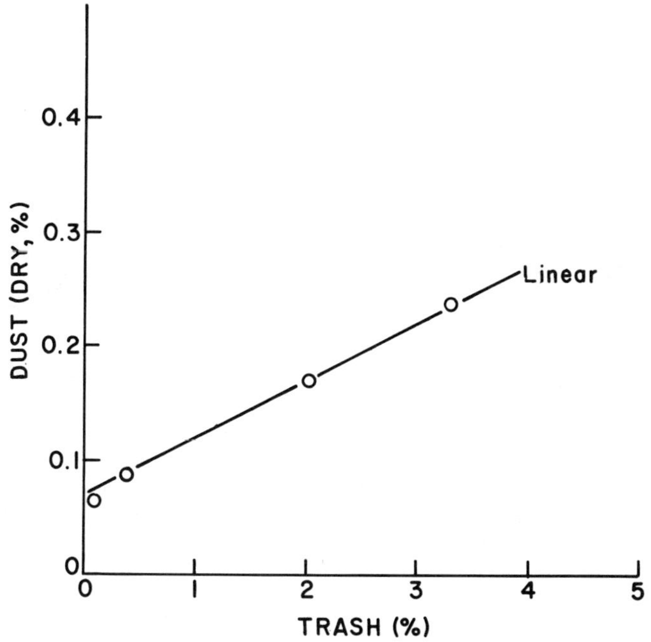

Figure 5. Variation of dust and trash content.

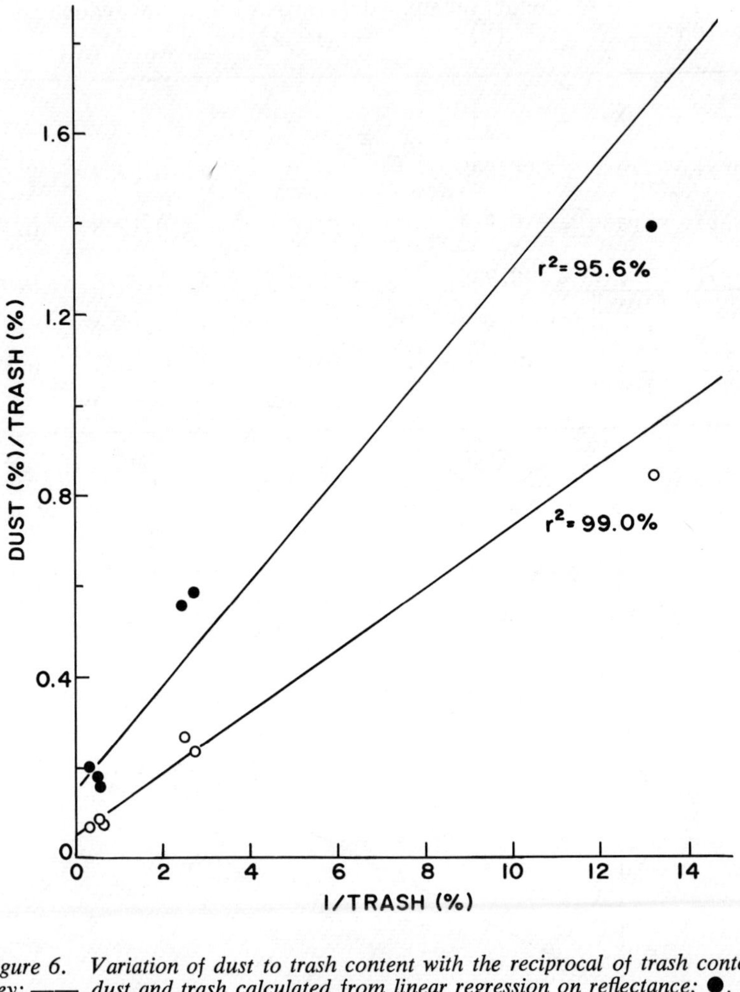

Figure 6. Variation of dust to trash content with the reciprocal of trash content. Key: ——, dust and trash calculated from linear regression on reflectance; ●, observed dust (wet) and trash; and ○, observed dust (dry) and trash.

and trash in six carefully selected cottons correlated significantly with both visible light reflectance and ln (1/visible light reflectance). Airborne dust levels of five of the samples also correlated significantly with both reflectance functions. Variations of dust content between the grades exceeded within- grade variances. Dust content correlated significantly and positively with trash content.

Light measurement offers the combined capability of rapidly predicting by nondestructive means dust and trash content in cotton and airborne dust level. Of course, the standard error of estimate is not a practical statistic based on only six cottons and is not reported in this feasibility paper.

Other statistical inferences are possible, however, about characteristics of a population of cotton samples from a study of six randomly selected from the population. We conclude that the particulate-reflectance relationship is a very strong one and that the model of Equations 6 and 7 is a "highly likely candidate" even though there is no evidence in this paper that it is superior to the model obtained by replacing ln (1/R) with R.

The approach to using light to relate or predict particulate propensity of cotton in the gin and in the textile mill appears eminently feasible. Additional work is in progress with a population of over fifty samples in order to verify the reported findings. Vertical elutriator dust levels, and dust and trash contents in the cottons will be correlated with light measurements. Dependence of the correlation coefficient (r) on the wavelength of incidence light is being investigated. Light transmitted through a cotton sample offers several advantages over the reflectance technique and is also being studied.

Acknowledgements

We greatfully acknowledge trash analysis by Mrs. Cynthia Lichtenstein, dust (dry assay) by Mr. Jimmie Sandberg, and dust (wet assay) by Mrs. Shirley Armand.

Disclaimer

Mention of company names or products does not constitute endorsement by the United States Department of Agriculture.

Literature Cited

1. Federal Register 1978, 43, 27350-418.
2. Amercian Society for Testing and Materials, Annu. Book ASTM Stand. 1977, Part 33, p 428-434.
3. Taylor, R. A. Proc. 1980 Beltwide Cotton Prod. Res. Conf. 1980, p 259-265.
4. Kasdan, H. L. Proceedings of the 1977 Electro Optics/Laser Conf. 1977, p 256-262.

5. Lyons, D. W.; Barker, R. L. Text. Res. J. 1976, 46, 135-9.
6. Kubelka, P.; J. Opt. Soc. Am. 1947, 38, 448-57.
7. Norris, K. H.; personal communication.
8. Anderson, J. D.; Baker, R. V. Trans. ASAE 1979, 22, 918-21, 925.
9. American Society for Testing and Materials, Annu. Book ASTM Stand. 1977, Part 33, p 576-583.
10. Shofner, F. M.; Hyde, R. E.; Duckett, K. E. Proc. 1981 Beltwide Cotton Prod. Res. Conf. 1981, p 48-52.
11. Thibodeaux, D. P.; Baril, A. J. Text. Res. J., in press.
12. Montalvo, J. G., Jr. Proc. 1981 Beltwide Cotton Prod. Res. Conf. 1981, p 53-54.

RECEIVED January 20, 1982.

7

A Standardized Method for Vertical Elutriator Cotton Dust Sampling

ANN L. WALKER and ELLIS E. PARDUE[1]

The Hanes Group, Consolidated Foods Corporation, Winston–Salem, NC 27102

Specific equipment and techniques used by The Hanes Group for vertical elutriator cotton dust sampling are discussed. Some accessories were developed for convenience, but the approach to site selection, filter handling, orifice calibration, and training of sampling personnel were important in obtaining vertical elutriator data with coefficients of variation less than 10%. One new sampling method was investigated also, and plant data showed that it was equivalent to the vertical elutriator method. The alternative instrument used was a Portable Continuous Aerosol Monitor (PCAM) manufactured by ppm, Inc., and dust concentrations measured with the PCAM were 5-15% lower than values obtained with standard vertical elutriators. Calculations and examples for TWA exposures, equivalency tests, and vertical elutriator coefficients of variation are included.

Two factors are important if valid analytical data is to be generated. One is equipment or instrumentation; the other is technique. These two factors are always interrelated, since techniques are at least partially determined by the capability of the equipment (Tables I and II).

Cotton dust sampling is a plant site test, normally involving unsophisticated field equipment, ever-changing plant conditions, and technician-level labor in performing many functions. However, with adequate equipment and attention to technique, we have found that good quality data can be obtained for each survey. The purpose of this paper is to share with you some of the instrumentation, equipment modifications and techniques we have studied and employed to obtain vertical elutriator (VE) data with average coefficients of variation less than 10%.

[1] Current address: Route 8, Box 5202, Winston-Salem, NC 27106.

0097-6156/82/0189-0085$6.00/0

TABLE I

Cotton Dust Sampling Equipment

VE Rack	Stopwatch
Vertical elutriator	Walter crucible holder
Vacuum pumps	Balance (to 1 microgram)
Orifices	Tweezers
Chains and/or brackets	Modified arbor press
Thick walled rubber tubing	Filter support stand
Hose connectors	Static eliminator
Electrical tape	Diagrams of plant layout
Ladder	Employee lists
Storage cart	
Filter boxes	
Filters, backup pads, cassettes, shrink bands	
Filter data sheets and pens	
Wet test meter, bubble tube, rotameter, and manometer	
Assorted spare parts; pumps, fuses, orifices, etc.	

TABLE II

Basic Procedures for Cotton Dust Monitoring

1. Define process area
2. Define work areas within each process area
3. Select and prepare sampling sites
4. Define employee job classifications
5. Define time-in-work-areas for each job classification
6. Obtain current list of all employees in each job classification
7. Obtain production, ventilation and system design information
8. Clean elutriators
9. Calibrate orifices
10. Weigh filters and assemble cassettes
11. Calibrate personnel pumps
12. Obtain 6-8 hour elutriator samples in each work area during each shift of operation
13. Obtain personnel total dust samples for representative employees in noncompliance areas
14. Reweigh filters
15. Calculate dust concentrations for each site and shift
16. Calculate employee TWA exposures for each job classification and shift
17. Notify employees and management of results
18. Clean equipment for next survey

Sampling Site

Perhaps the most basic and important part of the techniques in cotton dust sampling is the process of choosing sampling sites. In the rush to obtain VE results, it is easy to overlook certain conditions in the workplace. Meaningless data can often be traced to nonrepresentative sites.

Instead, the first step should be a thorough review of processes, machinery variations, employee job functions for all affected job classifications, dust generation points, dust control equipment, and air handling systems (1). With this data in hand, and an accurate layout of the plant, one can begin the three-stage process of selecting plant sampling positions.

Process Areas. The first stage is easy: divide the plant into specific process areas, such as opening, carding, roving, spinning. The second stage draws upon the accumulated information to determine whether or not a given process area should be subdivided into several work areas (Figures 1 and 2). This decision is based on answers to the following types of questions:

1. Are dust levels consistent throughout the area? Do certain areas tend to have higher or lower dust concentrations due to machinery dust generation points, waste handling operations, etc.?
2. How do air handling systems and dust control units affect dust levels throughout the area?
3. Where do employees spend most of their time?
4. What job functions tend to generate the most dust?
5. How many different job classifications are represented in a given area, and are their work patterns similar or different?

Site Selection. The third stage examines each work area for suitable and representative sites. The number of sample sites depends on work area size, dust consistency, equipment generation points, and any other factors that seem appropriate to consider. Since process areas may be subdivided to assist in the calculation of employee time-weighted average (TWA) exposures, it is necessary to have at least one VE in each work area where cotton dust is present. Larger numbers of sample sites per work area give more representative information about dust levels throughout the area, but usually there must be a compromise between the amount of data that might be desirable and the amount of time, effort and equipment available to obtain necessary information. Some problems to avoid in choosing sampling sites are as follows: strong air currents, locations protected from normal air currents, areas with shutdown machines, and locations that interfere with machinery operation or maintenance, traveling cleaners, material handling, or employee efficiency (1). Column and wall locations should be carefully examined, since peculiarities in air currents often give

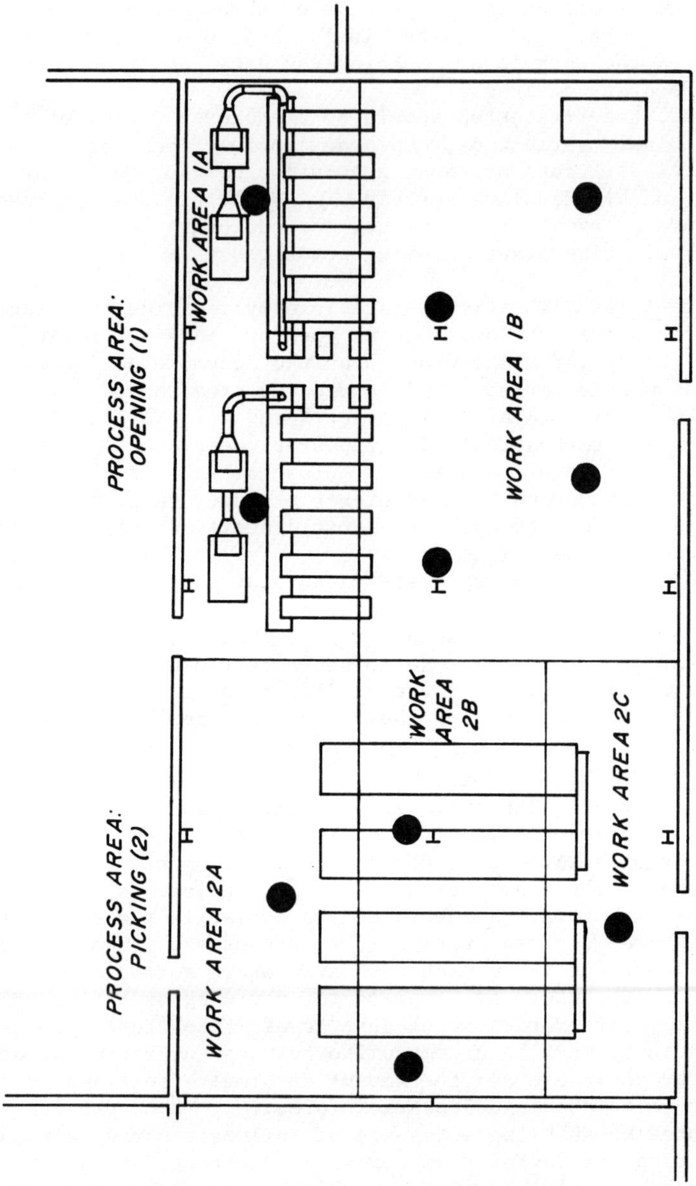

Figure 1. Sample plant layout of opening and picking process areas including subdivisions into work areas and sampling locations.

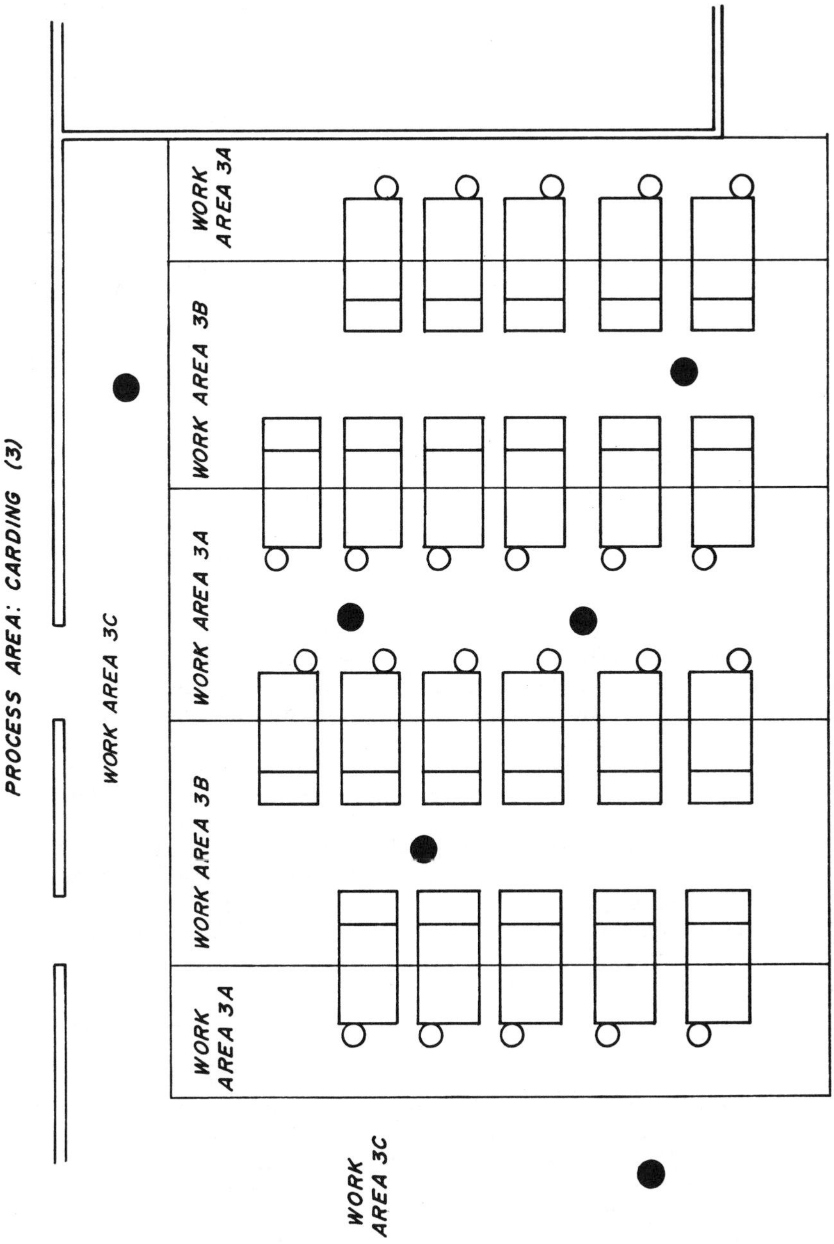

Figure 2. Sample plant layout of card room subdivided into five sections representing two work areas with sampling sites.

low dust levels at such sites. The goal is to choose locations that best represent the dust exposures of employees without interfering with either the employee job functions or the process machinery operation.

The final preparation step is to provide a bracket or chain and an electrical outlet at each selected site. Since we expect the need for dust sampling to continue for an indefinite period of time, we have established permanent sample locations with the necessary utilities.

Equipment

Vertical Elutriator. The basic piece of equipment for cotton dust sampling is the vertical elutriator, or VE for short (Figure 3) (2). It is essentially a hollow cylinder which is sized to act as a settling chamber for dust particles larger than 15 um diameter when used with a flow rate of 7.4 Lpm. Our own set of twelve VE's includes several from each of three suppliers, including Famco, General Metal Works, and our inhouse sheet metal shop. Batson also makes VE's. Although the VE is simple and rugged, it is also bulky, so we have tried to make it convenient and easy to use. The Gast vacuum pump is neatly mounted on brackets that extend above the elutriator. The brackets also accommodate the chains and S-hooks used to hang the VE in the plant. We have also designed a small switch box with an on/off toggle switch and a slo-blow quick disconnect fuse for the pump. The fuse arrangement alone has reduced hassle and headache time considerably.

The VE and pump require minimal routine maintenance. In the field, the motor is wiped off at each filter change to remove accumulated lint. The inside of the VE is checked each day to see if any lint buildup is present. The bottom and top of the VE are plugged with hollow plastic stoppers when not in use to discourage employee tampering and to reduce dust and lint accumulation. At the completion of each survey, the VE's and pumps are given a thorough compressed air cleaning, and about once a year they get a soap and water scrubbing. As a last measure of convenience, we built a roll-around cart to hold the twelve VE's and simplify transportation arrangements.

Filters. The filter unit consists of a three-piece polystyrene cassette, a backup pad and a filter (Figure 4) (2). These parts can be obtained from several firms, including Gelman, Millipore, and Glasrock. A cellulose shrink bank which we obtain from MSA, or various kinds of tape can be used to seal the base filter holder and center extender ring to prevent air leaks. It is convenient to label the cassette by writing on the bottom of the shrink band, although identification marks can be made directly on the cassettee base itself. Before the shrink band is put on, the base and center ring of the cassette must be firmly pushed together to hold the backup and filter in place. Although

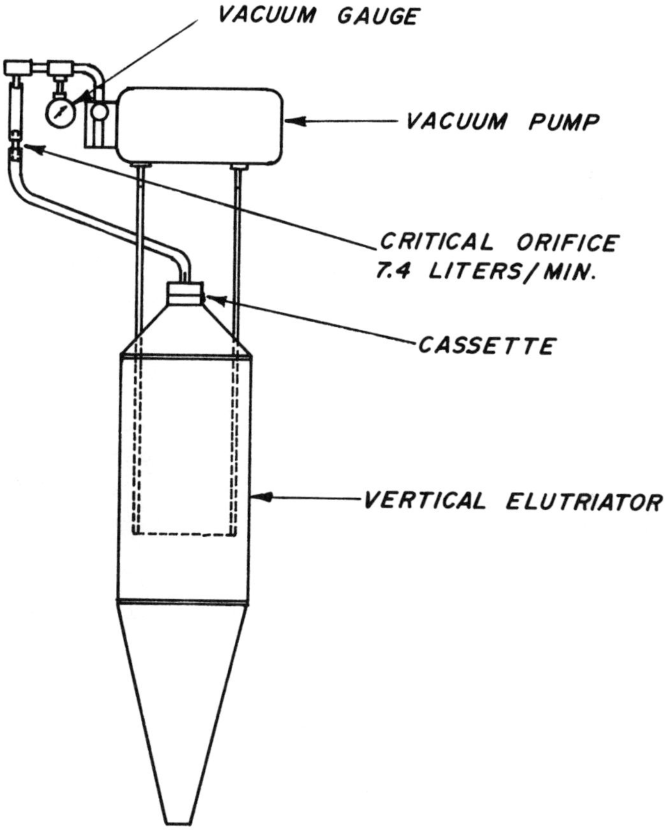

Figure 3. Vertical elutriator schematic. (Drawing courtesy of the National Cotton Council)

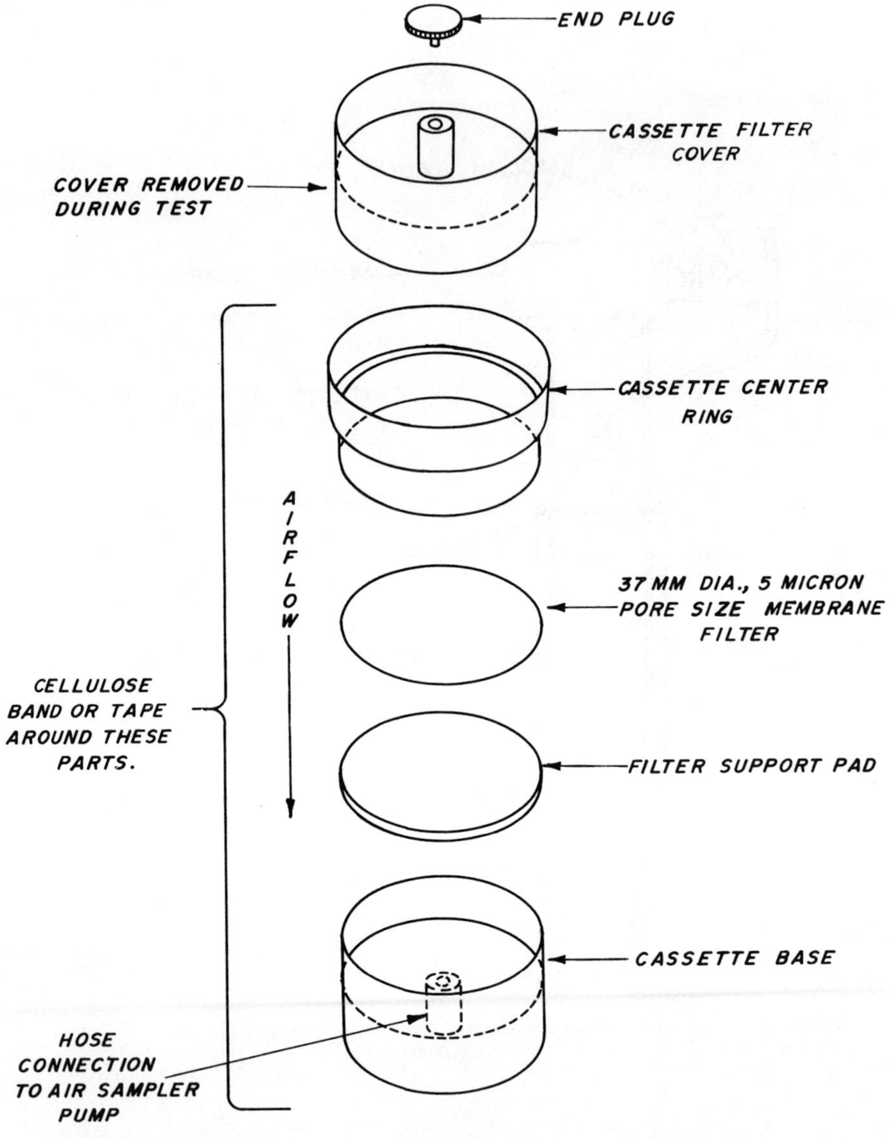

Figure 4. Expanded view of standard three-piece filter cassette. (Drawing courtesy of the National Cotton Council)

the heel of the hand works fine, we have modified a small arbor press to help apply consistently adequate pressure (Figure 5). Sufficient pressure is indicated by a noticeable pressure ring around the edge of the filter when the center ring is removed. Too much pressure is indicated by a cracked cassette, and too little by the absence of the ring on the filter edge.

Laboratory Operations

Weighing. The filters are not desiccated prior to weighing, and are always handled with nonserrated tweezers. Since it is easy to build up static charges on the filter, a static eliminator is necessary. These should be replaced at about six month intervals, since there is some question about their useful lifetime. The balance itself is critical, and must be capable of weighing to 1 ug in order to obtain reliable results. We use a Mettler M5, but there are more current digital readout, electronic balances on the market today by manufacturers including Mettler, Cahn, Sartorious, and Perkin-Elmer.

Since the filters are not desiccated, it is important to have a balance room with reasonably consistent temperature and humidity. Filters should be allowed to equilibrate 16-24 hours before weighing. Filters with dust should be allowed to equilibrate in the 3-piece cassettes with both end plugs out. Actually, a bottom end plug is totally unnecessary, and even the top plug is not critical. Once the filters have been used to collect dust, they should be handled carefully, always in an upright position to avoid losing the dust or lint. The top and center rings are removed using a small blade to slit the shrink band and a screwdriver to pry them apart. The filter base is then placed on the filter support stand (Figure 5) and tweezers are used to separate the filter from the backup pad and transport it onto the balance pan. Even in this operation, it pays to avoid heavy breathing, unnecessary rough handling of the filter, or other circumstances which could tend to scatter the dust before it can be weighed.

Eight to ten percent of the filters weighed are not used for sampling, and those cassettes are never opened during the plant sampling survey. They are controls, and the average control delta weight is used to correct all other filter delta weights prior to calculating dust concentrations. If the average control delta weight is a negative number, it is added to dust weights, and vice-versa. In addition, the range and standard deviation of the control weights are considered to be an indicator of reliability for the entire survey.

We normally reuse cassette pieces, although each part is checked for damage. The most common causes of attrition are cracks in the center rings, and loose hose connections on the cassette base. We check each base with a metal hose connector to insure that the fit is still tight. These hose connectors were ob-

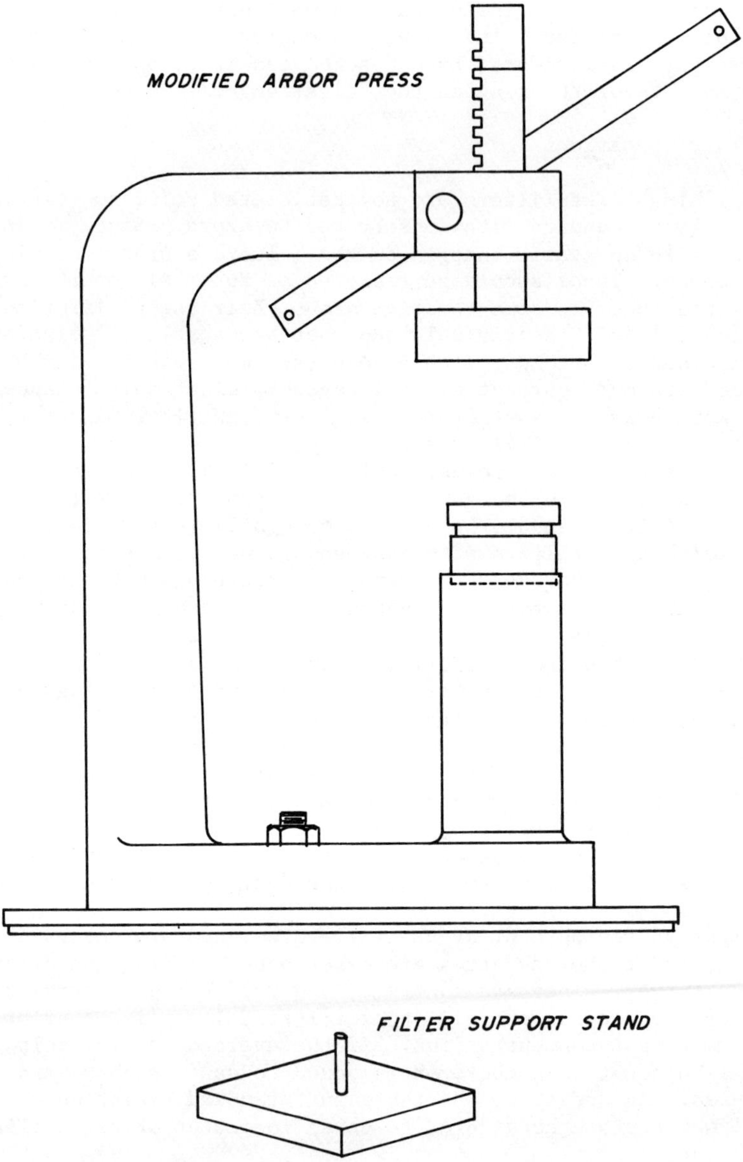

Figure 5. Schematic of arbor press modified for cassettes and filter support stand.

tained from Bendix, and we drilled them out slightly larger with a #47 bit (0.078 inches) to lower the pressure drop through the connector.

Orifice Calibration. The flow rate is regulated by an orifice designed to provide a constant 7.4 ± 0.2 Lpm of air through the filter. This combination of VE size and flow rate should allow the system to collect only the respirable dust fraction; that is, particles with diameters of 15 um or less. The orifice is calibrated as a part of the entire VE assembly (Figure 6), rather than isolating the filter and orifice (Figure 7). This allows us to measure flow rates under conditions that most closely resemble actual sampling conditions. A Walter crucible holder is used to connect the wet test meter to the bottom of the VE. This sampling train gave us flow rates 0.15-0.20 Lpm lower than the previous sampling train without the VE.

The metal orifices we use were purchased from Millipore and drilled out to obtain desired flow rates. Plastic or nylon orifices, however, are available from General Metal Works. The flow rates of metal orifices are dependent on pump vacuum until the pressure drop reaches 17" of mercury. At this point the flow becomes critical and is independent of pressure drop as long as the vacuum is equal to or greater than 17" of mercury. The plastic orifice has a different design, and reaches critical flow with only 10" of mercury pump vacuum (Figure 8).

In the field, a rotameter connected to the crucible holder is used to monitor flow rates each day. We recently invested in a direct-reading rotameter with a range of 3-21 Lpm, and we anticipate better recognition of flow problems during sampling surveys.

We are currently checking orifices prior to each survey with the direct reading rotameter, and washing them in isopropyl alcohol afterwards. Every six months, the calibration checks are performed with the wet test meter. As long as field checks and rotameter calibration checks agree with the bi-annual wet test meter calibration results, we feel the orifices are performing accurately.

It is necessary, however, to correct for volume if the calibration tool is not a true primary calibration source. Our wet test meter is supposed to be accurate within ± 0.5%, and the volume has been calibrated by personnel at the University of N.C. at Chapel Hill against their primary standard. There are also small differences in flow rates if there are large temperature changes between the calibration site and the sampling site (3).

Plant Sampling

With the equipment calibrated and in good working order, it must be transported to the sampling site. This is no small task, when the luggage includes a rack of twelve VE's, tubing and belts for personnel sampling, a battery charging station for the person-

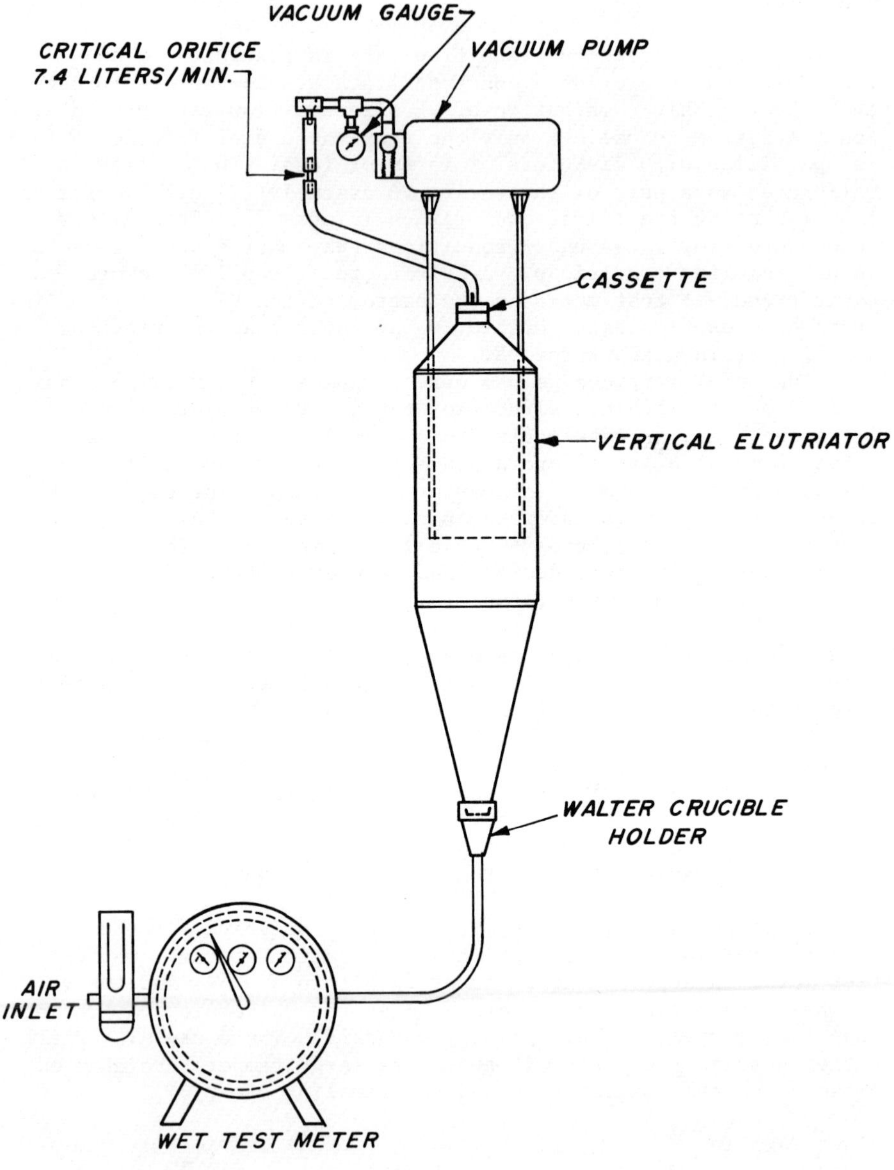

Figure 6. Modified calibration train. (Drawing courtesy of the National Cotton Council)

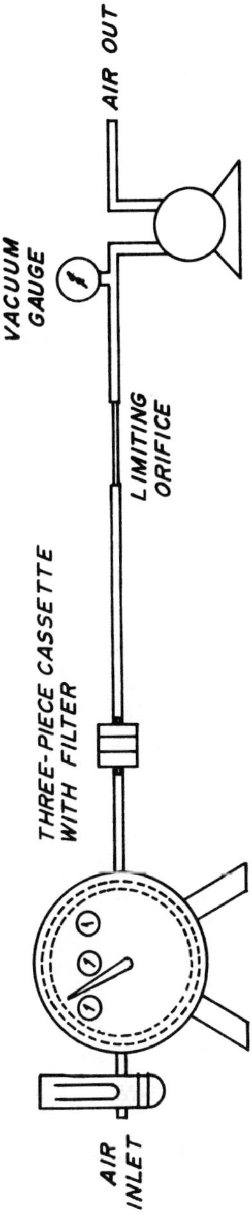

Figure 7. Standard calibration train. (Drawing courtesy of the National Cotton Council)

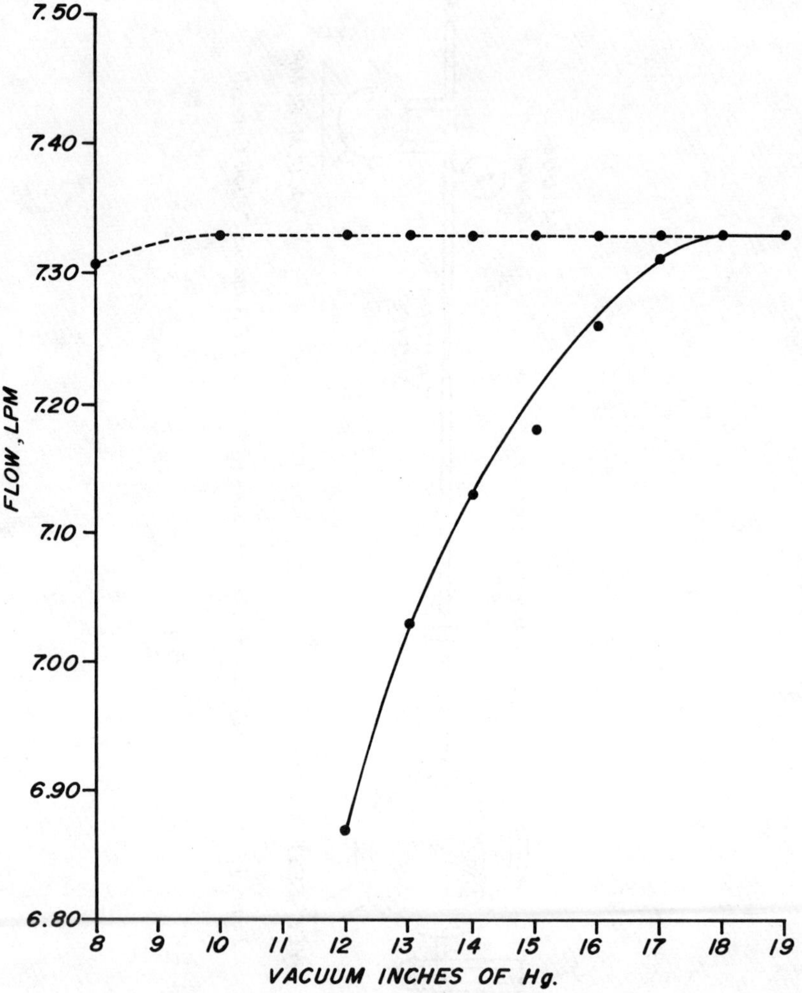

Figure 8. Pressure drop vs. flow rate. Key: – – –, general metal works orifice;——, millipore orifice.

nel pumps, electrical tape for sealing the cassette to the VE top, rotameter for field calibration, spare tubing, spare orifices, spare pumps and fuses, data sheets and pens, and a ladder (Table I). We therefore designed a second roll-around cart to hold everything not already attached to the VE. Once at the plant, samples are taken at the previously identified locations for a minimum 6-hour period during each operating shift. This means changing filters at some unusual hours, utilizing either technicians or plant personnel. We have always been concerned with the potential loss of accuracy that could occur by using plant personnel who are unfamiliar with scientific principles in general and cotton dust sampling techniques in particular. We have found that adequate training is the key. We have utilized the plant foreman to change filters and the results have been most satisfactory.

Employee Exposure

Since the end result of this sampling survey is to determine employee 8 hour TWA exposure, the dust concentration in each work area must some how be identified with each employee who works in that area. We accomplish this by identifying all job classifications and the average amount of time that each job class spends in any given work area. Nondust areas such as breakrooms or offices are also taken into account. If an employee enters the plant at 7:00 a.m. and leaves at 3:00 p.m., his time-in-grid breakdown should account for eight hours of time, or 100% of his work day. For each grid, there should be a dust level that can be used to compute dust exposure according to the length of time spent in that grid or work area (Table III).

After all data has been compiled to show TWA values this information is then shared with employees using a computerized employee exposure form. This concludes the task of dust measurement by means of the standardized vertical elutriator method.

Alternate Sampling Method

New sampling methods may result in eventual changes to these procedures. One such candidate method is the Portable Continuous Aerosol Monitor (PCAM) manufactured by ppm, Inc., which utilizes a small vertical elutriator (SVE) and correspondingly low flow rate of 1.85 Lpm. Although other instruments are available, this is the only one we studied. Any alternate sampling technique must first be proven equivalent to the vertical elutriator (2). This is usually accomplished by sampling each area of the mill with a combination of new sampling instruments and VE's to prove that the alternate method gives data within ± 25% of the VE data (Figure 9 and Table IV). Agreement between two or more VE's has often been a major problem in equivalency testing, but most of the data generated using our standard VE procedures gave % CV figures well below 10% (Table V).

TABLE III Sample Calculations

Cotton Dust Concentration

$$\text{ug/m}^3 = \frac{(\text{ug Final Filter Wt} - \text{ug Original Filter Wt}) \pm \text{ug Control Wt}}{(\text{L/m}) \times (\text{Min}) \times (\text{m}^3/1000\ \text{L})}$$

Employee TWA Exposure

Sample Job Classification: Card Tender

Work Area 3A:	% Time = 50	Dust = 300 ug/m^3
Work Area 3B:	% Time = 35	Dust = 350 ug/m^3
Work Area 3C:	% Time = 5	Dust = 150 ug/m^3
Breakroom Area:	% Time = 10	Dust = 0 ug/m^3

$$\text{TWA} = \frac{\Sigma(\%\ \text{Time in Area})(\text{Dust Conc. in Area})}{100\%\ \text{Time}}$$

$$\text{TWA} = \frac{(50\%)(300) + (35\%)(350) + (5\%)(150) + (10\%)(0)}{100\%}$$

$$\text{TWA} = 280\ \text{ug/m}^3$$

TABLE IV Equivalency Testing Calculations

Equivalency is defined as:

$$0.75 \leq R_L \leq 1.25 \text{ for 95\% of Samples}$$

$$R_L = \frac{X}{\text{Avg LVE}}$$

Where: R_L = Equivalency Ratio

X = Dust Concentration Calculated from Alternate Method.

Avg LVE = Avg Dust Concentration from Multiple Large Vertical Elutriators.

Area	Avg R_L
Opening	0.86 ± 0.07
Picking	0.87 ± 0.05
Carding	0.95 ± 0.07
Drawing	0.85 ± 0.04
Roving	0.86 ± 0.08

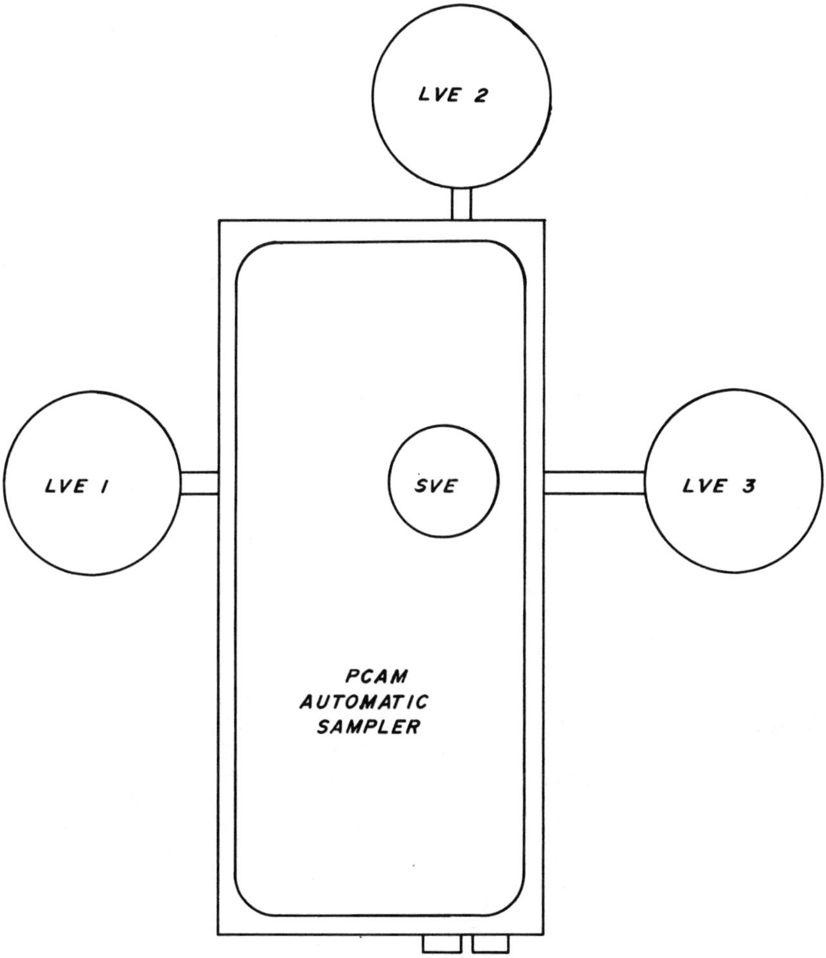

Figure 9. Schematic of PCAM equivalency testing rig showing the relationship of large vertical elutriators to PCAM small vertical elutriator.

TABLE V

Large Vertical Elutriator Data

(Coefficient Of Variation With 3 LVE's)

		ug/m^3					
Location	Shift	LVE 1	LVE 2	LVE 3	Avg	% CV	Avg % CV
Opening	2	223	235	230	229	3	7 ± 7
	3	152	134	126	137	10	
	1	264	262	267	264	1	
Picking	2	214	253	222	230	9	5 ± 3
	3	235	257	261	251	6	
	1	257	263	253	258	2	
Carding	2	386	464	409	420	10	4 ± 3
	3	401	420	401	407	3	
	1	330	341	333	335	2	
Drawing	2	207	219	207	211	3	3 ± 1
	3	184	195	190	190	3	
	1	200	190	194	195	3	
Roving	2	176	182	198	185	6	7 ± 5
	3	150	154	123	142	12	
	1	134	143	140	139	3	

Experience and common sense have helped us to refine the procedures for cotton dust sampling to obtain accurate and representative samples. The low coefficients of variation among multiple VE samples indicate that proper attention to equipment and techniques does result in quality data.

Literature Cited

1. Neefus, J.D.; Lumsden, J.C.; Jones, M.T. Jr. Am. Ind. Hyg. Assoc. J. 1977, 38, 394-400.
2. Federal Register 1978, 43, 27380-99.
3. Leidel, N.A.; Busch, K.A.; Lynch, J.R. "Occupational Exposure Sampling Strategy Manual"; DHEW (NIOSH) Pub. No. 77-173: Cincinnati, 1977; p 90-91.

RECEIVED December 15, 1981.

8

Procedures for the Determination of Humidifier Contributions to Respirable Dust Levels in the Workplace

F. M. SHOFNER

ppm, Inc., Knoxville, TN 37922

CAM or PCAM equipment may be used for the rapid and accurate determination of atomizer solids contributions to textile workplace dust levels. Experience with low solids water provided by both reverse osmosis and deionizer equipment is described. In certain cases, these determinations may be made in less than one day and sometimes even without the use of low solids water equipment.

Earlier publications have described the discovery of humidifier solids residue contributions to respirable cotton dust levels in the textile processing workplace (1,2) and the magnitude of the humidifier component χ_{at} and approximate costs for its control in textile operations (2,3,4). We report here Aerosol Contribution Procedures (ACP) for quantitative determination of χ_{at} using CAM or PCAM equipment and three examples of plant experience.

Respirable cotton dust is defined in the OSHA standard by the Large Vertical Elutriator (LVE) sampler which is the reference gravimetric method (5). Thus, theoretically, any particle having aerodynamic equivalent diameter (AED) $\leq$ 15μm (design "cut-off" for the LVE) is, apparently, respirable "cotton dust". Practically, any particle ascending the VE and collected by the membrane filter or electro-optically weighed by the CAM method is defined as cotton dust. It was clear to many investigators that apparent, respirable cotton dust could originate with many aerosol sources, other than cotton dust from textile processing machinery, such as oil mist, air pollution, forklift exhaust, humidifier residues, etc. One of the first constituents to receive theoretical and experimental attention by this author and his colleagues was humidifier residues.

The first experimental demonstration of the magnitude of χ_{at} was performed with the CAM System at the N.C. State University model card room in November 1979 (1,2). Subsequently, several in-plant demonstrations have been made with the CAM System, with

0097-6156/82/0189-0105$06.00/0

PCAM's, and with vertical elutriators, and some of these results have been published (4,6,7). The CAM and PCAM methods have proven to be quite powerful for quantitative determination of χ_{at} and other constituents of respirable dust (8). These determinations have been used to evaluate feasibility of engineering controls or to establish sound data to be used to possibly subtract the χ_{at} component from apparent cotton dust levels.

In two of the three plant examples, LVE's were run simultaneously with CAM or PCAM equipment for purposes of establishing equivalency according to the OSHA criterion and according to more detailed procedures given in the "Protocol Paper" (9). CAM/LVE equivalency was demonstrated in both these cases. It was not possible to use LVE's in the third test.

OSHA has recognized the capability of the CAM and PCAM method in responding equivalently to cotton dust as the LVE method. Two major textile manufacturers have received permission to use CAM and PCAM equipment in place of LVE's and it is quite possible that a broader approval by Federal and State OSHA's will be given.

Aerosol Contribution Procedures

The objective of these Aerosol Contribution Procedures (ACP) is to determine humidifier solids residue contributions, χ_{at}, to apparent workplace respirable dust levels so feasibility of engineering control or exclusion strategies may be evaluated. By engineering control of χ_{at} is meant that low solids water is used for humidification. This can be a very cost-effective means of control. Generally, χ_{at} is the component which should receive first attention when cost-prioritizing the various components of multiconstituent, respirable cotton dust.

By exclusion or subtraction it is meant that the explicitly-determined value for χ_{at} may be subtracted from the aggregate or total respirable dust measured in the workplace. Logic for subtraction necessitates the assumption that the χ_{at} component does not contain the causative agent for byssinosis. Determinations need to be made biannually for each process in case the exclusion or subtraction strategy is allowable and used.

Permissibility of subtraction is currently under OSHA review. If subtraction is allowed, the biannual determinations can be made simultaneously with the biannual compliance test, thus reducing test costs.

It is important to recognize that χ_{at} is known to be dependent upon air-conditioning parameters, including those influenced by seasonal conditions. The question therefore arises: "What χ_{at} should be subtracted?"

The focus of our analyses and experimental procedures has been upon identification and quantitative determination of the atomizer component *per se*. Greater emphasis is placed upon the actual workplace dust level when the atomizer component has been removed by engineering controls or when it has been subtracted. In some cases, the workplace dust level is below the applicable PEL for cotton dust when the atomizer component is excluded.

A simple example will clarify the point. Consider wintertime operation, having all inside air and heavy evaporation in order to control conditions. Contrast this with summertime operation having a large fraction of outside air with outside environmental conditions such that little humidification is required. (Furthermore, solids levels in the humidifier water tend to be higher in winter than summer, in some cases.)

The following respirable dust readings are representative of certain weaving operations:

	χ_{normal}	χ_{at}	$\bar{\chi}$
Wintertime Extreme	1000	800	200
Summertime Extreme	500	300	200

χ_{normal} is normal or total respirable aerosol dust concentration, χ_{at} is the atomizer or humidifier component, and $\bar{\chi}$ is the remaining workplace dust level when the humidifier component has been excluded.

Clearly the humidifier component is very different but it is really the $\bar{\chi}$ component with which we are concerned with regard to the assessment of worker exposure.

It follows that the aerosol contribution procedures are specific to air-conditioning parameters and that the χ_{at} component is to be excluded from the total dust level χ_T under a given set of conditions. It would obviously be improper to determine χ_{at} in the wintertime and use it for subtraction in summertime.

The following procedures have evolved from field testing or from predictive methods using either CAM or PCAM equipment and are in order preferred for accuracy and realism of the determination. However, the nature of the process or circumstances of the test condition controls which of the procedures is used. In many cases, testing over several days is possible and desirable. In other cases, the tests can only last a few minutes, otherwise processing would be interrupted and process conditions would become atypical.

Aerosol Contribution Procedure #1 (ACP-1). In this procedure, the humidification system is operated with low solids water and the textile machinery operation and work practices remain normal. Figure 1 shows the hypothetical time behavior of workplace dust levels as given by ERF-corrected PCAM readings (ERF = Equivalency Refinement Factor which is developed from the integral 37mm cassette built into CAM and PCAM sensors as required and described for official testing (8).) The transition from normal dust levels to low solids dust levels $\bar{\chi}$ normally requires of the order of an hour. Thus in a reasonably short period of time, one may obtain results as illustrated in Figure 1 and which permit determination of the atomizer component χ_{at}:

$$\chi_{at} \gtrsim \chi_{normal} - \bar{\chi} \quad (1)$$

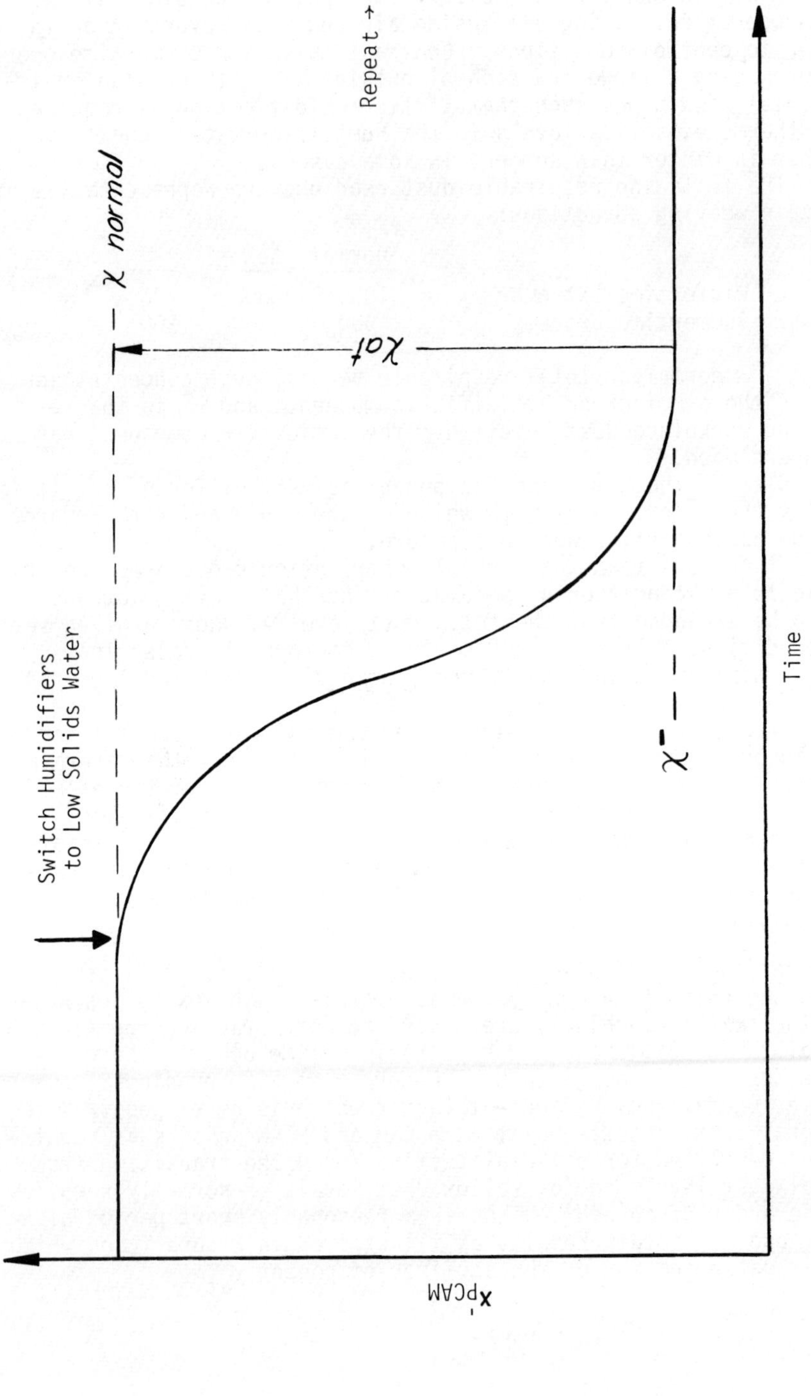

Figure 1. Illustration of χ_{at} by use of low solids humidifier water.

The approximation in Equation 1 is due to assuming that the solids concentration in the low solids water is zero. The determination is therefore conservative.

Equation 1 may be corrected for the actual low solids concentration using the χ_{at} equation to be described below (2). For example, it is sometimes found that even though very low solids water is supplied to the atomizer plumbing system, higher solids concentration can result due to redissolution from the pipe walls.

The errors in this approximation are usually tolerable if the normal solids concentration is more than 10 times the actual atomized low solids water solids concentration. This obviously necessitates a determination of the solids concentration in the atomized water at or from the atomizer.

In some cases, the atomizer component is much larger than the workplace dust levels χ^{-}. In this case it is necessary to establish that the applicable ERF's for normal and subtracted conditions are the same.

This ACP is the preferred one over the following three because it best simulates normal processing with the only difference being the solids concentration in the atomized water.

Aerosol Contribution Procedure #2 (ACP-2). In some cases it is impractical for technical or cost reasons to supply low solids water for ACP-1. In other cases, it is useful to obtain a quick but rough estimate relative to the viability of provision of low solids water.

In this hypothetical determination illustrated in Figure 2, the humidifiers are simply turned off if processing can tolerate this for approximately ½ to 2 hours, typically. χ_{at} is then determined according to

$$\chi_{at} \gtrsim \chi_{normal} - \chi^{-} \tag{2}$$

Again χ_{at} is determined in a conservative manner. The approximation is due primarily to the failure to reach steady-state condition.

The principal merit of this less expensive approach is that frequently it can be shown that the PEL is easily and cost-effectively achievable.

This procedure is usually not viable for processes with low air turn-over rate and/or poor filtration. One key feature is that the humidifier "off" condition should approach a reasonable steady-state character. However, it may be unnecessary to achieve steady-state if first it is clearly shown that dust levels fall well below the PEL.

In some processes, especially those with low air turn-over rate and poor filtration, it is unclear in the time allowable by process constraints that the PEL can be achieved. In other words, the process may not operate normally for more than two hours

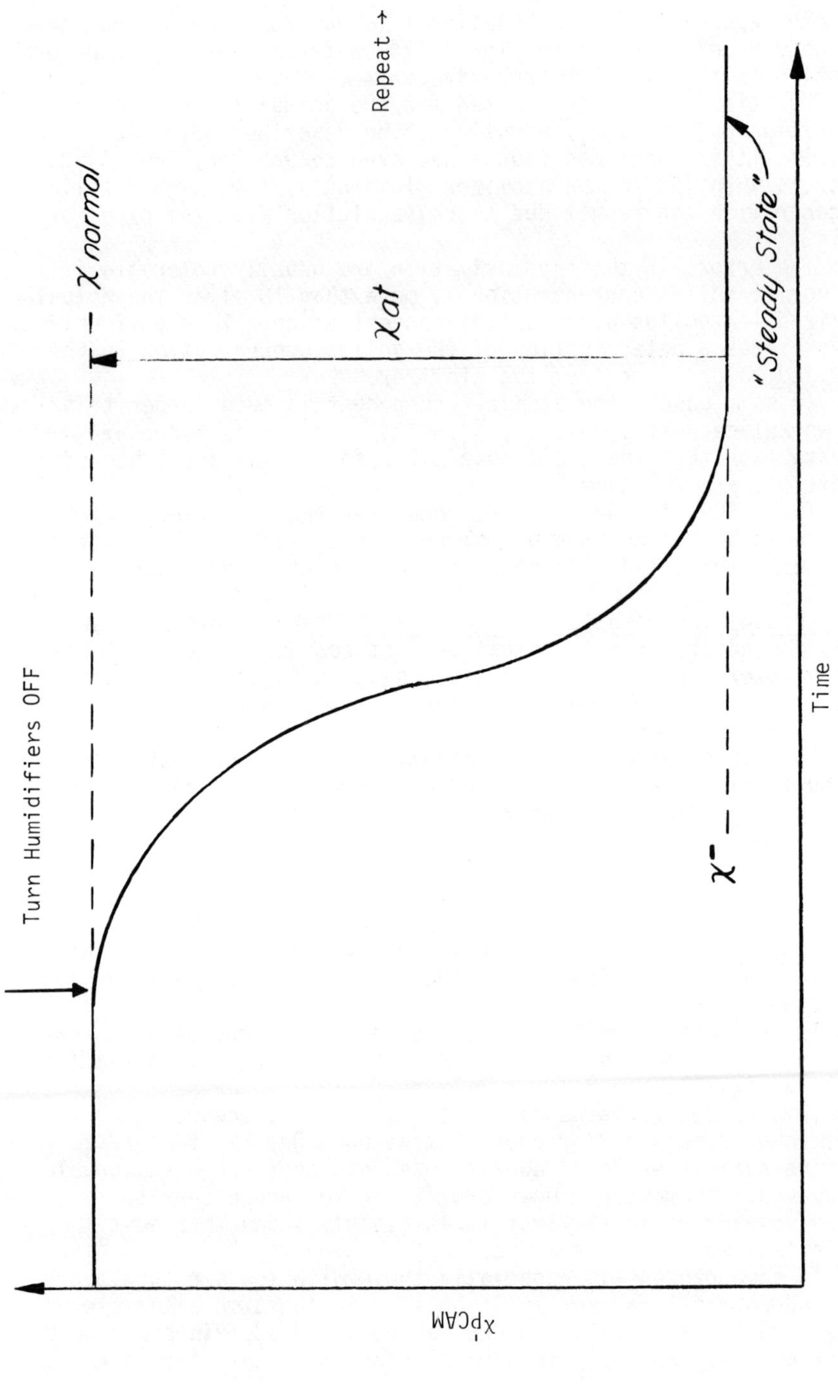

Figure 2. Illustration of χ_{at} by turning humidifiers off.

without humidification. As a matter of interest, many textile department managers feel strongly that process conditions will be intolerable for off-times greater than 30 minutes. This may be subject to question but the "off" time constraint will be the principal limitation to this procedure. Finally, if long humidifier "off"times are used, it must be ascertained that cotton processing remains approximately normal. For example, it is possible that dust levels in ring spinning might first fall when the humidifiers are turned off, in response to elimination of the χ_{at} component, but then rise again due to increased difficulties of fiber processing (increased "ends-down", electrostatic imbalances, etc).

Aerosol Contribution Procedure #3 (ACP-3). On weekends or during other plant standing times, extended exploratory test intervals are possible. In this procedure, with the plant's textile machinery standing but all air-handling and air-conditioning equipment in normal operation, the humidifiers are turned off and on repetitively as illustrated hypothetically in Figure 3. Taking due note to achieve steady-state conditions in both the baseline standing conditions, the atomizer component is estimated according to

$$\chi_{at} \approx \frac{\bar{\tau}_{normal}}{\bar{\tau}_{standing}} (\chi_{standing} - \chi_{baseline}) \quad (3)$$

$\chi_{baseline}$ is the workplace respirable dust concentration with all air-moving equipment running normally but with the textile processing machinery off and with the humidifiers off. $\chi_{standing}$ is the same except the humidifiers are turned on.

$\bar{\tau}_{normal}$ and $\bar{\tau}_{standing}$ are the average on-time fractions for the humidifiers in the above-defined conditions. For examples, if atomizer nozzles are on for 60 seconds and off for 30 seconds, $\tau_{on} = 60/(60 + 30) = 0.67$. (See Equation 7.)

Evidently, the atomizer contribution under normal conditions is scaled to that determined under plant-standing conditions according to the water consumption rate. Typically, $\bar{\tau}_{standing} < \bar{\tau}_{normal}$ since humidification requirements are lower under plant-standing conditions. It is emphasized that this assumption needs to be carefully checked as well as the assumption that the solids concentrations under plant-standing and plant-operating conditions are the same. It is noted that several implicit assumptions to this procedure can be violated, thus invalidating the determination.

Aerosol Contribution Procedure-Prediction (ACP-P). Although the following equations have in several cases, with one of them reported here, served as accurate predictors, the assumptions are

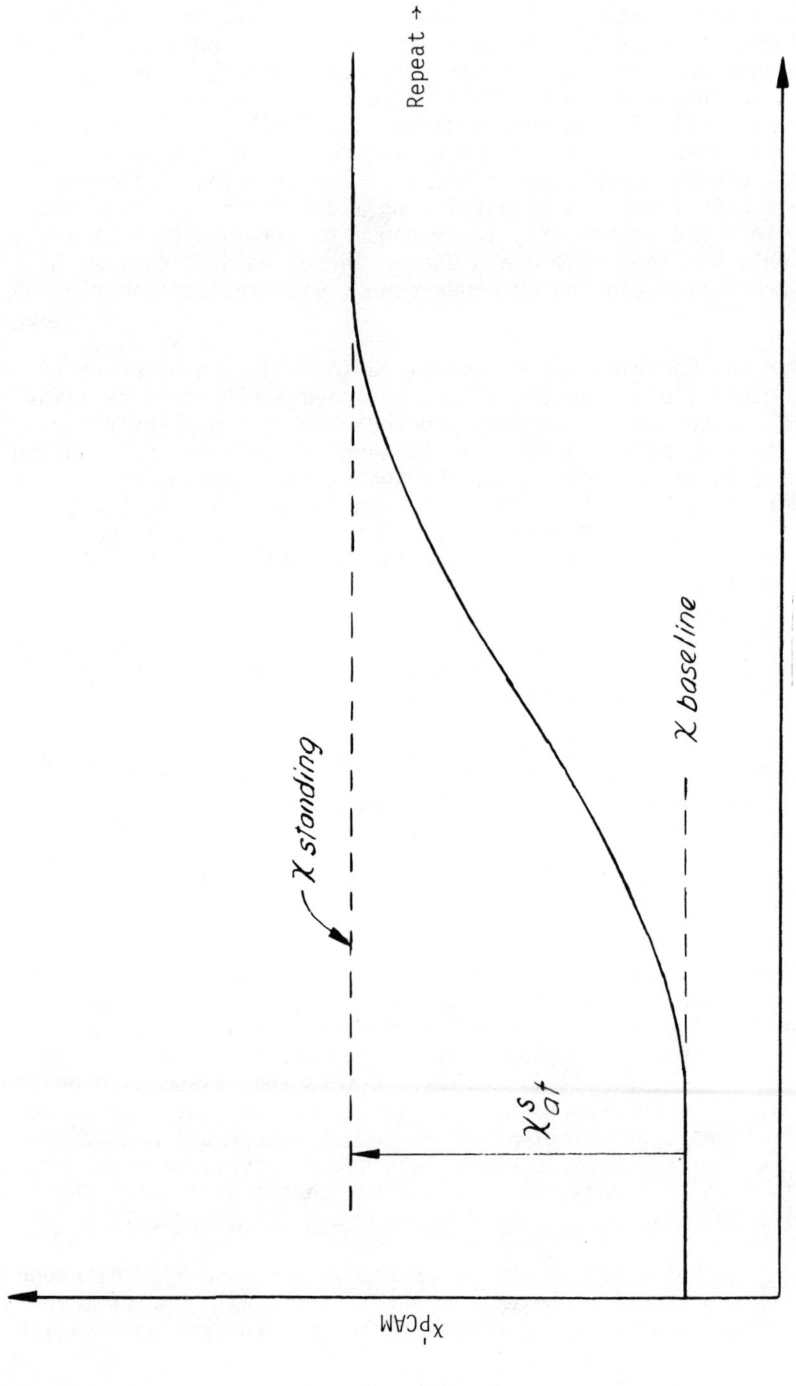

Figure 3. Illustration of χ_{at} under plant standing conditions.

so numerous as to render the theoretical predictions useful only for ball park estimations. This equation (2) is

$$\chi_{at} = 267 \frac{NW\tau C}{Q\ (1-F)\rho}, \quad \mu g/m^3 \tag{4}$$

and may be restated as

$$\chi_{at} = 1.337 \times 10^5 \frac{(GPM)\ C}{Q\ (1-F)} \tag{5}$$

In these equations, C is the humidifier solids concentration in ppm, Q is the total air-conditioned flow rate in CFM, F is the total, single path penetration efficiency of the air-handling equipment, ρ is the density of water (= 1gm/cm^3), GPM is the humidifier flow rate in gallons per minute, N is the number of humidifier nozzles or heads, W is the weight rate in pounds per hour emitted by each humidifier unit, and τ, as above in Equation 3, is the humidifier on-time fraction.

Equation 5 is preferred but requires the water flow rate in GPM. Equation 4 may be used with equal confidence if W and τ are accurately known. It is cautioned that actual atomization rate W may be materially different than original specifications.

The interested reader may consult the literature(2) for development of this equation and selected examples. In the first case reported below, results are given on ACP-1 and ACP-P. By comparing these results, insight into the cause of χ_{at} and its relationship to air-conditioning parameters are provided. Elaborations on the definitions of F, τ, and C will be more effectively made in the framework of this and the other examples.

We provide below examples illustrating each of these procedures.

Selected Examples

Carding, Spinning, Weaving: Atomizers on RO versus City Water; ACP-1, ACP-P. Table I contains the results of an extensive CAM study extending over two weeks in a 100% cotton plant. The plant has a split system using atomizers for supplementary humidification to that provided by an air washer.

The test procedures were to operate the atomizers for one day on normal city water and then operate them on low solids water provided by reverse osmosis equipment. The test periods coincided with normal 8-hour shifts and typically consisted of six hours, eight hours, and eight hours, thus allowing two hours for the city to RO transition, and vice versa. There were two CAM sensors in spinning and in lower weaving. One sensor was placed in each carding and upper weaving. Two sensors were also installed to isokinetically sample the inlet and exit of the air washer. (RO = low solids water via reverse osmosis equipment.)

Column 11 gives the normal dust concentration found from the average of several replications on city water. Column 10 gives

TABLE I
Comparison of Predicted and Measured Atomizer Solids Residue Contributions

1	2	3	4	5	6	7		8		9	10	11
PROCESS AREA	Q KCFM	N ATOMIZER HEADS	W #/Hr	F	$\overline{\tau}_{at}$ [c]	$\overline{C}$, ppm		X_{at} [f] µg/m³		ΔX_{at} [e] Predicted µg/m³ ACP-P	ΔX_{at} [d,e] Measured µg/m³ ACP-1	X_{normal} [d] µg/m³ (city)
						City	RO	City	RO			
Carding	32 [a]	19 [b]	9	0.2	.41	104	14	76	10	66	74	200
Spinning	95	68	15	0.2	.41	104	14	153	21	132	115	291
Upper Weaving	37	66	9	0.2	.86	104	14	479	65	414 } 378	384 } 359	654 } 659
Lower Weaving	47	79	9	0.2	.75	104	14	394	53	341 }	334 }	665 }

a Excludes flow from card cleaning system

b Atomizers actually in roving and drawing. These influence carding dust readings because of return flows to air washer and through card cleaning system to air washer.

c Simple average of τ_{at} for process area. Combined RO and city water conditions.

d ERF-corrected CAM readings from 12 6 to 8 hour runs.

e Note that these entries are necessarily <u>differences</u> between city and RO water operation

f Equation used for prediction:

$$X_{at} = 267 \frac{N\ W\ \tau\ C}{W\ (1-F)\rho}, \quad \mu g/m^3$$

the decrease measured when the atomizers were operated on RO water. That is, for example in weaving, the average apparent cotton dust concentration with the atomizers operating on city water was 659$\mu g/m^3$. When the atomizers were operated on low solids water from the RO unit, the dust levels fell to $\bar{\chi}$ = 300 $\mu g/m^3$, thus giving the measured decrement $\Delta\chi_{at}$ of 359$\mu g/m^3$.

The balance of Table I is devoted to providing the input parameters for the χ_{at} equation. That is, we now address ACP-P and the reliability of its predictions. Equation 4 provides an estimation of the humidifier component. This equation demonstrates the relationship between solids in the humidifier water and apparent cotton dust levels in the workplace. It provides considerable insight into what may be done to control them cost-effectively.

For this discussion, each of the terms in Table I is obvious in its definition in the appropriate columns. Some elaboration is worthwhile on penetration efficiency F, atomizer on time τ_{at}, and solids concentration C.

Penetration efficiency is defined as

$$F = \chi_{after}/\chi_{before} \tag{6}$$

and is a measure of the efficiency with which dust penetrates filter media or is otherwise lost as the air is circulated by the air-handling system. Evidently, F is in reality a distributed parameter and can be specialized to F(d), giving the penetration efficiency as a function of particle size. Here we are interested in the penetration efficiency of micron-sized solids residue particles in a complete pass. Consider a test cubic meter of air. It is supplied by the air-conditioning system, further humidified by the supplementary atomizers, transported over the workers and process machinery, returned to the air-conditioning equipment where it is filtered, reconditioned, and then resupplied. This assumes the plant is on 100% inside air.

For these calculations, a representative value of 0.2 was used. This was substantiated with the two sensors in the air washer.

Alternatively stated, the losses for the atomizer solids residue particles in a complete single pass is 80%. This is reasonable because this particular air washer system had good inlet filtration media.

The atomizer on time τ is a parameter describing the duty cycle of the atomizers:

$$\tau = \frac{\text{On Time}}{\text{On Time + Off Time}} \tag{7}$$

In the usual design, humidistats call for supplementary atomizer water in order to achieve a desired processing workplace humidity. The atomizers are turned on and off by applying compressed air to the atomizer heads which usually aspirate the water from a gravity feed system. Note that the average atomizer on time is much lower in carding and spinning, where they are accidentally equal, than in weaving. There was no appreciable difference in τ_{at} for RO versus city water operation. A water meter also monitored the total flow to all atomizers. The agreement between the predicted and measured water flow rates was only fair.

The total solids concentration in parts per million is designated as C. In most cases, as in Table I, this is inferred from electro-metric determinations of conductivity, which respond only to dissolved solids. Usually, suspended solids are small. It is noted however, that it is total solids which contribute to workplace apparent dust levels.

Column 7 indicates that the city water concentration had an average value of 104 whereas the atomizer supply line (near the end) concentration had an average for thest tests of 14ppm. Column 8 applies the χ_{at} prediction equation for both conditions and column 9 gives the predicted decrease in going from operation on city water to operation on RO water.

According to the Aerosol Contribution Procedures, the experimental data of column 10 follow ACP-1 and the predicted data of column 9 follow ACP-P.

Columns 9 and 10 may therefore be compared as the predicted and measured versions of the same parameter. Noting the various assumptions made, the agreement is remarkable.

When the input parameters to the χ_{at} prediction equation are satisfactorily known, it may be used for estimation purposes. We emphasize that explicit determination, according to ACP-1, is usually needed for thorough evaluation of the feasibility of engineering controls. An experimental determination is especially needed for each process, twice each year, for subtraction of the χ_{at} component, if that is allowed.

Weaving: Atomizers on DI versus Well Water; ACP-1. Figure 4 shows the well water to DI transition for a weaving operation on 100% cotton and for which the air-conditioning consists of a "dry duct". That is, the weave room environmental conditions are controlled by a mix of inside and outside air and humidity is controlled solely by atomizers. Low solids water was provided with dual bed, cation/anion deionization (DI) equipment.

In this dramatic case, it is seen that the PCAM analog output readings fall from approximately $1400\mu g/m^3$ to under $200\mu g/m^3$. In this case, within 30 minutes after DI was applied to the system, the decrease was observed and in 1½ hours, the levels were under $200\mu g/m^3$. (The PEL in weaving is $750\mu g/m^3$.) The $\chi(t)$ behavior is dominated by the time required for the DI to displace the well water in the gravity feed system.

An anomalous situation developed in these tests. It was estimated, based on the solids content of the well water, that the deionizer bottle should not exhaust until after 100 hours of

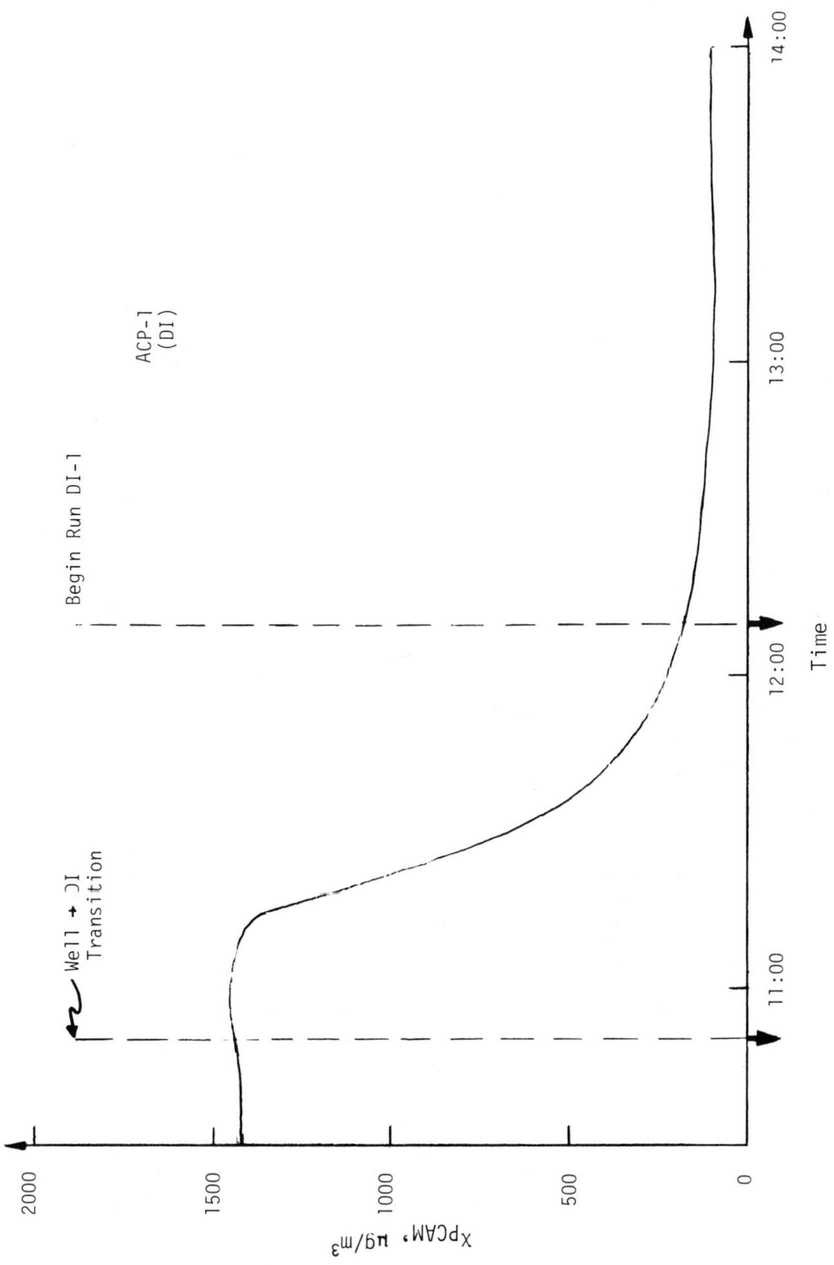

Figure 4. ***Weaving humidifiers operating on well and DI water.***

operation. It was observed after approximately 30 hours of operation that the workplace dust levels began to again increase. It was determined that the quality of the water from the DI unit was still satisfactory, however, as measured by the conductivity.

Figure 5 shows the workplace dust level at the end of run DI-3 where it is seen that the levels had risen to approximately 900μg/m^3 even though the water conductivity was still satisfactory. The bottles had operated for about 40 hours. A second set of bottles was placed in operation and it is seen that the room dust levels again fell to below 200μg/m^3, in the same fashion that the dust levels fell when the first set of bottles was applied.

It follows from this observation, and from other tests on water parameters, that the workplace dust levels are not totally measured by conductivity or dissolved solids in the DI output. It was found that the solids concentration in atomizer line conductivity had risen at the end of DI-3. A full explanation of this anomaly is not now available. There is some information to suggest that the behavior is due to changing pH in the DI output, even though the conductivity or dissolved solids of the DI output water remained good.

Weaving: Humiducts on Well Water; ACP-2, ACP-3. Figure 6 shows a weave room test wherein it was not practical to install low solids water. In this test, the atomizers were either operated normally or turned off for 30 to 45 minutes (ACP-2) or the looms stood and the atomizers were left on and turned off (ACP-3). The air-conditioning consists of humiducts operating on relatively high water hardness. The humiducts had good return air filtration but no mist elimination.

At A, on Figure 6, the water to the spinning disc atomizers was turned off for a period of 30 minutes. The workplace dust levels fell from approximately 1150μg/m^3 to 460μg/m^3. During this same time the workplace humidity fell from 78% to 70%.

At B, the humidifiers were turned off for approximately 45 minutes, during which the dust levels fell from about 1100μg/m^3 down to about 520μg/m^3.

The χ_{at} component for this one PCAM sensor was derived by taking the average of the normal conditions (1140) and subtracting the average for the humidifier off condition (χ^{-} = 520), or χ_{at} = 1140 - 520 = 620μg/m^3. This is according to procedure ACP-2. Two other PCAM's placed within the weaving area showed the same trend.

This χ_{at} determination should be less than the actual χ_{at} value since steady-state dust levels in the "humidifier off" condition (χ^{-}) were probably not realized. That is, the actual χ^{-} is most probably lower, or χ_{at} is larger.

Between C and D on Figure 3, ACP-3 was implemented. At C, the plant went into a standing condition. It is noted that the dust levels fell as the looms stopped. The humidification sys-

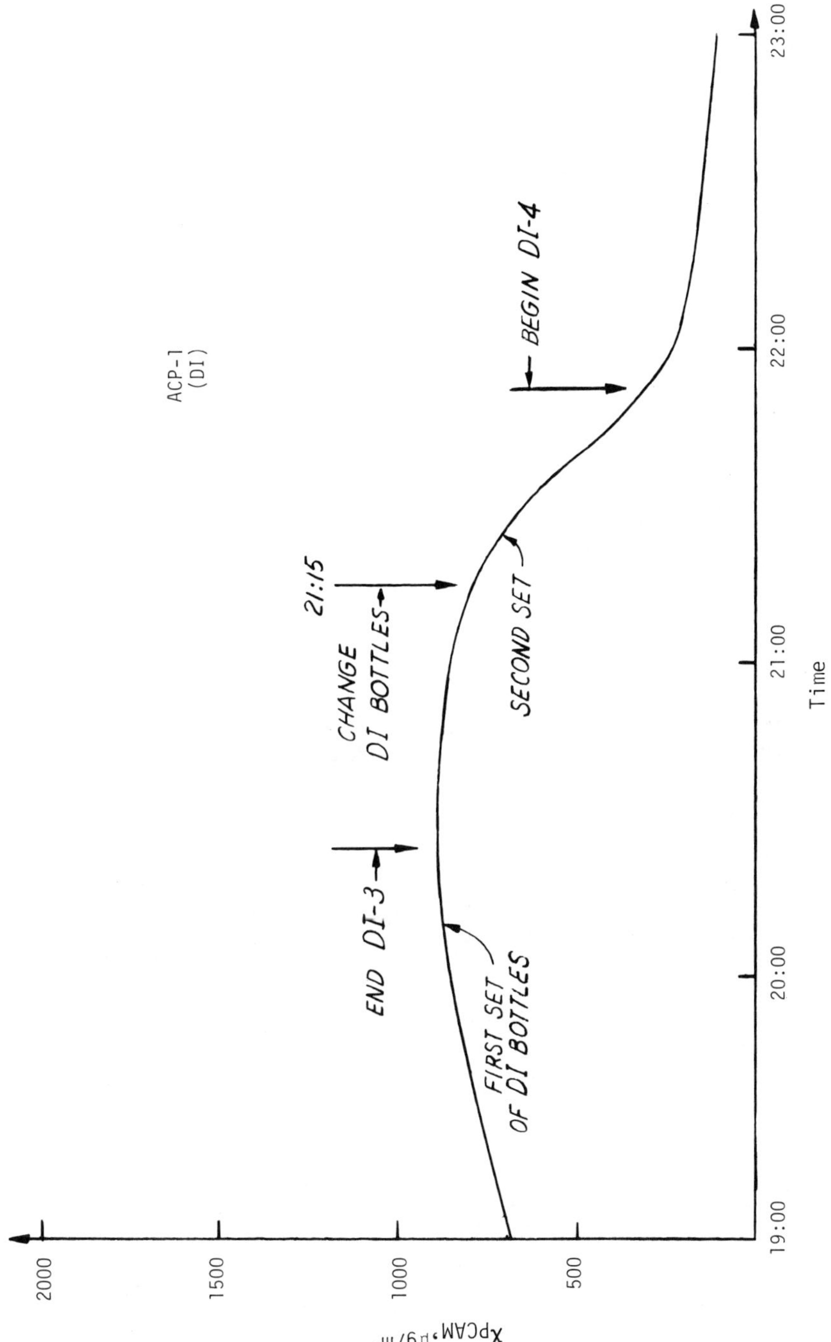

Figure 5. Anomalous behavior of χ_{at} on DI water.

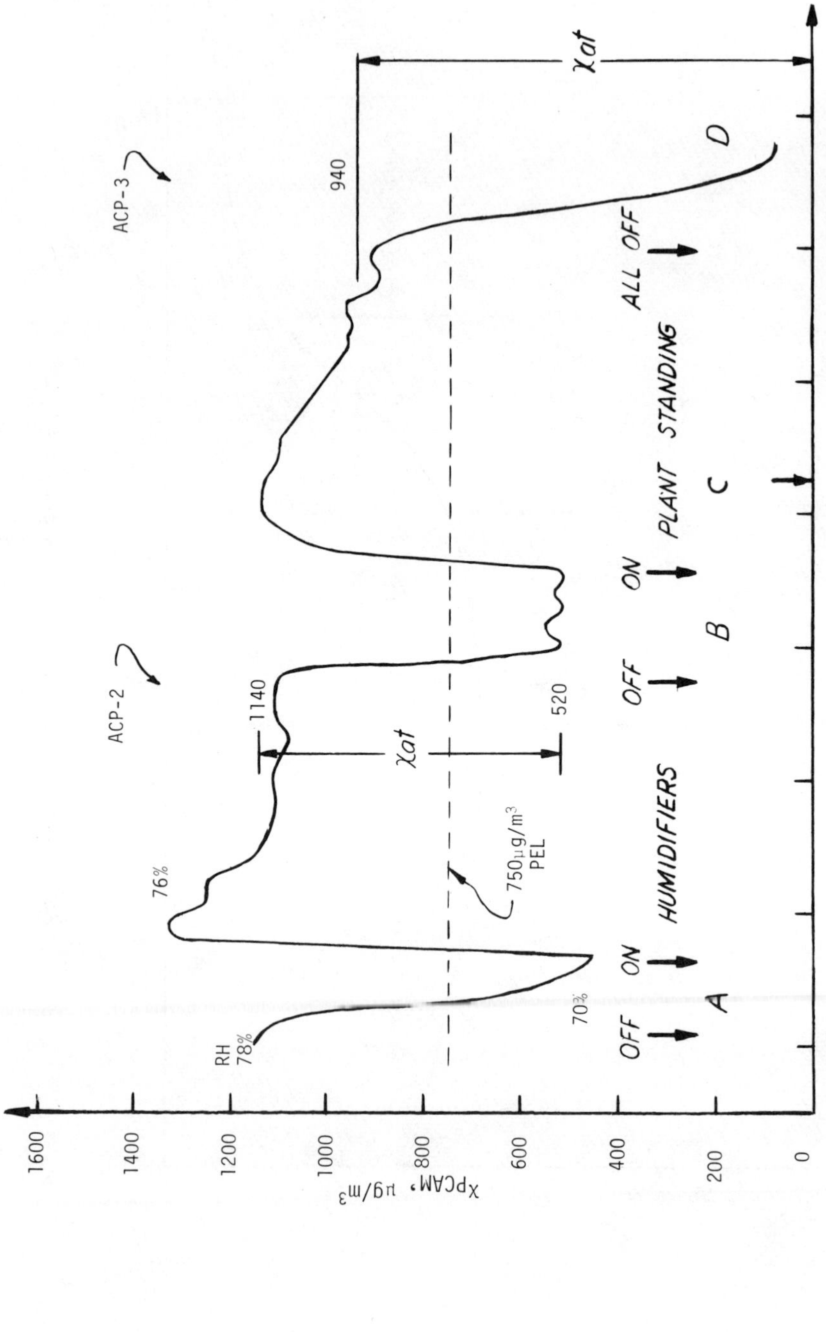

Figure 6. Determination of χ_{at} by turning atomizers off and on.

tem remained in operation. It was found that the atomizers were continuously operating, contrary to expectations, and with a higher duty cycle than for normal operation, for this particular PCAM location. A brief but intense effort was launched to place the humidifiers back in normal operation such that the humidity would be controlled to the normal workplace level of around 75 to 80%. This was finally accomplished approximately 8:30 to 8:45PM and the χ value at that time ($940\mu g/m^3$) is taken as the standing contribution.

At 9PM all humidifiers in the workplace were shut off and the dust levels rapidly decreased toward zero. According to ACP-3, the $\chi_{at} \leq 940\mu g/m^3$. This places an upper limit on the component whereas the earlier determined value is a lower bound. Thus for this sensor the true χ_{at} lies between 620 and $940\mu g/m^3$.

Conclusions

The humidifier solids residue contribution χ_{at} can be a major component in the textile processing workplace. It is characteristically largest in those processes requiring high humidity.

χ_{at} is definitely not cotton dust, as demonstrated experimentally by the data reported here. In many processes, elimination of this component by engineering control or by exclusion yields workplace dust levels well below the PEL.

The CAM/PCAM method was utilized in the discovery and much of the characterization of the χ_{at} and other components in the textile workplace. Those examples serve to illustrate the utility of such measurements for identification of workplace aerosols and evaluation of the effectiveness of engineering controls.

In order of confidence and realism in the χ_{at} determination, ACP-1 is preferred over the others. This is true if the χ_{at} determinations are to be used for engineering control design or for subtraction, if this strategy is allowed by OSHA.

If subtraction of χ_{at} is allowed, the determinations can and should be made with each 6 month compliance test.

Further, for both engineering controls design or for subtraction, due account of the seasonal variation of χ_{at} must be made.

Clearly, these methods and procedures are applicable to humidifier residue contribution in other manufacturing processes.

There are four basic methods by which to provide low solids water in the quantity and of the quality required for engineering control of χ_{at}: (1) reverse osmosis (RO); (2) deionization (DI); (3) boiler condensate; and (4) distillation. Each plant situation requires a thorough engineering and economic analysis but in general, the order given is preferred. Distillation is too energy-expensive as is boiler condensate unless heat exchangers are employed. DI requires the handling of caustic and acid for regeneration, by personnel unfamiliar with these materials.

Since the total capital plus operating costs are roughly the same for RO and DI, it follows that RO is generally the preferred choice.

Acknowledgements

I am indebted to the several textile firms whose data are reported here and, especially, to the technical personnel who supported the evolution of these procedures and their publication.

Literature Cited

1. Batra, S.K.; Fornes, R.E.; Hersh, S.P. Textile Research Journal 1980, 50, 454-5.
2. Shofner, F.M.; Miller, Jr., A.C.; Kreikebaum, G. Proceedings of the ASME Symposium on Cotton Dust 1980, p 33-37.
3. Leonard, M.H.; Hersh, S.P.; Batra, S.K.; Dyer, C.L. Proceedings of the Fifth Special Session on Cotton Dust, Beltwide Cotton Conference 1981, p 32-37.
4. Roberts, E.C.; Rossano, A.J.; McKay, D.L. Textile Research Journal 1980, 50, 699-700.
5. Federal Register 1978, 43, 27350-463.
6. Textile Week March 24, 1980, p 5.
7. Roberts, E.C.; Rossano, Jr., A.J.; McKay, D.L. Textile Research Journal 1981, 51, 471-6.
8. Shofner, F.M.; Neefus, J.D.; Smoot, D.M.; Beck, J.M. Proceedings of the International Symposium on Aerosols in the Mining and Industrial Work Environment 1981, in press.
9. Shofner, F.M.; Kreikebaum, G.; Miller, Jr., A.C. Proceedings of Fifth Special Session on Cotton Dust, Beltwide Cotton Conference 1981, p 55-62.

RECEIVED March 10, 1982.

9

Real Time Measurement of Particle Size Distribution of Airborne Cotton Dust by Light Scattering

S. P. HERSH, S. K. BATRA, and W.-W. LEE

North Carolina State University, School of Textiles, Raleigh, NC 27650

The particle size distribution (PSD) of airborne cotton dust has been measured in real time by light scattering while processing cotton in a model card room. The light sensing particle counter was coupled to a multichannel analyzer. With this instrumentation it is possible to identify components of the dust as originating from vegetable matter in the cotton, mineral matter from humidifiers, or background dust. The influence of various dust control techniques such as adding dust suppressing lubricants to the cotton or using an electrostatic precipitator as a second stage filter was also studied. For example, it has been found that dust in the size range from 2 to 4.5 μm is more efficiently removed (95-98%) by the use of a dust suppressant additive than is larger (~90%) or smaller (~70%) size dust.

Measurement of the particle size distribution (PSD) of airborne cotton dust by traditional methods has been a rather tedious and time consuming undertaking. Manually sizing and counting magnified images of dust particles collected on a filter is, by nature, wearisome. With image analysers the task becomes much simpler, but this technique still requires dust to be collected on a filter over an optimum period of time. Fractionation with cascade impactors is unsuitable since lint, because of its aerodynamic characteristics, is collected on all stages. The mass of the lint frequently overwhelms that of the fractionated equant dust particles. Coulter counters suffer from the problem of having to remove dust from the filter and the attendant unknown effects of agglomeration and dispersion when doing so. Also many of the dust components are soluble in the electrolytes used.

In contrast to the techniques just enumerated, measurement of the PSD by light scattering offers many advantages. Foremost of these is the ability to measure the particles while they are air-

0097-6156/82/0189-0123$06.00/0

borne and thereby to eliminate the problems of aggregation and dispersion. In addition, measurements can be made quickly, generally within 60 seconds. The utility of the technique is demonstrated by the development of several cotton dust mass samplers which utilize light scattering for the sensing mechanism (1,2).

Measuring Instrumentation

The basic instrumentation in the present work is a Royco Model 225/518 High Concentration Particle Counter. The location of the air inlet and light sensing unit of the instrument in the card room has been described previously (3). The inlet was fitted with a vertical elutriator preseparator designed to prevent particles >15 μm aerodynamic diameter from entering the light sensor. Thus the collection efficiency of this instrumentation as a function of particle size should be similar to that of the Vertical Elutriator Cotton Dust Sampler.

The counting unit of this instrument is limited to five channels. Although it is possible to derive the PSD of the sampled dust from only five channels, it has been shown that a histogram containing at least seven cells is necessary to obtain satisfactory agreement between PSD's measured by light scattering and those measured by manually counting dust particles collected simultaneously on filters (4). To obtain this amount of information on the standard instrument, it is necessary to first take a one-minute sample and then recalibrate the instrument for a second set of diameters. A second sample is then measured assuming the dust PSD does not change during the 15-minute interval required for the recalibration.

To eliminate the need for recalibration during a measurement and to obtain additional information, the Royco instrument was supplemented with a Nuclear Data ND-60 Multichannel Analyser (MCA). The amplified signal of the Royco 225 (which is proportional to the amount of light scattered from each particle) was connected to the input of the MCA which can count and classify pulsed input signals into as many as 2048 channels and display the results on a cathode ray tube (CRT). This number of cells is of course much more than required to determine the PSD. The data were therefore grouped into eleven cells whose limits were consistent with those used earlier (5), and the counts in these cells were then printed on a Texas Instruments 743 KSR Data Terminal interfaced with the MCA.

In preliminary evaluations a Nuclear Data ND-PSA Particle Sizing Amplifier (PSA) was interfaced between the Royco and the MCA. The PSA, which could serve as either a linear or logarithmic amplifier, was operated in the log mode to develop an output signal which would be more nearly proportional to the log of the particle diameter and spread the small-diameter particle count over a larger number of channels. The distribution displayed on the CRT would have been in that case more nearly comparable with the normal graphical representation of the PSD. It was found, however, that the PSA merely introduced additional noise to the Royco signal and did not increase the reliability of the count of small-diameter particles. For these reasons, use of the PSA was discontinued.

Experimental Procedure

Dust Sampling and PSD Analysis. One minute samples taken at a flow rate of 0.1 ft^3/min at intervals ranging from five to fifteen minutes were analysed. Sampling began as the card was started for each run but about 30 minutes before cotton was fed and the Pneumafil lint capture system was turned on. It ended when processing of the cotton was stopped. (Details of the card room layout, equipment and operating procedures have been described previously (6).) A surge in particle count usually occurred as cotton entered the card and the Pneumafil system started circulating the previously settled dust. In five to ten minutes, however, the count would fall to a reasonably steady level. The results reported below are for the relatively steady-state condition. (Detailed descriptions of the changes in dust concentration which occur during and after processing have been reported elsewhere (4,7).)

The PSD's measured were expressed in terms of the mean diameter and standard deviation of the log normal distribution calculated in two different ways. First they were calculated algebraically as the geometric mean diameter (on a number basis) $\bar{d}_{g,n}$ and as the geometric standard deviation σ_g. Second, they were determined from cumulative log normal probability plots using well documented standard procedures (see, for example, references 8, 9). The algebraic calculations of the distribution parameters included all cells of the histogram while those obtained from the cumulative plots were sometimes based on only a part of the cells. When the distribution was multimodal, the latter calculations included only the values from the distribution with the smaller diameter, and no attempt was made to adjust the percentage count for the number of points in the larger diameter distribution(s). Other factors reported are the number of particles per 0.1 ft^3, the dust concentration measured with the Vertical Elutriator Cotton Dust Samplers (VE), the nature of the cumulative plots, and for multimodal distributions, the percent of particles in the distribution with the smaller diameter.

Mock Runs--No Cotton Processed. In addition to the measurements described above, a set of experiments was carried out to assess the amount of background dust in the card room. A considerable amount of the respirable dust measured in the card room has been reported to come from the solids contained in the water supplied to the atomizers used to maintain the relative humidity (10). The spray drying of the atomized water droplets form particles of solid residue which also are collected by the samplers. To determine the PSD of the dust contributed by the atomizers, mock runs were made with (A) the humidifiers and the Pneumafil lint capture system (PN) off, (B) only the PN on, (C) only the humidifiers on, and (D) with both on. During these mock runs the air conditioner and card were operated, but no cotton was processed.

Results and Discussion

Mock runs. Results of all the measurements are summarized in Table I, and histograms of the distributions observed for two of the mock runs are shown in Figures 1 and 2. The corresponding cumulative distribution curves are shown in Figure 3.

The geometric mean diameters (number basis) $\bar{d}_{g,n}$ for the mock runs calculated algebraically (including all cells) range from 1.30 to 1.44 μm. The highest value was obtained when the atomizers were on and the PN was not. The slight increase in $\bar{d}_{g,n}$ over that observed when the PN was running (1.44 compared with 1.32 μm) was expected since it has been shown previously that the PN system selectively removes smaller diameter particles from the card room (4,7). The cumulative distribution curves indicate the distributions to be bimodal except for the mock run made with only the PN on. The small diameter end of the latter curve was concave down suggesting that smaller particles were being removed selectively.

The mean diameters $\bar{d}_{g,n}$ of the smaller diameter distributions calculated from the cumulative curves are about 0.1 μm greater than those calculated algebraically. Because the higher diameter distributions contain no more than 3% of the particles counted (and sometimes less than 0.05%), no attempt was made to resolve the two distributions present. Applying a correction for the particles in the upper distribution would have a negligible effect on $\bar{d}_{g,n}$ and σ_g calculated from the cumulative curve for the smaller diameter distribution.

Although the six cells with diameters >3.17 μm contain only a small fraction of the total number of particles counted, the numbers in the cells are remarkably consistent as noted in Table II. The possible significance of this observation will be discussed later.

TABLE I
Parameters of Particle Size Distributions Measured by Light Scattering

		Distribution Parameters				Cumulative Plot			
		Algebraic		Cumulative					
Run	Conditions[a]	$d_{g,n}$ (μm)	σ_g	$d_{g,n}$ (μm)	σ_g	Nature	b	No. of Particles	Dust Conc. (μg/m^3)
A	H off, PN off	1.30	1.40	1.42	1.22	Bimodal	97.1	25,730	47
B	H off, PN on	1.39	1.50	1.45[c]	1.28	Bimodal[c]	x	16,058	82
C	H on, PN off	1.44	1.39	1.52	1.28	Bimodal	99.96	436,376	376
D	H on, PN on	1.32	1.39	1.42	1.24	Bimodal	99.29	174,923	248
E	Cotton 1	1.63	1.76	1.63	1.84	Linear	-	168,249	1403
F	PET Staple	1.04	1.31	1.08	1.30	Bimodal	98.9	262,464	377
G	Cotton 2	1.88	1.58	1.85	1.44	Nearly Linear	99.56	554,638	1234
H	0.48% Texpray	1.44	1.48	1.45	1.28	Bimodal	90.3	79,482	364
I	1.09% Spraycot	1.43	1.44	1.44	1.26	Bimodal	91.92	89,226	187
J	Cotton 3	1.64	1.59	1.62	1.48	Nearly Linear	99.95	433,791	1931
K	0.60% Milube N-32	1.27	1.40	1.09	1.56	Bimodal	96.0	109,645	177
L	Cotton 4, ESP off	1.82	1.66	1.80	1.58	Nearly Linear	x	304,819	660
M	Cotton 4, ESP on	1.71	1.69	1.65	1.60	Nearly Linear	x	122,281	219
	G minus H	1.96	1.57	1.90	1.40	Bimodal	65.5	475,107	870
	J minus K	1.78	1.60	1.85	1.62	Nearly Linear	x	324,146	1754
	L minus M	1.89	1.63	1.90	1.66	Linear	-	182,538	441
	D minus B	1.31	1.37	1.43	1.22	Linear	-	158,865	166

Footnotes on next page.

TABLE I Footnotes.

[a]H = humidifier, PN = Pneumafil lint capture system, PET = poly(ethylene terephthalate), ESP = electrostatic precipitator. Physical properties of cottons 1, 2, 3, and 4 are: Class 43, 51, 82, 43, -; Micronaire 4.4, 4.1, 3.0, 5.5; Shirley Analyzer total trash 6.1%, 4.9%, 7.7%, 2.4%.

[b]Percent of observed particles contained in the smaller diameter distribution.

[c]Approximate value because cumulative distribution curve for the lower diameter distribution was curved concave to the diameter axis.

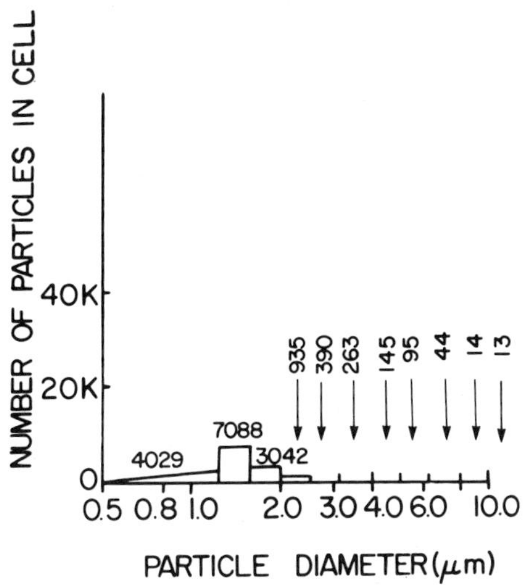

Figure 1. Particle size histogram of dust collected during mock run (no cotton being processed) with humidifier off and Pneumafil lint capture system on. Conditions: $\bar{d}_{gn,}$, nonlinear; 16,059 particles; VE, 80 $\mu g/m^3$.

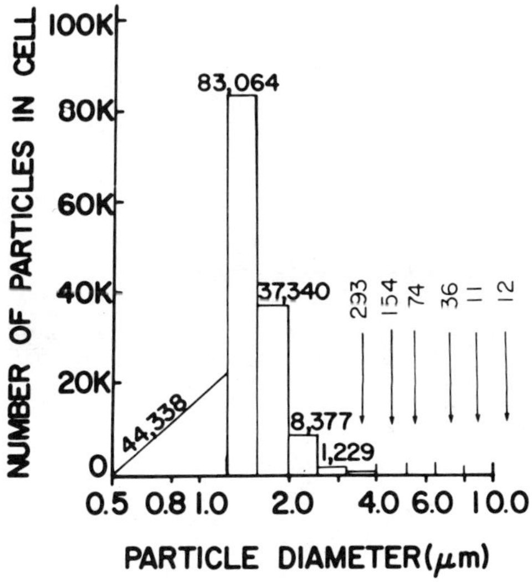

Figure 2. Particle size histogram of dust collected during mock run (no cotton being processed) with humidifier and Pneumafil lint captive system on. Conditions: $\bar{d}_{g,n}$, 1.32 μm; σ_g, 1.39; 174,923 particles; and VE, 250 $\mu g/m^3$.

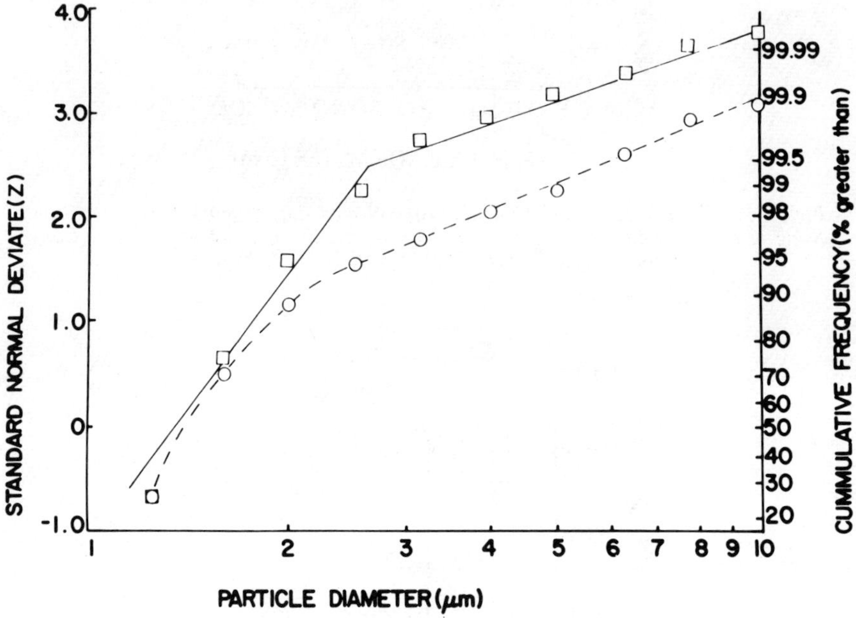

Figure 3. Cumulative distribution curves of distributions shown in Figures 1 and 2. Key: □, *humidifier on, PN on;* ○, *humidifier off, PN on.*

TABLE II

Particle Counts in Six Largest Diameter Histogram Cells (number counted in 0.1 ft^3 sample)

	Cell Midpoint (Diameter, μm)						Particle Count		
								Upper 6 cells	
Run[a]	3.6	4.5	5.7	7.1	9.0	11.3	Total	No.	(%)
B	263	145	95	44	14	13	16,059	574	3.57
D	293	154	74	36	11	12	174,923	580	0.33
F	382	199	125	40	14	10	262,464	780	0.30

[a]See Table I for processing conditions.

Processing of Cotton and PET Staple Fiber. The histograms obtained while processing 100% cotton and 100% poly(ethylene terephthalate) staple fiber (PET) are shown in Figure 4. The cotton was class 43 (strict low middling), 4.4 micronaire and contained 6.1% trash as measured by the Shirley Analyser. The PET was type 310 Fortrel, 1.5 denier, and 1.5 inch staple length. Cotton with a relatively high trash content was selected deliberately as a control in experiments designed to evaluate techniques for reducing dust generation. The results reported in Table I (runs E and F) show that although the concentration of dust engendered while processing the cotton was 271% greater than when processing the PET, the number of particles present was 36% less. The diameters $\bar{d}_{g,n}$ of dust from the cotton and PET were 1.63 and 1.04 μm respectively. The observed σ_g for the cotton was also greater, which suggests that many more larger diameter particles are generated when the cotton is processed. This conclusion is further supported by the histograms shown in Figure 4.

The presence of a large number of small-diameter particles during the PET run is at least partially attributable to the use of four atomizers (instead of the normal two) to maintain a high enough humidity to permit the PET to be processed. The $\bar{d}_{g,n}$ of the dust measured during the PET run is considerably smaller than that observed during the mock run, a fact which suggests that the PSD of aerosols generated by water atomizers is quite variable. Indeed, the diameter of the particles would be expected to vary with the concentration of solids in the water and the size of the droplets formed. These factors could change considerably over time and with changing humidification requirements based on outside ambient conditions.

Even though the scale of the histograms shown in Figure 4 suggest that no particles are present in the PET run with diameter >2.6 μm, particles in this size range were indeed present. The actual particle count, shown in Table II, is remarkably close to that reported for the mock runs. The agreement between the counts

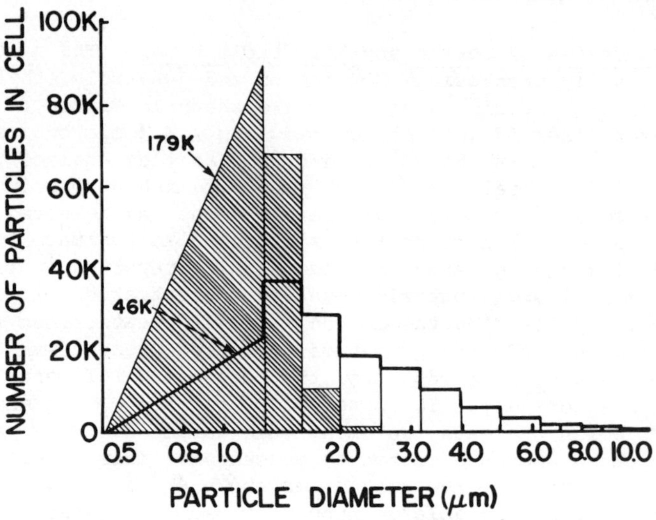

Figure 4. Particle size histograms of dust collected while processing cotton and poly(ethylene terephthalate) (PET). Key: ▧, 100% PET; VE, 377 μg/m³; N, 262,464; □, 100% cotton; VE, 1400 μg/m³; N, 168,249.

in the six highest diameter cells, representing in one case only 0.3% of a count of 262,464 (that for the PET run), suggests that the resolution of the counting and sizing system employed is remarkably good.

The cumulative distribution curve of the cotton histogram is linear through the entire size range (up to 99.94% of the particles counted). The PET curve, on the other hand, is bimodal as shown in Figure 5. When the bimodal distribution is resolved into its two components using the method described by Taylor (11), the cumulative distribution plot of the larger diameter distribution, part of which is shown in Figure 5, is linear. The fact that the number of particles included in this distribution (2051) is only 0.78% of the total particles counted and that the cumulative curve for these particles is linear again shows the sensitivity of the instrumentation in measuring the particle count and size. The mean and standard deviation of the upper distribution diameter is 2.9 µm and 1.58, respectively.

The histograms of the resolved distributions, plotted on a log scale to show the number of particles in the high diameter cells, is shown in Figure 6.

Effect of Dust Suppressing Lubricants. The authors have studied the influence of dust suppressing additives on the dust generating characteristics of cotton (12). These studies were concerned primarily with the concentration of the dust generated during processing. In this paper the PSD of the dust obtained from a few of these runs will be examined.

The effects of applying 0.48% of Texspray Compound and 1.09% of Spraycot 8853 are summarized in Table I. In both cases there is a marked drop in the number of particles (an average of 84.8%) and in dust concentration (70.5% for the Texspray and 84.8% for the Spraycot). The $\bar{d}_{g,n}$ calculated algebraically decreases from 1.88 µm for the control cotton to 1.44 µm for the two lubricated cottons. The cumulative probability curves of the dust emitted from the cottons containing additives become bimodal. These changes in the nature of the cumulative distribution curves suggest that the fraction of particles removed is not constant for all diameters.

Table I also illustrates the effect of adding 0.60% of Milube N-32 to a low grade, low micronaire and high trash content cotton. The histograms and cumulative distribution curves of the control and treated cottons are shown in Figures 7 and 8. The results are similar to those found for the other cottons containing additives in that there is a drop of 74.7% in particle count and of 90.8% in dust concentration. The presence of the additive lowers $\bar{d}_{g,n}$ from 1.62 to 1.09 µm (based on the cumulative plots). The cumulative distribution of the stock cotton is linear (except for the lowest diameter cell) over a range including 99.95% of the particles and that of the additive-treated cotton is bimodal. The smaller

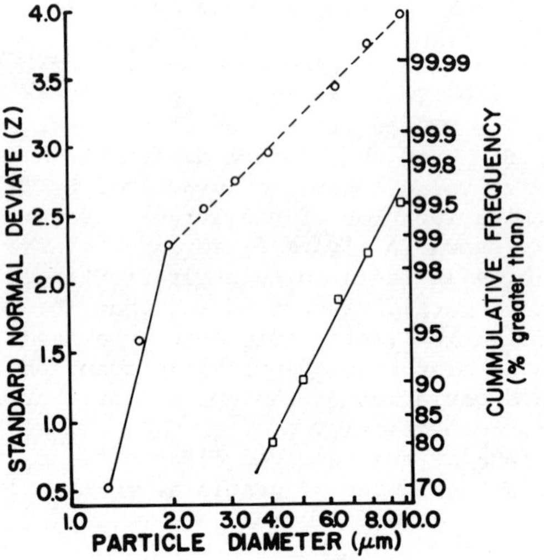

Figure 5. Cumulative distribution curves of dust collected while processing 100% PET. Key: ○, original bimodal curve; $\bar{d} = 1.08$ μm, $\sigma = 1.30$; □, curve for distribution having the larger diameter as resolved by the Taylor method(11); $\bar{d} = 2.9$ μm, $\sigma = 1.58$. The latter curve includes points for diameters ≥ 4 μm.

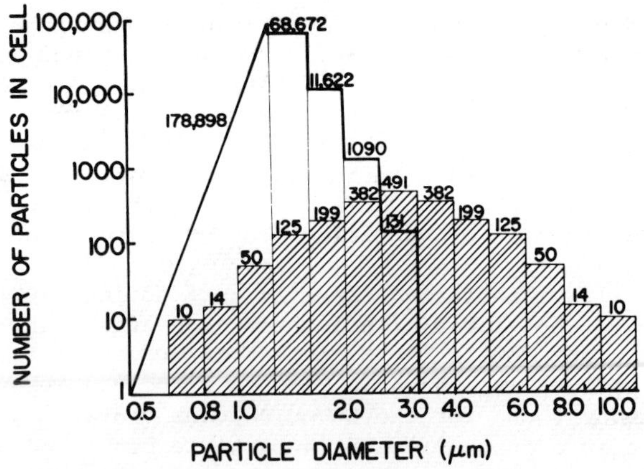

Figure 6. Particle size histograms of dust collected while processing cotton control and PET. Logarithmic particle count. Key: ▨, 100% PET, $\bar{d} = 2.9$ μm, $\sigma = 1.58$, $N = 2051$; □, 100% cotton, $\bar{d} = 1.08$ μm, $\sigma = 1.30$, $N = 260,413$.

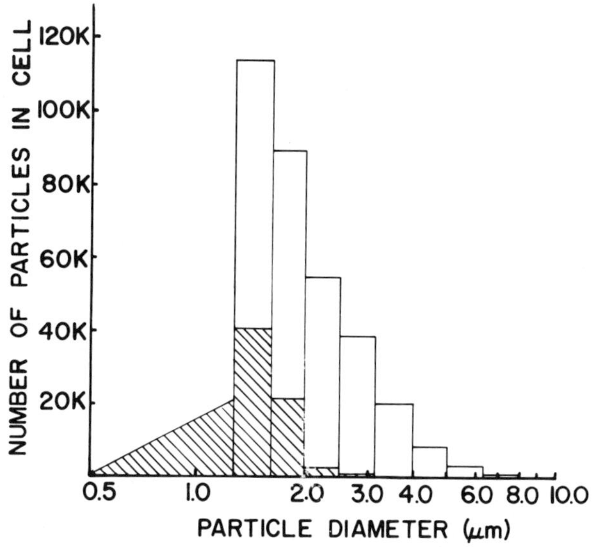

Figure 7. Particle size histograms of dust collected while processing cotton control and cotton containing 0.60% of additive A (Milube N-32). Key: ▨, *100% PET, 0.6% A, 180 μg/m³, N = 109,645;* □, *100% cotton, 1.930 μg/m³, N = 433,791.*

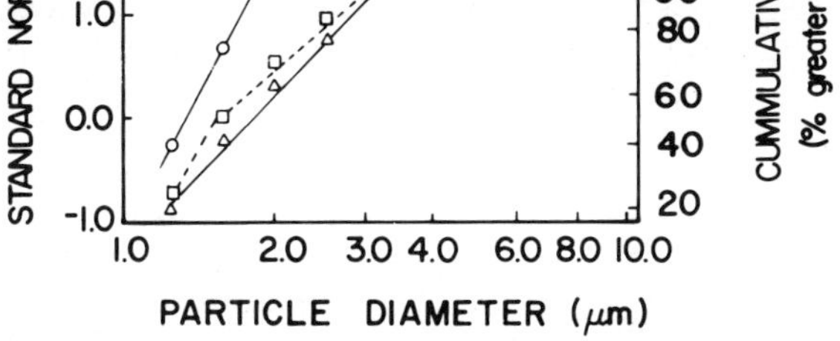

Figure 8. Cumulative distribution curves of distributions shown in Figure 7. Key: □, *cotton control;* ○, *0.60% Milube N–32;* △, *distribution of dust removed from card room atmosphere when Milube N–32 is added to cotton.*

diameter distribution, however, is linear over 96.0% of the particle count.

The fraction of particles removed as a function of particle diameter by the application of Texspray and Milube N-32 are illustrated in Figure 9. The greatest fraction of particles removed are those having diameters from 2 to 4.5 µm (95-98%). Removal efficiency decreases to about 90% for the larger particles (10 µm diameter) and to about 70% for the smaller diameters.

Effect of In-line Electrostatic Precipitator. The effectiveness of two types of electrostatic precipitators (ESP) in reducing the concentration of cotton dust in the card room during processing was described earlier (12). One of these, the SMOG-HOG reduced the dust concentration by an average of 67% (from 810 $\mu g/m^3$ to 264 $\mu g/m^3$). The PSD parameters measured during two of the eight runs made are listed in Table I, and the corresponding cumulative distribution curves are shown in Figure 10. The drop in $\bar{d}_{g,n}$ is only about 0.1 µm (from 1.82 to 1.71 µm), much less than the drop of 0.4 µm observed on the cottons processed containing additives. The cumulative curves are linear except for the lowest cell.

The fraction of particles removed by the ESP as a function of diameter is also shown in Figure 9. Removal efficiency is greatest for 2.3 µm diameter particles (70%). The fraction removed at all diameters is considerably less than that removed after applying additives. The theoretical removal efficiency curve for an ESP as a function of diameter has a minimum at about 0.25 µm (13,14); however, experimental observations show the minimum to actually range between 2 to 5 µm (15). Thus, the removal efficiency of the ESP observed here is consistent with similar measurements reported in the literature.

Size Distribution of Particles Removed. The number and size of particles removed from the card room atmosphere by applying an additive or by the ESP can be determined by subtracting the individual cell counts observed during these runs from those observed during the control runs. The parameters of the "removed" distribution are reported in Table I. The cumulative distributions of the particles removed for a typical example of each type are shown in Figures 8 and 10 by the lines denoted with "delta" symbols. The parameters of the PSD of the particles removed from the card room atmosphere by applying 0.6% of Milube N-32 (Figure 8) were $\bar{d}_{g,n}$ = 1.78 µm and σ_g = 1.60. The cumulative curve consists of two linear portions with nearly the same slopes (σ_g = 1.54 and 1.70 for the smaller and larger diameter segments respectively). For the untreated cotton, $\bar{d}_{g,n}$ = 1.64 µm and σ_g = 1.59.

As shown by the difference curve in Figure 10, the PSD of the dust collected by the ESP has $\bar{d}_{g,n}$ = 1.90 µm and σ_g = 1.66, values not much different from those of the original cotton ($\bar{d}_{g,n}$ = 1.82 µm and σ_g = 1.66).

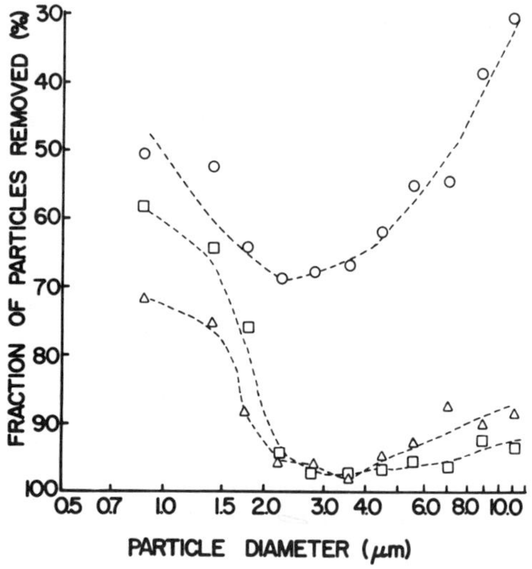

Figure 9. Reduction in number of dust particles in card room as a function of diameter. Fraction removed compared with control when processing cotton with 0.60% Milube N–32 applied (□), 0.48% Texspray applied (△), and electrostatic precipitator in filter system (○).

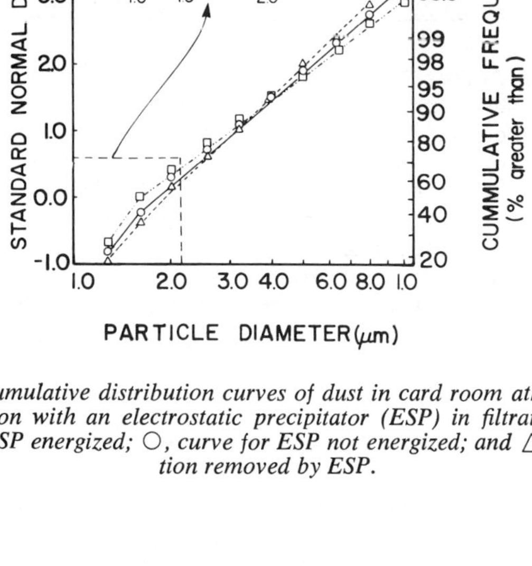

Figure 10. Cumulative distribution curves of dust in card room atmosphere while processing cotton with an electrostatic precipitator (ESP) in filtration line. Key: □, curve for ESP energized; ○, curve for ESP not energized; and △, size distribution removed by ESP.

Possible Sources of Dust Components. The results presented above suggest that the dust present in the card room can be separated into three basic categories: (1) dust arising from the spray drying of water from the atomizing humidifiers which has $\bar{d}_{g,n}$ of about 1.4 µm and σ_g of 1.4; (2) dust arising from the processing of cotton having $\bar{d}_{g,n}$ of around 1.7 µm and σ_g of around 1.6; and (3) "background" dust having a $\bar{d}_{g,n}$ of around 3.0 µm and σ_g of 1.6 [the dust observed as the larger diameter distribution when processing PET (Figure 6) and in the mock runs (Table II)]. In addition, a fourth distribution having $\bar{d}_{g,n}$ of 0.29 µm and σ_g of 1.70 (but with a mode of 0.44 µm) was observed in a clean library environment from particle size measurements of dust collected on Nuclepore filters (4). A distribution having the same mode (0.44 µm) was also observed in dust collected in the card room while processing cotton. A distribution having a mode of <0.19 µm was also present in the library dust. These latter measurements were made by Scanning Electron Microscopy since the lower limit of detection by light scattering is around 0.5 µm. These components and their distribution parameters are enumerated in Table III.

TABLE III

Particle Size Distribution and Source of Dust Components Found in Model Card Room and Library

No.	Source	Distribution Parameters $\bar{d}_{g,n}$ (µm)	σ_g	Particles per m^3
1	Library, lower diameter	<0.19	-	-
2	Library, higher diameter	0.39	1.7	40
3	Card room, atomizer	1.4	1.4	500
4	Card room, cotton	1.7	1.6	900
5	Card room, background	3.0	1.6	2

Whitby and Cantrell (16) report that aerosols collected near the surface of the earth are trimodal in nature. As listed in Table IV, these consist of distributions arising from (1) the direct emission of primary products from combustion having $\bar{d}_{g,n} \cong 0.02$ µm; (2) coagulation of the aerosols from (1), or the condensation of reaction products or water on the aerosols from (1), having $\bar{d}_{g,n} \cong 0.16$; and (3) larger particles arising from natural sources such as wind blown dusts (desert), sea spray, volcanos and plant particles and man-made particles from mechanical processes with an average $\bar{d}_{g,n}$ of 2.9 µm.

A comparison of the aerosol sources listed in Tables III and IV suggests that the second distribution listed in Table III having a $\bar{d}_{g,n}$ of 0.39 µm corresponds to the second distribution listed in Table IV and represents aerosols arising from coagulation and condensation. Similarly, distribution 5 in Table III apparently coincides with the third sample of aerosols listed by Whitby and Cantrell as arising from natural and man-made sources. It is conceivable that the first distribution listed in Table III corresponds to the first source listed in Table IV. This statement cannot be made with certainty, however, since the resolution of the SEM technique used was not high enough.

It should be noted that distribution 5 (Table III) could not be detected in the card room when any of the control cottons were being processed because the large number of particles generated during processing (several hundred thousand) completely overwhelmed the small number of particles present as distribution 5 (~2000). (It should be remembered that the cottons used for the experiments reported here were deliberately selected for their high trash content and potential for high dust generation.)

Because of the small separation between the modes of the distributions arising from the atomized water droplets and the cotton, it would be difficult to resolve these two distributions. In principle, one possible way to resolve them might be to subtract the count obtained in a mock run in which the humidifiers are running from the count obtained when cotton is also being processed. In practice, however, this procedure may not be feasible because the amount of humidification required during the day and from day-to-day varies so much.

TABLE IV
Trimodal Nature of Surface Aerosols as Proposed by Whitby and Cantrell (16)

No.	Source	Distribution Parameters $\bar{d}_{g,n}$ (µm) Range	Average	σ_g
1	Primary products from combustion	-	0.017	1.74
2	Condensation of reaction products or water on particles from (1) or coagulation of particles from (1)	0.08-0.37	0.16	2.05
3	Particles from natural sources (such as wind blown dusts from deserts, sea spray, volcanos and vegetation) and man-made from mechanical processes.	1.6-11.5	2.9	2.33

Conclusions

It has been demonstrated that this technique for measuring the PSD by light scattering in real time is sensitive, reproducible and can provide valuable information about the nature of the dust and the mechanisms of dust generation and removal. Moreover, the data obtained can help in establishing equivalency between cotton dust samplers. It should also aid in determining how equivalency is affected by the PSD of the cottons processed since the PSD is expected to vary with grade, processing stage and even with the method of dust control employed.

Acknowledgement

This study was supported by NIOSH Grant No. 5 R01 OH 00744-03 and by Cotton Incorporated. The authors are grateful for this assistance and for the materials supplied by the following companies: Cotton Incorporated (cotton); Fiber Industries Inc. (Fortrel PET staple fiber); Texaco, Inc. (Texspray Compound); Vickers & Sons, Ltd. (Spraycot 8853); ICI Americas, Inc. (Milube N-32); and United Air Specialists (SMOG-HOG).

Literature Cited

1. Shofner, F. M.; Miller, A. C. Jr.; Kreikebaum, G.; Kerlin, T. W. Proc. Third Special Session on Cotton Dust Research 1979, p 75-85.
2. Chansky, S. H.; Lilienfeld, P.; Witsee, K. Proc. Second Natural Fibers Textile Conference, 1979, p 18-21.
3. Hersh, S. P.; Fornes, R. E.; Anand, M. Am. Ind. Hyg. Assoc. J. 1979, 40, 578-87.
4. Hersh, S. P.; Fornes, R. E.; Batra, S.; Anand, M.; Johnson, R. H. Proc. Third Special Session on Cotton Dust Research 1979, p 67-74.
5. Fornes, R. E.; Kleinfelter, M. M.; Hersh, S. P. J. of Engineering for Ind., Trans. ASME 1977, Series B 99, 56-60.
6. Hersh, S. P.; Fornes, R. E.; Caruolo, E. V. Proc. Topical Symp. on Cotton Dust 1975, p 376-394.
7. Anand, M., M.S., Thesis, North Carolina State University, Raleigh, NC, 1978.
8. Dallavalle, J. M. "Micrometrics: The Technology of Fine Particles"; Pitman: New York, 1943.
9. Irani, R. R. and Callis, C. F. "Particle Size: Measurement, Interpretation, and Application"; Wiley: New York, 1963.
10. Batra, S. K.; Fornes, R. E.; Hersh, S. P. Textile Res. J. 1980, 50, 454-5.
11. Taylor, B. J. R. J. Animal Ecology 1965, 34, 445.

12. Hersh, S. P.; Batra, S. K.; and Fornes, R. E. Proc. ASME Textile Industries Division Symposium on Cotton Dust Measurement, Monitoring and Control 1980, p 23-31.
13. Bethea, R. M. "Air Pollution Control Technology"; Van Nostrand Reinhold: New York, 1978, p 226-227.
14. Masuda, S. Inst. Phys. Conf. Ser. No. 27 1975, 154-172.
15. Batel, W. "Dust Extraction Technology"; Technicopy: Stonehouse, Glos., England, 1976, p 78-79.
16. Whitby, K. T.; Cantrell, B. Proc. of the International Conference on Environmental Sensing and Assessment, IEEE 1975, p 1-6.

RECEIVED January 20, 1982.

ETIOLOGY AND EPIDEMIOLOGY

10

Mechanisms in Byssinosis: A Review

CAROL E. O'NEIL, BRIAN T. BUTCHER, and JOHN E. SALVAGGIO

Tulane University Medical Center, Department of Medicine, New Orleans, LA 70112

Byssinosis, a respiratory disease of cotton, flax, and jute workers is characterized clinically by shortness of breath, cough, and chest tightness on Mondays or the first day a worker returns to work after a time off. Although described for more than a century, both the underlying pathogenesis and etiology(s) of the disease remain obscure. Four main mechanisms have been proposed: enzyme mediated, immunologic response, endotoxin activity, and nonspecific pharmacologic mediator release, to explain disease pathogenesis. This article reviews current and previous findings to support or refute the mechanisms proposed for byssinosis, as well as indicating possible approaches for future research.

Byssinosis is a respiratory disease of cotton (1,2), flax (3), hemp (4), and sisal (5) workers. In the acute phase it is characterized clinically by chest tightness, cough, and dyspnea, with or without wheezing, which occurs when first returning to work after time off. In the chronic phase these symptoms occur on all days and continue after cessation of dust exposure. The disease is not seen in workers exposed to other vegetable or animal fibers, such as kapok, silk or wool (6,7,8). In the United States alone, there are more than 94,810 separate cotton businesses in at least 20 states employing over 535,000 people (9) and it has been estimated that approximately 35,000 men and women in cotton textile mills suffer from work related disabling lung diseases (2). Adequate programs of prevention and control, of both the acute and chronic diseases, are urgently needed, but an understanding of the disease mechanisms involved is necessary to successfully accomplish these goals.

Although byssinosis has been recognized as a disease for more than a century, the underlying etiology and pathogenesis remain obscure. Four main mechanisms: enzyme mediated (10,11,

0097-6156/82/0189-0145$6.00/0

12), immunologic response (13), endotoxin activity (14,15), and non-specific pharmacologic mediator release (16,17) have been advanced to explain disease pathogenesis. These are discussed below.

Enzyme Mediated

Enzymes in Dust. Early findings showed that cotton dust contained protein (18) and several authors have demonstrated the presence of proteolytic enzymes in cotton mill dust (10,19,20). Statistically significant correlations have been shown between dust enzyme levels and post shift decline in forced expiratory volume in 1 second (FEV_1) (10,11,20,21). Enzyme activity has been shown over the pH range 3.0-10.0, with two peaks at pH 4.5 and 7.0 (11,20). It probably originates from numerous contaminating microorganisms, especially Aspergillus and Bacillus sp. (10,21). Acid enzymatic activity appears to be associated with unstained cotton seeds, while neutral enzyme activity is found in leaves. Clean, unstained cotton fibers contain no proteolytic activity (11).

Evidence against the involvement of dust enzymes is the finding that byssinosis does not occur in woolen mills which have an abundance of enzymes in the environment (7). Further, cotton willowing mills, which have high enzyme levels, have a low incidence of byssinosis. It is proposed, however, that enzymes may be responsible for the high prevalence of bronchitic symptoms (53%) among workers in these plants (19).

Despite these findings, mediation by enzymes present in dust remains an attractive hypothesis. Enzymes may exert their action in one of three ways: 1) an allergic mechanism like that shown in workers exposed to B. subtilis during detergent manufacture (22,23,24) where wheezing, shortness of breath, and/or rhinitis symptoms are shown to be mediated by specific IgE antibodies. 2) non-specific histamine release by enzymes from B. subtilis and A. oryzae found in cotton dust (11,25). In guinea pigs, pretreatment with enzyme causes histamine accumulation in lungs, liver, and ears. This enzyme-induced histamine synthesis occurs rapidly and is stored for at least 28 days, but, upon provocation inhalation challenge (PIC) with enzyme, histamine is released immediately from lungs. The histamine releasing ability of cotton dust enzymes is ten times that of a standard compound (21). 3) direct tissue injury from exposure to proteolytic enzymes. Enzymes can cause emphysema in experimental animals (26). Moreover, proteases degrade human lung tissue (27,28,29), causing emphysema or an emphysema-like pathology; however, no increase of emphysema has been noted in byssinotics.

Not all enzyme exposed workers develop byssinosis, however, suggesting that certain individuals are hypersusceptible. It is possible that antiproteases such as serum $alpha_1$ anti-trypsin (SAT) may play a role. SAT is an antiprotease capable of deactivating proteolytic enzymes normally released in the lungs by macrophages or polymorphonuclear leucocytes (PMNs) during phagocytosis or at the end of their life span (30,31). There is a high incidence of SAT deficiency in byssinotics compared with the general population (21,32). However, not all persons with SAT deficiency develop chronic obstructive pulmonary disease (COPD). There is less tendency to develop COPD if there is a concomitant protease deficiency (33). Therefore, in individuals with a partial SAT deficiency and normal protease levels, symptoms only occur when there is an interaction between environmental factors and hereditary disposition (34). It has been reported that members of some families are highly susceptible to flax dust and develop byssinosis, while others do not. This unknown genetic factor is so decisive that it overshadows duration of exposure to dust (35).

Cotton Dust Induced Enzyme Release. Alveolar macrophages and PMNs engulf particles or fluid droplets which penetrate to the alveoli and effectively remove them via the tracheobronchial tree or by other internal routes (36). Ingestible particles, when presented to phagocytes, attach to the cell membranes, via the Fc receptor. The cell's metabolism is altered from glycolysis to the hexose monophosphate shunt whereby it can produce highly reactive oxidizing agents (e.g. singlet oxygen and hydrogen peroxide). These agents, with the enhancement of luminol (5-amino-2, 3-dihydro-1, 4-pthalazindione), produce chemiluminescence (37). Measurements of luminol-dependent chemiluminescence are useful in assessing effects of environmental pollutants on the functional behavior of alveolar macrophages (38). Cotton bract extracts inhibit sheep alveolar macrophage chemiluminescence by 90% in a dose dependent fashion. This inhibition is attributed to a direct action of the extracts and their chemical fractions on the chemiluminescence mechanism (39).

Aqueous extracts of cotton bract and mill dust are leucotactic (15,40). In experimental animals, aqueous extracts of cotton dust (AECD) attract PMNs to airways in a dose dependent fashion beginning at 3 hours, and reaching a peak at 18-24 hours. Macrophage levels immediately drop and remain low until 18 hours post-exposure when a modest increase occurs. Cell infiltration, with subsequent release of intracellular enzymes and mediators, is thought to be important in the pathology of byssinosis (15).

It is postulated that chemotactic agents leach from respirable cotton dust particles in the small bronchioles. AECD recruit PMNs to the lung in the following sequence: connective tissue beneath the basal lamina, between airway cells, and, finally, into the lumen. Chest tightness is also correlated with leucocyte recruitment (41). Although it has been proposed that extracellular lysosomal enzymes from PMNs cause the symptoms of byssinosis by initiating release of histamine and/or other chemical mediators (25), it has not been shown that cotton dust actually liberates histamine from PMNs.

Purification of dust extract yields a compound consistent with the structure $C_{16}H_{20}O_3$. This compound accounts for a slow type of chemotactic activity seen with crude cotton dust extracts (42) suggesting that, rather than exerting a direct chemotactic effect, formation of chemotactic factors or cytotaxins may be induced. Repeated steam distillation removes the chemotactic activity (42). Since steaming cotton has been shown to significantly reduce the byssinogenic potential of cotton dust, it is tempting to speculate that this uncharacterized compound is, at least partially, responsible for disease and the chemotaxins play a major role in byssinosis. Quercetin, a polyphenolic compound present in cotton plants, has been reported to enhance recruitment of PMNs (40) but other work disputes this (42). Such differences probably reflect extraction procedures or choice of animals since there is a difference between guinea pigs and hamsters with respect to the time sequence of cell infiltration, with PMN recruitment proceeding more rapidly in guinea pigs (43).

Exposure to endotoxin aerosols also produces phagocyte recruitment *in vivo*. Endotoxins are common cotton contaminants (44). *In vitro*, they are directly chemotactic, but *in vivo*, they may also interact with airway cells to generate chemotactic factors.

PMN infiltration also occurs following exposure to some common microbial cotton contaminants (*Enterobacter aerogenes* (44), *Klebsiella pneumoniae* or *Escherichia coli*), but not others (*B. subtilis*) (45). Cotton dust extracts pretreated at 80°C and 100°C for 20 minutes cause successively higher leucocyte responses, indicating that the chemotactic effect is not solely affected by viable bacteria (46). Thus, while the increase seen in PMNs may not, by itself, represent a pathological alteration, it could be of importance in the later development of pathological effects.

Complement. Complement is an extensive series of glycoproteins and protein inhibitors whose function includes major cytolytic effects, mediation of opsonization, and modulation of inflammatory responses. Activation of this system plays an important role in host defense leading to destruction of microorganisms. It also results in generation of anaphylotoxins which induce mediator release and "split products" that mediate membrane damage, either directly through structural alteration or indirectly, via cell chemotaxis and regulation.

Cotton dust activates complement *in vitro* by both the classical (antibody dependent) and alternative (antibody independent) pathways (12,47,48). It is proposed that endotoxins may be the agents responsible for complement activation (49). Cotton dust extractions maximizing endotoxin content are 10 times more potent than other extracts in activating complement (12). Activation of complement via the alternative pathway has also been demonstrated using several species of *Aspergillus*, a common cotton contaminant, but not by other fungal contaminants, including *Mucor*, *Penicillium* and *Hormodendrum sp*. (50).

If disease is mediated by non-specific activation of the alternative pathway, it does not explain why some mill workers, who are presumably exposed to equal dust levels, do not develop symptoms. One possible explanation is that there is host factor variability, such as end-organ sensitivity. It has also been proposed that pre-existing, non-specific bronchial hyper-reactivity may be important in development of byssinosis (51), but, to date, there is little evidence for this hypothesis (52-55).

Endotoxin Activity

It has been recognized that cotton fibers and dust are contaminated by both fungal and bacterial organisms (56-59) which produce endotoxins. Some microbial colonization occurs via insect punctures (59) before the bolls open, but the primary contamination source is from handling. Fresh samples of raw fiber have been shown to have as many as 4×10^6 bacteria per gram and 12×10^4 to 40×10^4 mold spores/gram. Unstored samples of cotton fibers contain large numbers of non-spore forming soil bacteria and molds, especially *Hormodendrum*, *Fusarium*, and *Alternaria sp*., but a large percentage of the original microflora die during long storage. *Aspergillus* and *Penicillium sp*. are present in smaller numbers but, when the cotton samples are stored, these spore forming bacteria predominate (58,59). Both gram positive and negative cocci and bacilli and bacterial spores are present in addition to molds. These include *Mucor*, *Rhizopus*, *Sporotrichium*, *Cladosporium* and *Aerobacter cloacae* (56).

Studies of mills processing raw cotton show that in cotton card rooms, most noticeably among the cards, the bacterial count is exceptionally high (up to several thousand/cubic ft.). Pre-carding areas have comparable counts, but spinning rooms are substantially lower (50-200/cubic ft). Air samples taken from canteens and offices have bacterial counts that are numerically similar to spinning rooms, but contain a strikingly different microflora. Mills processing rayon, where byssinosis is unknown, show bacterial counts of less than 10/cubic ft.; values indistinguishable from outside control counts (57).

Substantial numbers (5,000 to 22,000/m^3) of actinomycetes, particularly *Thermoactinomyces vulgaris* (60), are present in the atmosphere of mills. These organisms are known to be causative agents in other occupational lung diseases (61), specifically several forms of hypersensitivity pneumonitis.

There is no strong correlation between byssinosis and levels of viable bacteria in a given plant. Symptoms are, however, more compatible with those produced by endotoxins. Endotoxins are pathogenic agents produced by gram-negative bacteria and are primarily lipopolysaccharide (LPS) in nature.

In 1 ml of aqueous extract of cotton dust, there may be as much as 30 ug of endotoxin-like material; moreover, most dust extracts contain endotoxin. Cotton extracts are pyrogenic in rabbits, but daily injections produce tolerance, an effect similar to that of purified endotoxins. Further, rabbits made tolerant to injections of cotton extracts are also tolerant to I.V. injections of purified S. abortus equi endotoxin. Conversely, rabbits made tolerant to endotoxins are also tolerant to cotton extracts (62).

Histamine is released from whole rabbit blood by both cotton extracts and endotoxins, however, the ability of AECD to release histamine is greater than would be expected from endotoxin content alone. Antweiler (63), however, was unable to show in vivo histamine release by endotoxins obtained from cotton extracts in rabbits nor could he show an acute fall in blood pressure of cats after I.V. endotoxin injection, as occurred with subsequent injections of compound 48/80 or other dust extracts. He concludes that endotoxins are not responsible for any histamine releasing activity of cotton dust.

Boiling an acidified cotton extract does not lower its anaphylatoxin activity whereas endotoxins lose their activity by this procedure. Furthermore, it is argued that the endotoxin hypothesis is not compatible with the fact that different parts of the cotton plant contain different amounts of histamine liberating factor, particularly as plant parts which are more contaminated by handling, i.e. cotton hairs, have no histamine liberating activity.

In favor of the endotoxin theory is the demonstration that endotoxins are active if administered by aerosol (62,64), as is the agent of byssinosis. In a rabbit model, inhalation of either endotoxin or cotton dust extract produces histological patterns consistent with chronic bronchitis (65). Also, in a variety of animal species, fever and dyspnea occur after short periods of inhalation of endotoxins, but when endotoxin solutions are inhaled on two consecutive days, the second inhalation is without effect. This suggests tolerance to endotoxins, and parallels the Monday syndrome, characteristic of byssinosis (62).

Prevalence of byssinosis correlates better with airborne endotoxin concentration than with total dust (65). Also, gram-negative bacteria levels in the mill correlate well with disease (66). It has been hypothesized that endotoxins elicit symptoms of byssinosis by activation of both the classical and the alternative pathway of complement with subsequent release of anaphylatoxins, which lead to airway narrowing, and chemotaxins, which cause the influx of PMNs followed by release of lysosomal enzymes and, ultimately, tissue damage. In experiments with guinea pigs using bract, cotton, and gin mill trash extracts, there is a strong correlation between number of PMNs recruited to airways and level of endotoxin (67).

There are other ways in which endotoxins may act to produce cotton dust induced airway disease. These include: 1) an instrinsic toxicity due to lipid A, responsible for both pyrogenicity and tissue damage; 2) a hypersensitivity reaction involving anti-lipid A antibodies. Further, changes in mechanical properties of the lung could be explained by the release of histamine or serotonin caused by endotoxins.

A major argument against an endotoxin-like mechanism in byssinosis is the lack of fever (63). It is hypothesized, however, that exposure to endotoxin in cotton dust causes mill fever in new employees. With continued exposure, the worker becomes tolerant to this pyrexial action of the endotoxin, but other effects of the LPS predominate, including complement activation and release of leucotaxic substances, both of which may ultimately lead to tissue damage.

Immunologic

Another possible mechanism for byssinosis is the involvement of a specific hypersensitivity response. There are two major arguments for an allergic mechanism in byssinosis: 1) there is a lag time between first exposure to cotton dust and onset of symptoms, suggesting a sensitization period; and 2) not all individuals exposed to cotton dust develop byssinosis, suggesting possible genetic differences in host response or immunoglobulin class specific antibody forming potential. Studies concerning an immunologic pathogenesis of byssinosis have, however, yielded equivocal results.

Immunoglobulin (Ig) levels have been measured in the serum of cotton dust exposed asymptomatic and byssinotic workers in the textile industry and in non-dust exposed controls (68,69). Dust exposed workers have elevated mean total IgG levels compared with normals (68,69), and a statistically significant relationship between length of dust exposure and total IgG levels is reported (68). This increase in IgG levels is highly significant in workers exposed for periods of less than five years, but gradually loses significance until, after exposure periods of greater than 20 years, dust exposed individuals do not differ from controls. Even if significant, such increases in total IgG would be non-specific and afford little useful information regarding disease pathogenesis.

Workers exposed to lipopolysaccharides from office humidifiers and sewage plants (70,71) also exhibit elevated IgG levels and, in sewage workers, this response is dose dependent. Since endotoxin contamination of cotton is well documented (14), it suggests that the increased IgG levels seen in cotton workers may be due to endotoxin exposure. The possibility that this increase is due to specific IgG is slight in view of the fact that in other diseases, high specific IgG levels do not necessarily correlate with high total IgG values (72). No differences in IgA have been reported, but there is one report of statistical differences in IgM levels in Grade 2 byssinotics. Significantly higher IgD levels have been shown in Grade 1 byssinotics (68) although lower IgD levels have also been reported in byssinotics, compared with normals (69). Interestingly, elevated IgD levels have been reported in atopic individuals (73) and related allergic pulmonary diseases such as allergic bronchopulmonary aspergillosis (74). This is particularly interesting in light of recent studies of workers exposed to cotton linters, linking atopy with Monday decline in lung function (75).

Early studies of allergy in relation to cotton dust induced respiratory disease were reviewed by Prausnitz (18) who concluded, from results of skin testing, that a distinct "super-sensitiveness" to cotton dust protein was regularly present in cotton operatives suffering from respiratory disease. Some investigators feel that there is a common antigen in house dust and cotton linter extracts (76-78) and some toxic factors have been demonstrated in both house dust and linter extracts which may lead to false positive skin test results (76). Early skin test results with extracts of cotton dust, prepared by several methods, failed to demonstrate a difference between byssinotic and asymptomatic dust exposed workers (77). Delayed skin reactions occur in normals, byssinotics, and unaffected cotton mill workers, suggesting a direct toxic effect, rather than a Type IV, cell mediated hypersensitivity reaction. Workers from cotton mills demonstrated a higher incidence of positive skin tests to hemp, flax, and jute extracts than normals, suggesting the possibility of a common antigen among these fibers (52,53,79). Skin testing with fungal extracts, including fungal contaminants of cotton, e.g. *Mucor sp.*, *Aspergillus sp.*, or *Alternaria sp.*, also failed to correlate with disease activity (52,80).

A recent epidemiologic study of oil mill employees correlates Monday post shift decline in FEV_1 with immediate Type I skin test reactions to linter and/or cotton seed extracts in cotton linter exposed workers. Of the common inhalant allergens tested, only *Fusarium sp.* shows this trend. Atopic, linter exposed individuals have a significantly greater drop in FEV_1 over the working shift than non-atopics. Four allergens show this association: *Fusarium sp.*, *Alternaria sp.*, Johnson and Bermuda grass (75); the first three have been identified as cotton dust contaminants (81). Recently, in the same mill workers, specific IgE antibodies for cotton linters and seeds have also been demonstrated *in vitro* (82).

Provocative inhalation challenge has been used in an attempt to identify byssinogenic agents (52-54, 83-86). Results of these studies have been inconclusive, but most positive reactions appear to be due to endotoxin contamination of the dust, or to a toxic or irritant factor (52,53).

Other investigators have looked for the presence of precipitating or agglutinating antibodies against cotton antigens (13,47,48,83,87). Precipitating antibodies against cotton flower receptacles are demonstrable in sera of both card room workers and normal controls (13). The antigen responsible for the antibody response is the condensed tannin, 5,7,3',4'-tetrahydroxyflavan 3,4, diol (THF). However, this was later found to be a non-immunologic reaction when THF was shown to non-specifically react with the Fc fragment of IgG, which cannot bind antigen (88). Further studies show that stem and cotton card room dust extracts can also precipitate sera in a pseudo-immune fashion (47,89). This non-specific reaction is due to a polyphenolic tannin present in the cotton plant. Specific cotton dust antibodies have recently been demonstrated in hyperimmunized rabbits using double gel diffusion (87). Using crossed-immunoelectrophoretic techniques, at least forty separate antigenic components are identifiable in cotton dust extracts (90). Conflicting reports of the antigenicity of cotton extracts probably reflect differences in antigenic material present in extracts, the wide range of extraction techniques used and the degree of antigenic contamination of the different cottons (14,81,91,92). Dried plant materials contain a large number of organic and inorganic compounds, including amines, porphyrins, and pigments (93). It is erroneous to relate antigenic or disease potential to one isolated compound. Several elements may act synergistically or one compound may act as an adjuvant for others.

The fact that an isolated compound, in high concentration, provokes an immune response in experimental animals does not necessarily prove that it is present in high enough concentration in the working environment to induce an immune response in man. Further, production of antibodies in laboratory animals by parenteral injection of extracts may not be analogous to the occupational setting where workers are "sensitized" by inhalation. Attempts to sensitize animals using inhaled antigens have met with only limited success (94,95). Doses of material used to sensitize animals are also important. It has been shown, in mice, that low levels of antigen favor both primary and secondary IgE responses, whereas higher doses stimulate IgG production, but inhibit IgE formation (96,97).

Non-Specific Mediator Release

Another proposed mechanism of byssinosis is pharmacologic mediator release, especially histamine and 5-hydroxytryptamine (5-HT). Studies of histamine release following cotton dust exposure are complicated by the fact that cotton itself contains histamine (98), the majority of which is found in the dust particle fraction below 20 μ size (99).

In Vivo Human Studies. Increased histamine levels have been reported in the blood of both cotton and flax dust exposed workers. Histamine levels in all dust exposed workers are significantly greater than controls. In exposed workers, histamine levels further increase on re-exposure to dust on the first day of the working week, after a weekend off. On the second working day, blood histamine levels are reduced in asymptomatic workers, while values in byssinotics remain high. Histamine levels in workers with continuous dust exposure are lower than those with interrupted exposure suggesting that, in byssinotics, histamine formation is potentiated by a component(s) in the dust, and/or that the rate of histamine catabolism is lower in byssinotics than in non-byssinotics (68).

It has been demonstrated that healthy volunteers have significantly higher levels of the histamine metabolite 1-methylimidazole-4-acetic acid (MeIAA) in 24 hour urine samples, when challenged with unwashed cotton, than with washed cotton. There also are reports of histamine metabolites occurring in the blood of exposed workers (100-102).

Due to technical difficulties in detecting *in vivo* histamine release in humans, *in vivo* animal experiments or *in vitro* assays are often used.

In Vivo Animal Experiments. In guinea pig lung tissue, a statistically significant accumulation of histamine occurs over the weekend away from flax dust. Decreases in the histamine content of lung, liver, and ear of guinea pigs are detected after exposure of flax dust (103) but total histamine catabolizing activity is not significantly altered after exposure. In controls, methylating enzymes appear to be the major catabolizing agents, while in exposed animals, activity is due to diamine oxidase. Methylating enzyme activity reappears in these animals after one day of rest. In humans, however, histamine catabolism appears to be mediated by methylating enzymes (101).

Animals exposed *in vivo* to cotton dust show similar results. In excised tissues, histamine methylating enzymes fall to zero during exposure, but rise following a rest from cotton dust inhalation. In flax dust exposed animals, histamine activity initially increases. In guinea pigs, enzyme levels fall upon exposure, then rise after removal from exposure. Further, while flax exposed animals show a fall in total lung histamine content, with cotton dust exposure there is an increase. It should, however, be borne in mind that histamine release is not necessarily correlated with total lung histamine (103).

In Vitro Mediator Release. Although no pulmonary effects have been demonstrable in guinea pigs following inhalation of bract extract (104), contraction of isolated guinea pig ileum by extracts (105,106) has been reported. Aqueous extracts of cotton, jute, flax, and hemp cause contractions of isolated guinea pig ileum or tracheal muscle preparations which are similar in time of onset and duration to those produced by histamine. Contraction heights of muscle preparations by different extracts correlate with the prevalence of byssinotic symptoms in workers processing cotton, flax, sisal and jute. The antihistamine mepyramine maleate has little effect on contraction, suggesting that the response is not due to histamine release.

Delayed constrictor responses in guinea pig smooth muscle preparations following challenge with jute extract have been observed. The response diminishes with successive doses of extract as though some "store" is being depleted, until, finally, constriction is not seen. Cotton extract is a more potent contracting agent than jute.

Both histamine and 5-HT have been demonstrated in extracts: 5-HT is responsible for some of the bronchoconstrictor activity of cotton dust extracts. Brom-lysergic acid, a specific 5-HT inhibitor, partially reduces activity, suggesting the presence of an "unknown contractor." This does not appear to be acetylcholine or bradykinin. Thus, although histamine, 5-HT, and the "unknown contractor" can cause immediate contractor responses, delayed onset contractions may still be due to secondary release of histamine (105).

Cotton dust or plant extracts cause non-specific release of histamine from chopped human lung (107-111). Of the extracts tested, pericarps show no action while bract has the strongest activity. It should be noted, however, that although the lungs appear macroscopically normal, the tissue is obtained from patients with either pneumothorax, tuberculosis, or bronchogenic carcinoma removed at autopsy or surgically up to 16 hours prior to the experiment. An animal model of histamine release using chopped lung tissue may overcome the difficulty in working with human lung tissue. Studies of histamine release from various animal lungs have yielded conflicting results (16,109,112-114). Cotton dust extracts release histamine from human and pig lung. Cow and sheep lung also give good release. No *in vitro* histamine release has been demonstrable from isolated mouse, rat, guinea pig, or cat lungs and only low levels are released from monkey and rabbit lung. There are also marked intraspecies variations in sheep, cow, and horse specimens.

In pig lung tissue, the magnitude of response is, in part, associated with the low degree of catabolism of exogenous histamine shown by this species. Further, the main pathways for catabolism of histamine are similar for man and pig, but are different in ruminants. Additionally, pig lung and human lung have similar histology, indicating that the pig may provide a good model to study cotton induced histamine release *in vitro*.

Histamine release from pig lung occurs in response to extracts from cotton pericarp, seed, leaf, root and bract (112). Extracts of sisal release histamine from both pig and human lung, but the reactivity is less than cotton dust extracts. The use of chopped lung for histamine assay is not always reliable, however, nor is it sufficiently sensitive.

Pig platelets have recently been shown to release histamine when exposed to cotton dust or plant extracts (115) and this assay compares closely with chopped lung assays. Mill dust and gin trash extracts give some release and extracts of leaves from other plant sources, including pecan and grape, give similar reactions. Byssinosan (116), an aminopolysaccharide isolated from cotton dust, and THF antigen (83) are relatively inactive. The tannins, quercetin and catechin, show low activity (117). While histamine releasing activity is mainly associated with high molecular weight fractions, they are not necessarily the same ones responsible for antigenic or chemotactic activity, indicating the possibility that several mechanisms may be responsible for byssinosis.

It is not known if platelets are actually involved in byssinosis; however, a reduction of platelets has been shown in cotton mill workers on the first day of the work week (118). One problem with animal models, however, is that while, in humans, virtually all the total blood histamine is contained within the basophils (119), in some common laboratory animals, such as the rabbit, much of the histamine may come from other sources, such as platelets (120).

Adrenergic Responses. Cotton dust extracts liberate histamine from rat peritoneal mast cells. This reaction cannot be blocked by antihistamines; however, epinephrine ($1 \times 10^{-9}M$) and norepinephrine ($1 \times 10^{-8}M$) are effective blockers, suggesting a role of the adrenergic system (121). Further evidence for a role of the adrenergic system in byssinosis comes from experiments using blocking drugs. Hitchcock (107) has demonstrated histamine release by methylpiperonylate, isolated from bract. Propranolol, a β-blocking agent, stimulates this histamine release but both isoproterenol, a β-adrenergic agonist, and theophylline, a phosphodiesterase inhibitor, inhibit release.

Cotton dust extracts have been shown to affect cyclic nucleotide levels (122). Guinea pig lungs, in response to AECD, show a decrease in cAMP levels with a concomitant increase in cGMP. Further, there is a high correlation ($r = 0.95$) between lung histamine levels and cAMP/cGMP ratios. Other workers (123) have shown stimulation of cAMP in human peripheral blood lymphocytes in response to AECD.

Prostaglandins. AECD also influences prostaglandin (PG) levels, notably $PGF_{2\alpha}$ (121). Mean values of $PGF_{2\alpha}$ and its major metabolite, 15-keto-13,14-dihydro-$PGF_{2\alpha}$, in guinea pig lung, increase with increasing doses of AECD (124). Cotton bract and leaf extract elicit production of both $PGF_{2\alpha}$ and PGE by rabbit alveolar macrophages *in vitro*. Production of $PGF_{2\alpha}$ is fifteen times that of the control culture (125). $PGF_{2\alpha}$ can produce moderate pulmonary vascular resistance, decreased pulmonary tidal volume, increased airway resistance, and contraction of bronchial smooth muscle. Many of these symptoms are seen in byssinosis (124).

Summary

In summary, it can be seen that there are multiple in vivo and in vitro effects of cotton dusts in man and experimental animals which may result in mediator release, complement activation, antibody formation, endotoxin effects and related phenomena. Whether any of these, singly or in combination, are operative in disease pathogenesis in man remains a matter of speculation at present. Development of a workable animal model of byssinosis and provocative inhalation challenge studies in persons having byssinosis, with careful monitoring of physiological effects and mediator release would help answer some of these questions. Several other possible mechanisms may prove to be operative but, as yet, they remain to be evaluated. Among these are in-depth studies of possible subcellular effects of cotton dust extracts on leukotrienes and thromboxanes and the release of cell activating factors. Such studies will, however, not likely be meaningful without prior or concomitant development of well characterized and/or purified biological materials from cotton dusts.

Acknowledgment

This work was supported by NHLBI grant HL-15092, NIAID grant AI-13401, USDA-SEA cooperative agreement 5B-7B30-9-128 and cooperative agreement 81-847 of Cotton Incorporated.

Literature Cited

1. Ayer, H. E. "CRC Critical Reviews" Environ. Control 1971, 2, 207-41.
2. Bouhuys, A; Schoenberg, J. B.; Beck, G. J.; Schilling, R. S. F. Lung 1977, 154, 167-86.
3. Bouhuys, A.; Hartogensis, F.; Korfage, H. J. H. Brit.J. Industr. Med. 1963, 20, 320-3.
4. Barbero, A.; Flores, R. Arch. Environ. Hlth. 1967, 14, 529-32.
5. Gilson, J. C.; Stott, H.; Hopwood, B. E. C.; Roach, S. A.; McKerrow, C. B.; Schilling, R. S. F. Brit. J. Industr. Med. 1962, 18, 9-18.
6. Uragoda, C. G. Brit. J. Industr. Med. 1977, 34, 181-5.
7. Cinkotai, F. F. Amer. Industr. Hyg. Assoc. J. 1976, 37, 234-8.
8. Zuskin, E.; Valic, F.; Bouhuys, A. Amer. Rev. Resp. Dis. 1976, 114, 705-9.
9. Mann, L. American Textiles R/B edition 1978, 19-23.
10. Braun, D. C.; Scheel, L. D.; Tuma, J.; Parker, L. J. Occup. Med. 1973, 15, 241-4.

11. de Treville, R. T. P. Industrial Health Foundation 1971, 1-14.
12. Wilson, M. R.; Sekul, A.; Ory, R.; Salvaggio, J. E.; Lehrer, S. B. Clin. Allergy 1980, 10, 303-8.
13. Massoud, A.; Taylor, G. Lancet 1964, 2, 607-10.
14. Rylander, R.; Lundholm, M. Brit. J. Industr. Med. 1978, 35, 204-7.
15. Rylander, R.; Nordstrand, A. Brit. J. Industr. Med. 1974, 31, 220-3.
16. Evans, E.; Nicholls, P. J. Agents and Actions 1974, 4, 304-10.
17. Hitchcock, M.; Piscitelli, D.M.; Bouhuys, A. Arch. Environ. Hlth. 1973, 26, 177-82.
18. Prausnitz, C. London. Spec. Report Series, 1936, 212, 1-73.
19. Chinn, D. J.; Cinkotai, F. F.; Lockwood, M. G.; Logan, S. H. M. Ann. Occup. Hyg. 1976, 19, 101-8.
20. Tuma, J.; Parker, L.; Braun, D.C. J. Occup. Med. 1973. 15, 409-19.
21. Jurgiel, J. A; Ryckman; Edgerly; Tomlison; associates "ATMI/IHF study of U. S. cotton textile workers," Amer. Conf. Govern. Industr. Hygienists, 1975, p 131-48.
22. Cashner, F.; Schuyler, M.; Fletcher, R.; Ritz, H.; Salvaggio, J. Toxicol. Appl. Pharmacol. 1980, 52, 62-8.
23. Flindt, M. L. H. Lancet 1969, 1, 1177-81.
24. Pepys, J.; Wells, I. D.; D'Souza, M. F.; Greenberg, M. Clin. Allergy 1973, 3, 143-60.
25. Tolos, W. P.; Richards, D.E.; Scheel, L. D. Amer. Industr. Hyg. Assoc. J. 1975, 36, 272-7.
26. Marco, V.; Mass, B.; Merzane, D. R.; Weinbaum, G.; Kimble, P. Amer. Rev. Resp. Dis. 1971, 104, 595-8.
27. Janoff, A.; Zeligs, J. D. Sci. 1968, 161, 702-4.
28. Lazarus, G. S.; Daniels, J. R.; Brown, R. S.; Bladen, H. A.; Fullmer, H. M. J. Clin. Invest. 1968, 47, 2622-9.
29. Ziff, M.; Gribetz, H. J.; Lospalluto, J. J. Clin. Invest. 1960, 39, 405-12.
30. Eriksson, S. Acta. Scand. (Suppl. 432) 1965, 177, 1-85.
31. Keuppers, F.; Bearn, A. G. Proc. Soc. Exp. Biol. Med. 1966, 121, 1207-11.
32. Harley, R. A. "Patho-physiological studies in byssinosis," Amer. Conf. Govern. Industr. Hygienists, 1975, p 136.
33. Stokinger, H.E.; Scheel, L.D. J. Occup. Med. 1963, 15. 564-573.
34. Galdston, M; Janoff, A.; Davis, A. L. Amer. Rev. Resp. Dis., 1973, 107, 718-27.
35. Noweir, M. H.; Amine, E. K.; Osman, H. A. Brit. J. Ind. Med. 1975, 32, 297.
36. Rylander, R. Scand. J. Resp. Dis. 1971, 52, 121-8.
37. Allen, R. C.; Loose, L. D. Biochem. Biophy. Res. Comm. 1976, 69, 245-52.

38. Ziprin, R. L. Infect. and Immun. 1978, 19, 889-92.
39. Greenblatt, G. A.; Ziprin, R. L. Amer. Industr. Hyg. Assoc. J. 1979, 40, 860-5.
40. Kilburn, K. H.; Lynn, W. S.; Tres, L. L.; McKenzie, W. N. Lab. Invest. 1973, 28, 55-9.
41. Merchant, J. A.; Halprin, G. M.; Hudson, A. R.; Kilburn, K. H.; McKenzie, W. N., Jr.; Hurst, D. J.; Bermazohn, P. Arch. Environ. Hlth. 1975, 30, 222-9.
42. Lynn, W. S.; Monoz, S.; Campbell, J. A.; Jeffs, P. W. Ann. NY Acad. Sci. 1974, 221, 163-73.
43. Hudson, A. R.; Kilburn, K. H.; Halprin, G. M.; McKenzie, W. N. Amer. Rev. Resp. Dis. 1977, 115, 89-95.
44. Rylander, R.; Snella, M.-C. Amer. Conf. Govern. Industr. Hygiensts 1975, p.101-9.
45. Rylander, R.; Snella, M.-C.; Garcia, I. Scand. J. Resp. Dis. 1975, 56, 195-200.
46. Rylander, R.; Nordstrand, A.; Snella, M.-C. Arch. Environ. Hlth. 1975, 30, 137-40.
47. Kutz, S. A. Ph.D. Thesis, Univ. W. VA, Morgantown, W. VA., 1978.
48. Kutz, S. A.; Olenchock, S. A.; Elliot, J. A.; Pearson, D. J.; Major, P. C. Environ. Res. 1979, 19, 405-14.
49. Morrison, D. C.; Kline, L. F. J. Immunol. 1977, 118, 362-8.
50. Marx, J. J.; Flaherty, D. K. J. Allergy Clin. Immunol. 1976, 57, 328-34.
51. Wilson, M. R.; Salvaggio, J. E. J. Allergy Clin. Immunol. 1980, 65, 319-21.
52. Gavrilescu, N.; Popa, V.; Preda, N.; Teculescu, D.; Avrarm, A.; Nicolau, G. Allergie und Asthma 1969, 15, 26-31.
53. Popa, V.; Gavrilescu, N.; Preda, N.; Teculescu D.; Plecias, M.; Cirstae, M. Brit. J. Industr. Med. 1969, 26, 101-8.
54. Hamilton, J. D.; Halprin, G. M.; Kilburn, K.H.; Merchant, J. A.; Vjda, J. R., Arch. Environ. Hlth. 1973, 26, 120-4.
55. Navratil, M.; Roth, Z. Institut d'hygiene des Mines Revue 1973, 141-6.
56. Furness, G.; Maitland, H.B. Brit. J. Industr. Med. 1952, 9, 138-45.
57. Drummond, D. G.; Hamlin, M. Brit. J. Industr. Med. 1952, 9, 309-11.
58. Prindle, B. Text. Res. 1934, 5, 11-31.
59. Prindle, B. Text. Res. 1934, 4, 555-69.
60. Lockwood, M. G.; Attwell, R. W. Lancet 1977, 2, 45-6.
61. Salvaggio, J. E. Clin. Allergy 1979, 9, 659-68.
62. Pernis, B.; Vigliani, E. C.; Cavagna, C.; Finulli, M. Brit. J. Industr. Med. 1961, 18, 120-9.
63. Antweiler, H. Brit. J. Industr. Med. 1961, 18, 130-2.
64. Snell, J. D., Jr. J. Lab. Clin. Med. 1966, 67, 624-32.
65. Cavagna, G.; Foa, V.; Vigliani, E. C. Brit. J. Industr. Med. 1969, 26, 314-321.

66. Cinkotai, F. F.; Lockwood, M. G.; Rylander, R. Amer. Industr. Hyg. Assoc. J. 1977, 38, 554-9.
67. Rylander, R.; Snella, M.-C. Brit. J. Industr. Med. 1976, 33, 1975-80.
68. Noweir, M.H. Amer. Industr. Hyg. Assoc. J. 1979, 40, 839-59.
69. Kamat, S. R.; Taskar, S. P.; Iyer, E. R.; Naik, M.; Kamat, G. R. J. Soc. Occup. Med. 1979, 29, 102-6.
70. Rylander, R.; Haglind, P.; Lundholm, M.; Mattsby, I.; Stenqvist, K. Clin. Allergy 1978, 8, 511-6.
71. Rylander, R.; Andersson, K.; Belin, L.; Berglund, G.; Bergstrom, R.; Hanson, L.; Lundholm, M.; Mattsby, I. Schweiz. Med. Wschr. 1977, 107, 182-4.
72. Patterson, R.; Schatz, M; Fink, J; DeSwarte, R.; Roberts, M.; Cugell, D. Amer. J. Med. 1976, 60, 144-51.
73. Butcher, B. T.; Salvaggio, J. E.; Leslie, G. A. Clin. Allergy 1975, 1, 33-42.
74. Leslie, G.A.; Martin, L.N. "Cont. Topics in Mol. Immunology" Plenum, New York, 1978, pp. 1-49.
75. Jones, R.N.; Butcher, B.T.; Hammad, Y.Y.; Diem, J.E.; Glindmeyer, H.W.; Lehrer, S. B., Hughes, J. M.; Weill, H. Brit. J. Industr. Med. 1980, 37, 141-6.
76. Cayton, H. R.; Furness, G.; Jackson, D. S.; Maitland, H. B. Brit. J. Industr. Med. 1952, 9, 303-8.
77. Coulson, E. J.; Stevens, H. J. Allergy 1940, 11, 537-56.
78. Cayton, H. R.; Furness, G.; Maitland, H.B. Brit. J. Industr. Med. 1952, 9, 186-96.
79. Fetisova, A. A.; Titova, S. M.; Aleksandrova, O.G. Gigiyena Truda i Professionalnye Zabolevaniya 1970, 14, 19-22.
80. Voison, C.; Jacob, M.; Furon, D.; Lefebvre, J. Poumon 1966, 22, 529-38.
81. Morey, P. R.; Bethae, R. M.; Wakelyn, P. J.; Kirk, I. W.; Kopetzky, M. T. Amer. Industr. Hyg. Assoc. J. 1976, 37, 321-8.
82. Butcher, B. T.; Lehrer, S. B.; O'Neil, C. E.; Hughes, J. M.; Salvaggio, J. E.; Weill, H. J. Allergy Clin. Immunol. 1979, 63, 213.
83. Taylor, G.; Massoud, A. A. E.; Lucas, F. Brit. J. Industr. Med. 1971, 28, 143-51.
84. Oehling, A.; Gonzalez de la Reguera, I.; Vines Rueda, J. J. Respiration 1972, 29, 155-60.
85. Neal, P.A.; Schneiter, R.; Caminita, B.H. JAMA 1942, 119, 1074-82.
86. Buck, M. G.; Bouhuys, A. Lung 1980, 158, 25-32.
87. Sekul, A. A.; Ory, R. L. Text Res. 1979, 49, 523-5.
88. Edwards, J. H.; Jones, B.M. Ann. NY Acad. Sci. 1974, 221, 59-63.
89. Kutz, S. A.; Mentnech, M. S.; Olenchock, S. A.; Major, P. C. Environ. Res. 1980, 22, 476-84.
90. O'Neil, C. E.; Butcher, B. T.; Hughes, J. M. Proc. 1981 Beltwide Cotton Prod. Res. Conf. 1981, p. 3-6.

91. Tuffnell, P. Brit. J. Industr. Med. 1960, 17, 304-6.
92. Morey, P. R.; Sasser, P. E.; Bethea, R.M.; Kopetzky, M. T. Amer. Industr. Hyg. Assoc. J. 1976, 37, 407-12.
93. Cooke, T.F. Text. Res. J. 1979, 49, 398-404.
94. Weicher, K.; Nay, R.; Reisman, R.; Arbesman, C. E. Fed. Proc. Fed. Amer. Soc. Exp. Biol. 1968, 27, 367.
95. Patterson, R.; Kelly, J.F. Int. Arch. Allergy Appl. Immunol. 1973, 45, 98-109.
96. Levine, B. B.; Vaz, N. M. Int. Arch. Allergy Appl. Immunol. 1970, 39, 156-71.
97. Maia, L. C.; Vaz, N. M.; Vaz, E. M. Int. Arch Allergy Appl. Immunol. 1974, 46, 339-44.
98. Maitland, H. B.; Heap, H.; MacDonald, A. D. H.M.S.O. London Appendix VI, 1932.
99. Haworth, E.; MacDonald, A. D. J. Hyg. 1937, 37, 234-42.
100. Bouhuys, A.; Barbaro, A.; Lindell, S.-E.; Roach, S. A.; Schilling, R. S. F. Arch.Environ. Hlth. 1967, 14, 533-44.
101. Edwards, J.; McCarthy, P.; McDermott, M.; Nicholls, P.J.; Skidmore, J. W. J. Physiol. 1970, 208, 63-4.
102. McDermott, M.; Skidmore, J. W.; Edwards, J. Intern. Conf. Resp. Dis. Text. Workers, Alicante, Spain, 1968, 133-136.
103. Noweir, M.H.; Abdel-Kader, H. M.; Maker, A. B.; El-Gazzar, R. J. Egypt. Pub. Hlth. Assoc. 1976, LI, 148-62.
104. Antweiler, H. Ann. NY Acad. Sci. 1974, 221, 136-40.
105. Davenport, A.; Paton, W. D. M. Brit. J. Industr. Med. 1962, 19, 19-32.
106. Nicholls, P. J. Brit. J. Industr. Med. 1962, 19, 33-41.
107. Hitchcock, M. Ann. NY Acad. Sci. 1974, 221, 124-31.
108. Nicholls, P. J.; Nicholls, G. R.; Bouhuys, A. "Inhaled Particles and Vapors," Pergamon, New York, 1967, 69-74.
109. Evans, E.; Nicholls, P. J. J. Pharm. Pharmac. 1974, 26 Suppl., 115-6.
110. Douglas, J. S.; Zuckerman, A.; Ridgway, P.; Bouhuys, A. Intern. Conf. Resp. Dis. Text. Workers, Alicante, Spain, 1968, 148-55.
111. Bouhuys, A.; Lindell, S.-E. Experientia 1961, XVII, 211-4.
112. Evans, E.; Nicholls, P. J. J. Pharm. Pharmac. 1973, 25 Suppl., 141-2.
113. Evans, E.; Nicholls, P. J. Comp. Gen. Pharmacol. 1974, 5, 87-91.
114. Nicholls, P. J.; Evans, E.; Valic, F.; Zuskin, E. Brit. J. Industr. Med. 1973, 30, 142-5.
115. Ainsworth, S.K.; Neuman, R. E.; Harley, R. A. Brit. J. Industr. Med. 1979, 36, 35-42.
116. Mohammed, Y. S.; El-Gazzar, R. M.; Adamyova, K. Carb. Res. 1971, 20, 431-5.
117. Ainsworth, S.K.; Neuman, R. E. Proc. 1977 Beltwide Cotton Prod. Res. Conf. 1977, p. 76-8.
118. Bomski, H.; Otawski, J.; Bomsha, H. Internationales Archiv fur Arbeitsmedizin 1971, 27, 309-23.

119. Galli, S. J.; Dvorak, H. F. "Comprehensive Immunology," Vol. 6,Plenum, New York, 1979, 1-53.
120. Benveniste, J.; Henson, P. M.; Cochrane, C. G. "The Biological Role of the Immunoglobulin E System," U.S. D.H.E.W., 1973, 187-205.
121. Antweiler, H. Ann. Occup. Hyg. 1959, 1, 152-6.
122. Elissalde, M.H. Jr.; Greenblatt, G. A. Amer. Ind. Hyg. Assoc. J. 1979, 40, 1067-74.
123. Butcher, B. T.; O'Neil, C. E.; Reed, M. A. Proc. 1981 Cotton Prod. Res. Conf. 1981, p. 9-11.
124. Ellisalde, M. H. Jr.; Greenblatt, G. A.; Ziprin, R. L. Amer. Ind. Hyg. Assoc. J. 1980, 41, 382-4.
125. Fowler, S. R.; Ziprin, R. L.; Elissalde, M. H. Jr.; Greenblatt, G. A. Amer. Ind. Hyg. Assoc. J. 1981, 42, 445-8.

RECEIVED December 15, 1981.

11

Etiologic Agents and Pathogenic Mechanisms in the Acute Byssinotic Reaction

STERLING K. AINSWORTH and PATRICIA A. PILIA

Medical University of South Carolina, Department of Pathology (Immunopathology), Charleston, SC 29425

Inhalation of cotton dust has long been known to cause a pulmonary disease termed byssinosis. This chapter is a comprehensive review of etiologic agents and pathogenic mechanisms of the acute byssinotic reaction. The chemical properties of cotton mill dust are described, and the various active agents proposed in the literature to produce the acute byssinotic reaction reviewed, together with their pathogenic mechanisms. This includes studies of immunoglobulin levels in animals and man, complement activation by both immunologic and non-immunologic means and investigations of possible hypersensitivity to cotton dust. Also reviewed and discussed are the active agents found in extracts of cotton mill dust and cotton bract which might be responsible for histamine release, chemotaxis and bronchoconstriction.

The population of workers in the cotton industry at risk of contracting byssinosis includes workers in areas for carding, spinning and other dust producing operations. The cardinal acute symptoms of chest tightness, shortness of breath, coughing and wheezing were described as early as the mid 1800's by Mareska and Heymann (1). More recently the findings of a reduction in FEV_1 (2), peripheral leukocytosis, slight elevations in body temperature and leukocyte recruitment to air passages (3) have been added to the list of recognizable symptoms. These acute symptoms typically develop after exposure to the dust, and are seen particularly on Mondays following a weekend away from the work environment; in addition, they are reversible and gradually subside over a period of several days of continued exposure or upon leaving the work area. Acute symptoms differ primarily in degree and duration from chronic symptoms, which appear after several years of occupational exposure. The more severe chronic symptoms are irreversible and persist even in a dust-free atmosphere.

0097-6156/82/0189-0163$06.00/0

In general, workers with irreversible chronic byssinosis or chronic obstructive lung disease smoke and have been employed in the industry for 10 or more years. We can assume that repeated, acute reactions in the lungs have a cumulative damaging effect. At this time, however, information linking the acute reaction and chronic byssinosis is lacking, as is a thorough understanding of the lung pathology, causative agent(s) and pathogenesis.

Laboratory exposure to dust clouds and dust extract aerosols results in chest tightness, dyspnea and decreases in both expiratory flow and dynamic lung compliance (4). Bouhuys et al. showed that aerosols of cotton dust extract inhaled by man produced reversible small-airway obstruction within 10 minutes (5); the same effects were noted in cardroom workers exposed to dust on Mondays, i.e. decreased maximum expiratory flow rates and increased airway resistance (6). These changes are compatible with narrowing of small airways as the principal effect of acute dust exposure.

The large majority of people at risk are affected when toxic dust concentrations are high. Healthy people exposed for the first time to dust or dust extract respond as severely as long term workers (5). Experiments have also shown that following a single exposure to cotton dust or aerosol inhalation of an aqueous dust extract, exposure repeated 24 hours later has no effect (5,7). These findings indicate that the etiologic agent(s) is water soluble, and that prior immunologic sensitization is not necessary. Individual differences are notable; for instance, in dusty workrooms where reactive workers experience chest tightness, marked tachyphylaxis and acute lung changes, some workers show no symptoms. This suggests a genetic predisposition to either toxic, pharmacologic or immunologic adverse mechanisms.

Within 30 minutes of their administration, β-adrenergic drugs often reverse most of the functional deficit in Monday morning byssinotics. As there is no mucous secretion, airway smooth muscle contraction is considered the primary response. Exposure of man to histamine aerosols produces pulmonary function changes similar to those seen after exposure to dust extract. However, exposure to histamine aerosol invariably initiates constriction of smooth muscle more rapidly than exposure to cotton dust (<15 minutes), and dissipates within minutes, while the acute effects of inhalation of cotton dust and dust extracts lasts for hours. The slowly developing and prolonged effects of dust and extracts suggest that mediators other than histamine are involved.

Small airway constriction and recruitment of leukocytes on pulmonary surfaces are prominent, documented responses to the inhalation of cotton dust. Currently, one or both of these effects are generally ascribed to endotoxin (8-10), to antigen-antibody reactions (11), to lacinilene C-7 methyl ether (12, 13), to a low molecular weight (~1000 daltons), neutral, highly water soluble substance that is stable in boiling water and found in cotton bracts (14), to chemotaxins present in cotton mill dust extracts (15, 16) or to histamine releasing substances (17).

Work in this laboratory has been directed toward assessing the causative agent(s) and pathogenic mechanisms in the acute byssinotic reaction. Our investigations of toxic, immunologic and pharmacologic mechanisms have led to the development of several bioassay techniques germane to the eventual understanding of this disease process. These bioassays have been important in ascertaining 1) histamine releasing substances, 2) smooth muscle bronchoconstrictors, 3) chemotaxins, 4) endotoxin and 5) complement activators. In particular, we have concentrated our efforts on three observed responses of the human lung following the inhalation of cotton dust, namely lung smooth muscle constriction, leukocyte recruitment into airways (3) and the reputed histamine release (18). This chapter will review our findings and the pertinent findings of others regarding the etiology and pathogenesis of byssinosis, the use of extracts of cotton mill dust and cotton bract and the importance of bioassays for understanding the disease process.

Chemical Properties of Cotton Mill Dust

Studies in cotton textile mills have shown that the incidence of byssinosis can be correlated with the average concentration of fine cotton dust (2, 19, 20) and with the number of years of occupational exposure (19-21). The causative agent in byssinosis has been shown to be a water extractable, filterable, nonvolatile agent (40°C) that can be retained on dialysis (22). The active byssinogenic agent appears to be present chiefly in the cotton bract, the leaf-like structure surrounding the cotton boll (also a prominent component of cotton mill dust (20)), because 1) water soluble extracts cause an FEV_1 drop (18, 23), and 2) the byssinogenic agent can be partially deactivated by steam.

Wakelyn et al. (24) reviewed the complex chemical composition of cotton mill dust (CMD) found in various processing operations. Substantial chemical variation exists in CMD collected from different mills and different processing rooms, and even from different areas within the same processing room. Dust composition varies in the proportion of all plant parts, i.e., leaf, bract, capsule and lint, as well as of fiber, fungi, bacteria, inorganic materials and material from other contaminating vegetation. Attempts to link spores of bacteria or fungi to the pathogens of byssinosis have not been successful (25, 26), although these microbiological contaminants cannot be excluded as potential sources of water soluble substances capable of contributing to the acute byssinotic response.

Our studies have shown that cotton dust extracts contain deoxyribonucleic acid (DNA) and ribonucleic acid (RNA) (27). DNA is present in varying concentrations in cardroom cotton dust (28) and emanates from bacteria, fungi, protozoa and plant cells. DNA might be important in the pathogenesis of byssinosis, as minute amounts can cause complement conversion.

Immunological Studies

Immunoglobulin Studies in Man. Previous studies of the etiology of byssinosis have proposed an immunological pathogenic mechanism. Massoud and Taylor (11) reported higher titers of serum antibodies in byssinotic cotton mill workers than in non-byssinotic workers. They suggested that higher titers of antibody combine with a cotton dust antigen, and that symptoms are either produced directly by antigen-antibody complexes or indirectly by release of pharmacological substances.

Recent studies by Noweir (29) showed elevated IgG concentrations in flax workers, whether free of respiratory symptoms, byssinotic or emphysematous. IgM and IgD were also significantly higher in some groups of byssinotics. No changes were noted for IgE and IgA. Similar results were seen in cotton workers. No significant difference in concentrations were seen between sera samples drawn pre-shift or 2 hours post-dust exposure on Monday or Tuesday. IgG values proved to be highest in mill workers employed less than 10 years, and showed no relationship to the level of dust exposure. Furthermore, IgG levels decreased in workers exposed for greater than 10 years; with exposure greater than 20 years, IgG levels returned to normal. Noweir suggests that precipitating antibodies in grade II byssinotics deteriorate due to the advanced stage of the disease, but this is unconvincing as an explanation because antibodies have a short half life (days), are constantly replenished by plasma cells and show essentially no altered structure in otherwise healthy individuals.

Our studies of serum levels of IgG, IgM, IgA, IgE and complement (30) drawn from byssinotic and nonbyssinotic mill workers at different times during the work week (Monday a.m. preshift, 4 hours post-exposure, and Friday p.m.) did not deviate from normal ranges (see Table 1). This is in agreement with results obtained by Edwards and Jones (31), which do not suggest an immunological mechanism (Type I or III) for the pathogenesis of byssinosis. Our results also agree with Noweir's findings of no differences in the immunoglobulin concentrations between samples obtained on the first pre-shift after the weekend, two hours post exposure or on the second day of the work week within each worker group (control, exposedsymptom free, byssinotic grades I and II, and emphysematous). In addition, Noweir's results showed no correlation between immunoglobulins and dust exposure.

Noweir suggested that high levels of IgG indicate the presence of precipitating antibodies in the sera of workers exposed to cotton dust (29). However, these suggestions and the inference that a Type III reaction is responsible are highly unlikely, because both our data and Noweir's show no weekly change. Moreover, our results demonstrate no significant serum complement change. This is important for, if a Type III antigen-antibody reaction were the pathogenic mechanism, one would expect the following: a) antigens or haptens would elicit high titers of

TABLE I
Mean Immunoglobulin Concentrations in Sera of Byssinotic and Non-Byssinotic Cotton Mill Workers At Different Time Intervals

Subjects	Age(yrs)	Number	MAM[a]	MPM	FPM
			IgG (mg/dl)[b]		
Normal White Males	20-29	4	1223	1119	1020
	30-39	4	1223	1295	1072
	40-49	3	890	817	647
Byssinotic White Males	40-49	3	1242	1130	1323
	50	11	1137	1133	1057
			IgA (mg/dl)[b]		
Normal White Males	20-29	4	276	229	228
	30-39	4	270	229	218
	40-49	3	265	218	186
Byssinotic White Males	40-49	3	307	227	292
	50	11	289	288	272
			IgM (mg/dl)[b]		
Normal White Males	20-29	4	167	155	147
	30-39	4	64	65	66
	40-49	3	139	143	134
Byssinotic White Males	40-49	3	65	66	68
	50	11	98	91	75

[a] MAM, Monday A.M., MPM, Monday P.M., FPM, Friday P.M.

[b] Immunoglobulin levels in all categories fall within normal ranges (IgG, 616-1543; IgA, 71-417; IgM, 57-343). There are no statistical differences (< 0.05) between byssinotic and non-byssinotic subjects or between times samples were taken.

specific antibodies; b) following specific antibody production, a precipitous drop in serum complement should occur; c) sera from controls and non-byssinotics should not react; and, d) clinical radiologic and histologic findings should correlate. None of these conditions are met, however, and it is therefore highly unlikely that immune complexes (antigen-antibody-complement) mitigate the byssinotic reaction.

In Vitro and Animal Immunoglobulin Studies. When injected intramuscularly, extracts of cotton are immunogenic in rabbits, and show both true and pseudoimmune precipitating reactions (32, 33). However, in rabbits exposed to cotton dust by inhalation, as in man, no precipitating antibodies are detected (34).

Taylor et al. (35) isolated a condensed polyphenol which they considered to be a cotton antigen. Precipitin and passive agglutination tests were used to show significant differences in mean (serum) titers (not specific immunoglobulins) between cardroom workers and controls and between byssinotic and non-byssinotic cardroom workers. However, this study did not assess the contribution of each antibody class, and no attempt was made to explain why high antibody titers were seen in normal (control) subjects never exposed to cotton. The authors did note the possibility that all individual sera would react with the condensed tannin "antigen."

Edwards and Jones (31) identified the condensed tannin extracted from cotton plant bracts as a tannin-like polymer of 5, 7, 3', 4' tetrahydroxyflaven 3-4 diol (THF). They demonstrated nonspecific precipitation with IgG, IgM, IgA, five myeloma IgG's and positive gel diffusion reactions with heavy and light chains, Fab and Fc pieces of IgG. Nevertheless, they refuted this reaction as a true antigen-antibody reaction, and subsequently suggested that byssinosis was not an immune complex mediated pulmonary disease.

Sera of cotton mill workers have been found to yield positive immune precipitation reactions with antigens of cotton dust, plant debris and microbial contamination in dust, in particular cotton dust, carpel and stem antigens (29). The highest positive precipitation occurred with grade II byssinotics, while a diminished response occurred with grade III byssinotic sera, suggesting that antibodies might deteriorate during the course of disease. Precipitating antibodies to cotton antigens were also found in non-byssinotics, with the carpel extract exhibiting the greatest reaction with all sera tested. It was suggested that bract and leaf play no role in antibody induction, and postulated that "antigens" present in carpel may be the causative agent(s) in producing the byssinotic response.

In 1971, Edwards and Jones showed that non-specific non-immunological reactions occurred between plant extracts and normal human sera (31). Noweir (29) repeated studies in byssinotics similar to ones performed by Massoud and Taylor (11) and Taylor et al. (35), and demonstrated similar findings, i.e. normal, byssinotic and non-byssinotic sera precipitated with substances from cotton dust, carpel and stem antigens. Again, however, no attempts were made to assign the precipitating sera to specific immunoglobulins, or to determine complement levels and specificity of the reactions as recorded by Edwards and Jones (31) and Kutz et al. (33). Moreover, neither Kutz et al. (33) nor Ainsworth et al. (30) could demonstrate true precipitating antibodies against cotton plant and dust antigens in cotton workers and byssinotics. Kutz further examined extracts of stems and cardroom cotton dust to precipitate certain serum proteins in cotton mill workers. All control worker and rabbit sera tested precipitated against the cotton "antigens" and tea leaf "antigen." Plant polyphenolic tannins were demonstrated to be the lipoprotein and gamma-globulin precipitating substances (33).

Thus our studies and others show that findings are not consistent with an immunological pathogenesis of byssinosis. Some findings remain suspicious, however, and need further study, especially in the area of atopy.

Hypersensitivity to Cotton Dust. An allergic pathogenesis for byssinosis was proposed by Bouhuys et al. (6). While the acute byssinotic reaction has few similarities to asthma, a short period of exposure followed by constriction of lung smooth muscle, drop in FEV_1, chest tightness and symptoms that are partially abolished by antihistamines are experienced by both asthmatics and byssinotics. However, mill workers who have a proven allergy to cotton dust by history and symptoms demonstrate an acute reaction within minutes of exposure, while byssinotic cotton mill workers usually require four to six hours to demonstrate a much milder reaction. This difference might be explained by the type of mediator released, i.e. slower reacting mediators in the case of byssinosis. If an allergic (atopic) mechanism were involved in the acute byssinotic reaction, serum IgE values would be elevated. Our results with sera from byssinotics and control subjects (nonbyssinotic cotton mill workers) showed no statistical difference between mean values of serum IgE levels for the two groups and three different time intervals (Monday a.m.-pre-shift, 4 hours post exposure and Friday p.m.) during the work week (Table II). Similar studies by Noweir also failed to demonstrate a significant difference in IgE concentration (29).

Further assessment of atopy in the pathogenesis of the acute byssinotic reaction necessitates purification of well characterized and standardized cotton dust antigens, and the development of an allergy specific test (RAST) to measure serum IgE antibodies to cotton dust allergens. Such developments would allow correlation of skin tests, clinical history, dust exposure, FEV_1 and serum IgE level with specific IgE to cotton dust allergens.

Passive cutaneous anaphylaxis studies of byssinotic and non-byssinotic sera in our laboratory and similar studies in rabbits exposed to inhalation of cotton dust (34) have demonstrated uniformly negative results. Thus, to date, the results obtained eliminate atopy from consideration; however, the development of an allergen test specific to cotton dust is crucial to obtaining the final and definitive answer.

TABLE II
Mean IgE Concentration in Sera of Byssinotic and Non-Byssinotic Cotton Mill Workers at Different Time Intervals

Subjects	Number	IgE (U/ml)		
		MAM[a]	MPM	FPM
Non-Byssinotics	29	82	82	78
Byssinotics	28	81	76	70

[a]MAM, Monday A.M.; MPM, Monday P.M.; FPM, Friday, P.M.

Mechanisms of Complement Activation. Complement is a major mediator of the inflammatory response. Complement recruits and enlists the participation of humoral and cellular effector systems, induces histamine release from mast cells and directs migration of leukocytes (chemotaxis), in addition to producing phagocytosis and the release of lysosomal constituents from phagocytes.

There are two parallel, but entirely independent pathways leading to activation of the terminal, biologically important portion of the complement sequence. These mechanisms of activation, termed the classical and alternative pathways, are triggered by different substances. The two pathways converge at C3 (midpoint) while the remainder of the reaction sequence, involving the reactions of C5 through C9, is common to both pathways.

There is now an abundance of *in vitro* data demonstrating that the complement system can be activated by several substances of both low and high molecular weight without the presence of specific antibody. Thus, in addition to classic IgE mediated mechanisms of histamine release from basophils and tissue mast cells, there are non-immunologic mechanisms capable of inducing mediator release *in vitro*, including: the β-adrenergic blocking properties of simple chemicals, such as toluene diisocyanate (TDI), the histamine releasing properties of enzymes, polypeptides, ligands, seed proteins and polycationic amines; and the complement activating properties of other low molecular weight substances, such as plicatic acid, tannins and radiographic contrast media.

The classical pathway may be activated immunologically by antigen-antibody complexes and aggregated immunoglobulins, and non-immunologically by a number of chemically diverse substances, including DNA, C-reactive protein, Staphylococcal protein A, trypsin-like enzymes and certain cellular membranes (Table III).

Interestingly, many of the major activators of the classical and alternative complement pathways are of bacterial origin. Cotton dust is known to contain significant bacterial contamination, and also contains proteolytic enzymes, DNA, plant polysaccharides, polyanions and polycations. Therefore, it is not inconceivable that a number of agents are responsible for complement activation by cotton dust. Activation occurs by direct binding of Cl to these substances or, in the case of such enzymes as the fibrinolytic enzyme plasmin, by direct proteolytic attack on the Cl molecules. Of special interest to those investigating etiologic agents and mediators in the acute byssinotic reaction is the fact that a relatively small stimulus to complement activation may lead to generation of these biologically potent products. The alternative pathway (or properdin pathway) may be activated immunologically by human IgA and some human IgG and IgE molecules, and non-immunologically by certain complex polysaccharides, lipopolysaccharides, trypsin-like enzymes and cobra venom.

TABLE III
Activation of the Complement System

Mediator	Classical	Alternative
Immunologic	IgG, IgM and aggregated Ig's	IgA, IgG, (some) IgE
Non-immunologic	Trypsin-like enzymes	Trypsin-like enzymes
	DNA	Lipopolysaccharides
	Staphylococcal protein A	Plant polysaccharides
	C-reactive protein	Cobra venom factors
	Viruses	Bacterial cell wall
	Bacterial cell wall	Viruses
	Polyanions and polycations	

Cleavage of C'3 into C3a and C5 into C5a results in peptide fragments with chemotactic and histamine releasing biological properties. These fragments have been demonstrated to be as effective as IgE in releasing histamine from human basophils and mast cells. Further activation of C5, C6 and C7 ($\overline{C567}$) is also chemotactic. The chemotaxins (C3a, C5a, $\overline{C567}$) and anaphylatoxins (C3a, C5a) are effective in the recruitment of polymorphonuclear leukocytes through blood vessel walls, the release of histamine from blood borne basophils and tissue mast cells, and the possible contraction of lung smooth muscle. These functions are summarized in Table IV.

TABLE IV
Biologic Effects of Complement Activation

C4a C2	Kinins (increase vascular permeability and contract smooth muscle)
C3a	Chemotactic activity Histamine release Kinin-like activity (contracts smooth muscle)
C5a	Chemotactic activity Histamine release Lysosomal enzyme release
$\overline{C567}$	Chemotactic activity

In vitro studies indicate that cotton mill dust extracts do activate complement by the alternative pathway. Kutz *et al.* (36) proposed that endotoxin is not the only agent responsible for complement activation, as microgram rather than nanogram quantities of purified endotoxin are required to induce the degree of complement activation observed with crude cotton dust extract. Several investigators (36, 37) have thus proposed endotoxin together with other hemolytically active substances as the causative agents. Mundie *et al.* (38) in our laboratory recently reported the *in vitro* activation of classical and alternative complement pathways by crude and purified cardroom cotton dust extract. Crude cardroom cotton dust extract was separated into high and low molecular weight fractions. The component of cotton dust that results in complement activation was shown to be retained by the UM10 Diaflo Ultrafiltration membrane and to precipitate in the presence of 20% ammonium sulfate. Serum C3 crossed immunoelectrophoresis in EGTA-Mg^{++} buffer demonstrated activation of the alternative pathway by the high molecular weight fraction but not the low molecular weight fraction. Hemolytic C1 consumption tests using antibody-and C4-coated sheep erythrocytes showed strong evidence of classical pathway activation. Many other agents exist in CMD extracts that have the potential to cause complement conversion, including endotoxin, bacterial proteolytic enzymes, bacterial cell wall components, DNA, polyanions and polycations (39).

Endotoxin inhalation has been proposed to explain symptoms of the acute byssinotic reaction (8) and implicated as the causative agent (10). A variety of bacteria are present in cotton mill dust (40), many of which produce endotoxins. Quantitation of endotoxin in cotton mill dust by Morey et al. (41) revealed concentrations of a magnitude that might be adequate to initiate biological effects. Effects of endotoxins on alternative and classical pathway complement activation can be critical to histamine release and the simultaneous recruitment of polymorphonuclear leukocytes (PMN). Endotoxin does not produce PMN recruitment without complement activation conversion of Clq or C3. Thus the definitive study will be to assess human byssinotic sera for Clq and C3 conversion. If Clq or C3 conversion does not occur, endotoxins and other materials could be removed as possible causative agents in cotton mill dust for bronchoconstriction and chemotaxis of PMN via complement conversion. However, such studies may not be as simplistic as perceived, inasmuch as attempts to demonstrate a decrease in serum complement in exposed workers or in persons exposed during bronchoprovocation challenge have not been successful; where changes in complement were detected, such as were reported following infusion of radio-contrast media, no clinical abnormalities were noted (42). In this recent study, blood had to be obtained from the aorta after the injection of the contrast media to demonstrate a complement decrease. Studies of animals inhaling cotton dust in our laboratory and others indicate that complement consumption does not occur (34, 38); however, no data has yet been gathered on complement conversion during exposure to cotton dust in byssinotics.

The work of Braun et al. (43) was instrumental in demonstrating that various proteolytic enzymes were contained in cotton dust; however, the low concentration inspired in 1 to 2 hours would be unlikely to initiate the acute byssinotic reaction directly as was proposed. On the other hand, proteolytic enzymes from bacterial degradation can trigger the complement cascade. Cinkotai (44) investigated the prevalence of trypsin-like proteases in cardroom air. He showed a high degree of association between the trypsin-like enzymes in the cardroom dust of 1-2 and 2-4 micrometer particles and the prevalence of byssinosis. These results indicate that a concentration of a pathogenic agent in the 1-4 micrometer particle fraction exists, much of which consists of viable microorganisms carrying proteolytic enzymes. This study did not measure complement concentration or mention the operative mechanism in producing byssinosis. Obviously, a hypothesis may be generated from our present knowledge that the mechanism could involve alternative complement pathway activation by trypsin-like proteases.

Our data showing normal serum complement levels in cotton mill workers (normal and byssinotic) does not support a complement activation mechanism for the pathogenesis of byssinosis, but the data does not eliminate the possiblity of complement activation in the etiology of byssinosis (Table V). As complement activation is a local reaction, small amounts of complement fragments sufficient to cause the acute byssinotic reaction could be generated locally. Serum drawn by venipuncture, however, may not demonstrate evidence of the activation because of the diluting effect of the systemic circulation.

TABLE V
Mean Complement (C3) Concentrations in Sera of Byssinotic and Non-Byssinotic Cotton Mill Workers at Different Time Intervals

Subjects	Age(yrs)	Number	C3 (mg/dl)		
			MAM[a]	MPM	FPM
Normal White Males	20-29	4	164	160	145
	30-39	4	156	129	123
	40-49	3	142	145	110
Byssinotic White Males	40-49	3	145	114	111
	50	11	149	145	140

[a]MAM, Monday A.M., MPM, Monday P.M., FPM, Friday, P.M.

Involvement of complement activation in the etiology of the acute byssinotic reaction could explain the pathogenic mechanism of histamine release, non-histamine-mediated bronchoconstriction, chemotaxis, endotoxin and bacterial proteolytic enzyme action. Bronchoconstriction experienced in the acute byssinotic reaction might be attributed to the combined action of C3a and C5a mediated histamine release and non-histamine mediated kinin activity. The presence of PMN in the nasal airways of byssinotics might be explained by the chemotactic action of C5a and the $C\overline{567}$ complex.

Histamine Releasing Agents in Extracts of Cotton Mill Dust and Cotton Bract

The concentration of plant histamine in 5 mg of respirable dust would have to be increased more than three orders magnitude to produce the acute symptoms of byssinosis (45). The etiological agent(s) in dust must of necessity be in extremely low concentrations and be potent pharmacological substances, because inhalation of less than 5 mg dust/8 hr triggers symptoms. Determination of a major histamine metabolite (1,4-methylimidazole acetic acid (MeIAA)) in the urine of reactive workers suggests that histamine is released and metabolized (18). Known histamine releasing agents are listed in Table VI.

Potential etiologic agents in cotton dust that release histamine are shown in Table VII. Some of these are effector molecules having potent biological effects in minute concentrations, i.e. peptides, which may act directly to affect chemotaxis and leukocyte recruitment, and also to release histamine and stimulate respiratory smooth muscle contraction. These bifunctional effector molecules are of major importance in considering pathogenic mechanisms in byssinosis.

TABLE VI
Mediators of Histamine Release

Complement fragments C3a, C5a
Peptides
Kinins
C3b immune adherence to platelets with release of factor 3
C5b attaches to platelets to cause lysis with release of histamine C5b platelet factors ⟶ activated Hageman factor activated Fletcher ⟶ Kallikrein ⟶ Kininogen ⟶ Kinins
Aggregated IgE and A (mucosal surface) lacks C probably
Arachidonic acid can lead to synthesis of PG's , thromboxanes, and leukotrienes in the lung and aggregation of platelets and release of histamine from platelets

TABLE VII
Potential Etiological Agents in Extracts of Cotton Mill Dust That Effect Histamine Release

A. Histamine release via activation of classical or alternate complement pathways

Endotoxins (LPS) from gram negative organisms.
Proteolytic enzymes
Polyanions
Polycations
DNA
Staphylococcal A protein

B. Histamine release via direct activation

Peptides (N-formylmethionyl)
Polyphenols and Tannins
  Tannic acid
  Quercetin
  Catechin
  Ellagic acid
  Rutin
Trimethylamine
Scopoletin
Metasilicates
Laciniline C-7 methyl ether

C. Histamine release via IgE (atopic hypersensitivity - Type I)

Antigen (hapten or complete) via IgE mediated release of histamine from basophils and tissue mast cells (complement independent).

Direct histamine releasers present in cotton mill dust are listed in Table VII-B. A major problem in the study of byssinogenic agents in CMD has been the question of suitable assay systems. These assays have ranged from inhalation by human volunteers, leukocyte recruitment in the lungs of animals in vivo, chemotaxis in Boyden chambers, to histamine release by chopped lung tissue. The latter method has been used in a number of productive studies and has led to the findings that histamine is one of the mediators in the acute byssinotic reaction.

Unfortunately in our laboratories (46) and in other's (47), the use of chopped lung tissues has appeared excessively laborious, not always reliable and extremely insensitive (48). We subsequently devised a simple, sensitive and reliable bioassay procedure using pig platelets for the assessment of histamine releasing factors in cotton mill dust (46).

The platelet histamine release assay demonstrated that cotton mill dust extract, cotton bract extract, cotton leaf extract, dialyzed CMD extract, polyphenols, compound 48/80, rutin, trimethylamine HCl, quercetin, catechin, tannic acid, ellagic acid and sodium metasilicate all release histamine directly (48). Thus not only do tannin compounds induce histamine release, but they may also form higher molecular weight polymers and contain components that survive acid hydrolytic conditions (48). Tannins are widely distributed in the plant kingdom.

Silicate is another type of widely distributed substance that induces the release of histamine from platelets. It is a common constituent of plant tissues in the form of dissolved hydrous silica or silicic acid (24), which may contribute to the byssinotic syndrome. Cotton bracts contain 0.4-0.8% silica (24). For many of the byssinogenic substances, nanogram concentrations are sufficient to release histamine (48).

It is now known that N-formylmethionyl (NFMet) peptides are strongly chemotactic for PMN and macrophages and cause the release of histamine in human basophils. Thus, like the complement derived C3a and C5a anaphlylatoxic (histamine releasing) fragments, N-FMet peptides also possess direct histamine releasing properties. Histamine release proceeds through a mechanism unrelated to IgE activation of basophils and tissue mast cells. The histamine releasing ability of these peptides correlates well with their chemotactic activity (49).

Chemotactic Agents in Extracts of Cotton Mill Dust

Table VIII lists a variety of substances that are known chemotaxins. Chemotaxins attract white blood cells, primarily neutrophils, eosinophils and macrophages, to a specific site by causing directed movement. Once these cells arrive they phagocytize and degrade invading microorganisms, and/or release hydrolytic enzymes which can cause subsequent tissue injury. These cells also release bronchoconstrictors, which provides another mechanism worthy of consideration.

TABLE VIII
Chemotactic Factors

- Proteins
  - Complement fragments
    - C3a
    - C5a
    - $\overline{C567}$
  - Coagulation proteins
    - Plasminogen activator
    - Fibrinopeptide B
    - Prekallikrein
  - Other proteins
    - Random coil proteins (e.g., casein)
    - IgG hydrolysis products
    - Cell-bound antigen
- Lipids and other molecules
  - Products of lipid peroxidation
  - Prostaglandins
  - Bacterial filtrate factors
  - N-Formyl methionyl peptides
  - Cyclic purine nucleotides
  - Transfer factor
  - Lymphokines

Gram negative bacteria are natural contaminants of fibrous plant material. In processes where cotton is agitated, i.e. during rapid machining, bacteria on the cotton fibers often become airborne, and the workers involved in dusty areas may be exposed to concentrations of bacteria as high as 10^7 bacteria/m^{-3} (50, 51).

A number of factors stimulate migration of leukocytes and reside in CMD (Table IX). Various strains of gram negative bacteria, especially those of Enterobacter and Klebsiella, produce potent chemotaxins. These organisms, isolated from cotton dust and administered to guinea pigs, initiate PMN migration in airways (52); however, isolated gram positive bacteria or suspensions from these organisms and to various molds produces no reaction. Various gram negative bacteria possess lipopolysaccharides (LPS) which differ greatly in their ability to recruit leukocytes. Several bacterial LPS isolated from cotton were tested by exposing guinea pigs to aerosols and counting the number of free lung cells at 24 hours. Chemotaxis was found to be dependent on dose and species of bacteria and LPS inhaled (52).

TABLE IX
Chemotaxins in Cotton Dust Extracts

Exert effects directly:	Exert effects indirectly through complement activation:
1. Bacterial N-formylmethionyl peptides	1.Endotoxins
2. Lacinilene C-7-methyl ether[a]	2.LPS (purified endotoxin)
	3.DNA
	4.Bacterial filtrate factors

[a]Recently shown by Ainsworth and Neuman not to be chemotactic (16).

Some factors, such as NFMet peptides and other chemotaxins, exert their effects directly on cells, while chemotaxigens attract cells indirectly through activation of complement and production of C3a, C5a or C567. Studies in our laboratory have shown that potent chemotaxins reside in aqueous extracts of CMD (15). Further studies have shown these chemotaxins to be anionic, m.w. 200-2000 daltons, stable in boiling water and acid hydrolyzable (16). These properties are consistent with characteristics of peptides, particularly N-FMet peptides. These are potent chemoattractants of bacterial origin and are potential cotton dust chemotactic etiologic agents. We have suggested that polypeptides might be the causative agent in byssinosis (15). Cotton dust is heavily laden with bacteria (40, 41), and their products (peptides) are chemotactic at concentrations as low as 10^{-11} M (on the order of 10^{-5} µg/ml) (53). Biological effects could easily be effected by inspiration of such potent substances. A further significant property of the peptides is their capacity to induce specific secretion of lysosomal enzymes from leukocytes (53-55) with the possible sequelae of pathologic lesions, i.e. bronchitis and emphysema. In byssinosis, however, emphysema is probably a result of the inhalation of cigarette smoke, and not of cotton dust (56).

The structure of NFMet peptides is peculiar to bacterial metabolism as intermediaries in protein biosynthesis. The biologic response to NFMet peptides may be part of a defensive mechanism against bacterial infection. The chemotactic factor(s) in cotton dust appears to be a small molecular weight peptide, consistent with the view that peptides, in general, are usually low molecular weight biological effectors. Direct evidence that this naturally occuring bacterial chemotaxin is an N-formylated peptide awaits further work. The purification and identification of chemotaxin(s) in cotton dust are being pursued in our laboratory, and these products are being similarly investigated in an animal model and compared with NFMet peptides.

Human plasma kallikrein has also been described as being directly chemotactic for human neutrophils (57). Kallikrein incubated with the complement component C5 generates chemotactic activity, providing a further mechanism for C5 activation. C5a is the most active and probably the most biologically important of the complement derived chemotactic and anaphylatoxic peptides.

Some agents are bifunctional, causing the release of histamine and recruiting leukocytes. Bifunctional mediators include bacterial peptides, endotoxins, DNA, C3a, C5a and bradykinin. Each of these substances can exert dual effects. This may either occur directly, as in the case of bacterial peptides and bradykinin causing chemotaxis and bronchial smooth muscle contraction, or indirectly, as endotoxin and DNA conversion of complement. C3a and C5a act indirectly as complement fragments to effect histamine release, which in turn contracts bronchial smooth muscle. However, both appear to act directly to effect chemotaxis with C5a, the more potent fragment.

Bradykinin, a chemotaxin and muscle constrictor, is activated by enzymatic cleavage. At present, blood clotting anomalies in byssinosis have not been described, indicating that it is unlikely that this substance plays a role, although aggregation of RBC by CMD extracts has been reported in our laboratory (58).

Clinical studies of cotton mill workers who had previously demonstrated a decreased expiratory flow measured by flow volume curves and FEV_1 during cotton dust exposure showed an increase in WBC to 25.5% after 4 hours of exposure. Segmented neutrophils increased most (33%), while eosinophil mean counts did not change. The ratio of segmented neutrophils to epithelial cells from nasal mucosal swabs increased from 0.56 before to 1.84 after 4 hours of exposure. Peripheral blood and PMN counts increased upon exposure to cotton dust, and PMN were recruited to the nasal mucosa. Chest tightness and decreased flow were temporarily correlated with leukocyte recruitment following cotton dust exposure (2).

In studies on hamsters and guinea pigs exposed to aerosols of crude and refined extracts from cotton mill trash and CMD, Kilburn et al. (59) has further demonstrated recruitment of PMN beneath the basement membrane and on luminal surfaces of intrapulmonary airways and tracheas. When administered as aerosols or dust, polyphenolic extracts from cotton trash and pure and oxidization-polymerization products of quercetin also recruit PMN from the trachea to terminal bronchioles in hamsters (60).

In addition, lacinilene (synthetic and natural), reputed by Kilburn to be chemotactic and to be the byssinotic agent, has recently been evaluated in our laboratory for chemokinetic and chemotactic activity (16, 61). In our studies, lacinilene does not possess chemotactic or chemokinetic activities. Interestingly, the agent used to solubilize lacinilene in Kilburn's studies (Pluronic Polyol F68, a polypropylene glycol) does not possess chemotactic activity, but is a new class of chemokinetic compounds (16). The chemokinetic activity of the polyol probably explains why lacinilene was reported as the "chemotactic-byssinogenic" agent by these investigators.

Bioassay of Bronchoconstrictor Substances in Extracts of Cotton Mill Dust and Cotton Bract

In 1962, Davenport and Paton (62) studied the chemical and biological properties of extracts of two different samples of cotton dust. They described an active component in these extracts which constricted smooth muscle of rat gastrointestinal tract and guinea pig trachea. The rat stomach strips were the most sensitive to cotton dust extract (CDE) and to 5-hydroxytryptamine (5HT). Brom-lysergic acid partially antagonized the effect of CDE over the stomach strips, but failed to antagonize the CDE constrictor effect over rat duodenum and guinea pig trachea. Atropine and Mepyramine maleate were ineffective in all tissues. The active component described was soluble in water, insoluble in methanol, chloroform, acetone, ethanol and petroleum ether and possessed high K^+ levels. It also had both basic and acidic groups in a ratio of 2 basic: 1 acidic, and was dialysable, resistant to boiling and not destroyed by the action of proteolytic enzymes.

In blood bathed preparations, animals injected with CDE released a substance into the blood stream that elicited relaxation of rat duodenum muscle but had no effect on rat stomach muscle. The onset was slow which, added to other findings, led these investigators to postulate a kinin-like substance to be the mediator released.

Mohammed (63) reported that acetone treatment of aqueous cotton dust extract caused the precipitation of several sugars and an aminopolysaccharide. The sugars were present in concentrations equal to those which exhibited contractile activity on guinea pig ileum. Our experiments to date have failed to demonstrate contractile activity in the acetone precipitate of either the cotton dust or cotton bract extracts (64).

Nicholls and Skidmore (65) demonstrated that dust collected from mills with a higher prevalence of byssinosis caused greater smooth muscle contractile activity than dust from mills with a lower prevalence. Recently, Russell et al. (66) used an isolated tissue bath to measure canine trachealis muscle contraction caused by cotton bract extracts (CBE). Morey et al. (67) showed that cotton bract represents 20-43% of the cotton dust total; thus, the findings of Paton and Davenport using cotton dust agree in principle with Russell et al., who used cotton bract. Davenport and Paton (62) found a percentage of the activity of CDE represented by a 5HT-like component, but they also found at least one more active substance in the CDE than Russell et al. (66).

We have gained considerable knowledge in our laboratory of bronchoconstrictors in bract and dust. A comparison of rat bladder, colon, ileum and stomach sensitivity to 5-HT showed the stomach to be the most sensitive tissue to extracts as has been reported by others (62).

Cotton dust and cotton bract extract contracted smooth muscle with forces equivalent to a 0.32 ± 0.05 µg/ml concentration of 5HT and 0.7 ± 0.1 µg/ml concentration of 5-HT, respectively (68). However, cotton bract extracts were blocked by methysergide, a 5-HT antagonist, while cotton dust extracts were not. Diphenhydramine, a histamine antagonist, failed to significantly affect either of the extracts (68).

Acetone precipitated CDE and CBE caused minimal contraction of the rat stomach smooth muscle. The supernatant retained most of the active substance (64). Butanol, however, did extract the active components of both CBE and CDE (69). Ethyl acetate, which will extract 5HT from an aqueous solution (64), was unsuccessful in removing the active components. These findings are in agreement with Russell et al. (66), who used this procedure to demonstrate that the active component of bract was "5HT-like." The active agent(s) in extracts of the dust and bract were demonstrated to have a molecular weight below 20,000.

In comparing 5HT equivalent values for CDE and CBE, it might be suggested that part of the contraction resulting from CDE is due to the 20-40% bract in the dust. We have shown that the contraction caused by cotton dust extract is different from the contraction caused by cotton bract extract. CBE was blocked by methysergide. A methysergide concentration that would block $75 \pm 2\%$ of 5 HT activity would block $59 \pm 6\%$ of CBE activity and only $12.6 \pm 4\%$ of CDE activity (68). This suggests that the two extracts operate at different receptor sites on the smooth muscle, and that the nature of their active component(s) would be different. Histamine, which is known to be present in cotton dust, is not responsible for the contractile activity in these preparations (68).

Though the contractions caused by cotton dust and cotton bract have important differences, there are also similarities between their chemical properties. It is doubtful that either of the active agents are proteins because pronase has no affect on the extracts and they are labile even at $4^{o}C$. In addition, both active substances were extracted with butanol (69).

Recent smooth muscle constrictor studies performed in our laboratory in collaboration with Dr. Marion Buck at Yale University have yielded interesting results. Various fractions were first tested in human volunteers for bronchoconstrictor activity and then bioassayed by the rat stomach strip isolated organ bath technique. The fractions demonstrating constrictor activity in man correlated precisely with the constrictor activity in the isolated organ bath. This effect was antagonized by methysergide (69).

As the major clinical manifestation of the acute byssinotic reaction is a drop in FEV_1, it is interesting to speculate that the bronchoconstriction observed in cotton mill workers may be in part or in full the result of constrictor substances in inhaled cotton dust.

If the receptors involved in the acute byssinotic reaction can be determined, pharmacologic blocking agents may be used to treat affected cotton mill workers or, conversely, preprocessing of cotton to eliminate the constrictor might prove feasible.

Conclusions

In recent years, rapid strides have been made toward understanding the composition of cotton mill dust, causative agents and pathogenic mechanisms. Studies on composition and chemistry have demonstrated significant differences in cotton dust emanating from various types of cotton plants, different harvest times, harvest techniques and geographical area of cultivation. The causative agent is seemingly ubiquitous in friable vegetable materials which, when machined, rapidly produce particles of respirable size and thus byssinosis in flax, hemp, and cotton workers.

Bioassays have been instrumental in furthering our understanding of etiologic agents and pathogenic mechanisms in byssinosis, in particular, bioassays of histamine releasing substances, chemotaxins, and bronchoconstrictors isolated from extracts of dust. Bioassays have helped to define parameters of biological activity of dusts, as well as the immunological, physiological, pharmacological and pathological reactions of cells and muscle tissue. The acute byssinotic reaction will be better understood when such bioassays are more closely correlated with human reactor studies, and in turn, both human and bioassay results correlated with an appropriate animal model.

Acknowledgments

This research was supported by funds from Cotton Incorporated, Cotton Foundation, and the South Carolina Lung Association. Dr. Pilia is a recipient of a National Kidney Foundation Postdoctoral Fellowship. The authors gratefully appreciate the editorial assistance of Janet Vesterlund and the secretarial assistance of Charlotte Spain.

Literature Cited

1. Mareska, J.; Heymann, J. Ann. Soc. Med. de Gand. 1945, 16, 5-245.
2. Merchant J.A., Lumsden, J.C., Kilburn, K.H., O'Fallon, W.M., Ujda, J.R., Germino, V.H., Hamilton, J.D. Dose Response in Cotton Textile Workers. J. Occup. Med. 1973, 15, 222230.
3. Merchant, J.A., Halprin, G.M., Hudson, A.R., Kilburn, K.H., McKenzie, W.N., Hurst, D.J., Bermazohn, P. Responses to Cotton Dust. Arch. Environ. Health 1979, 30, 222-229.
4. Bouhuys, A.; Heaphy, L.J., Jr.; Schilling, R.S.F.; Welborn, J.W. N. Eng. J. Med. 1967, 277, 170-175.
5. Bouhuys, A.; Lindell, S.E.; Lundin G. Brit. Med. J. 1960, 1, 324-326.
6. Bouhuys, A.; Van Duyn, J.; Van Lennep, H.J. Arch. Environ. Health. 1961, 3, 499-509.
7. McDermott, M.; Skidmore, J.W.; Edwards, J. "2nd International Conference on Respiratory Diseases in Textile Workers"; Alicante, Spain, 1968, p 13-36.
8. Cavagna, G.; Foa, V .; Vigliani, E.C. Br. J. Ind. Med. 1969, 26, 314-321.
9. Pernis, B.; Vigiliani, E.C.; Cavagna, G.; Finulli, M. Br. J. Ind. Med. 1961, 18, 120-129.
10. Bergstrom, R.; Haglind, P.; Rylander, R. "Proceedings, 1980 Beltwide Cotton Production Research Conference"; National Cotton Council of America, Memphis, Tenn., 1980, p 22-25.
11. Massoud, A.; Taylor, G. Lancet 1964, 2, 607-610.
12. Kilburn, K.H.; Lynn, D.; McCormick, J.P.; Schaefer, T.R. "Proceedings, 1979 Beltwide Cotton Production Research Conference"; National Cotton Council of America, Memphis, Tenn., 1979, p 19-20.
13. Lynn, W.S.; Munoz, S.; Campbell, J.A.; Jeffs, P.W. Ann. N.Y. Acad. Sci. 1974, 221, 163-173.
14. Buck, M.G.; Bouhuys, A. "Proceedings, 1980 Beltwide Cotton Production Research Conference"; National Cotton Council of America, Memphis, Tenn., 1980, p 31-34.
15. Ainsworth, S.K.; Neuman, R.E. "Proceedings, 1980 Beltwide Cotton Production Research Conferences"; National Cotton Council of America, Memphis, Tenn., 1980, p 14-18.

16. Ainsworth, S.K.; Neuman, R.E. Am. Rev. Respir. Dis. 1981 124, 280-284.
17. Antweiler, H. Ann. Occup. Hyg. 1960, 2, 152-156.
18. Bouhuys, A. In Breathing, Grune and Stratton: New York, p 416-
19. Fox, A.J.; Tombleson, J.B.L.; Watt, A.; Wilie, A.G. Br. J. Ind. Med. 1973, 30, 48-53.
20. Criteria for Recommended Standard. . . Exposure to Cotton Dust. U.S. Dept. HEW, PHS. CDD, NIOSH, 1974. (HEW Publication No. (NIOSH) 75-118) Washington, D.C.
21. Imbus, H.R.; Suh, M.W. Arch. Environ. Health 1973, 26, 183-191.
22. Hamilton, J.D.; Halprin, G.M.; Kilburn, K.H.; Merchant, J.A.; Ujda, J.R. Arch. Environ. Health 1973, 26, 120-124.
23. Antweiler, H. Ann. N.Y. Acad. Sci. 1969, 158, 136.
24. Wakelyn, P.J.; Greenblatt, G.A.; Brown, D.F.; Fripp, V.W. Am. Indust. Hygiene Assoc. J. 1976, 37, 22-31.
25. Tuffnell, P. Br. J. Ind. Med. 1960, 16, 307-309.
26. Zakhdov, A.Z.; Schraiber, L.B.; Gol'eva, I.V.; Katsenovich, L.A.; Samsonov, A.P. Hyg. Sanit. 1965, 30, 344.
27. Ainsworth, S.K.; Neuman, R.E. "Proceedings, 1977 Beltwide Cotton Production Research Conference"; National Cotton Council of America, Memphis, Tenn., 1977, p 62-64.
28. Ainsworth, S.K.; Neuman, R.E. Unpublished results.
29. Noweir, M.H. Chest 1981, 79, 62S-67S.
30. Ainsworth, S.K.; Mundie, T.G.; Pilia, P.A. "Proceedings, 1981 Beltwide Cotton Production Research Conference"; National Cotton Council of America, Memphis, Tenn., 1981, pp 78.
31. Edwards, J.H.; Jones, B.M. J. Immunol. 1973, 110, 498-501.
32. Sekul, A.A.; Ory, R.L. "Proceedings, 1979 Beltwide Cotton Production Conference"; National Cotton Council of America, Memphis, Tenn., 1979, p. 30-31.
33. Kutz, S.A.; Mentnech, M.S.; Olenchock, S.A.; Major, P.C. Chest 1981, 79, 56S-58S.
34. Kutz, S.A.; Mentnech, M.S.; Mull, J.C.; Olenchock, S.A. Arch. Environ. Health 1980, 35, 205-10.
35. Taylor, G.; Massoud, A.A.E.; Lucas, F. Br. J. Ind. Med. 1971, 28, 143-151.
36. Kutz, S.A.; Olenchock, S.A.; Elliott, J.A.; Pearson, D.J.; Major, P.C. Envir. Res. 1979, 19, 405-414.
37. Wilson, M.R.; Sekul, A.; Ory, R.; Salvaggio, J.E.; Lehrer, S.B. Clin. Allergy 1980, 10, 303-308.
38. Mundie, T.G.; Ainsworth, S.K.; Boackle, R.J. Society for Experimental Biology and Medicine Southeastern Section, Charleston, S.C., (abstr.) Abstracts 5, p 14, 1980. (Manuscript, In Press, 1981).
39. Morey, P.R.; Bethea, R.M.; Kirk, I.W.; Wakelyn, P.J. Cotton Dust, Proc. of a Topical Symp.; 1975, Cincinnati, p 237.
40. Fischer, J.J. "Proceedings, 1979 Beltwide Cotton Production Research Conference"; National Cotton Council of America, Memphis, Tenn., 1979, p 8-10.

41. Morey, P.R.; Fischer, J.J.; Sasser, P.E. "Proceedings, 1980 Beltwide Cotton Production Conference"; National Cotton Council of America, Memphis, Tennessee, 1980, p 68-9.
42. Cogen, F.C.; Norman, M.E.; Dunsky, E.; Hirschfield, J.; Zweiman, B. J. Allergy Clin. Immunol. 1979, Suppl. 64:299-303.
43. Braun, D.C.; Scheel, L.D.; Tuma, J.; Parker, L. J. Occupatonal Med. 1973, 15, 241-244.
44. Cinkotai, F.F. Am. Industrial Hygiene Assoc. J. 1976, 37, 324-338.
45. Ainsworth, S.K.; McCormick, J.P.; Neuman, R.E. "Proceedings, 1979 Beltwide Cotton Production Research Conference; National Cotton Council of America, Memphis, Tenn., 1979, p 21-29.
46. Ainsworth, S.K.; Neuman, R.E.; Harley, R.A. Br. J. Ind. Med. 1979, 36, 35-42.
47. Greenblatt, G.A. "Proceedings, 1977 Beltwide Cotton Production Research Conference"; National Cotton Council of America, Memphis, Tenn., 1977, p 71-72.
48. Ainsworth, S.K.; Neuman, R.E. "Proceedings, 1977 Beltwide Cotton Production Research Conference"; National Cotton Council of America, Memphis, Tenn., 1977, p 76-79.
49. Hook, W.A.; Schiffman, E.; Aswanikumar, S.; Siraganian, R. P. J. Immunol. 1977, 117, 594-596.
50. Fisher, J.J.; Battigelli, M.C.; Foarde, K.K. "Proceedings, 1979 Beltwide Cotton Production Research Conference"; National Cotton Council of America, Memphis, Tenn., 1979, p 13-14.
51. Lundholm, M.; Rylander, R. "Proceedings, 1979 Beltwide Cotton Production Research Conference"; National Cotton Council of America, Memphis, Tenn., 1979, p 11-13.
52. Helander, I.; Salkinoja-Salonen, M.; Rylander, R. Infect. Immunity 1980, 29, 859-862.
53. Showell, H.J.; Freer, R.J.; Zigmond, S.H.; Schiffmann, E.; Aswanikumar, S.; Corcoran, B.; Becker, E.L. J. Exp. Med. 1976, 143, 1154-1169.
54. Becker, E.L.; Showell, H.J.; Henson, P.M.; Long, S.H. J. Immunol. 1974, 112, 2047-2054
55. Becker, E.L.; Showell, H.J. J. Immun. 1974, 112, 2055-2062.
56. Pratt, P.C. Chest 1981, 79, 495-535.
57. Wiggins, R.C.; Giclais, P.C. (abstr.) Fed. Proc. 1980, 39, 1049.
58. Ainsworth, S.K.; Neuman, R.E. (abstr.) Am. Rev. Respir. Dis. 1978, 117, 217.
59. Kilburn, K.H.; Lynn, W.S.; Tress, L.L.; McKenzie, W.N. Lab. Invest. 1973, 28, 55-49.
60. Kilburn, K.H. Ann. N.Y. Acad. Sci. 1974, 221, 335-339.
61. Neuman, R.E.; Ainsworth, S.K., J. Reticuloendothelial Soc. 1980, 28, 305-312.
62. Davenport, A.; Paton, W.D.M. Br. J. Ind. Med. 1962, 29, 19-32.

63. Mohammed, Y.S.; El-Guzzah, R.M.; Adamyova, K. Carbohydrate Res. 1971, 20, 431-435.
64. Ainsworth, S.K.: Unpublished results.
65. Nicholls, P.S.; Skidmore, J.W. Br. J. Ind. Med. 1975, 32, 289-296.
66. Russell, J.A.; Gilberstadt, M.L.; Rohrback, M.S. (abstr.) Am. Rev. Respir. Dis. 1981, 124, 252.
67. Morey, P.R. "Proceedings, 1977 Beltwide Cotton Production Research Conference;" National Cotton Council of America, Memphis, Tenn. 1977, 10-11.
68. Mundie, T.G.; Cordova-Salinas, M.A.; Bray, V.J.; Ainsworth, S.K. "Proceedings, 1982 Beltwide Cotton Production Research Conference," National Cotton Council of America, Las Vegas, Nevada, 1982.
69. Mundie, T.G.; Buck, M.; Cordova-Salinas, M.A.; Neuman, R.E.; Ainsworth, S.K. "Proceedings, 1982 Beltwide Cotton Production Research Conference," National Cotton Council of America, Las Vegas, Nevada, 1982.

RECEIVED February 24, 1982.

12

Cotton Bract and Acute Airway Constriction in Humans

MARION G. BUCK

Yale University, School of Medicine, Department of Internal Medicine, New Haven, CT 06510

On Monday or on the first work day after an absence, cotton textile workers experience acute symptoms of chest tightness, shortness of breath and cough accompanied by a decrease in $FEV_{1.0}$, MEF40%(P), and other pulmonary function parameters indicative of airway narrowing. This response to inhaling cotton dust, which characterizes the early stages of byssinosis, can be reproduced in the laboratory by inhalation challenge of healthy human volunteers with aqueous extracts of cotton bracts(1g bracts/6 ml H_2O). Bracts (the leaf-like structures surrounding the stem of the cotton boll) are a major component of the mill dust. On first exposure to bract extract, 60% of our volunteers responded with decreases in $FEV_{1.0}$ of 5% or greater and corresponding MEF40%(P) decreases of 20% or greater. The response was reproducible in subsequent challenges delayed one week or longer. None of our volunteers had ever had a previous exposure to cotton dust. The causative agent(s) is not known. We have used inhalation challenge in volunteers who are responders as a bioassay for detection of airway constrictor activity in purified bract extracts. Crude aqueous extracts contain 60 mg dry weight material per milliliter. Precipitation of protein by methanol, removal of anions by DEAE chromatography, and extraction with ether reduces the dry weight material to 10 mg/ml and this purified extract retains 70% of its original airway constrictor activity. Tests are positive for the presence of sugars and amino nitrogen. Size exclusion chromatography has shown that airway constrictor activity is associated with the less than 1,000 molecular weight fraction.

0097-6156/82/0189-0187$6.00/0

Bract (modified leaf structure surrounding the stem of the cotton boll) is the principal plant trash component in cotton mill dust (1). It contains a potent airway constrictor substance for humans (2). Aqueous extracts of cotton bract (or mill dust) when inhaled by susceptible humans induces acute symptoms of chest tightness, shortness of breath and cough accompanied by a decrease in lung function (2,3). This response is similar to the characteristic Monday response of textile workers in the early stages of byssinosis. The response is seen in healthy humans never before exposed to cotton dust (2). The response is further characterized by a delay of 90-120 minutes for maximum effect (2). This is unlike the well known bronchoconstrictor agent histamine which acts within minutes and is overwith in less than one hour (4). The histamine content of bract is insufficient to provoke a bronchoconstrictor response in healthy persons. However, bract has been shown to cause histamine release from human lung tissue. The bract agent(s) may react directly with airway smooth muscle, but more likely, the 90 minute delay for maximum effect is the time it takes for the responsible bract agent(s) to react with susceptible lung cells and cause their release of bronchoconstrictor mediator(s) such as histamine and/or others such as SRSA or prostaglandin (5,6). These in turn react with the airway smooth muscle. The initiating causative agent(s) remains unknown. Such chemically diverse compounds as endotoxin (7), lacinilenes (8), glycoprotein (10), byssinosan (9), ellagic acid and sodium metasilicate (5) have been postulated as possible causatives of byssinosis. With the exception of endotoxin, however, none of these compounds have been tested for their effect on human airways. To date there is no animal model for byssinosis. Assay systems which have been used include histamine release *in vitro* by chopped lung tissue (11), histamine release by hamster platelets (5), chemotaxis (12), leucocyte recruitment in the lungs of animals *in vivo* (13), perfused guinea pig lung (6), and response of rabbit-aveolar macrophages (14).

Because cotton bract and cotton dust may contain several chemical compounds which, if in high enough concentration, may have some kind of biological action which may not be related to byssinosis, we use inhalation challenge in healthy human subjects as our assay method for determining the airway constrictor activity of our bract extracts in our search for the causative agent(s). This method has the advantage that we are looking at a biological activity which is directly related to one of the major symptoms of byssinosis - acute airway constriction in humans. We have prepared partially purified extracts of cotton bracts which retain the ability to induce airway constriction in our subjects. The characteristics of these extracts are discussed.

Materials and Methods

Preparation of cotton bract extracts. Figure 1 is a flow chart showing our procedures for preparing the various bract extracts. Dried bracts (frost killed) were hand picked just prior to harvest from cotton fields in the Lubbock, Texas area. These were stored at room temperature. Extracts were freeze-dried and stored at -4°C. For inhalation challenge by our subjects each extract was reconstituted with water or saline, as indicated, at a concentration equivalent to the standard crude extract. This insured that for challenge purposes components were not concentrated as purification progressed.

Assay of acute airway constriction in humans. From area universities, we recruited healthy volunteer subjects (no respiratory symptoms, no history of asthma), ages 18-36 yrs., males, females, smokers, and nonsmokers. Airway constrictor effects of the bracts extracts were assayed by comparing lung function values obtained from recordings of partial and maximum expiratory flow-volume (PEFV, MEFV) curves (15,16)before and at 30 min. intervals for a 2½ - 3 h period following a 10 min. inhalation of the aerosolized extract. An example of the curves obtained is shown in Figure 2. These were recorded with a pneumotachograph-integrator device (17)and an XY recorder: ordinate: expiratory flow rates, abcissa: expired volume. The subject first inspired to about 65% of the vital capacity (VC) - the exact level is not crucial and may vary from about 60-75% of VC - the subsequent forced expiration to residual volume yielded the PEFV curve. Without interruption, the subject next inspired maximally, and then again expired forcefully and maximally to residual volume, recording the MEFV curve. Forced vital capacity (FVC), forced expiratory volume in 1 s ($FEV_{1.0}$), MEF50% and MEF40% were measured from the MEFV curve. MEF50% and MEF40% are instantaneous flows at lung volumes corresponding to 50% and 40% of the forced vital capacity (maximum inspiration= 100% FVC). MEF40%(P) is the instantaneous flow on the PEFV curve at 40% remaining VC. Forty percent VC values were used to avoid peak transients on the PEFV curves at larger lung volumes. To compare responses to bract extract aerosol we used the MEF40%(P) value where the 40% VC volume for each subject day was computed as an average from 5 control (before aerosol inhalation) MEFV curves of that day. This 40% volume was used throughout the test period. When airway constriction occurs any changes in FVC are small relative to changes in MEF40%(P) and the 40% volume is always measured from the point of maximum inspiration on the MEFV curve.

Aerosols of less than 1μm diameter droplets were generated from bract extracts and saline by use of the Dautrebande D30 nebulizer.

Thin Layer Chromatography (TLC). Commercially available (Whatman LK6D, linear-K) silica gel (40Å) plates of 250 μm thickness were used. These were developed in chloroform:acetone: formic acid (80:19:1). Spots were detected by UV light and iodine vapor.

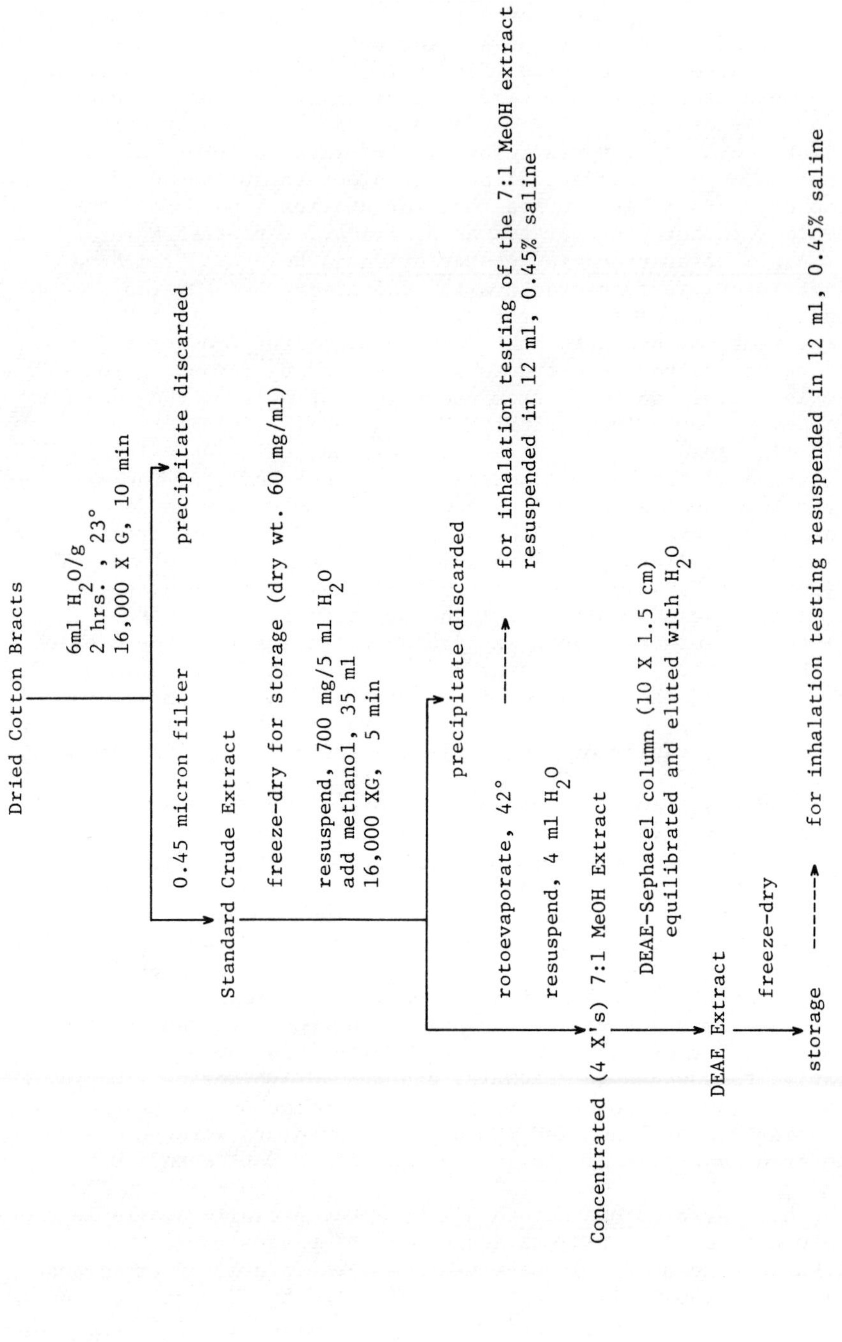

Figure 1. Procedures for preparing cotton bract extracts.

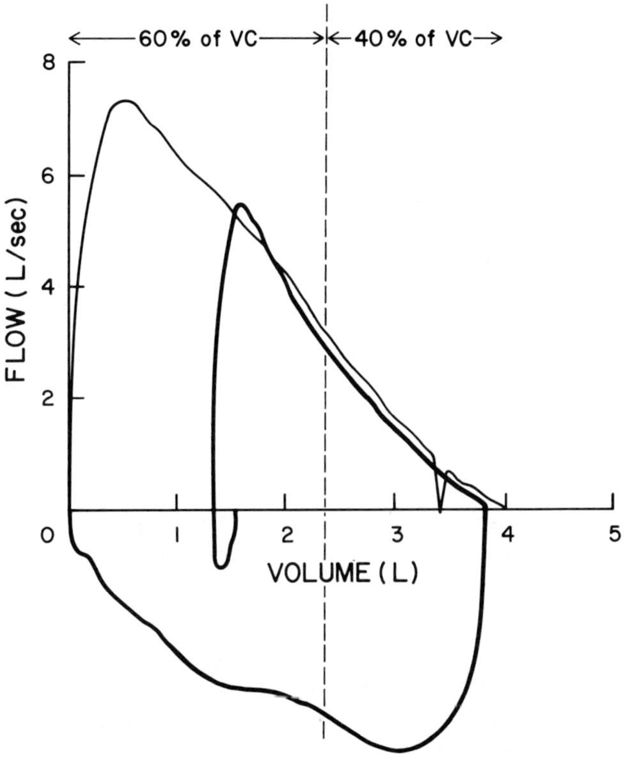

Figure 2. Maximum (MEFV; thin lines) and partial (PEFV; heavy lines) expiratory flow-volume curves by a healthy 25 year old female subject.

The lung volume level for measurement of MEF40% and MEF40%(P) is shown by the dashed vertical line. Point of maximum inspiration is indicated by the zero point on volume axis. The v shaped pen deflection near full expiration on MEFV curve is the one second time marker for measurement of $FEV_{1.0}$. The entire expiration–inspiration–expiration maneuver was recorded uninterrupted.

Results and Discussion

Lung function changes on exposure to aerosols of cotton bract extracts. From a group of 105 subjects (2) exposed by inhalation challenge to our standard crude bract extract, the responses of all but four were used to compare changes in the lung function parameters $FEV_{1.0}$ and MEF40%(P). The four subjects excluded were those with control $FEV_{1.0}$ values at or greater than FVC. For this comparison, our subjects are divided into two groups - those who had no or only a small response of less than an MEF40%(P) value of 20%, and those who responded to the crude extract with a 20% or greater decrease in MEF40%(P) and thus who clearly react to the bract extract with an acute airway constriction. We use this 20% cut-off to define responders in the selection of subjects to test the airway constrictor activity of subsequent purified extracts. Figure 3 shows that the maximum change in $FEV_{1.0}$ over the 120 minute test period of the non-responder group is -1.2% at 90 min. This compares to a slight increase in $FEV_{1.0}$ of 0.1% at 90 min. for the saline control group. The fifteen subjects challenged with saline as a control group were all responders, i.e. all responded to bract extract challenge with a 20% or greater decrease in MEF40%(P). The mean change in $FEV_{1.0}$ of the responder group following inhalation of bract extract was -7.5% at 90 min. This 7.5% decrease in $FEV_{1.0}$ for responders corresponds to a mean Δ $FEV_{1.0}$ of -307 ml ± 213 (SD). The Δ $FEV_{1.0}$ for the saline control group is +1 ml ± 75 (SD). The time of maximum decrease in $FEV_{1.0}$ at 90 min is the same as that seen for changes in MEF40%(P). MEF40%(P) is a more sensitive indicator of changes in airway caliber than $FEV_{1.0}$ (15) and as expected showed larger percentage changes in response to challenge by bract extracts. At 90 min., saline controls showed an increase in MEF40%(P) of 1.9% (mean Δ MEF40%(P) of + 37 ml/sec ± 197 SD), the non-responder group decreased by only 4.1%, and the responder group showed a mean decrease of 30.5% (mean Δ MEF40%(P) of -1039 ml/sec ± 462 SD).

We use the MEF40%(P) value to compare the airway constrictor activities of various bract extracts because of its greater sensitivity and thus the lack of a need to induce large decreases in airway caliber and corresponding discomfort in our subjects.

Table I is an attempt to compare the responses in lung function we observe with our naive subjects on exposure to cotton bract extracts with the responses reported in literature of both naive subjects and workers exposed to cotton dust. The comparison suffers from the fact that neither the exposure time or concentration nor the post-exposure time of $FEV_{1.0}$ readings are standardized for the different investigating laboratories. The various cotton dusts or extracts are not standardized either and the airway constrictor potency varies with the dusts. Bracts also vary in their potency. We have observed variations in potency with harvest year from the same location (Lubbock, Texas).

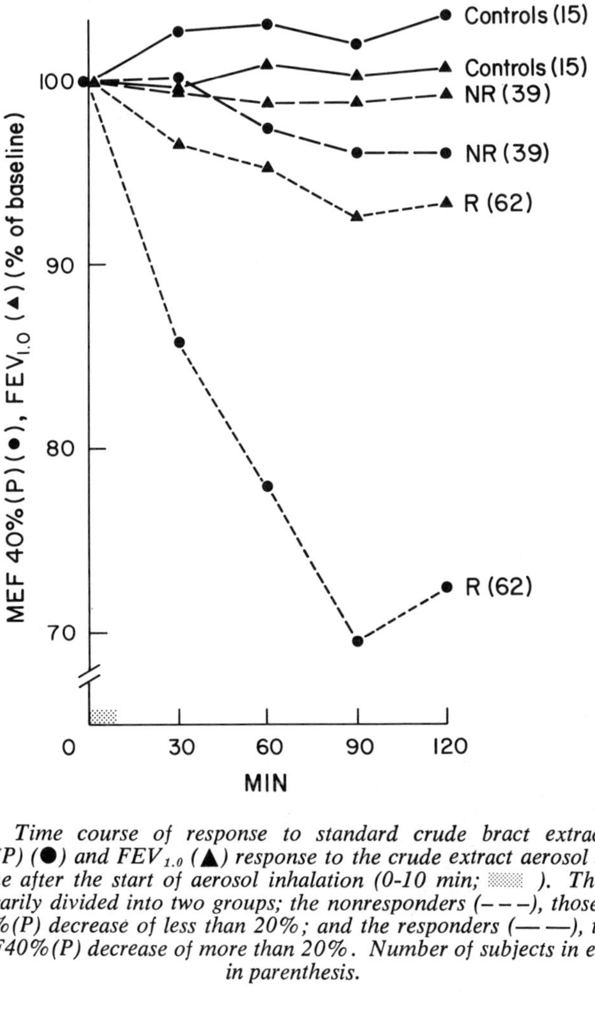

Figure 3. Time course of response to standard crude bract extract. Mean MEF40%(P) (●) and $FEV_{1.0}$ (▲) response to the crude extract aerosol as a function of time after the start of aerosol inhalation (0-10 min; ░). The subjects were arbitrarily divided into two groups; the nonresponders (– – –), those who had a MEF40%(P) decrease of less than 20%; and the responders (——), those who had a MEF40%(P) decrease of more than 20%. Number of subjects in each group in parenthesis.

TABLE I

Comparison of $FEV_{1.0}$ Changes with Exposure to Bract Extracts, Dust Extracts, and Dust

		$\Delta FEV_{1.0}$, post- pre-exposure					
		Naive Subjects		Workers			
				Bys[a]		Non-Bys	
Cotton Sample	Exposure Conditions	%	ml (±SD)	%	ml (±SD)	%	ml (±SD)
aqueous bract extracts (present study)	from 1g/6ml 10 min	-7.5	-307 (±213) (90 min after)				
aqueous cotton dust extract (24)	?				-276 (±227)		-172 (±120)
cotton dust (25)	standard Stonewall 1mg/m^3 6 hrs	-8.5	-271				
cotton dust (26)	mg/m^3 0.5 - 2.1			-2.4 to -12.0			
	0.6 - 4.0 4 hrs.	-0.1 to -8.8					
cotton dust (27)	mg/m^3 0.14 -1.35 6 hrs				+75 to -139		
cotton dust (28)	unwashed 0.91 mg/m^3 5 hrs.	-0.4		-10.2			
cotton dust (29)	mg/m^3 0.3 - 2.0 1 hour			-6.6	-139 (immed. after)	-5.4	-80 (5 hrs after)

[a]Byssinotic

The 1980 harvest illicited a 19% decrease in MEF40%(P) (n=4), whereas the same subjects showed a 40% decrease in MEF40%(P) to the 1979 harvest.

The extent of the response of our naive subjects to bract extracts is nevertheless similar to the finding of others for naive subjects exposed to cotton dust. Compared to a mean decrease in $FEV_{1.0}$ of 7.5% for our subjects Boehleche *et al.* observed a mean 8.5% decrease for his subject population exposed to cotton dust, Rylander *et al.* observed decreases ranging from 0.1 to 8.8% depending on dust concentration. In another study, however, Rylander *et al.* reported a much lower response of -0.4% to dust from unwashed cotton in naive subjects. The same dust induced a much larger response (10.2%) in cotton mill workers and others have found differences in responses between workers with and without byssinotic symptoms.

Purified cotton bract extracts. The sequence of purification steps used for this study involves as a first step the addition of methanol to a solution of the standard crude extract (SCE). A large amount of white precipitate forms composed presumably of proteins and other large molecules. This precipitate is removed by centrifugation. The resulting supernatant solution, after removal of methanol, was tested by inhalation challenge in subjects who responded to the standard crude extract with a 20% or greater decrease in MEF40%(P). This MeOH treated extract (designated 7:1 MeOH extract) induces an airway constrictor response which is 61% that of the standard crude extract (see Table II). The precipitate which forms in the presence of MeOH, when redissolved, contains only 22% of the activity. The second step in the purification sequence is the passage of the MeOH treated extract through an anion exchange column of DEAE-Sephacel. Elution with just water elutes all the constrictor activity from the column. None is bound by the anion-exchanger indicating the airway constrictor agent is not an anion. Left behind on the column are the brownish colored components. The airway constrictor activity of the DEAE eluate is 58% that of the standard crude extract. Thus essentially all the activity of the MeOH treated extract that was applied to the column was eluted.

The above 2 purification steps reduce the weight of the active extract by 3/4 (DEAE=15 mg dry wt/ml vs 60 mg dry wt/ml for the SCE).

In preliminary experiments we have further purified the DEAE eluate by extracting it with ether. The DEAE extract (dissolved in 0.45% NaCl) was shaken vigorously for 3 min. (4°C) with an equal volume of diethyl ether, the layers were separated and ether evaporated under a stream of N_2 from both the aqueous and ether phases, designated DEAE ether extract and ether layer respectively. An ether control was run at the same time using just 0.45% NaCl in place of the DEAE extract. As shown in Table III, extracting with ether had no effect on the airway constrictor activity of the DEAE extract. The percent activity after (97%)

TABLE II

Airway Constrictor Activity of Purified Cotton Bract Extracts

Sample	n[a]	% Airway Constrictor Activity mean ± SEM
7:1 MeOH Extract	22	61 ± 5
7:1 MeOH Control (No bract extract)	1	0
7:1 MeOH precipitate	6	22 ± 11
DEAE Extract	16	58 ± 8
DEAE Control (No bract extract)	2	0

[a]number of subjects tested with sample

TABLE III

Airway Constrictor Activity of Ether Extracted DEAE Purified Bract Extracts

Sample	n[a]	ΔMEF40%(P) 90 - 0 min exposure mean ± SEM ml/sec	%	% Airway Constrictor Activity[b]
Saline	2	+ 165 ± 165	+10 ± 10	
SCE[c]	3	-1117 ± 292	-33 ± 3	100
DEAE Extract	3	- 940 ± 224	-31 ± 6	94
DEAE Ether Extract	3	- 930 ± 116	-32 ± 4	97
Ether Layer	2	+ 500 ± 221	+24 ± 11	0
Ether Control	3	+ 180 ± 161	+11 ± 10	0

[a]number of subjects tested with sample

[b]$\frac{\Delta MEF40\%(P)_{Purified\ extract}}{\Delta MEF40\%(P)_{SCE}} \times 100$

[c]Standard Crude Extract

the ether extraction was the same as before (94%). No constrictor activity was found in the ether phase nor in the ether control. TLC (see Figure 4) revealed that several fluorescing compounds were removed by the ether. These were tentatively identified by their migration rates. The yellow fluorescent compound with an R_f of 0.60 was identified as lacinilene C methyl ether and it appeared to be completely removed by the ether. Lacinilene C (R_f 0.30, yellow fluorescence) was only partially removed. Scopoletin (R_f 0.42, fluorescence) was not removed.

This finding that removal of lacinilene, in whole or in part, does not decrease the airway constrictor activity of the DEAE extract, and that the ether layer containing these is devoid of activity tentatively suggests that these compounds are not involved with the acute lung function loss of textile workers.

In another preliminary effort we fractionated the DEAE extract as it was eluted from the DEAE column into 3 fractions. The fractions were arbitrarily collected according to the color eluting from the column:fraction 1, colorless, the first volume of 20 ml; fraction 2, yellow and red the next 2 volumes; and fraction 3, faint pink, the next 5 volumes. Fraction 2 contains the bulk of the dry weight, 13.7 mg dry weight/ml, fractions 1 and 3 contain only 0.45 mg/ml and 1.06 mg/ml respectively. Table IV shows that fraction 2 is the only fraction with airway constricting activity, neither fraction 1 eluting before, nor fraction 3 eluting after caused airway constriction. This fractionation procedure did not improve by much the purity of the constricting agent(s), however it showed that constrictor activity is associated with a specific fraction from the bract extract. It is, therefore, unlikely that the MEF40%(P) decreases we observe are due to laboratory contamination for example by bacterial endotoxin. Endotoxin is present on cotton bracts as they are harvested from the field and it has been postulated as a causative agent in byssinosis, but others have been unable to detect airway constriction in humans at the concentrations of endotoxin found in cotton dust (18,19). Limulus lysate assays have not yet been completed for our extracts. Several lines of evidence, however, argue against its being present in sufficient quantities in our extracts to cause the acute airway constrictor response observed in our subjects. Our volunteers are naive subjects, never before exposed to cotton dust of any kind. Of the more than 150 subjects (60% of whom are reactors) we exposed to cotton bract on their first session, not one complained of a fever subsequent to inhalation of our standard crude bract extract or to any of the subsequent purified extracts. Fever is the characteristic response of first time exposure to endotoxin (20). Precipitation by methanol is the first step for purification of the airway constrictor agent of cotton bracts used in this study, therefore, presumably any endotoxin present in our

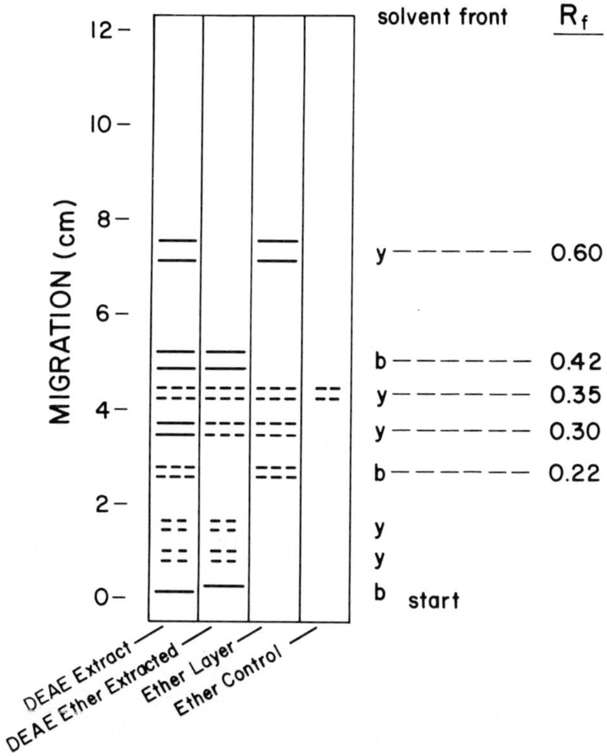

Figure 4. Thin layer chromatogram (TLC) tracing of the DEAE extract extracted with ether and controls on silica gel plates. Developing solvent was chloroform:acetone:formic acid (80:19:1). Plate was viewed under UV light. Equal concentrations of each sample were applied. Key: y, yellow fluorescence; b, blue fluorescence; ——, intense spots; – – –, less intense spots.

TABLE IV

Airway Constrictor Activity of DEAE Fractions of Bract Extracts

Sample	n[a]	ΔMEF40%(P) 90 - 0 min exposure mean ± SEM ml/sec	%	% Airway Constrictor Activity[b]
SCE[c]	5	-1058 ± 283	-34 ± 6	100
DEAE, Fr# 1	3	- 14 ± 14	+ 4 ± 4	0
DEAE, Fr# 2	5	- 522 ± 95	-24 ± 6	71
DEAE, Fr# 3	3	0 ± 1	+ 3 ± 2	0

[a]number of subjects tested with sample

[b]$\frac{\Delta MEF40\%(P)_{\text{Purified extract}}}{\Delta MEF40\%(P)_{\text{SCE}}} \times 100$

[c]Standart Crude Extract

standard crude bract extract would be precipitated and eliminated at this step. Methanol precipitation of endotoxins is a routine procedure for their purification (21). Endotoxins have a net negative charge (21) and would be expected to bind the DEAE-Sephacel column, whereas the airway constricting components in our purified DEAE extract are uncharged and are not bound by DEAE-Sephacel. In addition, we showed previously (2) that the agent in bract extracts which induces the acute lung function loss is of small molecular weight (< 1,000 daltons). This is in contrast to endotoxin which is a large molecule. Whether or not sublevels of endotoxin may play a synergestic role with other bract components is not known.

In addition to its small molecular weight and neutral charge, characteristics (previously shown (22)) of the airway constrictor agent(s) in our bract extracts include, a stability to heat (80°C, ½ hr), and acid (HCl, pH 2.0, 23°C, ½ hr) and alkali (NaOH, pH 12.0, 23°C, ½ hr). Constrictor activity is not destroyed by proteolytic enzymes papain or protease. The active constrictor agent(s) is highly soluble in water, less soluble in organic solvents such as methanol. Active extracts contain glucose (23) and possibly other hexoses and amino nitrogen. Chemical identification will require further purification and characterization. The precise role of the bract airway constrictor agent(s) in the disease state must await knowledge about the link between the acute and chronic phases of byssinosis.

Acknowledgments

We thank R.V. Baker and C. Brown (Lubbock, Texas) who supervised the collection of cotton bracts by members of Boy Scout Troop 103. This work was in part supported by the Physiology Institute, University of Utrecht, Utrecht, The Netherlands, and Cotton, Inc.

Literature Cited

1. Morey, P.R.; Sasser, P.E.; Bethea, R.N.; Kopetysky, M.T. Am. Ind. Hyg. Assoc. J. 1976, 37, 407-12.
2. Buck, M.G.; Bouhuys, A. Lung 1980, 158, 25-32.
3. Bouhuys, A.; Nicholls, P.J.; "Inhaled Particles and Vapors II" : Davies, C.N., Ed.; Paragmon Press: London, 1966: p77-84.
4. Bouhuys, A.; Jonsson, R.; Lichtnecker, S.; Lindell, S.E.; Lundgren, Lundin, C.; Ringquist, T.R. Clin Sci 1960, 19, 79-94.
5. Ainsworth, S.K.; Neuman, R.E.; Harley, R.A. Br. J. Ind. Med. 1979, 36, 35-42.
6. Elissalde, M.H.; Greenblatt, G.A.; Ziprin, Richard L. Am. Ind. Hyg. Assoc. J. 1980, 41, 382-4.
7. Rylander, Ragnar Chest 1981, 79, 34S-38S.

8. Stipanovic, R.O.; Wakelyn, P.J.; Bell, A.A. Phytochemistry 1975, 14, 1041-3.
9. Mohammed, Y.S.; Gazzar, R.M. El; Adamygva, K. Carbohydr. Res. 1971, 20, 431-5.
10. Evans, E.; Nicholls, P.J. J. Pharm Pharmacol 1974, 26 (Suppl). 115P-116P.
11. Bouhuys, A.; Lindell, S.E. Experientia 1961, 17, 211-15.
12. Kilburn, K.H.; McCormick, J.P.; Schafer T.R.; Thurston, R.J.; McKenzie, W.N. Proc. 1977 Beltwide Cotton Prod. Res. Conf. 1977, p 66.
13. Rylander, R.; Nordstrand, A. Br. J. Ind. Med. 1974, 31, 220-3.
14. Greenblatt, G.A.; Ziprin, R.L. Am. Ind. Hyg. Assoc. J. 1979, 40, 860-5.
15. Bouhuys, A.; Hunt, V.R.; Kim, B.M.; Zapletal, A. J. Clin. Invest. 1969, 48, 1159-68.
16. Bouhuys, A.; Mitchell, C.A.; Schilling, R.S.F.; Zuskin, E. Trans. N.Y. Acad. Sci. 1973, 35, 537-46.
17. Virgulto, J.; Bouhuys, A. J. Appl. Physiol. 1973, 35, 145-7.
18. Cavagna, G.; Foa, V.; Vigliani, E.C. Brit. J. Industr. Med. 1969, 26, 314-21.
19. Antweiler, H. Brit. J. Industr. Med. 1961, 18, 130-2.
20. Bradley, S.G. Ann. Rev. Microbiol. 1979, 33, 67-94.
21. Lüderitz, Otto; Galanos, C.; Lehmann, V.; Mayer, H.; Rietschel, E.T.; Weckesser, J. Naturwissenschaften 1978, 65, 578-85.
22. Buck, M.; Bouhuys, A. Chest 1981, 79, 43S-49S.
23. Shaick, F.van; Buck, M.; unpublished results.
24. Hamilton, J.D.; Halprin, G.M.; Kilburn, K.H.; Merchant, J.A.; Ujda, J.R. Arch Environ Health 1973, 26, 118-24.
25. Boehlecke, B.; Cocke, J.; Bragge, K.; Hancock, J.; Petsonk, E.; Piccirillo, R.; Merchant, J. Chest 1981, 79, 77S-81S.
26. Rylander, R.; Haylind, P. Proc. 1981 Beltwide Cotton Prod. Res. Conf. 1981, p 114-15.
27. Rylander, R.; Imbus, H.R.; Suh, M.W. Brit. J. Industr. Med. 1979, 36, 299-304.
28. Rylander, R. Chest 1981, 79, 34S-38S.
29. Battigelli, M.C.; Berni, R.J.; Sasser, P.E.; Symons, M.J. Chest 1981, 79, 86S-90S.

RECEIVED December 15, 1981.

13

Cotton Dust Exposure and Chronic Respiratory Impairment: An Epidemiological Controversy

MARIO C. BATTIGELLI

University of North Carolina, School of Medicine, Division of Pulmonary Medicine, Chapel Hill, NC 27514

In contrast to the documented effect of cotton dust on acute responses, the causation of chronic respiratory effects in occupationally exposed subjects has not been established. The OSHA cotton dust standard is based on the premise that sustained exposure may result in chronic respiratory problems. To test this hypothesis, the pertinent literature is reviewed and discussed in an attempt to decide if convincing epidemiological documentation exists to support a cause and effect connection between prolonged dust exposure and chronic respiratory impairment. There appears to be a need for additional studies to clarify this important aspect of occupational medicine.

With the promulgation of the OSHA mandatory standards for exposure to cotton dust (1), it is now assumed that prolonged exposure to cotton dust is a cause of chronic respiratory effects. Thus, there seems to have been a straightforward interpretation of complex and conflicting medical literature. This paper presents a review of the literature with emphasis on cause and effect relationship consistent with reported epidemiological data.

Historical

Let it be noted that the term byssinosis does not appear in any of the early writings. This term was introduced by L.H. Hirt in 1871 with a vague description of the dust effects on the pulmonary organ (2). Initiating a tradition of equivocations and errors which will keep recurring in the literature of byssinosis with perplexing regularity, the spelling edited by Hirt read "pneumoconiosis lyssinotica". A.A. Proust, the father of Marcel the novelist, spotted the error and provided the correction in 1877 (3). Proust, in fact,

0097-6156/82/0189-0203$6.00/0

did not offer a detailed description of the pathology attending dust exposure in textile mills and his succinct writing suggest that he had not seen any instance of this occurrence, a fact to be repeated later in the experience of many. To judge from Hirt's choice of classifying byssinosis among the pneumoconioses, lesions with prominent morphological derangements, one would conclude that this author expected obvious scarring of the lung associated with dust deposition, a view which has been largely dismissed by authoritative reporters (4, 5). Sir Thomas Oliver introduced this term in the medical literature in English language, again relating cotton disorder to pneumoconioses, and again providing no clear description of its pathology (6).

Epidemiology: U.K.

Since the early 1940s England and Wales have recognized byssinosis in their compensation scheme. The definition of the compensable disorder, however, has not been clearly given by any of the successive statements regulating this aspect of the British legislative provisions.

Even today, an official definition of the disorder, of adequate and detailed diagnostic value, is not given in any official documents. The relevant governmental literature repeats the conclusions of the H.M.H. Report of 1932 (7, 8) where a three stage clinical description is presented as the conclusion of rather conflicting and uncontrolled observations. It is widely recognized that the current interest in the health effects of cotton dust inhalation stems from the writing of Schilling (9 - 15). Schilling's studies, which have been gathered in the U.K., shed no light on the evolution of byssinosis from an acute to a chronic respiratory ailment.

Fox et al., examined 2556 cotton workers, processed by questionnaire and spirometry (16). A subset of these was examined in a similar fashion, on two distinct occasions, over a span of about two years. A gradient loss of spirometric performance seems to distinguish the workers exposed to cotton dust from those not exposed (control). An additional publication by the same authors comments on the relationship of the dust levels on the respiratory effect (17). The paper concludes in denying an effect of dustiness, in cotton exposure, on the frequency of bronchitis.

Fox et al., proceed, however, to describe a dose-effect relationship, in spite of the fact that the dust levels available to these authors were not prospective. They use levels of dustiness measured at the time of the survey. It should be stressed that the effect related by this curve does not include chronic or irreversible disorder, since the plot is based exclusively on reversible effects. Furthermore, the suggestion of a cumulative effect, which would appear supported by a frequency somehow proportioned to duration of employment (i.e., seniority), may not be justified.

These "effects", in fact, include sporadic manifestations, susceptible to secular trends in that the longer the tenure, the more likely the sporadic effect may be experienced.

Consistent with this observation is the fact, perhaps, that in the British experience, to date, chronic bronchitis is not compensable under the jurisdiction of the byssinosis scheme. The British Ministry of Pensions has issued a statement denying occupational significance to chronic bronchitis occurring in textile workers (18).

In cooperation with the Medical Inspectorate, investigators of the University of Manchester, Department of Occupational Health, conducted a similar survey, incorporating 1359 workers from 14 mills processing cotton goods, contrasted with 227 workers from two man-made fiber mills (19). This publication verifies the substantial frequency of acute respiratory complaints elicited by cotton dust inhalation, but the frequency of bronchitis does not seem to differentiate cotton workers from the man-made operatives. In a further communication the rate of decline of the ventilatory function is reported with observations covering a period of about three years (20). The mean decline for 595 cotton workers was 54 ml/year, differing from the mean of 32 ml/year observed in workers from the man-made fibers. Such a contrast would support the statement that exposure to cotton dust causes a more rapid decline in ventilatory function than exposure to a dusty ambient of different nature. However, the validity of this conclusion is questioned by the authors themselves. The lower yearly loss found in the control population results from the mean of two different values, one of which, observed in one of the two mills processing synthetic fibers, is undistinguishable from that of cotton workers.

Additional considerations further limit the support of these data in favor of a chronic effect on the respiratory health by the exposure to cotton dust. The annual decline of the FEV, the parameter taken as an index of ventilatory function, cannot be related to symptoms of bronchitis or of byssinosis, nor to current dust level (dust measurements obtained at the time of the survey). The prevalence of bronchitis appears related to years of exposure in women but not in men. Frequency of byssinosis (acute ventilatory discomfort) appears related to years of exposure (i.e., employment) in women, but not clearly in men. The separation of workers in respective groups of high and low exposure results somewhat meaningful for women but not for men. Altogether it seems that important selection factors, of uncontrolled nature, are influencing these different groups of workers, invalidating a straight-forward comparison.

Epidemiological Studies: U.S.

Two major sets of publications describe the experience in the United States. The first reports observations obtained on a group of textile workers (the exposed group) from cotton processing mills in North Carolina (21, 22). The other stems from studies which have contrasted textile workers from South Carolina with an eterogeneous group of "control adults" obtained in Connecticut and elsewhere (23).

North Carolina. In North Carolina the survey was conducted on the population of 22 textile mills, which included a number of cotton workers, the exposed group, compared to workers from departments processing synthetic-wool material, used as a control. (It is regretted that the published data do not present a precise estimate of the numbers of workers eventually analyzed since the tabulation totals are inconsistent and/or conflicting.)

The methods of survey consisted of questionnaire, spirometry and dust measurements. A major shortcoming of this survey is identifiable in the choice of the questionnaire. This instrument differs significantly from that introduced by the British investigators, missing the important qualifier on upper respiratory infections (question #8 of the MRC questionnaire). The diagnostic question on byssinosis is formulated in such a manner that the characteristic periodicity of the disorder is reduced to occurrences of sporadic frequency (once a year?). Most disturbing is the absence of report (and tabulation) of byssinosis grade 3 of the Schilling scheme (see ref. 37), a feature of this disorder which has been emphasized by international panels, as the possible epitome of the disabling phase of byssinosis. The mean differences in FEV between "exposed" and control groups amount to, at most, a 7 percent value, a gradient which can be hardly taken as significant index of impairment. Finally, dust exposure parameters are computed exclusively as dustiness at the time of the survey, irrespective of duration of exposure. Exposure measured in this format, in inhalation toxicology, particularly when chronic effects are sought, remains practically meaningless. Yet an entire paper is devoted to an elaborate analysis of dust effects, using current dustiness as the sole indicator of exposure (22). Frequency of chronic effects, such as dyspnea, obstructive disorders or even byssinosis grade 3 is not adequately documented in any representative sample.

South Carolina. Under the authorship of investigators from Yale, a group of publications have appeared, receiving a great deal of attention in the United States (23, 24, 25). Major deficiencies, regretfully, limit the informative value of these papers. Fundamentally the respective denominators wherefrom the samples studied derive, are largely unknown in number and composition. The selection of samples is obtained in a highly eterogeneous fashion, mixing members from one source (i.e., industrial files) with others recruited by words of mouth, etc. (23). The results reported amply confirm the perplexity suggested by the unorthodox methods. Frequency of dyspnea in older control subjects is zero in male nonsmokers and in female smokers. Among the exposed workers, frequency of symptoms is greater in younger workers than in older ones of corresponding smoking categories. The limitations of this study could be summarized with the comments reserved for selection biases by Feinstein (26).

Additional Observations

Spanish Hemp Workers. Data collected on hemp workers have been offered in support of chronic respiratory effects associated with cotton dust exposure. Historically, hemp workers constituted the first group to call medical attention to their respiratory effects (27). More recent studies done on hemp workers, however, suggest similar limitations of methodology as mentioned above. The recruitment of subjects leaves much perplexity about the representative character of the group, when the source population is not accounted or even remotely described (28, 29, 30). The exposure length is not assessed (some of the workers have less than two years tenure) and/or the status of "retirement" is used uncritically as an index of exposure (29, 30). The control group, chosen merely out of logistic convenience from farms and factories nearby, is pruned out of those workers with worst respiratory performance, under the "presumption" of being former hemp workers (30). Again, the criticism of Feinstein on arbitrary and unacceptable selection criteria is applicable to these data.

Further American Surveys of Textile Operatives. A study obtained on 470 employees of cotton mills, carefully processed with functional testing by body plethysmograph and with questionnaire was reported by Bradford and Ingram in Georgia in 1977 (31). The survey includes all the workers of the opening, picking, and carding divisions of the plants examined, in addition to workers from a rug manufacture. Multiple analysis of variance, based on dustiness, smoking history and length of employment, failed to detect major differences between exposed and control groups, in terms of spirometry or frequency of bronchitis. Significant differences, similarly, were not found when the workers were categorized according to their position in the processing of cotton (more dusty versus less dusty jobs). Only minor effects were identified within the interaction of smoking and cotton dust, on the basis of small airways function (density dependent compliance).

A survey of 486 textile workers, from three cotton mills and one man-made fibers plant, was completed by investigators of Tulane Medical School (32). Measurements of dust, of respiratory symptoms by the Schilling questionnaire and of ventilatory function were analyzed for correlation. The results indicated that current dust exposure and length of employment did not appear to influence the frequency of complaints, for byssinosis, at all grades. A mill factor, seemingly depending on variables differing from dust intensity or industrial process per se, emerged as probably significant. Baseline levels of pulmonary function did not correlate with dust levels or job position. In the same survey, frequency of chronic bronchitis in the exposed population did not result in excess over the expected value for the population studied (33).

A further study of 956 textile workers was obtained by Morgan in three mills in Georgia and North Carolina (34). Here again the tools of investigation consisted of a questionnaire (MRC modified by Schilling) and spirometry. The conclusions of the survey stressed that respiratory impairment was not particularly common among the workers exposed, nor that its prevalence differed between workers of diverging dust exposure. The author stated that "stringent proposed standard for cotton is unlikely to make a significant contribution to the prevention of respiratory disease".

Mortality Data

Although it is generally accepted that mortality data are not sensitive indicators of morbidity factors, a consistent or significant effect of cotton exposure on health should display some manifestations in mortality indices. This is certainly not the case for textile workers. To date, every effort devoted to the identification of a measurable influence of textile work on the mortality of its own operatives has failed to show any effect (35-38). Paradoxically, one of these surveys has concluded that more favorable mortality experience appears to characterize textile workers (38).

Frequency of Chronic Non Specific Lung Disorder in the U.S.

Part of the difficulty met in establishing the causative relationship between cotton dust exposure and chronic lung disorders (CNSPD)* stems from the very substantial frequency of these which occurs in the adult population in the United States. The occurrence of disabling dyspnea, for instance, is given with a frequency of 14.5 percent in the Anglo-white population surveyed in Arizona (39). The frequency of wheezing, present on most days of the year, is reported at 11.9 percent in Arizona and 9.9 percent in New Hampshire (39). Every survey carried out with proper methodology and incorporating an adequate number of subjects has converged in stressing the elevated frequency of chronic obstructive disorders. It should be noted accordingly that these frequencies, commonly occurring in the U.S., in the general population are compatible with those obtained in surveys of textile population. In certain population groups, not

*Chronic non-specific disorders, namely chronic bronchitis and emphysema.

distinguishable for dusty occupation, the frequency of productive cough (i.e., bronchitis) may exceed the value of 50% in adults (41). Frequencies of this magnitude, reported from the general population, are quite compatible with the analogous maxima observed in textile workers (i.e., 59% in workers 45 and older, reported by Bouhuys (23)).

Table I displays some results obtained by major surveys recently completed in the United States. Particularly when we consider the frequencies characterizing cigarette smokers, the numbers reported from the textile populations, displayed as evidence of the chronic effects of cotton dust, assume a new and sobering meaning.

TABLE I (39, 40)

Prevalence of Chronic Non-Specific Respiratory Diseases (%)

(Adults Age Adjusted)

	New Hampshire	Arizona	Michigan[a]
Males			
Non-smoker	12.8	21.6	11.9
Ex-smoker	20.6	42.2	11.3
Smoker	46.6	56.2	32
Total	33.3	42.4	--
Females			
Non-smoker	12.2	26.0	10.1
Ex-smoker	12.9	31.3	23.3
Smoker	27.1	46.8	18.1
Total	17.2	33.7	--

[a]The Michigan data include only chronic bronchitis and asthma, age 25-64.

An important consideration is due to certain factors which have been identified in the causation of these disorders and which are often neglected by commentators, namely the socio-economic determinants of chronic respiratory disorders (40, 42, 43). Differences of large magnitude underscore much higher mortality for the lower socio-economical classes, in respect to better economy groups, in men and women. Morbidity figures are similarly affected, with disproportional frequencies encountered in the lower economy groups, at about every indicator used. Although we do not understand entirely the specific origin of such risks, these important and conspicuous features should be carefully accounted for, before we either accept or dismiss occupational causes of lung pathology.

For these reasons, the assessment of lung morbidity (CNSPD)* in the textile population requires careful and painstaking methodologies, lest we end up with results that are not meaningful or informative. Careful design and adequate measurements, incorporating information on tenure, dust exposure and progression of respiratory disorder are not available to date for the textile population in the United States.

Conclusions

The review of published epidemiological data suggest that chronic respiratory effects have not been adequately documented for workers exposed to cotton dust. Chronic respiratory disorders are common in both the general and textile population. Because of many confounding factors (smoking, etc.), epidemiological surveys of cotton exposed workers require an adequate and unbiased data base, ideally obtained with a prospective approach, to verify the existence of a chronic effect. At variance with current opinion, a prudent assessment of the literature would, at worst, suggest a probable chronic respiratory effect of very limited degree.

These remarks are not intended as a deterrent against control measures, which are readily justified by the documented occurrence of acute ventilatory effects. It is suggested, however, that sufficient data do not exist to warrant extrapolation of existing epidemiological observations to chronic effect conclusions. Additional studies are recommended prior to such conclusions.

LITERATURE CITED

1. Federal Register 1978, 43, 27350-418.
2. Hirt, L. "Die Krankheiten der Arbeiter": Vol 1, Part 1; Hirt, Breslau, 1871, p 57.
3. Proust, A.A. "Traité d'Hygiène Publique et Priveé:; G. Masson: Paris, 1877, p 171.
4. Pratt, P.C.: Vollmer, R.T.; Miller, J.A. Arch. Env. Health 1980, 35, 133-8.
5. Landis, H.R.M. J. Industr. Hyg. 1925, 7, 1-5.
6. Oliver, T. "Dangerous Trades:; Murray: London; 1902; p 273.
7. Dpt. of Health & Social Security, "Pneumoconiosis and Allied Occupational Chest Diseases", H.M.S.O., London, 1967.
8. Byssinosis, Guidance Note M.S. 9, Health & Safety Executive, London, Dec. 1977.

9. Schilling, R.S.F.; Vigliani E.C.; Lammers B.; Valic F.; Gilson J.C. Proc. XVI Inter. Congr. Occ. Health, Madrid, Sept. 3, Excerpta Medica Found., Amsterdam, 1963, 2, p 137-45.
10. Schilling, R.S.F.; Hughes J.P.W.; Dingwall-Fordyce I. 1955, Brit. Med. J., i, 65-8.
11. Schilling, R.S.F., Brit. Med. Bull. 1950, 2, 52-6.
12. Schilling, R.S.F.; Hughes J.P.W.; Dingwall-Fordyce I.; Gilson J.C. Brit. J. Industr. Med. 1955, 12, 217-27.
13. Schilling, R.S.F., Lancet 1956, ii, 261-65.
14. Schilling, R.S.F., J. Occup. Med. 1959, 1, 33-8.
15. Rooke, G.B., personal communication.
16. Fox, A.J.; Tombleson J.B.L.; Watt A.; Wilkie A.G. Brit. J. Industr. Med. 1973, 30, 42-7.
17. Fox, A.J.; Tombleson J.B.L.; Watt A.; Wilkie A.G. Brit. J. Industr. Med. 1973, 30, 48-53.
18. Report on an Enquiry into the Incidence of Incapacity for Work, Ministry of Pensions & National Insurance, Part 2, #76-17-2, H.M.S.O., London, 1965.
19. Berry, G.; McKerrow C.B.; Molineux M.K.B.; Rossiter C.E.; Tombleson J.B.L. 1973, Brit. J. Industr. Med., 30, 25-36.
20. Berry, G.; Molineux M.K.B.; Tombleson, J.B.L. Brit. J. Industr. Med. 1974, 31, 18-27.
21. Merchant, J.A.; Lumsden J.C.; Kilburn K.H.; O'Fallon W.M.; Ujda J.R.; Germino V.H. Jr.; Hamilton J.D. J. Occup. Med. 1973, 15, 212-21.
22. Merchant, J.A.; Lumsden J.C.; Kilburn K.H.; O'Fallon W.M.; Ujda J.R.; Germino V.H. Jr.; Hamilton J.D. J. Occup. Med.
23. Bouhuys, A.; Shoenberg J.B.; Beck G.J.; Schilling R.S.F. Lung 1977, 154, 167-86.
24. Mitchell, C.A.; Schilling R.S.F.; Bouhuys A. Am. J. Epidem. 1976, 103, 212-25.
25. Bouhuys, A.; Beck G.J.; Schoenberg J.B. Yale J. Biol. Med. 1979, 52, 191-210.
26. Feinstein, A.R. Clin. Pharm. Ther. 1971, 12, 134-50.
27. Ramazzini, B. "De Morbis Artificum Diatriba"; W.C. Wright transl.; U. of Chicago Press: Chicago, 1940; p 257-61.
28. Bouhuys, A.; Barbero A.; Lindell S.E.; Roach S.A. Schilling R.S.F. Arch. Env. Health 1967, 14, 533-44.
29. Bouhuys, A.; Barbero A.; Schilling R.S.F. Am. J. Med. 1969, 46, 526-37.
30. Bouhuys, A.; Zuskin E. Ann. Int. Med. 1976, 34, 398-406.
31. Bradford, J.M.; Ingram R. Symposium on Grain Dust and Health, Saskatoon, Canada 1977, Nov. 7-9.
32. Jones, R.N.; Diem J.E.; Glindmeyer H.; Dharmajan V.; Hammad Y.Y.; Carr J.; Weill H. Brit. J. Industr. Med. 1979, 36, 305-13.

33. Brown Lung, Hearing before the Subcommittee of the Commission on Appropriation, U.S. Senate, 95th Congress, U.S. Gvt. Print. Office, Washington, D.C., 1978, pp 233-77.
34. Morgan, K.C. Statement presented at the Hearings on proposed cotton Standard, Washington, D.C., April 1977, (Mimeograph).
35. Daum, S. Cotton Dust Proc. Atlanta, Ga., 1974, Nov. 12-14, Am. Conf. Gvt. Ind., 1975.
36. Berry, G. Chest (Suppl.) 1981, 79, 11-15.
37. Merchant, J.; Ortmeyer, C. Chest (Suppl.) 1981, 79, 6-11.
38. Henderson, V.; Enterline P.E. J. Occup. Med. 1973, 15, 717-19.
39. Lebowitz, M.D.; Knudson R.J.; Burrows B. Am. J. Epid. 1975, 102, 137-52.
40. Higgins, M.W.; Keller J.B.; Metzner H.L. Am. Rev. Resp. Dis. 1977, 116, 403-10.
41. Lebowitz, M.D. Am. Rev. Resp. Dis. 1981, 123, 16-19.
42. Mueller, R.E.; Kelble D.L.; Plummer J.; Walker S.H. Am. Rev. Resp. Dis. 1971, 103, 209-28.
43. Gilson, J.C., Proc. Roy. Soc. Med., 63, 857-64, 1970.

RECEIVED February 19, 1982.

14

Some Possible Relations of Fungi in Cotton Fiber to Byssinosis

PAUL B. MARSH

U.S. Department of Agriculture, Agricultural Research Service
Biological Waste Management and Organic Resources Laboratory, Beltsville, MD 20705

MARION E. SIMPSON

U.S Department of Agriculture, Agricultural Research Service, Ruminant Nutrition Laboratory, Beltsville, MD 20705

Cladosporium herbarum and Alternaria sp., fungi well known for their occurrence as spores in outdoor air and also well known to physicians as causative agents of asthma, originate mainly from dead vegetation in fields but also grow on U.S. cotton fiber in preharvest weathering and enter cotton mills as common contaminants in most bales. The suspect role of bacteria as causative agents of acute byssinosis is considered plausible but fungi are also suggested as possible contributory causative agents.

Dust in the air of a mill engaged in the mechanical processing of cotton, flax, hemp, or certain other natural fibers is generally agreed to cause byssinosis (1-4). No specific causative agent of byssinosis in the dust, however, has yet been unequivocally identified (5). Certain bacteria dispersed from cotton fiber or bracts into mill air have been suggested to be a probable cause.

Cinkotai, Lockwood, and Rylander (6) measured levels of bacteria in the air of seven cotton spinning mills and five other types of mills in parallel with the use of a questionnaire to determine prevalence of byssinotic symptoms among workers and found that symptom prevalence exhibited high correlations with bacterial levels. Subsequently, Cinkotai and Whitaker (7) reported on the basis of tests involving over 1000 workers in 21 cotton spinning mills that prevalence of byssinotic symptoms again correlated significantly with the levels of bacteria in the air.

In a study involving over 5000 workers in 23 U.S. cotton spinning mills, Rylander, Imbus, and Suh (8) reported statistically significant correlations between dust levels and the decrease in measured lung function (FEV_1) during the work shift, but also noted that the level of correlation improved when bacterial levels in the fiber were included as a variable in the calculations.

From the evidence just cited, bacteria appear to be plausible suspects as a cause of byssinosis. In our view, however, fungi might also bear a causative relation to the disease. Published observations are summarized here which identify the population of fungi most frequently present on cotton fibers with fungi which are very common in outdoor air and which are widely recognized as a cause of asthma. It seems significant that byssinosis is frequently categorized as an "occupational asthma" (9, 10). Bouhuys (11) discusses byssinosis as "scheduled asthma in the textile industry".

Fungi Which Grow Frequently in Commercial Cotton Fiber

When samples of commercial cotton fiber are examined microscopically to detect any fungus growth present, some samples may be found which show little or no evidence of growth but also some are frequently found which do show such evidence. Growth is sometimes seen in the lumen, sometimes along the outer fiber surface, frequently in both positions (12). When present, the growth is almost invariably noted to involve one or more members of a group of fungi consisting of *Alternaria*, *Cladosporium herbarum*, *Fusarium*, *Colletotrichum gossypii*, *Aspergillus niger*, and *Rhizopus stolonifer* (13). Other fungi are relatively rare. The very limited population on weathered cotton contrasts sharply with the great number of fungal types in soils.

Some fungi are found especially in fiber from certain parts of the U.S. Cotton Belt (Table I). This geographical localization appears in certain cases to be related to physiological properties of the fungi involved. Thus, *Colletotrichum gossypii* is a fungus which requires liquid moisture for the dispersal of its spores; it is limited to fiber from the more humid eastern and mid-south parts of the Cotton Belt (13). It causes a plant

Table I

Fungi Found Frequently in U.S. Commercial Cotton Fiber and the Relation of Their Usual Occurrence in Fiber to the Geographical Areas of Cotton Production (13, 14, 15, 17)

Fungus	Areas of frequent occurrence in raw cotton: Southeast	Midsouth	Texas-Oklahoma	Western
Alternaria sp	+	+	+	+
Aspergillus niger	−	−	+	+
Cladosporium herbarum	+	+	+	+
Colletotrichum gossypii	+	+	−	−
Fusarium sp	+	+	+	+
Rhizopus stolonifer	−	−	+	+

disease called "anthracnose" which is localized in the more humid areas of cotton production throughout the world (15, 16). Aspergillus niger and Rhizopus stolonifer, on the other hand, have processes of spore dispersal which are adapted to drier conditions and which can proceed in the absence of liquid water; they tend to be localized in the fiber from the drier Texas-Oklahoma and western parts of the Belt (15). Alternaria, Cladosporium, and Fusarium appear to be more generally present in fiber from across the Cotton Belt. Cladosporium herbarum is frequently designated by the older term "Hormodendrum" in the medical literature.

The frequently observed occurrence of Alternaria, Cladosporium, and Fusarium in U.S. commercial cotton identifies this population with a population noted by Christensen and Kaufmann (18) in field-weathered cereal grains, a group of organisms which these authors report to include Alternaria, Cladosporium, Fusarium, Helminthosporium, and Curvularia, called by them "field fungi". The same authors note that the fungal population observed in similar seeds following damp storage, however, includes many other forms, notably many species of Penicillia and Aspergilli but also many other fungi. These are termed by them "storage fungi". Wallace (19) also indicates in respect to fungi found in cereal grains that: "The major field fungi are species of Alternaria, Cladosporium, and Helminthosporium."

Storage fungi, including many species of Penicillium, many Aspergilli other than A. niger, and many other fungi can grow in raw cotton fiber under experimental conditions in damp storage, but they have seldom been observed by the writers during examination of many samples of commercial cotton fiber over a period of several years; this experience presumably reflects the circumstance that storage moisture levels in baled cotton are generally too low in commercial practice to allow microbial growth.

The fact that the fungal population on dew-retted flax and hemp consists very largely of the same field fungi found on field-weathered cotton fiber was noted earlier; Alternaria and Cladosporium herbarum are prominent (17).

The high frequency of occurrence of Alternaria and Cladosporium as predominant forms growing on senescing leaves of many kinds of plants is described, with citations, by Hudson (20, 21).

None of the fungi observed frequently in field-weathered cotton (Table I) appears to pose any added threat of infection to a cotton millworker. With the exception of Colletotrichum gossypii, all are usually present in the general aerial environment encountered by most people. Rhizopus and other mucoraceous fungi can cause serious infections but these fungi are essentially omnipresent in the environment and infection appears to depend on the predisposed condition of the person rather than on any exceptionally high degree of exposure to the organisms (22). Aspergillus niger can cause annoying growth in the wax of the human ear but again the fungus is ubiquitous (23).

Fungi Present in Outdoor Air

Having noted the similarity of the fungus population in field-weathered cotton fiber to that in dead plant material in the field in general, we now note a striking parallel between the fungal population of field-weathered plants, i.e., the "field fungi" of Christensen and Kaufmann (18), and the dominant fungal forms usually encountered in outdoor air. The reason for this parallel seems evident, namely that most of the fungi in the air come from standing dead vegetation in the fields. Much relevant evidence is summarized, along with citation of original sources, in a book by Gregory entitled "Microbiology of the Atmosphere" (24). This author concludes in respect to fungi in the air that "Species of *Cladosporium* belong to the ubiquitous group. They dominate the daytime spora in temperate regions and in the moist tropics..." Also, "Much of the air spora comes from wild vegetation. ...It is doubtful whether the soil makes a substantial contribution to the fungus spore content of the atmosphere. ...It seems more likely that this air spora is derived predominantly either from moulds, plant pathogens, and other fungi growing on vegetation. ...In the soil, bacteria, Penicillia and Aspergilli predominate, but *Cladosporium* predominates in the air." The very much higher levels of Penicillia and Aspergilli in soil than in outdoor air at the same site is recorded in a paper by Dransfield (25).

The almost universal frequency with which *Alternaria* and *Cladosporium* (*Hormodendrum*) have been reported as dominant organisms in outdoor air throughout the U.S. has been documented by Morrow, Meyer, and Prince (26). A similar conclusion drawn from the literature of many countries is clearly evident from an extensive compilation of air sampling records by Roth (27). From observations on the air-spora in Northern Nigeria, Dransfield (25) reports: "Petri dish trapping over one year yielded records very similar to those in other parts of the world but the tropical genus *Curvularia* replaced *Alternaria*, which is more typical of cooler climates. The genera recorded most frequently were *Cladosporium* (36.8%), *Curvularia* (25.1%), *Fusarium* (8.2%), *Epicoccum* (5.8%), *Nigrospora* (4.3%), and *Pullularia* (4%)." The population of fungal spores in indoor air may be dominated by "storage" fungi in winter, according to Solomon (28).

Fungi That Cause Asthma and "Farmer's Lung"

In further pursuit of a train of observations which eventually relates fungi to pulmonary problems and suggests possible involvement in byssinosis, we note that most physicians concerned with asthma believe that fungus or "mold" spores in out-door air can cause asthmatic attacks in some persons with asthmatic tendencies. Two of the fungi which they cite most frequently as causes of such attacks are Alternaria and Cladosporium (22, p. 454), well known to us for their frequent growth on field-weathered cotton fiber. Such attacks in their patients are often associated by physicians with exposure of the individuals to air at times and in places where high air-borne mold spore levels are thought to have occurred.

A common situation relates to seasonal asthma attacks at the end of the summer when plants in the field have died and consequently become heavily infected with saprophytic fungi, this being followed by abundant release of spores into the air. Sometimes a short cold snap with a freeze which kills a great many plants in a short time may be followed by warmer weather during which infection and luxuriant growth of fungi occur on the dead plants, heavy spore loads are dispersed into the air and asthmatic attacks are common (29). Later, in regions where winters are cold, the fungal growth on the plants decreases greatly or ceases as the temperature drops, release of spores into the air becomes negligible and patients frequently experience a decrease in frequency or cessation of their asthmatic attacks. In a series of collections during winter periods with snow on the ground in Michigan, Solomon (30) never found more than 230 spore particles/cubic meter.

Available evidence on relations of asthmatic attacks in patients to spores in the air is found in a very large number of papers, only a few of which can be cited here (29, 31-40). Austwick (34) has stated "The spores of Cladosporium spp. are probably among the commonest in the outdoor air spora and are known to be associated with respiratory allergy. ...The genus Cladosporium is one of the best known groups of fungi concerned in respiratory allergy." An overview account is presented by Prince and Meyer (41) and many references by Roth (27). Biochemical studies have been reported on Cladosporium allergens by Aukrust (42) and Aukrust and Borch (43) and on Alternaria allergens by Vijay et al. (44).

Direct testing of asthmatic patients with extracts from molds, including Alternaria and Cladosporium (Hormodendrum) has shown that a high percentage of such individuals exhibited positive responses to intradermal and scratch tests of the skin and to inhalant provocation (45, 46). From these tests, along with the known frequency of Alternaria in air, the former investigators concluded in respect to bronchial asthma that: "...in Japan Alternaria is considered to be the most important of the mold allergens." Colen et al. (47) had previously observed prompt decreases in total vital capacity or forced expiratory volume at 1 second in seven seasonal asthma patients following administration of inhalant challenge with fungal antigens.

The subject of possible relation of the acute byssinotic response in a cotton mill to asthma in general and to atopy is one on which there appears to be relatively little information.

Certain investigators, however, have expressed interest in the matter recently. The possibility that a history of asthma may increase the probability of an acute byssinotic reaction to cotton dust is suggested by a paper by Hamilton et al. (48). The senior author of this paper had had asthma as a child. Promptly after exposure to the air in a dusty part of a cotton mill he exhibited pronounced shortness of breath with tightness in the chest and accompanying major temporary decreases in FEV_1 and arterial oxygen tension. The episode is described as "byssinosis". The authors remark: "It is unlikely that many textile workers with an initial response to cotton dust such as the one described here would remain working in dusty areas." Although the authors state that "It is not possible from the present study to conclude that a prior history of atopy confers sensitivity to cotton dust", the present writers were left with the impression that the authors suspect that such may be the case.

Jones et al. (49) also point to a possible connection between atopy and risk of byssinosis. Most but not all persons with extrinsic asthma exhibit atopy (50). From observations on 255 workers in four cottonseed crushing mills, Jones et al. (49) conclude that: "Atopy and exposure to dust were found to have significant interaction: large mean declines in FEV_1 and FEF_{25-75} occurred only in the workers exposed to linter dust who were also atopic." They also state: "These findings point to atopy as a risk factor in the bronchoconstrictor response to cotton dust aerosol, and, by inference, a risk in byssinosis. There is therefore a need to investigate atopy, particularly as that variable may interact with dust exposure, in cotton textile mills." The reader is left with the thought that perhaps "reactors" who exhibit symptoms of acute byssinosis in a cotton mill might be in some sense people who are not obvious asthmatics but who, however, have some minimal or borderline type of asthma or other mildly increased bronchial sensitivity. Merchant et al. (51) tested workshift declines in FEV_1 of workers exposed to cotton dust. In their summary they state: "The patterns of FEV_1 response over a week suggest that there are distinct individual patterns of response not dependent upon previous cotton dust exposure."

Some data from tests on grain-handlers may be relevant. It has been noted among grain handlers in Saskatchewan that this group had a lower proportion of atopic individuals than a matched population of teachers (52). The explanation offered was that persons who accepted and continued work as grain handlers were individuals with a naturally present resistance to the effects of inhaled grain dust. The authors state: "The teachers had a higher incidence of positive prick tests, a higher mean IgE level, and a greater proportion reacting to bronchial provocation tests with histamine and grain dust. ...These studies suggest what must be self-evident, namely that in Saskatchewan individuals who find that they are sensitive to grain dust avoid handling grain."

Mention is made here also of a phenomenon called "farmer's lung" which is associated with the inhalation of spores of actinomycetes and/or fungi, from moldy hay, usually by a farmer in his barn (53) but also by grain handlers exposed to grain which has undergone microbial heating (54). Such incidents, especially if repeated several times, may result in permanent lung impairment causing a person to be unable to undertake physical exertion. Some individuals are highly sensitive, others much less so. The organisms involved include types not known to be common in cotton. It seems conceivable, however, that the lung impairment associated with byssinosis might represent a situation in which damage occurs in small increments over a long period of time but is otherwise similar to the damage in the shorter but presumably more intense exposures in the farmer's lung situation. A review of the farmer's lung phenomenon, considered under the more inclusive term "extrinsic allergic alveolitis", is presented by Hargreave (55).

Summary and Conclusions

It is concluded on the basis of evidence cited here that bacteria are likely suspects in the continuing search for causal agents of byssinosis. It is further concluded, however, on the basis of circumstantial evidence summarized here that cotton fiber-inhabiting fungi may also have a relation to the causative process and that this possibility merits careful examination.

Acknowledgment

The authors thank Dr. James F. Parr for enthusiatic interest and encouragement. They also thank Joanne M. Kla and Ray Fisher for help in locating many of the references cited here.

Literature Cited

1. Bouhuys, A.; Barbero, A.; Schilling, R. S. F.; van de Woestijne, K. P. Am. J. Med. 1969, 46, 526-37.
2. Hunter, D. "The Diseases of Occupations"; Hodder and Stoughton: London, 1975; p. 1225.
3. Merchant, J. A.; Kilburn, K. H.; O'Fallon, W. M.; Hamilton, J. D.; Lumsden, J. C. Ann. Internal Med. 1972, 76, 423-33.
4. Valic, F.; Zuskin, E. Arch. Environ. Health 1971, 23, 359-64.
5. Cooke, T. F. Text. Res. J. 1979, 49, 398-404.
6. Cinkotai, F. F.; Lockwood, M. G.; Rylander, R. Am. Ind. Hyg. Assoc. J. 1977, 38, 554-9.

7. Cinkotai, F. F.; Whitaker, C. J. Ann. Occup. Hyg. 1978, 21, 239-50.
8. Rylander, R.; Imbus, H. R.; Suh, M. W. Brit. J. Ind. Med. 1979, 36, 299-304.
9. Pepys, J.; Davies, R. J. "Allergy: Principles and Practice": Middleton, E., Jr.; Reed, C. E.; Ellis, E. F., Eds.; G. V. Mosby Co.: St. Louis, 1978, p. 812-842.
10. Weill, H. "New Directions in Asthma": Stein, M., Ed.; Am. Coll. of Chest Physicians: Park Ridge, IL., 1975, p. 325-338.
11. Bouhuys, A. Lung 1976, 154, 3-16.
12. Simpson, M. E.; Marsh, P. B. Mycologia 1969, 61, 987-96.
13. Simpson, M. E.; Marsh, P. B.; Filsinger, E. C. Plant Dis. Rep. 1973, 57, 756-9.
14. Simpson, M. E.; Marsh, P. B. Plant Dis. Rep. 1971, 55, 714-8.
15. Simpson, M. E.; Marsh, P. B.; Filsinger, E. C. Plant Dis. Rep. 1973, 58, 828-32.
16. Marsh, P. B.; Simpson, M. E. "Public-Supported Cotton Research: Proceedings of Conference of Collaborators from Southern Agricultural Experiment Stations." USDA (U.S.) 1976, ARS-S-70, p. 22-30.
17. Marsh, P. B.; Bollenbacher, K. Text. Res. J. 1949, 19, 313-24.
18. Christensen, C. M.; Kaufmann, H. H. "Grain Storage: the Role of Fungi in Quality Loss"; Univ. Minnesota Press: Minneapolis, 1969; p. 153.
19. Wallace, H. A. H. "Grain storage: Part of a System": Sinha, R. N.; Muir, W. E., Eds.; AVI Publishing Co.: Westport, CN., 1973, p. 71-98.
20. Hudson, H. J. New Phytol. 1968, 67, 837-74.
21. Hudson, H. J. "Ecology of Leaf Surface Micro-organisms": Preece, T. F.; Dickinson, C. H., Eds.; Academic Press: New York, 1971, p. 447-455.
22. Rippon, J. W. "Medical Mycology. The Pathogenic Fungi and the Pathogenic Actinomycetes"; W. B. Saunders Co.: Philadelphia, 1974; p. 587.
23. Emmons, C. W.; Binford, C. H.; Utz, J. P.; Kwon-Chung, K. J. "Medical Mycology"; Lea & Febiger: Philadelphia, 1977; p. 592.
24. Gregory, P. H. "The Microbiology of the Atmosphere": John Wiley & Sons: New York, 1973; p. 377.
25. Dransfield, M. Trans. Br. Mycol. Soc. 1966, 49, 121-32.
26. Morrow, M. B.; Meyer, G. H.; Prince, H. E. Ann. Allergy 1964, 22, 575-87.
27. Roth, A. "Allergy in the World. A Guide for Physicans and Travelers"; Univ. Press Hawaii: Honolulu, 1978; p. 171.
28. Solomon, W. R. J. Allergy Clin. Immun. 1976, 57, 46-55.
29. Prince, H. E.; Morrow, M. B. Int. Arch. Allergy 1959, 15, 122-40.
30. Solomon, W. R. J. Allergy Clin. Immun. 1975, 56, 235-42.

31. Durham, O. C. "Aerobiology": Moulton, F. R., Ed.; Am. Assoc. Advan. Sci.: Washington, DC, 1942, p. 32-47.
32. Merksamer, D.; Sherman, H. J. Allergy 1958, 29, 60-71.
33. Liebeskind, A. Ann. Allergy 1965, 23, 158-61.
34. Austwick, P. K. C. Colston Papers 1966, 18, 321-37.
35. Goldfarb, A. A. Ann. Allergy 1968, 26, 321-7.
36. Adiseshan, N.; Simpson, J.; Gandevia, B. Aust. N. Z. J. Med. 1971, 4, 385-91.
37. Salvaggio, J.; Seabury, J.; Schoenhardt, E. A. J. Allergy Clin. Immun. 1971, 48, 96-114.
38. Lacey, J.; Pepys, J.; Cross, T. "Safety in Microbiology": Shapton, D. A.; Board, R. G., Eds.; Academic Press: New York, 1972, p. 151-184.
39. Shy, C. M.; Hasselblad, V.; Heiderscheit, L. T.; Cohen, A. A. "Environmental Factors in Respiratory Disease": Lee, D. H. D., Ed.; Academic Press: New York, 1972, p. 229-235.
40. Hobday, J. D.; Stewart, A. J. Aust. N. Z. J. Med. 1973, 3, 552-6.
41. Prince, H. E.; Meyer, G. H. Ann. Allergy 1976, 37, 18-25.
42. Aukrust, L. Int. Archs. Allergy appl. Immun. 1979, 58, 375-90.
43. Aukrust, L.; Borch, S. M. Int. Archs. Allergy appl. Immun. 1979, 60, 68-79.
44. Vijay, H. M.; Huang, H.; Young, N. M.; Bernstein, I. L. Int. Archs. Allergy appl. Immun. 1979, 60, 229-39.
45. Nakayama, Y.; Shimanuki, K.; Uehara, S.; Hirakata, A. Acta Paed. Jap. 1971, 13, 36-43.
46. Chen, C-Y.; Chuang, C-Y. J. Formosan Med. Assoc. 1973, 72, 47-56.
47. Colen, J.; VanArsdel, P. P.; Pasnick, L. J.; Horna, J. D. J. Allergy 1964, 35, 331-8.
48. Hamilton, J. D.; Germino, V. H., Jr.; Merchant, J. A.; Lumsden, J. C.; Kilburn, K. H. Am. Rev. Resp. Dis. 1973, 107, 464-6.
49. Jones, R. N.; Butcher, B. T.; Hammad, Y. Y.; Diem, J. E.; Glindmeyer, H. W., III; Lehrer, S. B.; Hughes, J. M.; Weill, H. Brit. J. Ind. Med. 1980, 37, 141-6.
50. McCarthy, O. R. Brit. J. Dis. Chest 1973, 67, 238-40.
51. Merchant, J. A.; Kilburn, K. H.; O'Fallon, W. M.; Hamilton, J. D.; Lumsden, J. C. Ann. Internal Med. 1972, 76, 423-33.
52. Gerrard, J. W.; Mink, J.; Cheung, S-S C.; Tan, L. K-t.; Dosman, J. A. J. Occup. Med. 1979, 21, 342-6.
53. Haller, R. de; Sutter, F., Eds.: "Aspergillosis and Farmer's Lung in Man and Animal"; Hans Huber Pub.: Bern, 1974, p. 329.
54. Dennis, C. A. R. "Grain Storage: Part of a System": Sinha, R. N.; Muir, W. E., Eds.; AVI Publ. Co.: Westport, CN., 1973, p. 367-387.
55. Hargreave, F. E. Canad. Med. Assoc. J. 1973, 108, 1150-54.

RECEIVED January 20, 1982.

ANALYSIS

15

The Relation of Microorganisms and Microbial Products to Cotton

JANET J. FISCHER

University of North Carolina, School of Medicine, Chapel Hill, NC 27514

Microbial species (fungi, gram negative bacteria, gram positive bacteria, thermophilic bacteria) and many microbial products (including enzymes and endotoxin) have been identified in "cotton" dusts and cotton bract extracts. A selective review of the literature outlines previous data on these microbial factors. Critical evaluation of the older references is attempted but is often impossible due to the absence of methological data. Viable gram negative microorganism counts and endotoxin levels are emphasized because they correlate with pulmonary function change. Data are presented on the levels of these microbial factors in the air of the carding room of mills (52,000 colony forming units of gram negative bacteria/m^3 of air and 1-2 μg of endotoxin/m^3), in the air of a model cardroom (20,000 colony forming units of gram negative bacteria/m^3 of air and 0.1 μg of endotoxin/m^3), and in various plant parts and "cotton" dusts.

Current concern about the relation of dust to pulmonary symptoms in the cotton industry has led to a resurgence of interest in the various constituents of "cotton" dust. As part of an ongoing study of the various factors that may play an etiological role in byssinosis, we have studied the microbial factors (organisms and their products). This review of the pertinent literature is selective and does not purport to be all inclusive. The initial approach was a critical analysis of the data, and this was carried out when possible. Many of the references did not supply enough data about methods to permit a critical evaluation. This is especially true for the data on fungi and gram-positive organisms. The paper concentrates on the counts of viable gram-negative organisms and the content of endotoxin because these correlate best with pulmonary function changes in workers.

0097-6156/82/0189-0225$6.50/0

A number of papers describe the types and quantities of microorganisms and their products in cotton, cotton plant parts and cotton mill dusts (1-37). Prausnitz (1) reported the presence of gram-negative bacteria in british cotton mills in 1936. Neal et al.(2) concluded that gram-negative microorganisms, or their products, caused an acute illness experienced by rural mattress makers. Tuffnell in 1960 (3) did not implicate bacteria as the causal agent of byssinosis. Antweiler in 1961 (4) rejected the gram-negative endotoxin hypothesis. In recent years other investigators have suggested that gram-negative bacteria and their endotoxins are a possible causal agent of byssinosis.

The literature is difficult to interpret because of a number of variables which are listed in Table I and because each reference usually addresses only one aspect of the problem. This review is selective and concentrates on papers where the details of the study method are given.

Table I
Variables Involved

Materials Studied
Raw cotton from
fields
gins
mills before carding
mills after carding
Cotton plant parts
leaf and bracts
seeds
pericarp
Weeds contaminating cotton
Cotton dusts
total airborne dusts
dusts from cardroom floors
dusts from dust filters
dusts from vertical elutriators (airborne respirable <15 μm)
Units of measurement
Media
Handling of specimen is often not listed
Classification of microorganisms
Various types of microorganisms or their products are studied
Animal and human experiments are often included

This paper consists of a review of the literature on microbiological (microorganisms and their products) composition of cotton and cotton dusts, and presentation of some data from our laboratory.

Materials and Methods for Data from our Laboratory

Cultures. On the premise that the materials in extracts of cotton and cotton bracts that led to bronchial constriction were water soluble, saline extract of cottons, dusts, and cotton plant parts were studied. Plant parts are weighed out and pulverized. Dusts are weighed out and suspended in saline and sonicated and vortexed. For airborne dusts, the active material is assumed to be associated with particles of a respirable size. Availability and ease of measurement led to the use of mixed cellulose acetate and nitrate vertical elutriator filters which capture particles <15 μm in size. Comparable counts are obtained with both six stage and two stage Andersen samplers, but the main method of measurement has been with vertical elutriator filters (pore size 0.45 or 0.8 μm) in the model cardroom and in the mills. The filters are extracted in saline and sonicated briefly and vortexed briefly to liberate the material from the fiber. Suitable serial dilutions of filter extract, dust, cotton, or plant parts extracts are made in saline and an aliquot of a milliliter is streaked out on appropriate media. Cultures are made on trypticase soy agar with actidione and incubated at 37°C for total bacterial counts, trypticase soy agar with actidione and vancomycin added and incubated at 25°C for gram-negative microorganism counts, and sabouraud agar with chloramphenicol and salt added and incubated at 25°C for fungi. Trypticase soy agar incubated at 60°C is used for counts of thermophilic organisms. The plates are incubated, colonies counted by colony type, and the results are calculated in cfu/g (colony forming units per gram) for cotton or plant parts and cfu/m^3 (colony forming units per cubic meter of air) for the vertical elutriator filter data.

Endotoxin Content. Specimens of the same types of material are also studied for endotoxin by a modification of the microtiter technique for the *Limulus polyphemus* amoebocyte lysate test. Samples are prepared using endotoxin-free saline or water to extract the material. Serial ten-fold dilutions were used to estimate the end point. This endotoxin-like activity was measured against an *E. coli* endotoxin standard obtained from Mallinckrodt (St. Louis, Missouri). The source of the endotoxin material in the cotton is from many different gram-negative microorganisms and the use of an *E. coli* standard gives only a rough quantitation of the amount present. The microtiter method is a modification of the original *Limulus* test described by Levin and Bang in 1964 and the method permits the detection of endotoxin in concentrations as little as 0.5ng. Twenty microliters of sample extract (or dilution) are added to twenty microliters of *Limulus* amebocyte lysate, in a microtiter plate and incubated at 37°C for sixty minutes and then ten microliters of 0.2% toluidine blue are added and gelation is read by tipping the plates after five minutes. Positive and negative controls are included. Endotoxin-like activity present is estimated per milligram of sample or per cubic meter of filtered air (if vertical elutriator filters are studied).

Overall Picture of Microbial Flora of Dusts

There are large numbers of gram-positive and gram-negative bacteria and fungi in various materials associated with cotton. Table II lists studies giving an overall picture of the microbial (viable organism counts) content of various cotton dusts. A few pertinent references are summarized.

Furness and Maitland (5) in 1952 did not study airborne dust but rather total dust from an air cleaning plant obtained by suction. They reported large numbers of gram-positive and gram-negative bacteria and fungi in this material. Drummon and Hamlin (6, 7) studied the total airborne dust measured by an impinger sampler in a cardroom and found large numbers of soil and water bacteria. Bacteria far outnumbered the fungi found. Oillng of the cotton at the pre-carding stages led to a reduction of fine particles to 40%, viable bacteria to 70%, and the weight of airborne solids to 79% of previous levels. The concentrations of airborne materials were not significantly different between Monday and other days in the week. Hamlin (8) identified the bacteria found in the air of cotton cardrooms in Drummond's initial study. The predominant viable bacteria were *Bacillus* species. Lacey (9) compared total airborne dust counts of particles with microbial counts. Actinomycete spores and bacteria comprised 10% of the particles. Eighty percent were unidentified. Fungal elements comprised 2% of the particles.

Battigelli et al. (10) found large numbers of bacteria, fungi, and thermophilic organisms in the airborne dust of the carding area. Cinkotai et al. (11,12) found large numbers of gram-positive and gram-negative bacteria and endotoxin in the total airborne dust from the cardroom of cotton mills. They interpreted their data to indicate that the prevalence of byssinosis correlated best with the concentration of airborne gram-negative rods and endotoxin and that there was no relationship to fungal counts.

Apparently Fischer (13) is the only investigator studying respirable airborne dust(collected by vertical elutriator, i.e. <15 μm). Cotton mill carding rooms have large numbers of viable gram-positive and gram-negative bacteria and fungi contained in the respirable dust.

Overall Picture of Microbial Flora of Raw Cotton in the Field

The flora of raw cotton in the field is different from that of raw baled cotton. Some data from the literature are summarized in Table III. Field-grown cottons and their plant parts contain many more gram-negative microorganisms and fungi than do greenhouse-grown cottons. The weeds that contaminate the cotton crop

TABLE II
Bacterial and Fungal Counts on Cotton Dust

	Material	Location	Bacteria	Fungi	Thermophilics	Units
Battigelli et al. (10)	airborne dust	cotton cardroom	1020-81460	40-48900	40-3640	cfu/m^3
Cinkotai et al. (11)	"	"	335-3500 (g neg) 4600-76900 (total)	1450-11,500	—	org/m^3
Furness & Maitland (5)	dust sucked up from aircleaning plant	"	millions/g (g pos & g neg)	millions/g	—	
Fischer (13)	respirable airborne	cardroom mills	1300-7000 (g pos) 2500-20,000 (g neg)	200-1200	—	cfu/m^3
Lacey (9)	airborne dust	opening area of all cotton mills	10% of particles	2% of particles	—	particles/m^3
Drummond & Hamlin (6)	airborne dust	cardroom	extraordinarily large numbers	large numbers (not comparable to bacteria)	—	—

TABLE III
Raw Cotton - Microorganisms

Ref.	Material	Bacteria	Fungi
Furness & Maitland (5) Prindle - 1934	freshly collected after storage	non-sporeforming soil org. sporeforming org.	Homodendrum, altemorium, Fusorium, Penicillium & Aspergillus
Heyn - 1957 (36)			
Flemming & Faison	seed cotton	220,000/g	
	gin cotton	1,200,000/g	
	bale cotton	7,000,000/g	
Prindle	raw cotton	37,000-520,000,000/g	
Fischer et al. (14)	cotton plant parts		
	field grown	leaves 34,000-180,000 cfu/mgm	750-1300 cfu/mgm
	greenhouse grown	leaves 13 - 90 cfu/mgm	5-17 cfu/mgm
	field grown cotton	4,300 cfu/mgm	6/1 cfu/mgm
	weeds	up to 8000 cfu/mgm	up to 1100 cfu/mgm
Marsh & Bollenbacher - 1949 (22)	field weathered storage		Altemorium, Clodosporium, Herborium, Fusarium, Aspergillus, Penicillium

contribute significantly to the gram-negative bacterial and fungal flora found in cotton (14). Bracts contribute large numbers of gram-negative microorganisms and comprise a significant amount of the trash in cotton (15). After the first killing freeze, the microorganisms on bract may increase 500 fold. This bract is non-green and contains approximately 500 million gram-negative rods per gram. Also after the first killing freeze, the friability of the bract increases from about 20-30% to 60% of the weight of the material converted into <250μm particulates.

As the cotton becomes poorer in quality, the gram-negative bacterial counts and the endotoxin levels increase markedly in the raw cotton, the hand cleaned fiber, and the leaf-like trash and seed trash that were removed from it (16). Tinged grades of cotton reach gram-negative microorganism counts of at least 150-160 million cfu/g.

Specific Microorganisms or Their Products

Gram-Positive Bacteria. There are large numbers of gram-positive rods in the airborne dust of the carding area whether total or respirable dust is studied. *Bacillus* species predominate (especially *subtilis*, *pumilis*, *cereus*, and *megatherium*) (5,8,13, 17,18). Counts do not correlate with dust levels or with prevalence of byssinosis. Culture filtrates of these organisms do not cause histamine release (13).

Tuffnell in 1960 (19) reported one byssinotic cotton mill worker who reacted to a dust prepared from the leaves and bracts of cotton plants and had a similar reaction (symptoms and a fall in maximal breathing capacity) to mill dust but no reaction to exposure to a dust containing *Bacillus pumilis*. Three byssinotic workers did not react to dusts of gram-positive bacteria or fungi but did react to dust from leaves of cotton plants (19). He concluded that there was no relation between total numbers of bacteria or fungi present in the air and the prevalence of byssinosis.

Fungi. Only a few of the many fungi references (2,3,5,9,10, 11,13,17,19-25) are summarized.

Battigelli et al. (10,17) found that fungi are common contaminants of cotton lint, cotton trash and cotton dust. The most numerous fungi are several varieties of *Aspergillus*. All parts of the plant are contaminated. Bract is often associated with high viable fungal counts. Fungal extracts do not cause significant histamine release from swine lung.

Braun et al. (20) demonstrated a drop in FEV_1. This correlated with fine dust levels and with concentration of chymotrypsin-like enzymes. The main source of these enzymes is said to be fungi, probably *Aspergillus* species. Many fungi are found on cotton plants and are related to degradation of the cotton fiber(22). The fungi found include *Aspergillus*, *Penicillium*, *Mucor* and others.

Cinkotai et al. (11) sampled the total airborne dust (Andersen impactor) in the cardroom of sevel cotton spinning mills and showed 1500 to 11,500 fungi/m^3. Cotton waste mills, a wool mill, and a tea packing factory had similar numbers of fungi while willowing mills had 22,500 fungi/m^3.

Fischer (13) sampled airborne <15 μm (from vertical elutriator filters) dusts in the carding area of mills.

Processing	Fungi (cfu/m^3) in thousands
100% cotton	0.2 - 1.2
50% cotton	0.1 - 1.0
0% cotton	<0.06

The fungi were variable in numbers and in types. Aspergilli included niger, glaucus and versicolor. Penicillium, Hemodendrum, Fusarium, Altenaria, and occasionally Rhizopus were also found. Fungal counts did not correlate with dust levels. Neither fungi or their culture filtrates caused histamine release (swing lung).

Tuffnell (3,19) studied seven workers who were challenged with various dusts. The dust containing A. niger produced no effect in the volunteer who had a drop in maximal breathing capacity when exposed to cotton leaf and bract dust and to mill dust (from cardroom extraction plant filters).

Welty et al. (25) described large numbers of viable fungi isolated (Andersen sampler) from air of a model cardroom. He used only fungal media so comparison with other types of organisms are not meaningful. The fungal species were Aspergillus, repens, A. niger, A. amstelodami, A. versicolor, A. restrictus, and other species of Aspergillus, Cladosporium, Penicillium and other fungi.

Thermophilic and Other Actinomyces. These are present in the air of the model cardroom and in the air of the carding area of mills (3,8,9,13,24,25). The data is very scanty because they are not adequately studied by most authors.

Gram-negative Bacteria. The significant data are summarized in Table IV. Cinkotai et al. (11,12) showed that the prevalence of byssinotic symptoms correlated best with gram-negative rod counts in the total airborne dust from cardrooms of cotton mills. This correlation could be increased by multiplying the bacterial counts by the years of exposure of the worker. These bacteria also correlated with the number of 2-4 μm particles and the amount of protease in the air.

Rylander and Lundholm (26) found the same types of gram-negative bacteria in raw cotton, cotton plant parts, and cotton from blending machines. Rylander et al. (18) found that there was a large increase in the leukocytes in guinea pig lungs after exposure to extracts from cotton and hay and that when different bacterial strains were tested, endotoxin producing strains caused the largest effect. The gram-negative rods constantly present were Enterobacter agglomerans, Pseudomonas syringae, and Agrobacterium. FEV_1 changes of mill workers showed a low correlation with dust levels and on improved correlation with the log number of the gram-negative bacteria cultured from the baled cotton (27,28).

Lundholm and Rylander (29) studied the total airborne dust bacteria in cotton mills in Sweden and in England. A 20% byssinosis prevalence correlated with bacterial counts of 3cfu/L in England and with 51cfu/L in Sweden. Rylander concluded that the ΔFEV_1 correlates best with the square root of the number of gram-negative bacteria per gram in bale cotton multiplied by the dust levels when the cotton is carded.

Neal et al. (2) described a "cotton bacterium" (probably an encapsulated enterobacterial species) that caused illness in rural mattress workers. He also pointed out that stained cottons have large numbers of gram-negative rods.

Fischer (13) studied the model cardroom at North Carolina State and various cotton mills. The gram-negative microorganisms were sampled by vertical elutriator filters to obtain measurements of viable airborne <15 µm bacteria. An Andersen sampler was used for total bacterial counts. The same types of organisms were found in the air of carding and spinning areas of the mill, the air of the model cardroom and in raw cottons. Table IV lists the counts comparing the respirable dusts of the mills and the model cardroom. Fischer showed that the dust levels in the mill cardrooms correlated with the viable airborne gram-negative microorganism count.

Carding Areas of Mills (1977-1978)

Dust mgm/m^3	# of Mills	gram-neg rods (25°C) cfu/m^3 in Thousands
0.10-0.239	8	6.7
0.24-0.40	6	30.5
>0.41	3	52.3

The gram-negative microorganism counts in the respirable dust were usually one log lower in the spinning than in the carding area of the mills. Endotoxin levels in the airborne respirable dust were also one log lower in the spinning than in the carding areas of the mills. The airborne dust levels of endotoxin corre-

TABLE IV
Gram-Negative Bacteria

Ref.	Material	Source	Counts	Organisms commonly found
Cinkotai et al. (11,12)	airborne dust	cardrooms of mills	1550-3500 (one volume 335)	Achromobacter Flavobacterium Aerobacter
Rylander & Lundholm (26)	waste cotton	cotton card	up to 10^8/g	Enterobacter agglomerans Pseudomonas syringae Agrobacterium species
Lundholm & Rylander (29)	airborne dust	cardroom		
		England	10cfu/L	
		Sweden	58cfu/L	
Neal et al. (2)	stained cotton	mattress factory	840,000,000/g	
	high grade cotton		13,000/g and 110,000/g	
	low grade cotton		79,000,000/g	
Fischer (13)	airborne respirable dust			
	a) model cardroom processing			
	100% cotton		52,000cfu/m^3	
	50% cotton		25,000cfu/m^3	
	0% cotton		490cfu/m^3	
	b) mills - processing			
	100% cotton		2500-20,000cfu/m^3	
	50% cotton		200-6000cfu/m^3	
	0% cotton		<60cfu/m^3	

lated roughly with the numbers of gram-negative microorganisms (13). Table V gives logs of gram-negative organisms, endotoxin levels, dust concentrations, ΔFEV_1, and percent of total cotton that is from the Memphis classing office for individual mills(30).

TABLE V
Carding - Individual Mills

cfu/m^3 of gram neg rods at 25°C means of logs	LPS ng/m^3	Dust mgm/m^3	ΔFEV_1 ml	% of Total Memphis
5.04	16.9	1.185	-61.0	75.0
4.59	1.6	0.309	-74.0	53.0
4.12	22.5	0.532	-45.4	100.0
4.06	135.0	0.384	-14.9	70.5
3.62	1.3	0.093	-32.8	35.0
3.35	11.9	0.194	-32.8	25.0
3.19	1.5	0.086	-54.0	38.3
2.62	0.8	0.104	- 5.0	17.5
≤2.60	0.2	0.609	+11.1	0.0

The airborne respirable gram negative rods in the mills varied with the percent cotton being processed and correlated well with the percent Memphis cotton being processed, and the dust level in mgm/m^3 and roughly with the grade of cotton being processed. For viable gram-negative rod counts $>10^3$ cfu/m^3 (i.e. > log 3) there is an inverse relationship to ΔFEV_1. For counts $<10^3$ cfu/m^3 of viable gram-negative rods, the ΔFEV_1 shows no appreciable change. The endotoxin levels are very variable but show a trend toward decreased values when the gram negative counts are low and when there are smaller changes in ΔFEV_1. Several attempts were made to modify the cotton being processed in the model cardroom and ascertain the resultant change in gram-negative rods and endotoxin in the airborne respirable dust. When blends of cotton and polyester were processed (see Table VI below), counts of gram-negative rods both on the lint and in the airborne respirable dust increased proportionately to the percent cotton in the blend. Dust levels also correlated with percent cotton in the blend (13).

TABLE VI
Cotton/Polyester Study

Blend[a]	gm negative rods		Lint[c]	Dust[d]
	Filters[b]	Andersen[b]		
0/100	0.49	2.6	14	.111
20/80	2.8	12	373	.160
40/60	6.4	38	600	.194
60/40	25.5	15	1230	.294
80/20	29	52	5350	.302
100/0	52	84	1900	.298

[a]percent cotton/percent polyester
[b]cfu/m^3 in thousands
[c]cfu/mgm in thousands
[d]mgm/m^3

Table VII shows the result of washing cotton and precleaning cotton. Precleaning by mechanical means resulted in some decreases in the gram-negative rod content of the lint and the resultant airborne respirable dust without significant change in endotoxin levels in these two materials. Washing at different temperatures resulted in marked decreases in gram-negative rod and endotoxin levels in the raw lint and the airborne respirable dusts (31). In a third study, steamed cottons had much less gram-negative rods than those treated with compressed air and this was reflected in a lower level of airborne respirable gram-negative rods in the model cardroom when the steamed cotton was processed (13).

TABLE VII
Washed Cotton Study

Treatment	gram neg rods		endotoxin	
	Cottons cfu/mg	Airborne Dusts cfu/m^3	Cottons ng/mg	Airborne Dusts ng/m^3
controls	939	2570	33.3	162
precleaned 2x	76	400	8.3	220
precleaned 2x and washed 60°C	<0.1	<180	0.32	18.6
precleaned 2x and washed 82°C	<0.8	<8	0.08	9.6

Fischer (31) also showed that in microbiological studies on cotton lints, the microorganism counts and endotoxin content were markedly decreased by scouring and bleaching or wetting followed by a hot water wash, but not by mechanical cleaning. When this washed cotton was carded, the airborne levels of gram-negative rods and endotoxin were reduced. This reduction was greater for gram-negative rod counts than for endotoxin levels.

Products of Microorganisms

Enzymes. Many proteolytic enzymes are formed by both *Bacillus* species (gram-positive organisms) and various species of fungi, especially *Aspergillus*. These have been implicated by byssinosis.

In 1973 Braun et al. (20) studied 1,000 workers in 18 mills. The highest incidence of symptoms and signs of byssinosis were not uniformly associated with the higher dust levels. The percent drop in FEV_1 correlated with the:

1. concentration of fine dust (mgm/m^3)
2. concentration of chymotrypsic-like enzymes in the fine dust

The source of the enzymes were from cotton seed (a small amount), from *Bacillus* species (intermediate amounts), and from fungi (large amounts probably from *Aspergillus*). The enzymes found in cotton dust caused histamine release that was reduced when enzyme activity was inhibited.

Chinn et al. (32) in 1976 pointed out that willowing mills have no byssinosis in spite of high dust levels (17-108 mgm/m^3) and high concentration of trypsin-like proteases (10.7 $\mu g/m^3$) in mill air. Total airborne dust was collected by cascade impactors.

Cinkotai (33) in 1976 reported that byssinosis correlates with the activity of trypsin-like enzymes in cardroom dust and with the concentration of 1-2 μm, and 2-4 μm particle fractions. These fractions contained the viable microorganisms carrying protealytic enzymes. The enzymes were also present in wool mills (no byssinosis) but were considered to be encapsulated in microorganisms.

In 1978 Cinkotai and Whitaker (12) added that byssinotic symptoms correlated with the protease in the airborne dust but more significantly with the gram-negative bacteria.

Histamine Liberation. This has often been considered the "final common pathway" to lung injury in byssinosis. Battigelli et al. (17) reported fungal extracts do not cause significant histamine release from swing lung. Cardroom waste from a pneumofil Vee-cell filter contains from 0.96 μg to 11.78 μg histamine per gram dust. In a handpicked series of bracts, the histamine content decreased markedly with the age of the plants as the pigmentation changed from green to non-green and the bacterial content increased.

Fischer et al. (21) documented that Bacillus cultures and their filtrates do not cause histamine release in swing lung.

Endotoxin. Endotoxin is the lipopolysaccharide that comprises a major portion of the cell wall of the gram-negative bacteria. The endotoxins from each species of bacteria are different but the lipid A moiety is similar for the Enterobacteriaceae, and has a similar series of biological actions regardless of its source. The lipid A material is different in some of the gram-negative rods present in cotton (i.e. in the Pseudomonas species). This variety of compounds makes quantitation of endotoxin difficult. Hence, it is usually measured by its biological activity as compared to a standard endotoxin (usually that of E. coli). (See Table VIII.)

Antweiler (4) in 1961 injected Salmonella abortus equi and E. coli endotoxins intraperitoneally into rats and looked for mast cells in the mesentery and the histamine content of the abdominal fluid. Negative results were obtained with amounts of the endotoxins (up to 10 μg) thought to be similar to that in cotton dust although large doses of endotoxin were known to cause rapid histamine release in cats and dogs. He concluded that endotoxins did not produce histamine release or the biological effect of cotton dust extracts.

In 1961 Pernis et al. (34) showed that histamine or histamine-like substances are liberated by endotoxins and by saline extracts of cardroom waste cotton by the guinea pig ileum method (a much more sensitive method than that used by Antweiler).

Pernis et al. (34) emphasized the following facts:

1. cotton extracts were pyrogenic in rabbits
2. cotton extracts could induce "tolerance"
3. rabbits tolerant to cotton extract were tolerant to endotoxin and vice versa
4. cotton extracts caused leukopenia followed by leukocytosis
5. 3.3 mgm of material isolated from 1 g of raw ordinary cotton extracted as if for endotoxin was pyrogenic and Schwartzman active
6. other activities were similar to those of endotoxins including liberation of histamine
7. human experiments with inhalation of endotoxins caused fever, malaise, decreased vital capacity

Cavagna et al. (35) in 1969 described the level of airborne endotoxins in cotton cardrooms (7.2 $\mu g/m^3$) and in hemp cardrooms (8.7 $\mu g/m^3$). Four out of fifteen volunteers showed a drop in FEV_1 with inhalation of 40-80 μg E. coli endotoxin. Rabbits exposed to 20 μg E. coli endotoxin/day or 2 mgm cotton extract/day responded with increased pulmonary resistance to a dose five times stronger after 20 weeks. They estimated that a textile worker breathes 40-50 μg endotoxin/8 hour shift, and pointed out the constant presence of endotoxin in cotton dusts.

TABLE VIII
Endotoxin

Reference	Material	Endotoxin Content	Method
Cinkotai et al. (11,12)	dust extract	0.2-1.60μg/ml	LAL
Cavagna et al. (35)	total airborne dust		
	cotton cardroom	7.2μg/m^3	skin necrosis in rabbits
	hemp cardroom	8.7μg/m^3	
Pernis et al. (34)	cotton lint[a]		
	rm. temp. extraction according to Antweiler	150-500μg/g	pyrogenic in rabbits
	phenol extraction	3000-11,000μg/g	pyrogenic in rabbits
Bergstrom et al. (37)	airborne respirable dust experimental cardroom	0.73μg/m^3	Shwartzman
Fischer (21,30,31)	cotton lint - unwashed	8-33μg/g	
	- washed	0.08-0.008μg/g	
	airborne respirable dust -model cardroom (different studies)	0.162-1.5μg/m^3 2.25μg/m^3	
	-mill cardroom	0.002-0.135μg/m^3	

[a]material probably not pure

Cinkotai et al. (11) measured the endotoxin content in the cardroom of seven cotton mills, and two cotton waste mills. None was found in a tea packing factory or a pipe tobacco factory and the level was low in the willowing mills. Byssinotic symptoms correlated with the level.

Fischer (13) showed that endotoxin levels in the respirable airborne dust (<15μm) are a log higher in the carding areas than in the spinning areas of cotton mills. Actual levels may reach 95 ng/m^3 in the carding areas.

Fischer (30) reported that airborne respirable endotoxin levels correlate (Spearman's coefficient of rank correlation) with the counts of gram-negative rods, with the percent of the total material processed that is Memphis cotton, and with the decrease in FEV, if these data are calculated only on mills where the carding areas are separate from the spinning areas.

Fischer et al. (21) demonstrated that the endotoxin content of raw cotton is significant (300 ng/gm lint) and is markedly decreased by washing and/or bleaching of the cotton, and by heating the cotton in hydrogen peroxide. Only prolonged high heat results in a complete loss (5 log decrease) of endotoxin activity from cotton dust.

Fischer (31) showed that mechanical precleaning plus washing, steaming plus washing, and steaming plus hot alkaline scour markedly decreased both the gram-negative organism counts, endotoxin content of raw cotton, and the respirable airborne dusts in a model cardroom when the cotton is carded. Precleaning alone is not very effective.

Summary

The microorganisms in cotton dust consist of large numbers of gram-positives or total bacteria, of gram-negative rod bacteria, and of fungi. This is the consensus of all references, whether total airborne dust, dust collected from an air-cleaning plant, or respirable airborne dusts are studied. Microorganisms comprise about 1% of total airborne cardroom dust by microscopic particle counting (9).

Gram-Negative Bacteria. The counts of total airborne gram-negative bacteria in the cardroom correlate with the prevalence of byssinotic symptoms, and also with the number of 2-4 μm particles in the air, and the amount of protease in the air. Up to 10^8 bacteria/g were found in waste cotton from the carding machine. Changes in FEV_1 in milliliters correlate best with the square root of the product of the number of gram-negative bacteria per gram of baled cotton and the dust level in milligrams. The level of airborne respirable gram-negative rods varied with the type and grade of cotton being processed with the dust level, and with the percent cotton in the blend. The spinning areas of the mills had a lower level of airborne respirable gram-negative rods.

Washing or steaming the cotton reduced the level markedly in the cotton lint, but only moderately in the air of the model cardroom. The same types of bacteria are found in raw cottons and the air of the mills, and the air of the model cardroom. Tinged grades of cotton have huge numbers of gram-negative microorganisms. Airborne respirable gram-negative bacterial counts correlate with the airborne endotoxin levels in cotton mills.

Gram-Positive or Total Bacteria. Bacillus species are the commonest bacteria in lint, raw cottons, cotton trash, and cotton dust, and may contribute to airborne levels of proteolytic enzymes, but the counts (while high) did not correlate with dust levels, and culture filtrates do not cause histamine release. Also, large numbers are present in wool mills and in willowing mills.

Fungi. Fungi are commonly found as contaminants of cotton lint, cotton trash, and cotton dust. Enzymes associated with fungi (mainly the aspergilli) are associated with a drop in FEV_1, but this work did not rule out the presence of endotoxin in those extracts. Large numbers of fungi are found in areas where there is no byssinosis. In cotton mills, fungal counts did not correlate with dust levels nor did the fungi cause histamine release. The fungal flora is very diverse and probably represents contamination during storage, harvesting, or processing because a different group of fungi are present on cotton that has weathered in the field before harvest. Human challenge with dust containing large numbers of Aspergillis niger did not cause the drop in maximal breathing capacity caused by mill dust.

Actinomyces. These organisms were not looked for adequately by most authors. They are certainly present in cardrooms and may be more frequent than the scanty data indicates. No one has shown any correlation with byssinotic symptoms or change in FEV_1.

Enzymes. Enzymes (proteolytic) derive from fungal and Bacillus organisms and are present not only in cotton mills but in wool and willowing mills. Byssinosis correlates with the activity of these enzymes and with the fine dust particles but this is the particle range that includes gram-negative microorganisms and their endotoxin. The correlation with the gram-negative microorganisms was more significant.

Histamine Liberation. Histamine liberation is not caused by fungal extracts, fungal cultures, Bacillus cultures, or their extracts, but is caused by cotton dust extracts and by known endotoxins when a sensitive method is used.

Endotoxin. The illness in the mattress workers using stained cotton (heavily contaminated by an encapsulated gram-negative bacteria) was probably an acute reaction due to the inhalation of endotoxin. Endotoxin levels of 7.2 $\mu g/m^3$ in cotton cardrooms correlate with a dose of 40-50 $\mu gm/8$ hour shift for a textile worker. Cotton dust extracts contain large amounts of endotoxin as does the air of model cardroom and the air of cotton mills. Byssinotic symptoms correlate with airborne endotoxin levels. Washing and steaming cotton reduces markedly this level of endotoxin in the raw cotton but only moderately in the airborne respirable dust in the model cardroom. In a sufficient dose endotoxin causes acute symptoms in people and leads to leukocyte recruitment in the lungs of animals. Enzymes from leukocytes or involvement of the complement system may be the pathway (as yet not proved) to cause a chronic disabling loss of pulmonary function.

Conclusions

The association of two factors does not prove a cause and effect relationship. One must be cautious in drawing conclusions from this diverse literature. The known facts about endotoxin are:

- -ubiquitous in its presence
- -represents previous growth of gram-negative microorganisms
- -is soluble
- -can be removed from cotton by washing
- -it is toxic
- -it causes recruitment of cells in animal lungs
- -it causes histamine release
- -there are many "endotoxins"
- -activity varies among endotoxins.

This leads to the hypothesis that byssinosis is the long-term (chronic) result of repeated acute episodes of lung injury. One factor in this injury may be inhalation of endotoxin. Endotoxins may act by triggering histamine release and subsequent bronchoconstriction.

Smoking and the presence of allergy (to fungal particles or other antigens) may both play a subsidiary role by increasing the fluid in the lungs and promoting the absorption of endotoxin.

Much work remains to be done. Especially crucial are studies relating endotoxin levels to pulmonary function changes in exposed individuals.

Acknowledgement

This review and our research were made possible through the generous support of Cotton, Incorporated of Raleigh and through the USDA/SRRC, New Orleans, Louisiana. The technical assistance of Karin Foarde has been invaluable throughout the conduct of this study. Many of the materials were kindly furnished by P. R. Morey, Department of Biological Science, Texas Tech University, Lubbock, Texas and P. E. Sasser, Cotton, Incorporated, Raleigh, North Carolina.

Literature Cited

1. Prausnitz, C. London Medical Research Council, HMSO, 1936.
2. Neal, P.A.; Schneiter, R.; Caminita, B.H. JAMA 1942, 119,1074-82.
3. Tuffnell, P. Brit J. Ind. Med. 1960, 17, 304-06.
4. Antweiler, H. Brit. J. Ind. Med. 1961, 18, 130-2.
5. Furness, G.; Maitland, H.B. Brit. J. Ind. Med. 1952, 9,138-45.
6. Drummond, D.G.; Hamlin, M. Brit J. Ind. Med. 1952, 9, 309-13.
7. Drummond, D.G.; Hamlin, M.; Donoghue, J.K.; Brownsett, F. Brit. J. Ind. Med. 1954, 11, 151-5.
8. Hamlin, M. Brit J. Ind. Med. 1952, 9, 311-13.
9. Lacey, J. Lancet, 1977, 2, 455-56.
10. Battigelli, M.C.; Fischer, J.J.; Craven, P.L.; Foarde, K.K. Am. Rev. Resp. Dis. 1976, 113(4), 100.
11. Cinkotai, F.F.; Lockwood, M.G.; Rylander, R. Am. Ind. Hyg. Assoc. J. 1977, 38, 554-9.
12. Cinkotai, F.F.; Whitaker, C.J. Am. Occup. Hyg. 1978, 21, 239-50.
13. Fischer, J.J. Proc. 1979 Beltwide Conference, 1979, p 8-10.
14. Fischer, J.J.; Battigelli, M.C.; Foarde, K.K. Proc. 1978 Beltwide Conference, 1978, p 110-113.
15. Morey, P.F.; Fischer, J.J.; Sasser, P.E. Proc. 1980 Beltwide Cotton Prod. Res. Conf. 1980, p 68-69.
16. Fischer, J.J.; Morey, P.R. Proc. 1979 Beltwide Conference, 1979, p 5-7.
17. Battigelli, M.C.; Craven, P.L.; Fischer, J.J.; Morey, P.R.; Sasser, P.E. J. Environ. Sci. Hlth. 1977, A 12, 327-39.
18. Rylander, R.; Nordstrand, A.; Snella, M.C. Arch. Environ. Hlth. 1975, 39, 137-40.
19. Tuffnell, P. Brit. J. Ind. Med. 1960, 17, 307-09.
20. Braun, D.C.; Schell, L.D.; Tuma, J.; Parker, L. J. Occup. Med. 1973, 15, 241-4.
21. Fischer, J.J.; Battigelli, M.C.; Foarde, K.K. Proc. 1979 Beltwide Conference, 1979, p 13-14.
22. Marsh, P.B.; Bollenbacher, K. Textile Res. J. 1949, 19, 313.
23. Pickard, R.H. J. Tex. Inst. 1930, 21, T595-T604.
24. Schwartz, H.J.; Chester, S.H.; Fink, J.N.; Payne, C.B.; Baum, G.L. Surg. and Allergy 1978, 40, 385-6.
25. Welty, R.E.; Gilbert, R.D.; Fornes, R.E. Tex. Res. J. 1977, 47, 38-48.
26. Rylander, R.; Lundholm, M. Brit. J. Ind. Med. 1978, 35, 204-7.
27. Rylander, R.; Lundholm, M. Proc. 1978 Beltwide Cotton Prod. Mech. Conf. 1978, p 113-15.

28. Rylander, R.; Imbus, H.R.; Suh, M.W. Brit. J. Ind. Med. 1979, 36, 299.
29. Lundholm, M.; Rylander, R. Proc. 1979 Beltwide Cotton Prod. Conf. 1979, p 11-12.
30. Fischer, J.J. Proc. 1980 Beltwide Conference, 1980, p 29-30.
31. Fischer, J.J. Textile Res. J. 1980, 50, 93-95.
32. Chinn, D.J.; Cinkotai, F.F.; Lockwood, M.G., Logan, S.H.M. Am. Occup. Hyg. 1976, 19, 101-08.
33. Cinkotai, F.F. Am. Ind. Hyg. Assoc. J. 1976, 37, 234-8.
34. Pernis, B.; Vigliani, E.C.; Cavagna, G.; Finulli, M. Brit. J. Ind. Med. 1961, 18, 120-9.
35. Cavagna, G.; Foa, V.; Vigliani, E.C. Brit. J. Ind. Med. 1969, 26, 312-21.
36. Heyn, A.N.J. Textile Res. J. 1957, 27, 591.
37. Bergstrom, R.; Haglind, P.; Rylander, R. Proc. 1980 Beltwide Cotton Prod. Res. Conf. 1980, p 22-25.

RECEIVED February 11, 1982.

16

Botanical Trash and Gram-Negative Bacterial Contents of Materials Utilized by the Cotton Industry

P. MOREY[1]

Texas Tech University, Department of Biological Sciences, Lubbock, TX 79409

R. RYLANDER

University of Gothenburg, Department of Environmental Hygiene, 40033 Gothenburg, Sweden

A comparison was made between the textile and non-textile cotton industries with respect to the amount of botanical trash and gram negative bacteria (GNB) entrained in materials being processed and levels of bacterial lipopolysaccharide (LPS or endotoxin) found in workroom air. Raw cotton used by the textile industry contained 0.2 to about 2% leaflike trash and an average of 5 x 10^6 GNB/g. Soft cotton mill wastes (SCMW) processed by waste recyclers and utilized by garnetters were characterized by large amounts of leaflike trash (5 to 20%) and entrained GNB levels of about 1 x 10^6/g. Average levels of LPS collected by vertical elutriator cotton dust samplers in oil mills, waste recyclers, and gins were lower (< 0.2 µg/m^3) than those typically found in cotton cardrooms (0.2 to 1 µg/m^3).

There is general agreement that the biologically active agent causing byssinosis is a lint contaminant derived either from the cotton plant itself or from a microbial contaminant of cotton. Work to define the active agent is required to improve the protection of workers and to modify the present proposed cotton dust standard (1) to one based on measurement of the active agent at the workplace.

A close relation between the extent of byssinosis and the contamination of cotton by GNB has been demonstrated in several studies (2,3,4). It has been shown that FEV_1 decrements in textile mills correlated best with the square root of the product of dust concentration and numbers of GNB in raw cotton (5). It has also been demonstrated that the cotton bract contains an agent or agents capable of eliciting acute respiratory responses during human challenge tests (6,7).

[1] Current address: Environmental Investigations Branch, NIOSH-ALOSH, 944 Chestnut Ridge Rd., Morgantown, WV 26505.

0097-6156/82/0189-0245$6.00/0

Bract and leaf trash materials are difficult to remove from cotton during ginning and comprise between ½ and 1% of the weight of a typical bale of strict low middling cotton (8). Thus bract and leaf trash components are present in sufficiently large amounts in raw cotton to function as botanical carriers of the suspect byssinotic agent(s).

The prevalence of byssinosis is less in nontextile cotton industries than in the cotton textile industry (1,2,9). It is thus of interest to determine the amount of botanical trash and GNB in materials processed by gins, oil mills, waste recyclers and garnetters. This study was undertaken to characterize the levels and types of botanical trash (especially bract and leaf components) and the number of GNB, in materials utilized in cotton yarn manufacturing and in cotton materials processed by gins, cottonseed oil mills, and cotton waste recyclers and garnetters. A further objective was to determine, whether larger numbers of GNB were present on the fiber or on the botanical trash components of various cotton materials, and whether washing in hot water effectively removed bacteria from these materials.

Materials and Methods

Cotton Materials and Botanical Trash Analysis. Cotton materials were collected from gins (raw seed cotton, cleaned seed cotton and raw lint) and from textile mills and U.S. Department of Agriculture - Agricultural Marketing Service (USDA-AMS) classing offices (raw cotton). Materials were also obtained from oil mills (cottonseed, hulls and linters) and from waste recyclers and garnetters [strips, sweeps, picker, mill motes, fly, SCMW mix, linters and gin motes]. All materials were analyzed for content of all nonfibrous botanical trash particles > 50 μm in size (10). The amount of leaflike trash (bract, cotton leaf and weed leaf) and total botanical trash was expressed as the percent of the weight of the sample.

Raw seed cotton was collected from the trailer or from the module at gins located in all major U.S.A. growing regions. Corresponding cleaned seed cotton samples were collected at the gin stand feeder (seed cotton at feeder) and after two stages of lint cleaning (raw lint).

Raw cottons in 1976 were obtained from 10 U.S.A. textile mills. In 1977 and 1979 raw cottons were collected from USDA-AMS classing offices in all major cotton growing regions of the U.S.A.

Cottonseed and seed hulls were obtained from two oil mills in West Texas and from one oil mill in California. Cottonseed samples were taken from the seedhouse, cleaning room and from the first, second and third-cut delinter machines. Seed hulls and linters were obtained from the hulling and baling areas respectively, of the same oil mills.

A number of cleaned SCMW as follows were obtained from 10 garnetters and from four waste recyclers from various U.S.A.

locations. Strips and fly are fibrous wastes from the card flats and from the lickerin screen of the card, respectively. Sweeps are fibrous wastes collected from under the card (sometimes called card motes) and from under spinning machines. Picker and mill motes are fibrous wastes left after the cotton has passed through picking and opening-picking, respectively. SCMW mix is a variable combination of any of the aforementioned SCMW. Samples of cleaned linters and cleaned gin motes were also obtained from the same waste recyclers and garnetters.

GNB Analysis. The following procedure was utilized to analyze for GNB entrained in cotton materials: One g of the material was added to 10 ml of sterile water with a few drops of 1% wetting agent (Saponine). The material was squeezed for 10 minutes in a special apparatus and serial dilutions were prepared from the liquid. One ml samples were inoculated on Drigalski agar plates (selective for gram negative rods) and incubated overnight at 37°C. The number of colony forming units was counted and the results expressed as GNB/g of material.

Endotoxin Analysis. Filters were obtained from vertical elutriator cotton dust samplers, operated according to standard procedures (1) in cardrooms from several cotton mills, and from cottonseed oil mills, cotton waste recyclers and cotton gins. The cottonseed oil mills from which vertical elutriator filters were obtained were located in Texas and California and were processing machine-picked cotton materials. Vertical elutriator samplers in oil mills were located in the cleaning, delintering, hulling and baling work areas. Waste recyclers and gins from which elutriator filters were obtained were located in the U.S.A. Southeast. Vertical elutriators in gins were set up at the gin stand and lint cleaning work areas. Elutriators in waste recyclers were located at various work areas including bale opening, blending and willowing.

After weighing the dust filters, the amount of endotoxin was determined by shaking them in 10 ml of pyrogen free water and preparing serial dilutions. Limulus lysate (Cape Cod Associates Inc.) was added to the dilutions according to the manufacturer's recommendations. The last dilution giving a stable clot was read as the *Escherichia coli* endotoxin equivalent concentration. Dilutions were also prepared with commercial *E. coli* endotoxin (*E. coli* 026-B26, Difco) to assess the accuracy of the production reference standard. The values were always found to agree closely with the stated values.

Localization of GNB on Botanical Trash and Fiber. Leaflike, bark, and seed trash materials > 50 μm were removed by hand from light spotted 1976 raw cottons grown in West Texas. These botanical trash materials plus the lint minus gross trash and samples of the original raw cottons were analyzed for content of entrained

GNB by the procedures given above. Similarily leaflike, seed, stem and bark trash materials were removed from linters, gin motes, blended stock and batting being processed by a garnetter in West Texas in 1977. Separated trash materials, fiber minus gross trash, and unsorted linters, gin motes, blended stock and batting were analyzed for entrained GNB levels. Finally, all botanical trash particles > 25 μm and most particles > 15 μm were removed by hand from two raw cotton samples, one of which had been washed at 66°C and the second of which was unwashed. Separated botanical trash and cleaned lint from each sample were analyzed for entrained GNB levels.

Results

An average of 1-2 x 10^6 GNB was found in the seed cotton received by gins and in seed cotton at the gin stand feeder (Table I). Considerable variability in GNB content was found between seed cotton samples as shown by the large standard deviations characteristic of materials received at the gin and entering the gin stand feeder. Raw ginned lint samples collected after two stages of gin lint cleaning contained about the same number of GNB on a weight basis as the seed cotton entering the gin stand feeder. By contrast, the delinted seed collected at the gin and sent to the oil mill contained about 1 x 10^5 GNB/g. The raw cottons utilized by the textile industry contained about 5 x 10^6 GNB/g.

Table I also shows the approximate amount of leaflike trash found in materials processed by the textile and nontextile cotton industries. Seed cotton at the gin contained about 2% (range 0.5 to 6%) leaflike trash. Raw cotton utilized by the textile industry contained on average about 0.8% leaflike trash. The best and the poorest grades of raw cotton were characterized by lesser (0.2 to 0.6%) and higher (1.5 to 3.5%) amounts of leaflike trash, respectively. The gin stand is a major partitioning point for leaflike trash entrained in the cotton processing stream. Thus, the cottonseed delivered from the gin to the oil mill contained < 0.1% leaflike trash. By contrast the lint even after several lint cleanings and baling (raw cotton) contained 0.8% leaflike trash.

GNB were found to be partitioned in the process stream in cottonseed oil mills when the linters are removed from the seed (Table I). Linters from oil mills and even cleaned linters used by garnetters contained about one order of magnitude more GNB than was found on seeds (at all stages of processing) and on seed hulls. As cottonseed at the oil mill is cleaned and delintered, the level of entrained leaflike trash decreased to < 0.05% (Table I, one sample only). Almost no leaflike trash remained in the seed hulls obtained at the huller separator. Linters removed from the seed at the oil mill and utilized by garnetters contained about 0.2% leaflike trash (Table I, 20 samples).

Cotton garnetters and waste recyclers process a variety of materials including SCMW from textile manufacturers, motes from

TABLE I

Content of Gram Negative Bacteria, Leaflike Trash and Total Trash in Materials Processed by Cotton Industries[†]

Industry and Material	GNB x 10^6 per g	% Leaflike Trash	% Total Trash
Ginning			
Raw Seed Cotton	1.0± 2.9 ab	2.6± 2.2 de	20.0± 17.8 cd
Seed cotton at feeder	1.8 ±3.6 ab	2.1 ±2.6 de	5.3 ± 3.7 de
Raw lint	1.8 ±4.2 ab	-	-
Textiles			
Raw Cotton	5.3±11.8 ab	0.8 ±0.8 e	2.8 ± 2.2 e
Oil Mills			
Seeds and seed hulls	0.1± 0.2 b	0.02±0.02e	1.1 ± 0.9 e
Linters ††	2.2± 3.8 ab	0.05 e	46.5 ab
Garnetters and Waste Recyclers			
Strips	0.3± 0.3 b	4.9± 3.8 ce	14.7 ± 8.5 cd
Sweeps	0.4± 0.5 b	9.1± 5.8 bc	20.8 ±11.0 c
Picker	0.4± 0.6 b	6.5± 2.6 cd	34.6 ±16.7 b
Linters	0.7± 1.8 b	0.2± 0.3 e	20.3 ± 8.2 c
SCMW mix	1.0± 1.7 ab	6.1± 4.8 cd	20.8 ±10.8 c
Mill motes	1.3± 1.7 ab	18.1± 9.3 a	41.0 ±16.2 b
Fly	2.8± 3.7 ab	7.1± 4.8 cd	16.2 ± 9.9 cd
Gin motes	7.9±23.3 a	11.8± 7.6 b	55.2 ±12.3 a

† Means within a column followed by the same letter are not significantly different at the 5% level according to the Duncan's Multiple Range Test.

†† Only one sample of oil mill linters was examined for botanical trash content.

gins and linters from oil mills. All garnetting raw materials listed in Table I were precleaned (at waste recyclers) prior to sample acquisition. Among cleaned garnetting raw materials, gin motes contained the highest number of GNB. An average of < 1 x 10^6 GNB/g was found in linters and some SCMW including strips, sweeps and picker. Gin motes and SCMW utilized by garnetters are characterized by high levels of entrained leaflike and total botanical trash.

Comparison of the average contents of leaflike trash and GNB in the different materials (Table I) processed by all cotton industries showed a lack of correlation between botanical and microbiological parameters ($r = 0.18$, $P = 0.55$). Thus, some cotton materials with a high leaflike trash content (e.g., strips, sweeps, and picker) contained low numbers of GNB while other materials with low leaflike trash contents (e.g., raw cotton, linters) had larger amounts of GNB. When raw cottons (1977 crop) were considered separately a somewhat better, but still nonsignificant correlation coefficient ($r = 0.48$, $P = 0.16$, $N = 43$), was obtained between contents of leaflike trash and GNB.

Among the 65 raw cottons examined, samples from the combined tinged-yellow stained color groups and from the poorest grade division (low middling) contained more entrained GNB than those from the white color group and the higher grade divisions, repectively (Tables II and III). The difference in GNB levels found in the white and combined tinged-yellow stained color groups was statistically significant. However, among raw cotton grade divisions, differences in GNB content were not statistically significant even though the poorest grade division contained significantly more leaflike and total botanical trash than found in cottons from better grade divisions (Table III).

In order to determine the location of GNB in cotton materials all botanical trash particles were separated from the lint of light spotted raw cottons (1976 crop) and also from fiber of linters, gin motes, blended stock and batting from a garnetter using a 60% linter - 40% gin mote blend. On a weight basis, significantly more GNB were found in botanical trash materials entrained in raw cottons than on the cleaned lint (Table IV). Cleaned lint and linters from garnetting samples contained fewer (though not significantly fewer) GNB than botanical trash (Table V).

Airborne endotoxin was collected in gins, waste recyclers, oil mills and textile cardrooms (Table VI) to see whether an airborne microbial parameter might correlate with the contents of leaflike trash and GNB entrained in materials being processed by various cotton industries. In gins, oil mills and waste recyclers levels of airborne endotoxin were significantly lower than those generally found in textile cardrooms.

Washing is reported to lower the content of the byssinotic agent(s) in raw cotton (11) and to lower the GNB level in bale size lots of raw cotton (12). All botanical trash particles > 25 μm were removed by hand from two middling white, 1979 raw cottons, one of which had been washed and the second of which was unwashed (Table VII). As with the 1976 samples (Table IV) considerably more

TABLE II

Bacteria Present in Raw Cotton Color Groups †

Color groups	GNB x 10^6
Plus, white	2.0 b
Light spotted, spotted	6.2 ab
Tinged, yellow-stained	14.3 a

† Means followed by the same letter are not significantly different at the 5% level according to the Duncan's Multiple Range Test.

TABLE III

Trash and Bacterial Contents in Raw Cotton Grade Divisions†

Grade Division	% Leaflike Trash	% Total Trash	GNB x 10^6 per gram of Sample ††
SM	0.23 b	1.29 b	0.1 a
M	0.35 b	1.60 b	4.1 a
SLM	0.72 b	2.03 b	4.6 a
LM	1.50 a	4.61 a	6.6 a

† SM = strict middling; M = middling; SLM = strict low middling; LM = Low middling. Means within a column followed by the same letter are not significantly different at the 5% level according to the Duncan's Multiple Range test.

†† Range of GNB content in samples: SM = 0 to 0.57 x 10^6; M = 0.06 to 21.8 x 10^6; SLM = 0.002 to 55.4 x 10^6; LM = 0.003 to 39.7 x 10^6.

TABLE IV

GNB Present on 1976 Light Spotted Raw Cotton from which Botanical Trash (> 50 μm) was Removed by Hand †

Sample	GNB x 10^6 ††
Raw Cotton	1.0 b
Clean lint	0.8 b
Botanical Trash	35.7 a

† Means followed by the same letter are not significantly different at the 5% level according to the Duncan's Multiple Range Test.

†† Seven raw cotton samples, 8 clean lint and 8 botanical trash samples. Range of content of GNB x 10^6 per g sample: Raw Cottons = 0.007 to 5.4; clean lint = 0.19 to 3.5; botanical trash = 0.08 to 125.4

TABLE V

Distribution of GNB on Garnetting Materials, Clean Fiber and Gross Botanical Trash †

Samples	GNB x 10^6 per gram sample††
Linters, gin motes, blended stock and batting	28.2 a
Lint and linters minus trash	0.8 a
Gross trash	16.2 a

† Means followed by the same letter are not significantly different at the 5% level according to the Duncan's Multiple Range test.

†† Range of content of GNB x 10^6 per g sample: Linters, gin motes, blended stock, and batting (N = 7) is 2.2 to 144.0; Lint and linters minus trash (N = 4) is 0.05 to 2.8; Gross (> 50 μm) trash (N = 7) is 0.01 to 94.0

TABLE VI

Endotoxin in Workroom Air in Various Cotton Industries †

Industry	Endotoxin ($\mu g/m^3$) ††
Cardroom	0.73 a
Waste Recycler	0.13 b
Gin	0.05 b
Oil Mill	0.02 b

† Collected by vertical elutriator cotton dust sampler.
†† Means followed by the same letter are not significantly different at the 5% level according to the Duncan's Multiple Range Test. N = 3 for cardroom; N = 6 to 8 separately for gins, oil mills and waste recyclers.

TABLE VII

Effect of Washing on Bacterial Content of Trash and Lint Removed from Raw Cotton†

Sample	GNB per g
Lint minus trash	1,100
Botanical trash	61,500
Lint minus trash (W)	< 100
Botanical trash (W)	< 100

† Middling raw cotton, 1979 crop, all botanical trash particles > 25 μm separated from raw cotton lint. W = washed

GNB were found on the unwashed botanical trash than on the unwashed clean lint (Table VII). Both the botanical trash and the cleaned lint from the washed sample had levels of entrained GNB < the threshold limit of sensitivity (100 GNB/g) detectable in our laboratory.

Discussion

It is likely that at least some of the variability encountered in the number of GNB present in seed cotton, raw lint and raw cotton samples (Table I) was the result of environmental, varietal and other cultural parameters since cotton samples were derived from each of the four major U.S.A. growing regions. Insufficient samples were available in this study to determine whether GNB levels were unusually high in any specific growing region. The somewhat higher bacterial content of raw cotton compared to that of raw ginned lint (Table I) was likely associated with the wider and different sampling base of the former (1977 and 1979 crop years, 65 samples) as compared to the latter (1979 crop year, 15 samples).

An important partitioning action occurs both on GNB and leaf-like trash as seed cotton moves through the gin stand. Most of these microorganisms and most of the leaflike trash follow the lint process stream and a lesser amount of these contaminants travel with the lintered seed to the oil mill (Table I). We have not yet attempted to make even a crude material balance for GNB and leaf-like trash in the cotton ginning industry because of the considerable variability in microbial and botanical contents in seed cotton samples (Table I). In addition, GNB and leaflike trash are likely removed from the seed cotton and lint processing streams at many points during gin cleaning, and these trash streams were not examined either microbiologically or botanically.

In cottonseed oil mills, GNB and leaflike trash are partitioned when linters are removed from the seed. Linters from oil mills and even cleaned linters used by garnetters contained about one order of magnitude more GNB than that found on seeds and on seed hulls (Table I). Linters also contained more leaflike trash than delintered seed and seed hulls. Presumably GNB are found in greater numbers on linters than on delintered seed in oil mills because of larger amounts of leaflike trash entrained in linters and/or because of the relatively huge fiber surface area available on linters for bacterial attachment.

The absence of a statistically significant correlation coefficient between the number of GNB and the content of leaflike trash in raw cottons appears difficult to reconcile with the current opinion that bract is the plant part that primarily carries the causative agent of byssinosis (6,7,10). However, it should be kept in mind that a bract from a cotton plant in the field contains widely differing levels (three orders of magnitude differences) of

GNB depending upon weather variables to which the plants were previously exposed (13). Thus bract materials in different raw cottons will carry variable levels of GNB depending upon the environmental history of the crop from which the raw cotton was derived (4,13). A given weight of bract particles from tinged and yellow-stained cottons will likely carry more GNB than the equivalent weight of bract in the same grade division of white raw cotton (Table II). Because of its abundance in raw cotton and raw cotton dust (8,10) bract can still be considered to be the major, although a somewhat variable, plant part carrier of microbial agents including GNB.

Prevalence of byssinosis in the cotton textile industry is reported to be higher than that found in cotton gins, cottonseed oil mills and the cotton garnetting - waste recycling industries. Thus vertically elutriated particulate levels of 200 $\mu g/m^3$ are associated with byssinosis prevalence levels of 12% in the textile industry (14) whereas in gins, oil mills and garnetting - waste recycling industries high dust levels (generally 1000 $\mu g/m^3$ or greater) are associated with prevalences less than 6% (1,9,15-18). The data from this study show similarity in GNB levels in seed cottons in gins, raw cotton used by the textile industry, linters in oil mills and fly, mill motes and SCMW mix used in garnetting. These findings do not seem to support the assumption that GNB or their endotoxins are a major cause of byssinosis. However, when airborne LPS levels collected by vertical elutriator cotton dust samplers near a textile card were compared with LPS levels in gins, cottonseed oil mills and cotton waste recyclers, the levels in the latter are significantly less than those found in the cardroom (Table VI).

An explanation for the occurrence of high numbers of entrained GNB in some cotton materials processed in industries (gins, oil mills, garnetters and waste recyclers) where byssinosis prevalence is low could be that the handling of these materials in nontextile industries is less vigorous mechanically than that occurring in the preparation areas of a cotton textile mill (19). Agents present in seed cotton and in the raw lint streams in ginning are less likely to become airborne because of the mild mechanical operations in a gin versus the severity of processing as on a textile card where lint and entrained trash are individualized and exposed to a high velocity airstream. Thus, low levels of airborne LPS might be anticipated in all nontextile cotton industries. In addition, low levels of airborne LPS are likely in garnetting-waste recycling cotton industries because some of the materials utilized (SCMW) have already been subjected to the aspiration systems of both gins and the preparative steps in yarn production. That SCMW contain high levels of leaflike trash and yet, on a weight basis, contain only about 1×10^6 GNB/g suggests that substantial amounts of microorganisms have been selectively removed in prior mechanical processing operations. Although the sampling base is small (Table VI) a preliminary conclusion is that increased prevalence of byssinosis may be associated with workplaces with high levels of airborne endotoxin.

Establishment of the location of microorganisms, that is, whether primarily on the fiber and or on the botanical trash entrained with the fiber, is of practical importance for attempts to remove GNB from cotton materials. This study shows that GNB are more highly concentrated on gross botanical trash found in cotton materials than on cleaned lint or linters. However, since the trash removal procedure involved separation of only those botanical fragments > 50 μm, it may be that some GNB on cleaned fiber are localized on smaller particles still entrained in the lint or linters.

While data in Tables IV and V show that GNB are more highly concentrated on separated trash than on cleaned lint or linters, it does not follow that removal of all gross trash from cotton materials will produce a material which involves a lower risk of medical symptoms among those exposed to the dust. Thus for raw cottons in Table IV assuming that 35.7×10^6 GNB occur on all botanical trash [2.8% of sample weight (Table I)] and 0.8×10^6 GNB remain on the lint (97.2% of raw cotton weight), simple calculations show that only about 56% of the total GNB content in raw cotton is localized on the gross trash. Removal of all gross trash from raw cotton will still leave about 44% of the GNB on the lint or on the fine particulate associated with the lint. Thus, extensive cleaning of these raw cottons either in the gin or in the preparative steps of cotton yarn production might not significantly lower the content of entrained GNB.

On the other hand, for the 60% linter - 40% gin mote blend in Table V similar calculations show that about 91% and 9% of the GNB are localized on gross trash and on cleaned lint-linters, respectively. The higher proportion of GNB associated with gross trash in garnetting materials is due primarily to the larger amount of total botanical trash characteristic of these materials (e.g., 55% for gin motes; 20% for linters, Table I). Additional cleaning in this garnetting operation (Table V) would likely lower the content of entrained GNB significantly.

The experience from the preliminary experiment on washing demonstrates that this is effective in reducing GNB to very low levels both on the gross botanical trash entrained in raw cotton as well as on the lint itself. Washing, as opposed to the mechannical removal of trash by extensive air cleaning operations, appears to offer a better means of lowering the levels of GNB found on both the trash and lint fractions of raw cotton.

Acknowledgments

These investigations were supported by funds made available to both authors by Cotton Incorporated. Many of the samples examined in this study were provided by John Zey of NIOSH, Robert Bethea of Texas Tech University, and Preston Sasser, William Lalor and Herbert Willcutt of Cotton Incorporated.

Literature Cited

1. Federal Register 1978, 43, 27350-418.
2. Cinkotai, F. F.; Lockwood, M. G.; Rylander, R. Am. Ind. Hyg. Assoc. J. 1977, 38, 554-9.
3. Neal, P. A.; Schneiter, R.; Caminita, B. H. J. Am. Med. Assoc. 1942, 119, 1074-82.
4. Rylander, R.; Lundholm, M. Brit. J. Ind. Med. 1978, 35, 204-7.
5. Rylander, R.; Imbus, H. R.; Suh, M. W. Brit. J. Ind. Med. 1979, 299-305.
6. Bouhuys, A. "Breathing"; Grune and Stratton: New York, 1974; p 416-40.
7. Bouhuys, A.; Nicholls, P. J. "Inhaled Particles and Vapours II": Davies, C. N., Ed.; Pergamon: New York, 1966: p 75-85.
8. Morey, P. R. Proc. Beltwide Cotton Prodn. Res. Conf. 1980, p 67.
9. Chinn, D. J.; Cinkotai, F. F.; Lockwood, M. G.; Logan, S. H. M. Ann. Occup. Hyg. 1976, 19, 101-8.
10. Morey, P. R. Am. Ind. Hyg. Assoc. J. 1979, 40, 702-8.
11. Merchant, J. A.; Lumsden, J. C.; Kilburn, K. H.; Germino, V. H.; Hamilton, J. D.; Lynn, W. S.; Byrd, H.; Baucom, D. Brit. H. Ind. Med. 1973, 30, 237-47.
12. Bergstrom, R.; Haglind, P.; Rylander, R. Proc. Beltwide Cotton Prodn. Res. Conf. 1980, p 22-5.
13. Morey, P. R.; Fischer, J. J.; Sasser, P. E. Proc. Beltwide Cotton Prodn. Res. Conf. 1980, p 68-9.
14. Merchant, J. A.; Lumsden, J. C.; Kilburn, K. H.; O'Fallon, W. M.; Ujda, J. R.; Germino, V. H. Jr.; Hamilton, J. D. J. Occup. Med. 1973, 15, 222-30.
15. Curtis, R.; Parnes, W. "Byssinosis, an Industrial Hygiene and Medical Survey of the Stearns and Foster Co., Lockland, Ohio"; NIOSH 1973; 15 p.
16. Federal Register 1978, 43, 27418-63.
17. Jones, R. N.; Carr, J.; Glindmeyer, J.; Diem, J.; Weill, H. Thorax 1977, 32, 281-6.
18. Piccirillo, R. E.; Zey, J.; Boehlecke, B.; Merchant, J. A. "Report No. 76-73-523"; NIOSH 1978; 9p.
19. Morey, P. R. Chest 1981, 79, 97S-101S.

RECEIVED December 15, 1981.

17

Analysis of Antigens in Cotton Dust by Immunological Methods

ANTONIO A. SEKUL and ROBERT L. ORY

U.S. Department of Agriculture, Agricultural Research Service
Southern Regional Research Center, New Orleans, LA 70179

Aqueous extracts of cotton dust and cotton bract induced the formation of specific precipitating antibodies in rabbits. The antisera cross-reacted with both extracts as well as with extracts of cotton stem, leaf, and burr, baled cotton and gin trash. Cross-reactivity was also demonstrated with extracts of flax, soft hemp, sisal, and jute. No antigen-antibody reaction was obtained with extracts of cottonseed hulls, cottonseed proteins, noncontaminated cotton lint, or house dust. No reaction was obtained between the antisera to dust and several commercial preparations of bacterial lipopolysaccharides believed to be present in cotton dust. With the exception of extracts from burr, none of the antigens reacted with preimmunization serum.

Dust generated in cotton textile processing plants is a hazard for some workers. Those that are susceptible and are exposed to cotton dust for a long period of time may be affected by a symptoms-complex known as byssinosis (1), a syndrome characterized by periodic coughing, wheezing, chest tightness, and decreased pulmonary function (2,3). The symptoms are more obvious on the first day back after a rest from exposure (Monday phenomenon). Prolonged exposure to the dust may cause irreversible respiratory impairment. The disease has also been described in workers in the flax and soft hemp industries (4,5,6), as well as in the sisal and jute industries (7-10). In its acute stage as well as in its chronic stage, byssinosis remains a major problem in the vegetable fiber processing industry. Byssinosis, however, is not understood in either its mechanism or specific etiology (11).

Accumulated evidence shows that in cotton mills, byssinosis is not caused by the cotton lint itself, but rather by foreign matter in the dust arising from the processing of raw fibers (12).

Cotton dust is a heterogeneous mixture of varied composition (13), but cotton bract has been identified as one of the major contaminants (32-52%) of the plant trash (14).

Many different agents and theories have been postulated to explain the causes of byssinosis. For example, proteolytic enzymes derived from cottonseed proteins, bacilli, and fungi, are thought to be associated with the disease (15). Numerous reports implicate histamine or histamine liberators (2, 16-19), mediators of smooth muscle stimulants (11,20), and pharmacologically-active substances such as lacinilene C-7 methyl ether, which causes leukocyte chemotaxis *in vivo* and *in vitro* (21). The possibility that gram-negative microorganisms and/or their lipopolysaccharides (LPS) may have a role in producing byssinosis has been studied with great interest. Several investigators have demonstrated that airborne gram-negative bacteria in cotton mills are closely associated with the prevalence of byssinotic symptoms among workers, but the exact role of these microorganisms in the etiology of the disease is not clear (22-25). Other workers (9, 16) stated that the action of cotton dust extracts was not typical of endotoxins (LPS) and that bacterial endotoxins were not present in the dust in quantities sufficient to be effective. Some investigators have suggested that antigenic material present in cotton dust may play an important role in the disease (26,27). A phenolic polymer 5,7,3'4'-tetrahydroxyflavan-3,4 diol isolated from cotton bract was thought to be the responsible agent (28). This polymer was later found to react with all human sera, with several myeloma IgG preparations, and with the isolated Fc piece of IgG on gel diffusion (29,30).

Recently, other reports have appeared (31), as well as our own studies (32), showing that cotton dust activates the alternate pathway of complement. Previous studies in this laboratory (33,34), showed that antibodies to water extracts of cotton dust, cotton bract, and a highly purified fraction of dust elicited positive immunological responses in rabbits.

This report describes our results on analyses of antigens in cotton dust and bract by immunological techniques, and discusses the possibility of applying these results to the development of a bioassay for active agents which may be related to byssinosis.

Material and Methods

Preparation of Aqueous Extract of Cotton Dust. Cotton cardroom dust was collected from V-cell filters in a commercial textile mill. A typical extraction was carried out by manually kneading 50 g of dust with 500 ml of deionized water for 5 min at 25°C and removing the liquor by centrifugation. The process was repeated twice with 250 ml of deionized water each time. The combined supernatant was filtered through filter paper by gravity and the filtrate (of final pH 8.3 without addition of buffer) was freeze-dried to yield fraction 1 (f-1). The major portion of f-1

(10g) was extracted three times with 50 ml portions of 85% methanol at 25°C for 30 min each time with stirring then filtered. The combined solution was evaporated to dryness under reduced pressure and labeled fraction 2 (f-2). The methanol-insoluble material was labeled fraction 3 (f-3). Five g of f-3 was dissolved in 50 ml of water and treated gradually with an excess of lead acetate (20 ml; 0.2M), with vigorous stirring. The lead acetate soluble material was treated by slowly adding 100 ml of a 0.4M solution of sodium sulfate (excess) with stirring and filtered. The filtrate was dialyzed for 72 hr at 4°C against several changes of deionized water. The solution was then freeze-dried to yield a purified fraction 4 (f-4). The lead acetate insoluble fraction was treated with sodium sulfide and the resulting solution was freeze-dried after dialysis to obtain fraction 5 (f-5). Fractions f-1, f-3, f-4, and f-5 were used to immunize rabbits.

Preparation of Aqueous Extract of Cotton Bract. Field-dried cotton bract, 10 g, picked directly from plants in a field near Lake Providence, Louisiana, was ground with mortar and pestle, extracted twice with 100 ml of deionized water at pH 7 for 30 min each time at 25°C with stirring. The extracts were combined and the solution was filtered; the filtrate was freeze-dried. This bract extract (bAg) was also used to immunize rabbits. Additional bAg was further purified by treatment with 85% methanol in a similar manner as with cotton dust.

Preparation of Other Antigenic Materials. Cotton plant tissues (stem, leaf, burr), cotton gin trash, baled cotton, clean cotton lint, both hand picked in the field and from plants grown in the greenhouse, cottonseed proteins, cottonseed hulls, house dust, and flax, soft hemp, sisal, and jute fibers, were extracted with deionized water. The purification process was, however, stopped to correspond to f-3 (see Figure 1).

Bacterial LPS used in this study were purchased from Sigma Chemical Co., St. Louis, MO., and were as follows: Escherichia coli serotypes 0.26:B6; 0127:B8 (prepared both by the phenolic and the TCA procedures); 0127:BB (by the butanol procedure); Serratia marcescens, and Shigella flexneri. The LPS were solubilized in water and used as antigenic materials.

Preparation of Rabbit Serum and Antiserum. Four white New Zealand rabbits (2-3 kg) were first bled to obtain normal serum (NS), then injected subcutaneously with a total of 2.5 mg of either f-1, f-3, f-4, or f-5 in complete Freund's adjuvant. After 10 days, booster injections of the same amount of antigen in incomplete adjuvant were given every 2 weeks for a total of seven injections. Antisera to dust fractions (AD) and to bract (AB) were pooled and concentrated approximately tenfold by 40% saturation with ammonium sulfate at 4°C. The precipitated

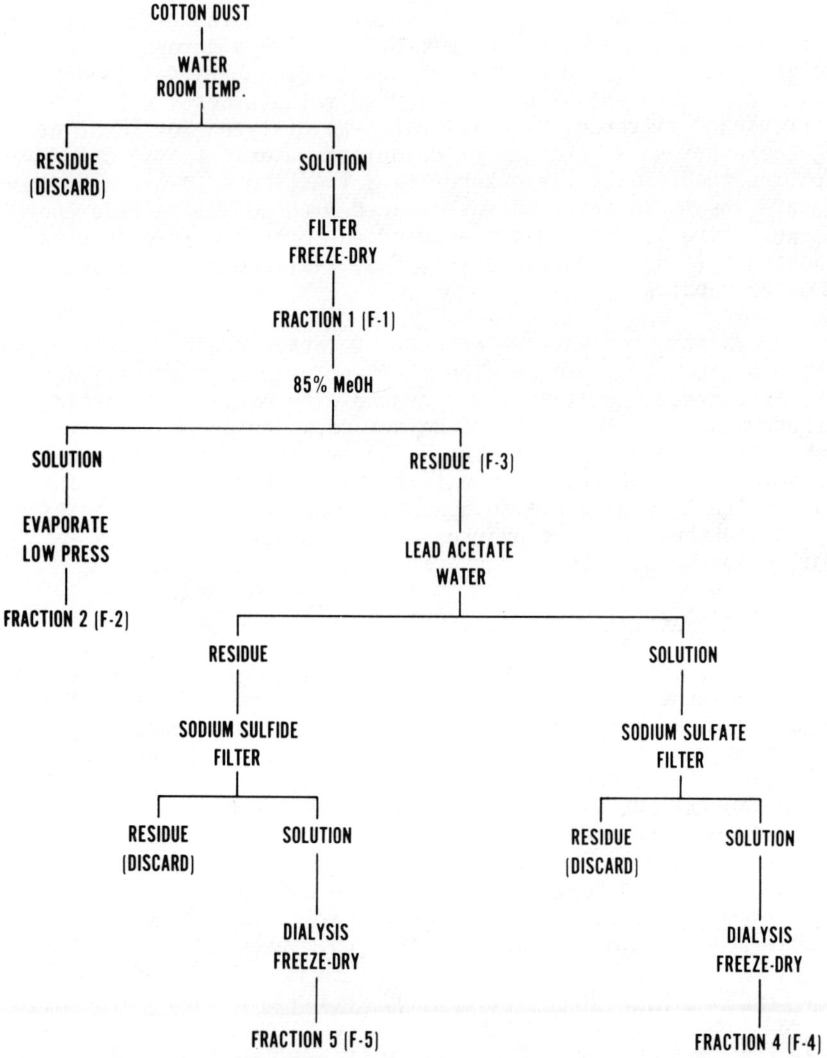

Figure 1. Fractionation of cotton dust. Room temp, 25°C; dialysis time, 5 days.

antibodies were resuspended in a minimal amount of 0.01M phosphate-buffered saline (PBS) at pH 7.2 and dialyzed exhaustively against several changes of PBS. NS was concentrated in a similar manner. AD, AB, and NS were used in double diffusion experiments to detect the antibodies.

Detection of Antibodies. The method used for detecting antibodies was the double diffusion technique in agarose. Agarose plates (8.5 x 9.5 cm) were prepared by pouring 10 ml of a 1% molten suspension of agarose in a barbital buffer of 0.02 ionic strength and pH 8.6 (35). After the gel had set, circular wells of 50 µl were punched out with a cork borer and filled once with the appropriate serum, antiserum, or antigenic material. The antigens were applied as 100 mg/ml solutions (except for burr, which was 25 mg/ml because of its gummy characteristic and difficulty in handling) in deionized water. Diffusion was allowed to proceed for 20-30 hr at 25°C. Plates were washed with either 0.2M sodium chloride or 0.15M sodium citrate for 24 hr prior to staining with 0.5% solution of amido black 10B.

Chromatography and Electrophoresis of Antigens. Cotton dust (20-30 mg) was dissolved in water and passed through a small column (30 x 1.5 cm id) packed with 3 g of Sephadex G-75 that had been preswelled in water. Chromatograms were obtained with an LKB Uvicord ultraviolet monitor and a chopper bar recorder. Volumes of 5 ml each were collected in test tubes with an automatic fraction collector. Two components were detected at 250 nm. Samples of 10 mg were analyzed by disc gel electrophoresis according to procedures described by Davis (36), and Zacharius (37).

Quantitation of Human IgG. Radial immunodiffusion technique (Tri-Partigen; Calbiochem-Behring Corp.) was used to measure normal serum and serum from byssinotic persons. After filling the wells, diffusion was allowed to proceed for 50 hr at 4°C. Precipitin rings were measured and the concentration of IgG in mg/dl was obtained from the Table of References supplied with the plates.

Results and Discussion

Figure 1 shows the flowsheet diagram for the fractionation of cotton dust. Active antisera were obtained with fractions f-1, f-3, and f-4. Fraction 2 was not active against antibodies to dust (f-1), and f-5 was immunogenically inactive. In Figure 2 double diffusion of cotton dust and bract antigens are shown against AD and NS. The continuous lines between bAg and f-4, and between f-3, and f-4 indicate a cross reaction of full identity is present in all three extracts. Similar results were obtained with AB. Figure 2 indicates that antigens in cotton dust and/or bract do not react with rabbit NS. This differs from the report (29) that cotton dust reacts with both byssinotic serum and normal serum. Both bract antigen and antigen from cotton dust react with cotton dust antibodies but they do not react with normal pre-immunization serum. This indicates that normal serum does not contain antibodies to either bract or cotton dust. These reactions differ from the pseudoimmune reactions reported by Edwards and Jones (30), because the cotton dust antigen(s) does not react nonspecifically with both normal and immunized rabbit sera. Precipitin arcs in a reaction of identity between antigens in bracts and dust in Figure 2 confirm that antigens present in dust are derived at least partly from cotton bract.

Typical electrophoregrams stained for protein and for carbohydrate are shown in Figure 3. The antigen in f-4 actually consists of two materials; a large, slow moving, diffuse band near the origin, and a much smaller, sharp band that migrates about two-thirds of the way down the gel. To determine the type of material present in the bands, a dual staining technique was employed. Coomassie blue was used to stain for protein and the Schiff's reagent to stain for polysaccharide. The larger slow moving band near the origin stained heavily for carbohydrate but lightly or not at all for protein. The smaller, sharp, fast moving band stained for protein but very lightly for carbohydrate. These results indicate that the active material in f-4 is glycoprotein in nature. When these separated fractions were tested for antigenicity against antibodies to cotton dust, it was found that both were active.

To determine if plant tissues other than bract contained these active antigens, hand-picked stem, leaf, and burr tissues were obtained from growing cotton plants, dried, then ground and extracted as described previously. Figure 4a compares immunodiffusion of burr, gin trash, leaf, stem, cotton dust, and cotton bract. Results indicate that the antigenic materials present in cotton dust and bract is also present in other plant tissues (stem, leaf, burr) and in gin trash collected before the cotton enters the textile mill cardroom. Immunodiffusion tests of the same fractions against normal rabbit serum showed that only the extract of burr produced a very diffuse precipitate against normal serum (Figure 4b). It is likely that burr contains the common active antigen found in other tissues. However, there are other materials, including a gummy extract of large molecular weight carbohydrate polymer, which are probably responsible for the only instance of nonspecific reaction with normal rabbit serum noted. The reaction between burr extract and dust antisera does not signify a greater concentration of antigen in burr compared to that in other extracts. Except for the burr extract, precipitin arcs formed between antigens in other tissues and antisera indicate that the antigens in the dust and plant tissues are the same and that the reaction is immunologically specific for antigens common to all. Since byssinosis has been reported

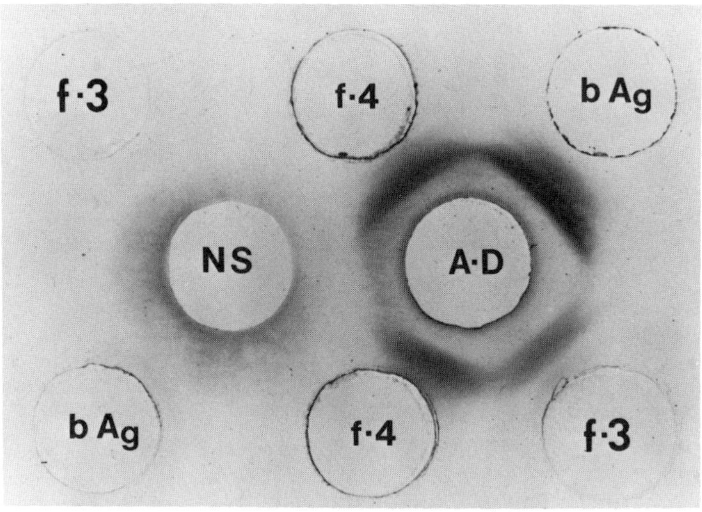

Figure 2. Double diffusion of cotton dust fractions and cotton bract extract against rabbit antiserum to dust (AD) and normal rabbit serum (NS). Conditions described in Material and Methods.

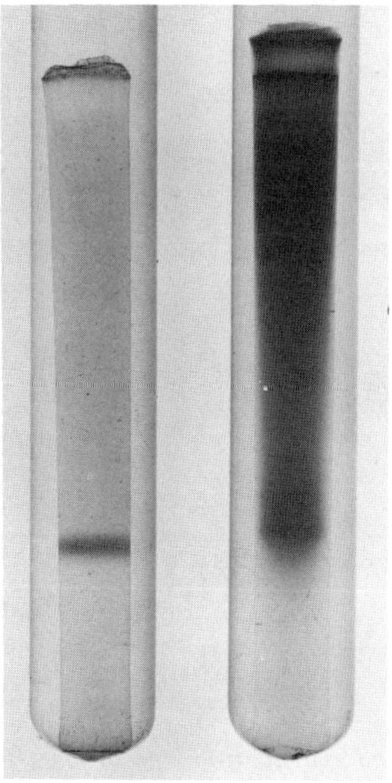

Figure 3. Gel electrophoresis of cotton dust fraction 4 stained for protein (left) and carbohydrate (right). Conditions described in Material and Methods.

a

b

c

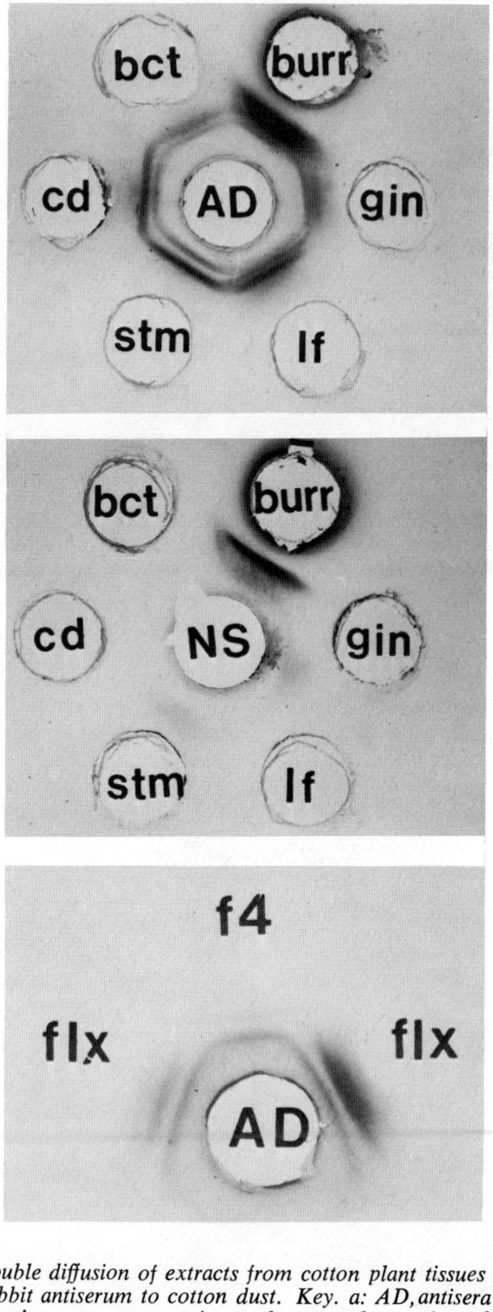

Figure 4. Double diffusion of extracts from cotton plant tissues and extract from flax against rabbit antiserum to cotton dust. Key. a: AD, antisera to dust; gin, gin trash; lf, leaf antigen; stm, stem antigen; cd, cotton dust antigen; bct, bract antigen; burr, burr antigen. b: NS, normal rabbit serum. c: flx, flax extract; f-4, cotton dust antigen. Conditions described in Material and Methods.

to occur in people working with other vegetable textile fibers, we tested the reaction of antibodies to dust with extracts of flax, soft hemp. sisal, and jute. Figure 4c shows a typical reaction of extracts from flax, f-4, and AD. In all instances, reactions of extracts from vegetable fibers other than cotton were positive with AD but negative towards NS.

There have been reports of reactions between house dust and cotton dust antibodies (38) and of allergens in cottonseed proteins by Spies et al. (39). Also, byssinosis is uncommon in cottonseed crushing mills. Therefore we looked for the presence of antigens in water extracts of house dust, cottonseed hulls, cottonseed kernel proteins and clean hand picked cotton fibers that had not been baled. The results in Figure 5 indicate that house dust does not contain antigens common to those found in cotton dust.

Results in Table I indicate that no immune precipitin reaction occurred between extracts of cottonseed hulls, cottonseed protein, or clean cotton fibers (picked from cotton grown in the greenhouse) and antibodies to cotton dust, bract, or normal serum. The reaction is positive to baled cotton, however. The antigens found in cotton dust or bract are not derived from cottonseed tissues, such as hulls or cottonseed proteins, or from clean cotton fibers, but from cotton plant parts other than the seed or fiber. There have also been reports (24,26) that possibly bacterial endotoxins produced by microorganisms growing in cotton, or associated with cotton might be implicated in the production of antibodies. We considered LPS produced from certain gram-negative organisms (some found on cotton, some found in soil) for common antigenicity to antibodies in cotton dust. Data in Table 1 indicate that these particular LPS tested do not cross-react with antibodies to cotton dust. This suggests that these particular endotoxins are not associated with the antigenic materials found in cotton dust or bract or that their concentrations were not high enough to be a factor in the production of active serum in rabbits.

To determine whether normal humans who have not been associated with textile mills produced immune reaction with antibodics to cotton dust or bract, 37 volunteers from the Southern Regional Research Center donated blood. The blood was collected, the serum was separated and concentrated approximately 7-fold then tested for antigen-antibody reactions. The majority produced no reaction at all but 5 did form what was referred to as a nonspecific or pseudoimmune reaction. When blood obtained from known or alleged byssinotics was compared with these pseudoimmune-reacting blood sera, the results showed (Figure 6a) that the material producing the antigen-antibody reaction in normals, does not cross-react with blood from the byssinotics. However, the two known byssinotic patients do show a reaction of identity (arrow; Figure 6b) between their blood sera and cotton dust antigen (cd). These two blood samples were obtained from

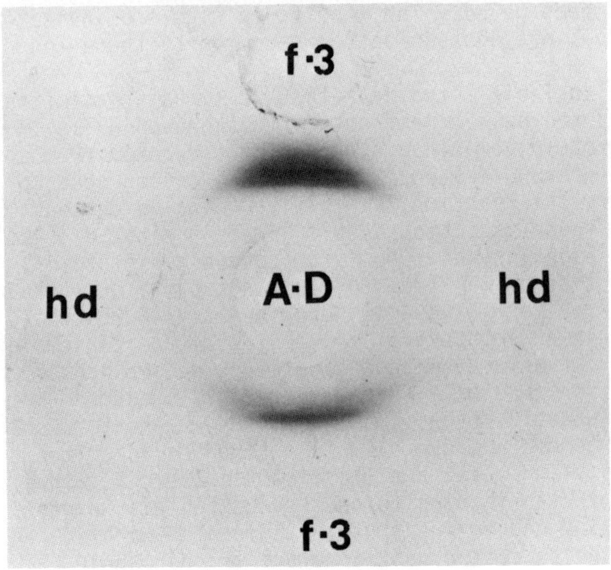

Figure 5. Double diffusion of cotton dust and house dust extracts against rabbit antiserum to dust (AD). Key: f-3, cotton dust antigen; hd, house dust extract. Conditions described in Materials and Methods.

Table I

Reactivity Between Rabbit Antisera to Cotton Dust and Bract, Normal Rabbit Serum, and Extracts of Cotton Dust, Cotton Tissues, House Dust, and Certain Bacterial Endotoxins.

Antigens	AD	AB	NS
Cotton Dust	+	+	-
Bract	+	+	-
Stem	+	+	-
Leaf	+	+	-
Burr	+	+	+
Gin Trash	+	+	-
Lint (Baled)	+	+	-
Lint (Clean)	-	-	-
Cottonseed Proteins	-	-	-
Hulls	-	-	-
House Dust	-	-	-
Endotoxins			
E. Coli 026:B6	-	-	-
0127:B8 (Phenol Extracted)	-	-	-
0127:B8 (TCA Extracted)	-	-	-
0137:B8 (Butanol Extracted)	-	-	-
Serratia marcescens	-	-	-
Shigella flexneri	-	-	-

(AD), antisera to dust; (AB), antisera to bract; (NS), normal serum; (+), positive reaction; (-), no reaction.

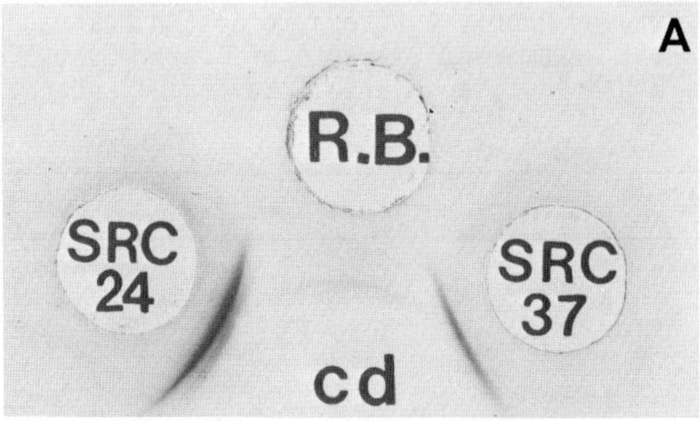

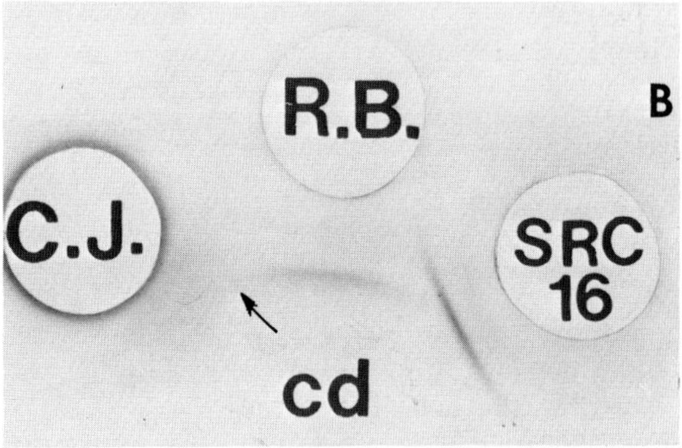

Figure 6. Double diffusion of cotton dust antigen against human sera. Key: SRC 24, 37, and 16, normal human sera; RB and CJ, sera from byssinosis patients. Conditions described in Materials and Methods.

byssinotic patients eight years apart. One sample was held in a freezer at -10°C and the other sample was freshly drawn. Nevertheless it confirms that these two people who had worked in cotton textile mills for many years, have antibodies to a common cotton dust antigen in their blood. They show a reaction of identity with cotton dust antigen. This suggests that the antigens which induced formation of these antibodies in the blood of the two patients are identical.

Kamat et al. (40) reported an examination of blood serum immunoglobulins from cotton mill workers having byssinosis or chronic bronchitis, and normal blood serum. They showed that normal patients had IgG levels averaging 1400 mg/dl, whereas blood sera obtained from byssinotics had a mean value of 1850 mg/dl. In a very limited exploratory way we examined blood of an SRRC normal patient, a normal IgG standard obtained from Calbiochem-Behring, and IgG levels from one of the byssinotics. Results in Figure 7 show that the diameters of the precipitin rings around the two normal sera are equal, but the diameter of the precipitin ring for the byssinotic blood is much larger. Using the table supplied with the standard IgG kit, the normal had a calculated IgG level of 1292 mg/dl compared to 1790 mg/dl for the byssinotic blood.

Summary

Reaction of antisera to cotton dust and bract antigens produced precipitin arcs which fused in a reaction of identity, indicating common antigenic determinants in the two materials. Cotton dust, bract, and a purified antigen separated from the dust give positive immune responses in rabbits. The immune response is specific only for rabbits that have been immunized with dust or bract extracts, not for normal rabbit serum. Sera obtained from normal human volunteers do not contain antibodies to antigens present in cotton dust or bract. Sera obtained from alleged byssinotic patients do contain antibodies specific for these antigens. With admittedly limited data it was indicated that serum obtained from an alleged byssinotic had an increased IgG level compared to the IgG level in normal blood. Antigens found in the dust and bract are also present in leaf, stem, and burr tissues of the cotton plant, but not in cottonseed hulls, kernel proteins, clean cotton fibers, certain bacterial lipopolysaccharides or house dust. The antigenic material was also found in other textile fibers such as sisal, soft hemp, jute, and flax.

Disclaimer

Mention of company names or products does not constitute endorsement by the United States Department of Agriculture.

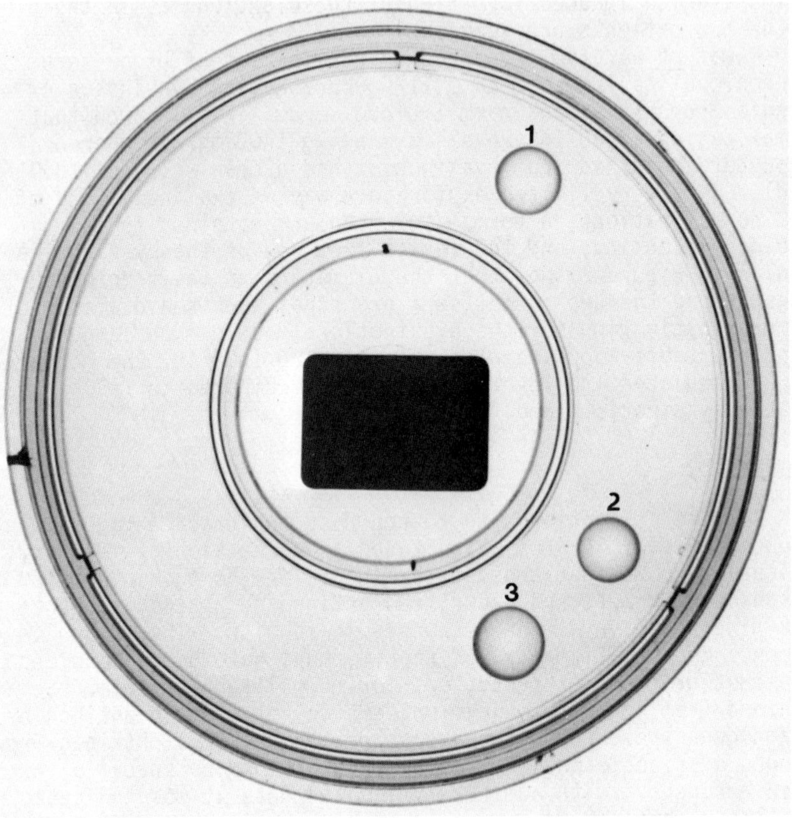

Figure 7. Immunodiffusion of normal and byssinotic blood sera against human IgG antibodies. Tripatigen plate contains antibodies to human IgG in gel. Key: well 1, control IgG serum provided with plates; well 2, normal human serum; well 3, serum from byssinosis patient.

Literature cited

1. Ayer, Howard E. Crit. Rev. Environ. Control 1971, 2, 207-41.
2. Bouhuys, A. Trans. N. Y. Acad. Sci. 1966, 28, 480-90.
3. Bouhuys, A.; Schoenberg, J. B.; Beck, G. J.; Schilling, R. S. F. Lung 1977, 154, 167-86.
4. Schilling, R. S. F. Lancet 1956, 2, 261-5-319-25.
5. Bouhuys, A.; Barbero, A.; Lindell, S. E.; Roach, S. A. Arch. Environ. Health 1967, 14, 533-44.
6. Zuskin, Eugenia; Valic, Fedor; Bouhuys, Arend. Lung 1976, 154, 17-24.
7. Mustafa, K. Y.; Lakha, A. S.; Milla, M. H.; Dahoma, U. Br. J. Ind. Med. 1978, 35, 123-8.
8. Nicholls, P. J.; Evans, E.; Valic, F.; Zuskin, E. Br. J. Ind. Med. 1973, 30, 142-5.
9. Nicholls, P. J. Br. J. Ind. Med. 1962, 26, 101-8.
10. Popa, V.; Gavrilescu, N.; Preda,N.; Tesculescu, D.; Plecias, M.; Cirstea, M. Br. J. Ind. Med. 1969, 26, 101-8.
11. Battigelli, M. C.; Craven, P. L.; Fischer, J. J.; Morey, P. R.; Sasser, P. E., J. Environ. Sci. Health 1977, A12, 327-39.
12. HEW publication No. (NIOSH) 75-118, 1974, 159 pp.
13. Wakelyn, P. J.; Greenblatt, G. A.; Brown, D. F.; Tripp, V. W. Am. Ind. Hyg. Assoc. J. 1976, 37, 22-31.
14. Morey, P. R.; Sasser, P. E.; Bethea, R. M.; Kopetzky, M. T. Am. Ind. Hyg. Assoc. J. 1976, 37, 407-12.
15. Braun, D. C.; Scheel, L. D.; Tuma, J.; Parker, L. J. Occup. Med. 1973, 15, 241-4.
16. Antweiler, H. Br. J. Ind. Med. 1961, 18, 130-2.
17. Edwards, J.; McCarthy, P.; McDermott, M.; Nicholls, P. J., Skidmore, J. W. J. Physiol. London 1970, 208, 63P-64P.
18. Evans, E.; Nicholls, P. J. J. Pharm. Pharmacol. 1974, 26, 115P-116.
19. Haworth, E.; Macdonald, A. D. J. Hyg. 1937, 37, 234-42.
20. Nicholls, P. J. Br.J. Ind. Med. 1962, 19, 33-41.
21. Northrup, S.; Presant, L.; Kilburn, K. H.; McCormick, J.; Pachlatko, P. Fed. Proc., Fed. Am. Soc. Expt. Biol. 1976, 35, P632.
22. Rylander, R., Mattsby, I., Snella, M-C. Chest 1979, 75S, 278S-9S.
23. Furness, G.; Maitland, H. B. Br. J. Ind. Med. 1952, 9, 138-45.
24. Cavagna, G.; Foa, V.; Vigliani, C. Br. J. Ind. Med. 1969, 26, 314-21.
25. Pernis, B.; Vigliani, C.; Cavagna, C.; Fenulli, M. Br. J. Ind. Med. 1961, 18, 120-9.
26. Massoud, A.; Taylor, G. Lancet 1964, 2, 607-10.
27. Oehling, A.; Gonzales de la Reguerra, I.; Vines Rueda, J. J. Respiration 1972, 29, 155-60.

28. Taylor, G.; Massoud, A. A. E.; Lucas, F. Br. J. Ind. Med. 1971, 28, 143-51.
29. Edwards, John H.; Jones, Brian M. J. Immunol. 1973, 110, 498-501.
30. Edwards, John H.; Jones, Brian M. Ann. N. Y. Acad. Sci. 1974, 221, 59-63.
31. Kutz, S. A.; Olenchock, S. A.; Elliott, J. A.; Pearson, D. J.; Major, P. C. Environ. Res. 1979, 19, 405-14.
32. Wilson, M. R.; Sekul, A. A.; Ory, R. L.; Salvaggio, J. E.; Lehrer, S. B. Clin. Allergy, 1980, 10, 303-8.
33. Sekul, A. A.; Ory, R. L. Fed. Proc. Am. Soc. Exptl. Biol. 1978, 37, P604.
34. Sekul, A. A.; Ory, R. L. Text. Res. J. 1979, 49, 523-5.
35. Axelsen, N. H.; Kroll, J.; Weeke, B. Eds.: "A Manual of Immunoelectrophoresis"; Universitetsforlaget: Oslo, 1973, reprinted 1975.
36. Davis, B. J. Ann. N. Y. Acad. Sci. 1964, 121, 404-27.
37. Zacharius, R. M.; Zell, T. E.; Morrison, J. H.; Woodlock, J. J. Anal. Biochem. 1969, 30, 148-51.
38. Berrens, L. "The Chemistry of Atopic Allergens," Publisher S. Karger: New York, 1971; p 71.
39. Spies, J. R.; Coulson, E. J.; Bernton, H. S.; Stevens, Henry. J. Am. Chem. Soc. 1940, 62, 1420-3.
40. Kamat, S. R.; Taskar, S. P.; Iyer, E. R.; Naik, M. J. Soc. Occup. Med. 1979, 29, 102-6.

RECEIVED January 20, 1982.

18

Secondary Metabolites of *Gossypium*: A Biogenetic Analysis

J. P. McCORMICK

University of Missouri, Department of Chemistry, Columbia, MO 65211

Some 310 secondary metabolites which reportedly have been found from the cotton plant are reviewed according to the biogenetic classifications of acetogenins, shikimates, terpenoids and steroids, nitrogen compounds, monosaccharides, and others which are not classified. Aside from synthesis for structural materials, the cotton plant apparently invests the energy expended on secondary metabolism primarily toward the formation of terpenoids. Of these, the sesquiterpenoids account for the majority and the cadinane group in particular is predominant. Alkaloids are conspicuously absent from the known *Gossypium* secondary metabolites, perhaps as a result of isolation techniques employed. Relevant to the byssinosis problem, assay of physiological activities might best be focused on the cadinane terpenoids, the flavanoid, coumarin and cinnamic acid phenols, and any alkaloids which may be found by future investigation.

Of the possible causes of byssinosis, the suggestion that one or more organic substances found in cotton dust may play a role remains a plausible hypothesis. Based on various biological assays of extracts obtained from cotton trash, much of the work performed to identify an organic causative agent has focused on a cadinane sesquiterpene, lacinilene C methyl ether (**178a**) and such related compounds as the parent phenol (**177**) and glyco-

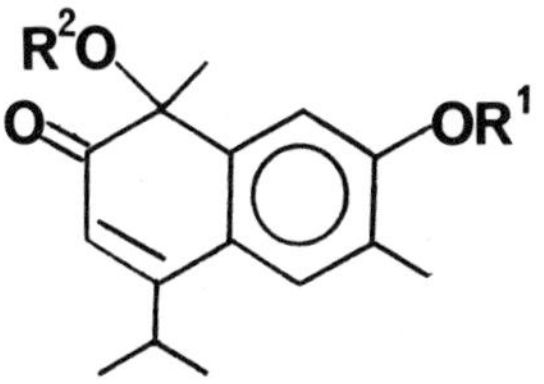

177 R^1 = H, R^2 = H
178a R^1 = Me, R^2 = H
178b R^1 = Me, R^2 = sugar

lacinilene compounds

0097-6156/82/0189-0275$7.50/0

side derivatives (**178b**) (1, 2, 3). However, the likelihood of these compounds' involvement in causing byssinosis has been questioned and to date no convincing evidence has been presented implicating them in the development of this disease. For this reason, it is timely to consider what other organic substances are known to be in the cotton plant. As well, it can be useful to consider which types of compounds have not been reported and to question whether such compounds really are absent or simply have not yet been found, owing to the nature of the methods and orientation of previous investigations.

Strictly speaking, it is the material in cotton dust which is of interest. However, only very small amounts of such airborne, small particulate matter has been available for examination. Thus, the reasonable assumption has been made that the organic composition of such dust is similar to that of its major components, which are derived from the dried, friable cotton plant parts: bract and leaf, pericarp, stem, and seed fragments (4). [Of these, the bract and leaf are the most abundant in raw cotton dust and therefore have received the most attention regarding composition (5).] Using this relatively sound justification, a number of groups have examined the organic composition of the cotton plant in varying stages of growth and senescence. One must be careful about drawing conclusions regarding the composition of cotton dust from studies of material in a state of development unlike that of cotton-derived material when it is generally processed. However, the focus of the present paper is on the general secondary metabolism of *Gossypium* as it can be surmised from the known organic substances reported to be in the plant. In this context, it is useful to consider results obtained from studies of cotton in various stages of growth and aging.

The purpose of this paper, then, is to present an organized summary of the known secondary metabolites of *Gossypium*, in order to provide a conceptual platform for further work toward identification of organic substances which may play a causative role in byssinosis.

Historical

A few groups have made substantial progress toward the identification of *Gossypium* secondary metabolites. Stipanovic, in collaboration with Wakelyn, Bell, and others, has identified several compounds, primarily cadinane sesquiterpenoids (17, 21 - 28, 31). Hedin's group has used gas chromatography-mass spectrometry to identify a wide variety of substances which may be derived from the cotton plant (8 - 10, 12, 13, 14, 20). Brzozowska, Hanower, and Tanguy have reported the structures of several phenolic compounds (15). Other investigators have made more focused, but significant contributions. Wakelyn, Greenblatt, Brown and Tripp have reviewed much of the early work in this area (16).

Approach

In the present discussion, the general scheme of biogenesis will be used as the basis for organization of the compounds reportedly found in *Gossypium*. Biogenesis is a term which refers to the general biological pathway(s) utilized by an organism for formation of secondary metabolites, those nonpolymeric substances produced which are not a part of the primary metabolism system. A schematic representation of the major components of such systems in plants is given in Figure 1. The organizational value of using such a scheme is readily apparent, since there are only a few major groups of secondary metabolites. More importantly, the members of a particular group share general structural features which may give them common properties and perhaps similar locations in a plant.

The weaknesses of this approach also should be pointed out. The classification system generally ignores specific functionality found in the compounds. To cite an example of particular relevance to *Gossypium* secondary metabolites, most of those classes listed in Figure 1 may contain phenolic compounds. As well, although some generalizations may be made concerning the common physiological activities of each of the groups of metabolites, the actual activities of a specific compound must be examined individually before any statements are made regarding that member of the group. Relating this to the goal of identifying causative agents of byssinosis, certain groups of compounds may be singled out as likely candidates for containing one or more culprits, but nevertheless the physiological activity of each isolated substance must be examined separately

Most all of the organic compounds which have been reported from studies of cotton plant parts and cotton trash have been included in this review. Only those which seem most unlikely to be cotton-derived natural products have been excluded. For example, the phthallates reported as "air space volatiles of the cotton plant" are likely artifacts derived from common plastics (9); some hydrocarbons found to be in cotton lint and waste probably came from a source obtained from petroleum (8); and aflatoxin is presumably a mold metabolite (36). A few other compounds have been excluded for similar reasons.

On the other hand, some compounds which are included may not be true *Gossypium* secondary metabolites. Not only are the sources mentioned above possible contributors of exogenous compounds which have been included in the accompanying Tables (I - X), but also it is quite possible that methods of isolation and analysis caused molecular transformation which created isomers of true metabolites or even caused more drastic alterations. The diversity of structures which are plausible natural products is so great that it is not reasonable to exclude many of those reported simply on the basis of structure assignment. For this reason, it can be expected that some errors of inclusion have been made.

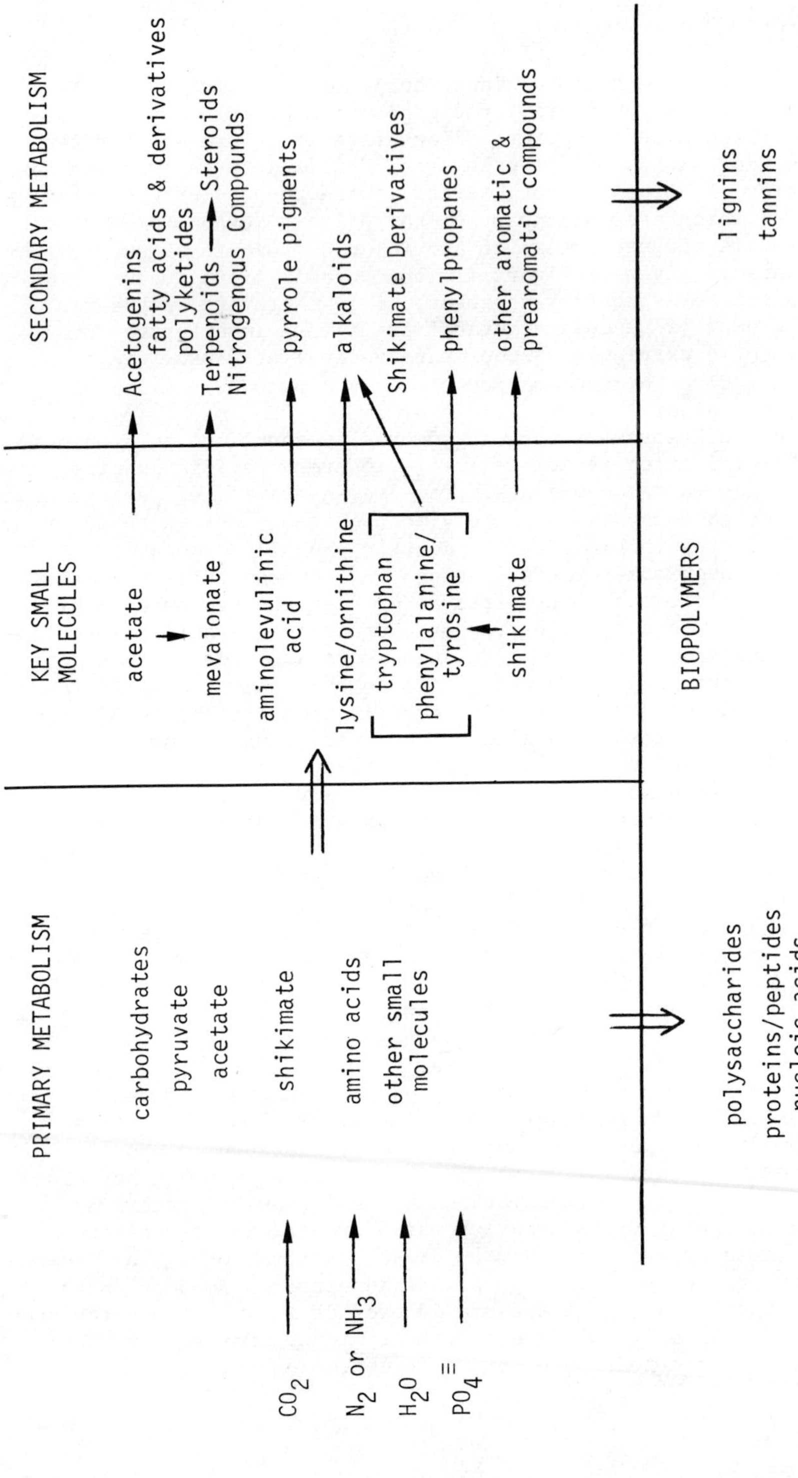

Figure 1. Generalized biogenesis scheme for plants.

Finally, it should be pointed out that in this review no attempt has been made to separate the results according to plant species or plant part. Both types of divisions would be useful, but practical considerations have precluded such a detailed analysis. Some reports cited, primarily those of Stipanovic and of Hedin, provide some of this type of information.

Secondary Metabolites of *Gossypium*

Acetogenins. Consistent with expectations based on the nature of the cotton plant, a number of fatty acids and related compounds have been characterized as components. Table I lists those which have been reported and which contain at least twelve carbon atoms in the linear chain. Much of such material is found in the seeds and in the waxes of the leaves and much is tied up as glyceride or as sterol ester (6). Of these fatty acids, palmitic

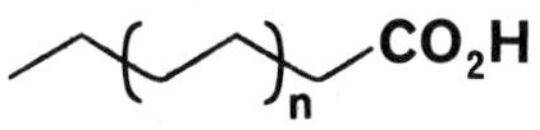

12, n = 6

18, n = 7

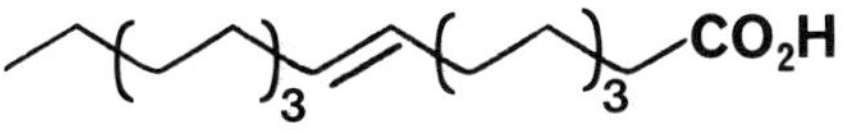

19

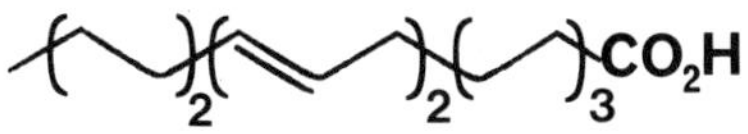

21

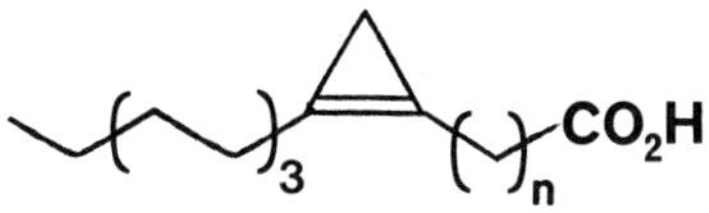

25, n = 6

26, n = 7

(**12**), linoleic (**21**), oleic (**19**) and stearic (**18**) acids are the predominant ones. Fatty acid substances having an odd number of carbons are generally less common; several appear in *Gossypium*. As well, the unusual cyclopropenoic acids malvaldic (**25**) and sterculic (**26**) acids are present and may have significant physiological activity (65).

The other acetogenins, shown in Table II, are a varied assortment of small molecule compounds which as a group contain alkene, alcohol, and carbonyl (acid, ester, aldehyde, and ketone) functionality. They are fairly typical substances with common structural features. Again, those compounds possessing an odd number of carbon atoms are less common, and biogenetically may be derived from a propionate starter unit.

Table I. Fatty Acids and Related Compounds.

Compound	Number	Reference
lauric acid	1	7
methyl laurate	2	43
dodecane	3	8
γ-tridecalactone	4	9
myristic acid	5	7
methyl myristate	6	43
tetradecane	7	9
n-pentadecene	8	47
3-methyltetradecane	9	10
pentadecanoic acid	10	8
pentadecenoic acid	11	45
palmitic acid	12	8
methyl palmitate	13	43
palmitoleic acid	14	45
margaric acid	15	8
heptadecenoic acid	16	8
heptadecadienoic acid	17	8
stearic acid	18	6
oleic acid	19	7
methyl oleate	20	10
linoleic acid	21	8
methyl linolate	22	10
linolenic acid	23	8
octadecatetraenoic acid	24	45
malvalic acid	25	46
sterculic acid	26	46
arachidic acid	27	45
eicosadienoic acid	28	47
eicosatrienoic acid	29	47
behenic acid	30	47
dicosadienoic acid	31	47
tricosane	32	48
pentacosane	33	48
heptacosane	34	48
octacosane	35	49
octacosanol	36	49
montanyl alcohol	37	50
nonacosane	38	48
triacontane	39	49
triacontanol	40	49
untricontane	41	48
dotriacontane	42	49
dotriacontanol	43	49
hexatriacontane	44	49

Table II. Other Acetogenins

Compound	Number	Reference
acetic acid	45	8
ethyl acetate	46	12
ethylene	47	51
butyraldehyde	48	8
γ-butyrolactone	49	8
valeric acid	50	52
hexyl crotonate	51	12
1-hexanol	52	8
hexanal	53	8
2,4-hexadienal	54	10
trans-2-hexen-1-ol	55	13
cis-3-hexen-1-ol	56	13
4-hexen-1-ol	57	13
trans-2-hexenal	58	8
caproic acid	59	45
γ-caprolactone	60	10
heptanal	61	8
1-octanol	62	9
6-octen-4-ol	63	13
2-octenal	64	8
caprylic acid	65	45
δ-capryllactone	66	8
1-nonanol	67	14
3-nonanol	68	9
nonanal	69	8
2-nonenal	70	8
trans, cis-2,6-nonadienal	71	8
nonanoic acid	72	8
methyl nonanate	73	43
γ-nonalactone	74	8
2-methyl-1-nonanol	75	9
3-methyl-1-nonanol	76	9
n-decane	77	8
n-decene	78	8
decanal	79	9
2-decanone	80	12
capric acid	81	45
6-undecanol	82	12
undecanoic acid	83	8
γ-undecalactone	84	8

Shikimates. The flavanoids, shown in Table III, have been investigated primarily by a few groups (15, 53 - 58). These structurally complex substances, which contain both acetogenin- and skikimate-derived portions, are of significant interest regarding characteristic physiological activities which make them suspect agents for involvement in byssinosis. In fact, quercetin (**85**) has been found to cause leucocyte recruitment through airway walls (37) and catechin (**101**) reportedly affects capillary fragil-

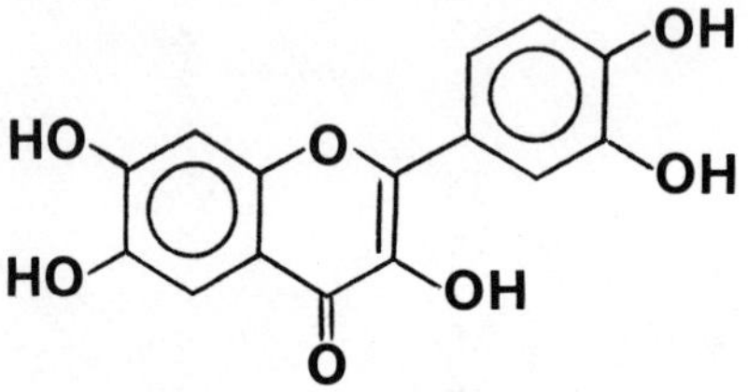

85

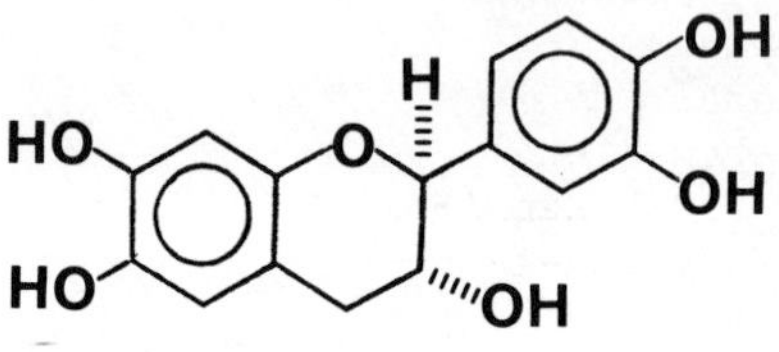

101

ity and permeability (38). Furthermore, these compounds possess considerable water solubility, a characteristic reportedly associated with the causative agent(s) in cotton dust (42).

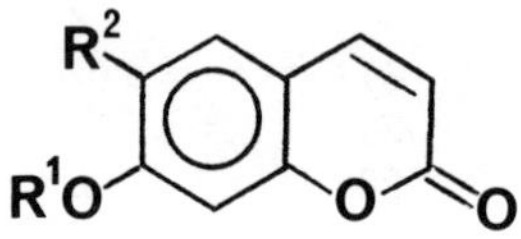

109, R^1 = H, R^2 = OMe
110, R^1 = glucosyl, R^2 = OMe
111, R^1 = H, R^2 = H

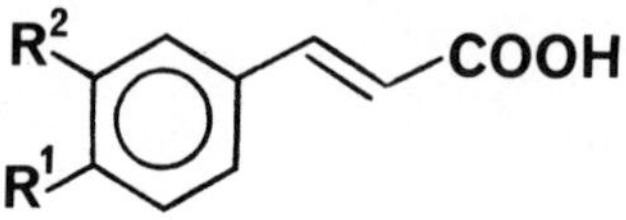

112 – 117
R^1, R^2 = OH, OMe, or Osugar

The phenylpropanes (C_6C_3 compounds) listed in Table III are a rather common group among plants. Scopoletin (**109**), scopolin (**110**), and umbelliferone (**111**) are very widespread coumarins. The cinnamic acid compounds (**112 - 117**) also are well known, common plant metabolites.

The remaining shikimates in Table III also are relatively simple, well known compounds. The phenolic structures of vanillin (**125**) and gallic acid (**127**) and the prephenolic structures of the common quinic acid (**128**) and chlorogenic acid (**129**) make them candidates for physiological activity. Gallic acid is the monomer for tannins, biological polymers found in the cotton plant (15, 37).

Table III. Shikimate Derived Compounds

Compound	Number	Reference
Flavanoids		
quercetin	85	15
quercetin rhamnoglucoside	86	15
quercetin glucoside	87	53
isoquercitrin	88	15
quercimeritrin	89	53
rutin	90	15
kaempferol	91	15
kaempferol glucoside	92	15
kaempferol rhamnoglucoside	93	15
kaempferol rutinoside	94	54
trifolin	95	54
gossypetin	96	15
gossypitrin	97	54
gossypin	98	54
herbacitin	99	55
herbacitrin	100	56
catechin	101	15
gallocatechin	102	57
1-epigallocatechin	103	57
gallocatechin gallate	104	57
epigallocatechin gallate	105	57
cyanidin	106	15
cyanidin-3-glucoside	107	58
leucocyanidin	108	15
C_6C_3 Compounds: Coumarins		
scopoletin	109	17
scopolin	110	15
umibelliferone	111	15
C_6C_3 Compounds: Cinnamic Acids		
cinnamic acid	112	18
p-coumaric acid	113	15
glucosyl *p*-coumarate	114	15
3-quinoyl p-coumarate	115	15
caffeic acid	116	15
ferulic acid	117	15
Other C_6C_3 Compounds		
phenylacetone	118	10
phenylpropionaldehyde	119	10

Table III. Shikimate Derived Compounds (Cont'd)

Compound	Number	Reference
C_6C_2 Compounds		
2-phenylethanol	120	13
phenylacetaldehyde	121	10
acetophenone	122	9
C_6C_1 Compounds		
benzyl alcohol	123	13
benzaldehyde	124	10
vanillin	125	8
salicylic acid	126	52
gallic acid	127	19
quinic acid	128	15
chlorogenic acid	129	15

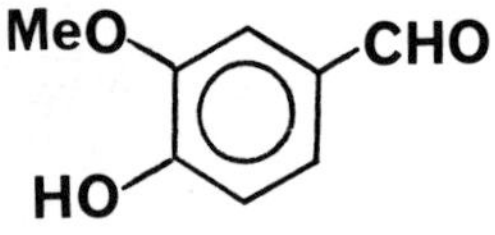

125

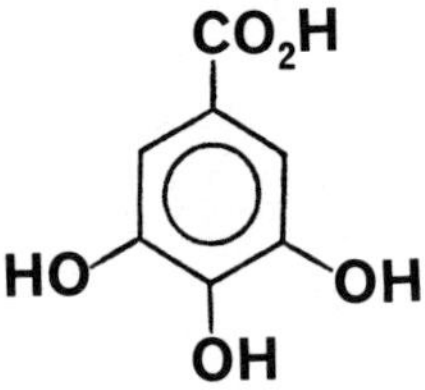

127

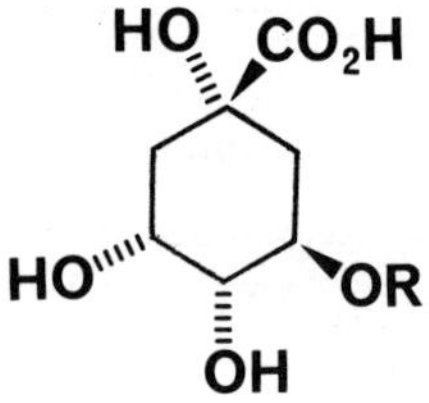

128, R = H

129, R = caffeoyl

Table IV. Hemiterpenoids

Compound	Number	Reference
2-methylbutanol	130	13
3-methylbutanol	131	8
3-methylbutanal	132	8

Terpenoids and Steroids. The information given in Tables IV-VII and the biogenetic relationships shown in Figures 2 and 3 speak for themselves. This class of compounds accounts for more than one-third of the known cotton plant secondary metabolites. The monoterpenoids listed in Table V, many of which have the para-menthane skeleton, are generally common compounds widely spread in the essential oils of plants.

The sesquiterpenes are the largest group of cotton-derived natural products which have been characterized. When the heliocides (**239** - **246**) are included, over 50 compounds in this class have been reported, 31 of which contain the cadinane skeleton. Importantly, these cadinane compounds include one implicated in byssinosis, lacinilene C methyl ether (**178**; vide supra) and others having significant physiological activities. For example, gossypol (**188**) is toxic to humans and is now known to have male anti-fertility activity (39, 40). Gossypol also is a natural insecticide, as are hemigossypolone (**185**) and its methyl ether

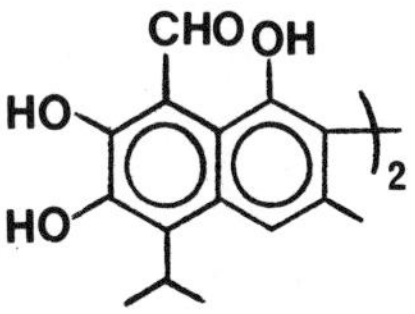

188

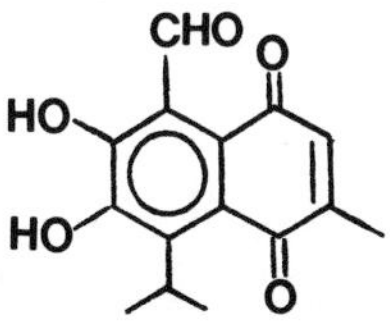

185

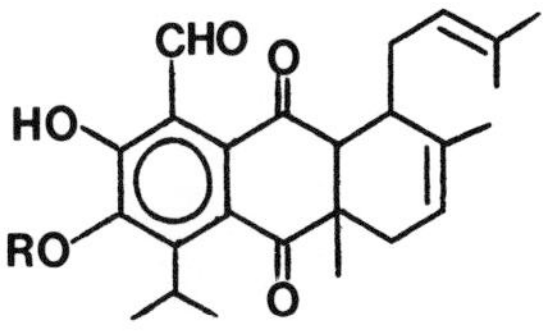

239, R = H

243, R = Me

Table V. Monoterpenoids

Compound	Number	Reference
Acyclic		
trans-β-ocimene	133	14
myrcene	134	20
citronellol	135	13
citronellal	136	10
geraniol	137	13
nerol	138	14
linalool	139	13
Monocyclic: p-methanes		
limonene	140	8
α-terpinene	141	8
γ-terpinene	142	14
terpinolene	143	8
α-phellandrene	144	8
β-phellandrene	145	8
α-terpineol	146	13
carveol	147	13
isopulegone	148	10
1-p-menthen-9-al	149	12
4-isopropylcyclohex-1-ene-1-carboxaldehyde	150	10
4-isopropylcyclohexa-1,3-diene-1-carboxaldehyde	151	10
perilla-aldehyde	152	8
carvacrol	153	10
thymol	154	10
cuminyl alcohol	155	10
cumic aldehyde	156	10
Bicyclic		
thujyl alcohol	157	10
α-pinene	158	14
α-pinene oxide	159	43
β-pinene	160	10
isopinocamphene	161	10
myrtenol	162	10
myrtenal	163	10
verbenone	164	10
borneol	165	14
isoborneol	166	13
camphene	167	14
α-fenchene	168	12
α-campholene aldehyde	169	10

Table VI. Sesquiterpenoids

Compound	Number	Reference
δ-cadinene	170	14
γ-cadinene	171	43
γ-muurolene	172	12
copaene	173	14
α-copaene alcohol	174	12
2,7-dihydroxycadalene	175	21
2-hydroxy-7-methoxycadalene	176	21
lacinilene C	177	22
lacinilene C 7-methyl ether	178	22
hemigossypol	179	23
6-methoxyhemigossypol	180	23
6-deoxyhemigossypol	181	24
desoxyhemigossypol	182	25
6-methoxydesoxyhemigossypol	183	25
raimondal	184	26
hemigossypolone	185	27
6-methoxyhemigossypolone	186	27
gossyrubilone	187	27
Dimeric Cadinanes		
gossypol	188	28
6-methoxygossypol	189	23
6,6'-dimethoxygossypol	190	23
gossypolone	191	30
gossypol alcohol	192	50
Bisabolanes		
α-bisabolene	193	8
α_2-bisabolene	194	8
cis-γ-bisabolene	195	14
1-methyl-4-(1-methylene-5-methylhexyl)-cyclohexa-1,3-diene	196	10
α-curcumene	197	10
α-bisabolol	198	13
β-bisabolol	199	13
bisabolene oxide	200	14

Continued on next page.

Table VI. Sesquiterpenoids (Cont'd.)

Compound	Number	Reference
Farnesanes		
farnesene	201	14
farnesol (E,E & Z,E)	202	12
nerolidol	203	13
Germacrane		
germacrone	204	10
Humulane		
α-humulene	205	14
Caryophyllanes		
caryophyllene	206	14
β-caryophyllene oxide	207	14
α-caryophyllene alcohol	208	10
Santalanes		
α-santalene	209	10
β-santalene	210	10
epi-β-santalene	211	10
Bergamotane		
trans-α-bergamotene	212	14
Guaiane		
δ-guaiene	213	14
Other		
abscisin II	214	44

Table VII. Other Terpenoids and Steroids

Compound	Number	Reference
Sterols and Steroids		
β-amyrin	215	47
β-amyrin montanate	216	47
cholesterol	217	59
campesterol	218	59
β-sitosterol	219	8
β-sitostanol	220	47
campesterol galactoside	221	59
stigmasterol galactoside	222	59
Carotenoids		
phytoene	223	60
phytofluene	224	60
α-carotene	225	60
β-carotene	226	60
lutein	227	60
isolutein	228	60
flavoxanthin	229	60
violaxanthin	230	60
auroxanthin	231	60
neoxanthin	232	60
neochrome	233	60
lycopene	234	47
Other Terpenoids		
β-ionone	235	13
strigol	236	61
strigyl acetate	237	62
vitamin A_1	238	60
heliocide H_1	239	27
heliocide H_2	240	27
heliocide H_3	241	27
heliocide H_4	242	27
heliocide B_1	243	27
heliocide B_2	244	31
heliocide B_3	245	31
heliocide B_4	246	27

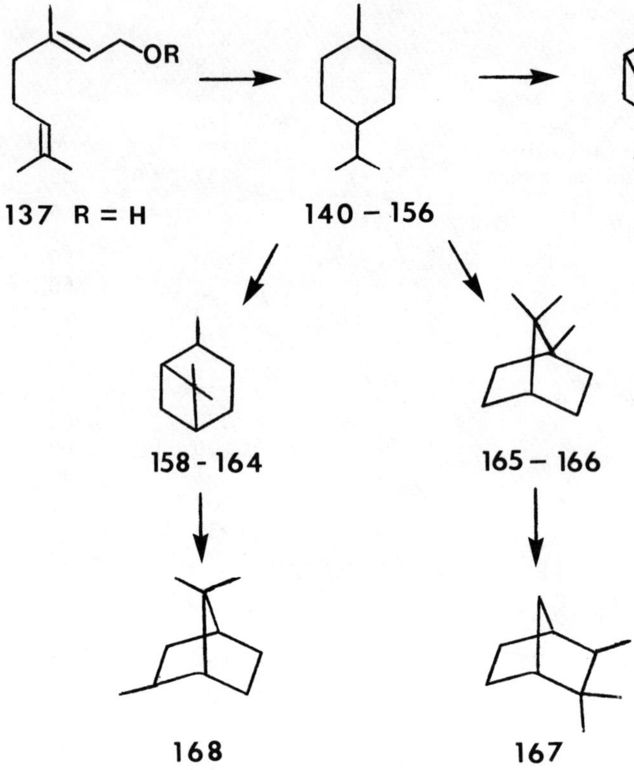

Figure 2. Biogenesis of monoterpene skeleta.

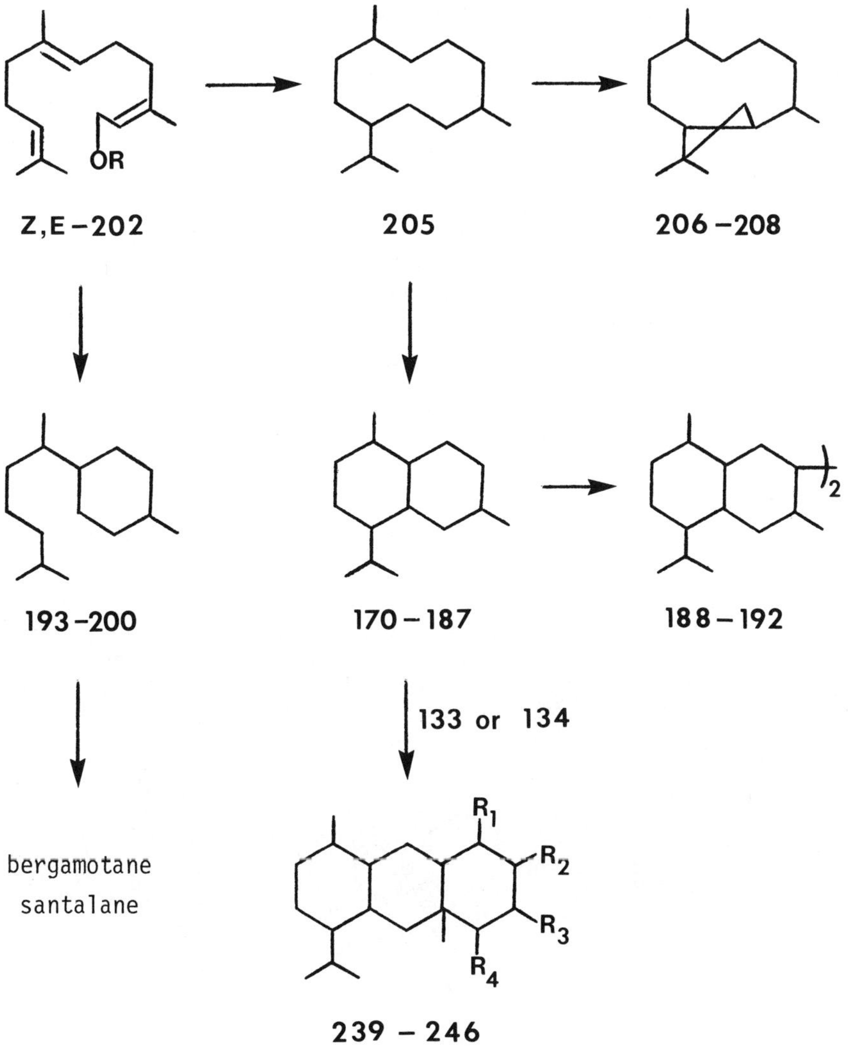

Figure 3. Biogenesis of predominant sesquiterpene and heliocide skeleta.

as well as the heliocides (**239** - **246**) (31). These heliocides are most interesting compounds, being adducts of the sesquiterpenoid hemigossypolone (**185**, itself an insecticide) and the common monoterpene hydrocarbons β-ocimene (**133**) or myrcene (**134**), which are gradually formed during plant aging (very possibly by a nonenzymic reaction). The "B" series consists of methyl ether derivatives of the "H" series.

As indicated in Figure 3, the cadinanes (**170** - **187**) are formed from the humulane (**205**) system, which also is the progenitor of the caryophyllanes (**206** - **208**). Of these last three compounds, caryophyllene (**206**) itself is of particular importance, since it can account for 20 - 25% of the essential oil of some samples (14). Other major constituents in the same sample were copaene (**173**, another cadinane) and α-humulene (**205**), each near 15%. It is therefore apparent that the pathway involving initial conversion of Z,E-farnesyl pyrophosphate to the humulane system is dominant in *Gossypium* terpenoid biogenesis.

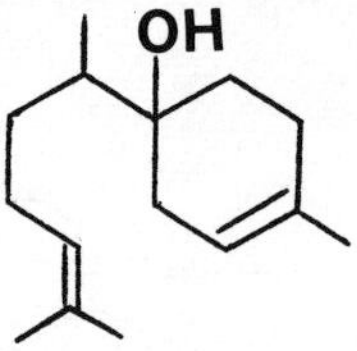

199

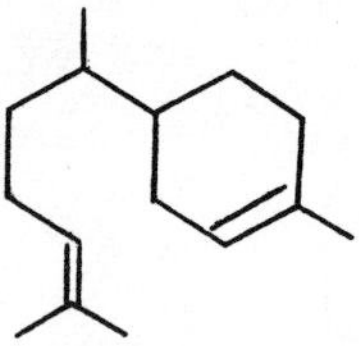

193

The bisabolanes, of which eight have been reported in these studies, also deserve special mention. Again, Z,E-farnesyl pyrophosphate is the putative progenitor. One study (13) reported β-bisabolol (**199**) to be about 34% of the volatile alcohol fraction, making it about 5% of the total essential oil. α-Bisabolene (**193**) is representative of the hydrocarbons of this group.

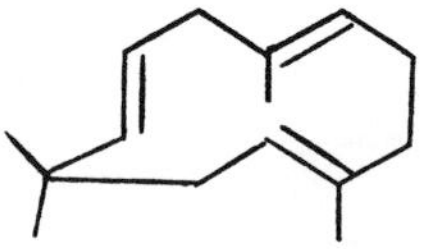

205

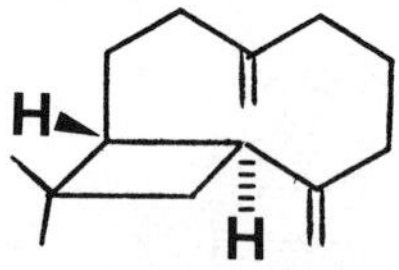

206

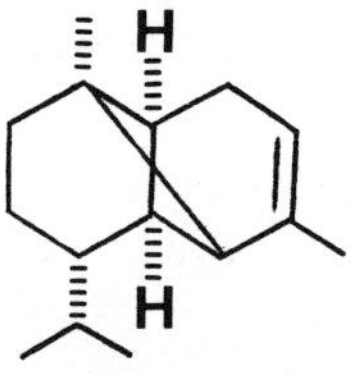

173

Studies of *Gossypium* metabolites have uncovered the occurrence of a few plant sterols, including the representative β-sitosterol (**219**) (8, 18, 47, 59). These widely occurring phytosterols arise by early formation of cycloartenol (not yet reported), which is then structurally modified. Some occur as glycosides.

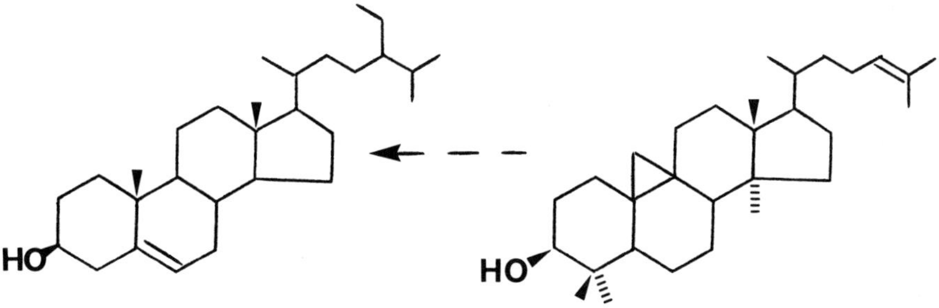

219 cycloartenol

Nitrogen Containing Compounds. This remarkably small group contains indole (**247**), an unusual derivative of indole (**249**), and the well known derivative serotonin (**248**), a neurologically active material endogenous to the central nervous system.

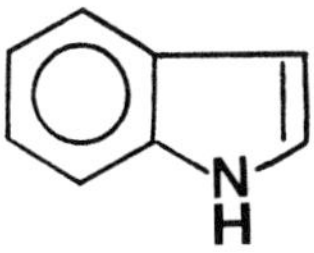

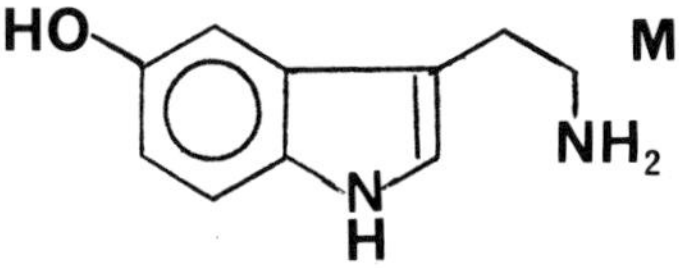

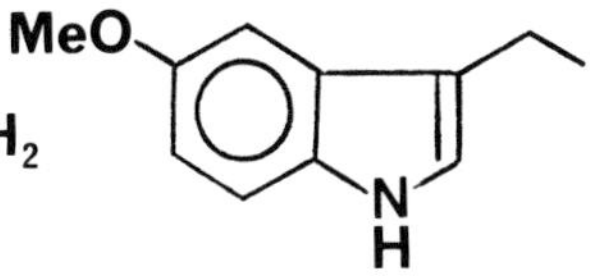

247 **248** **249**

Expectedly, the pyrrole pigments chlorophyll, as well as pheophytin a and b, have been characterized in *Gossypium* (33, 61).

Histamine (**253**), which is widely regarded as associated in some manner with byssinosis (41), is present in relatively small amounts in the cotton plant itself (34). Apparently much larger amounts are released in lung tissue which is exposed to byssinotic agents. (See Table VIII.)

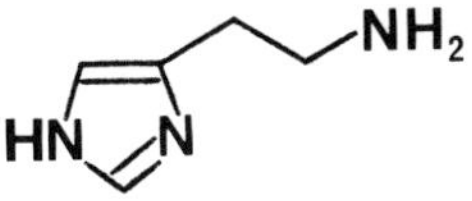

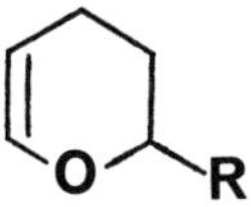

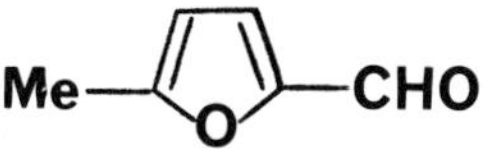

253

288, R = H
289, R = CHO

287

Monosaccharides. The monomeric carbohydrates which have been found in the cotton plant appear in Table IX and have been included because of an implication by one group that they may act as a causative agent of byssinosis (35). This report states that a mixture of D-mannose and D-fructose exhibited contractor activity using the guinea-pig ileum assay. Their report on isolation of byssinosan, an aminopolysaccharide, and its causative agent activity has had more impact and some regard this substance to be a leading candidate as a significant byssinotic agent. (42).

Biogenetically Unclassified Compounds. Table X contains the compounds which either are not easily classified biogenetically by inspection of the structure or which can arise by more than one pathway. In any case, they are generally small molecules containing common functional groups. Some may well be artifacts which have been improperly included (vide supra). In any case, none have been singled out as particularly strong candidates for byssinotic activity. On the other hand, compounds such as the dihydropyrans (**288** and **289**), methylfurfural (**287**) and other aldehydes may well possess damaging physiological activities and phenols commonly are toxic substances.

Discussion

General Biosynthesis of *Gossypium*. A substantial portion of the biosynthetic effort in the cotton plant is invested in formation of structural and functional substances: cellulose, lignins, tannins, and waxes, which are derived from some of the small molecule metabolites listed in the Tables: monosaccharides, phenylpropanes, flavanoids and fatty acid derived substances. Apart from the energy invested in making these structurally essential materials, the vast majority of biosynthesis activity characterized to date goes toward formation of terpenoids. These compounds putatively play ecological roles in many cases and as expected possess significant physiological activities.

It is clear that the sesquiterpenoid pathway proceeding through Z,E-farnesyl pyrophosphate accounts for most of the mevalonate utilization. While cyclization (Figure 3) of this compound may proceed to give bisabolanes and further derivatives, it is an alternative mode of step-wise cyclizations which forms the cadinanes, those sesquiterpenoids which appear to be most significant regarding potential toxic and/or byssinotic activities of the secondary metabolites.

Only a few sterols can be found among those compounds characterized, again emphasizing the sesquiterpenoid, and to a lesser extent the monoterpenoid, orientation of the plant's biosynthetic industry.

Table VIII. Nitrogen Containing Compounds

Compound	Number	Reference
Indoles		
indole	247	8
serotonin	248	32
3-ethyl-5-methoxyindole	249	9
Pyrrole Pigments		
chlorophyll	250	33
pheophytin a	251	61
pheophytin b	252	61
Other Compounds		
histamine	253	34
nicotinic acid	254	47
tetramethylpyrazine	255	10

Table IX. Monosaccharides

Compound	Number	Reference
2-acetamido-2-deoxyglucose	256	35
2-amino-2-deoxyglucose	257	35
arabinose	258	16
fructose	259	35
galactose	260	16
glucose	261	35
mannose	262	35
rhamnose	263	16
ribose	264	16
xylose	265	16
inositol	266	47

Table X. Miscellaneous Compounds

Compound	Number	Reference
acetone	267	8
isobutyraldehyde	268	62
2-ethyl-1-butanol	269	9
2-ethylbutyraldehyde	270	9
1-pentanol	271	13
1-penten-3-ol	272	13
4-hydroxy-4-methyl-2-pentanone	273	8
cyclopentanol	274	12
cyclohexanol	275	13
cyclohexanone	276	8
cycloheptanone	277	8
2-cyclohexadienyl-4-methylpentan-1-ol	278	10
2,4-dimethyl-2,4-heptadienal	279	43
2-methylfuran	280	9
2,5-dimethylfuran	281	10
2-butyl-4-methylfuran	282	8
2-butyl-4-vinylfuran	283	8
2-acetylfuran	284	10
2-isobutyroylfuran	285	10
α-furfuryl alcohol	286	12
5-methyl-2-furfural	287	8
dihydropyran	288	10
2,3-dihydropyrancarboxaldehyde	289	8
cyclohexanecarboxaldehyde	290	8
5-*tert*-butyl-3,3-dimethylindanone	291	10
oxalic acid	292	52
fumaric acid	293	52
succinic acid	294	52
malic acid	295	52
tartaric acid	296	52
glutaric acid	297	47
α-ketoglutaric acid	298	52
citric acid	299	52
phenol	300	8
o-phenylphenol	301	8
di-*sec*-butylphenol	302	8
2-phenoxyethanol	303	9
m-tolyl ethyl ether	304	8
ethylbenzaldehyde	305	9
m-tolualdehyde	306	10
o-methylacetophenone	307	10
p-methylacetophenone	308	12
p-ethylacetophenone	309	10
2,4-dimethylacetophenone	310	10

Perhaps most conspicuous by their absence from the list (cf. Table VIII) are the alkaloids. These substances, generally defined as nitrogen-containing secondary metabolites, are common plant products and usually have distinct physiological activities. Nevertheless, to date no reports seem to have appeared concerning the presence (or absence) of alkaloids as *Gossypium* metabolites.

Directions for Future Investigation. Consideration of the results summarized above permits some suggestions for further research concerning *Gossypium* derived byssinotic agents. The most obvious area of ignorance concerns the alkaloids: virtually none have been found. This is not surprising when the isolation techniques which have been employed are considered: steam distillation/gas chromatography, extraction with water and with low polarity solvents, guidance of isolation procedures using specific functional group reagents (such as was most effectively employed to uncover the terpenoid aldehydes in Stipanovic's work). While these procedures have been used profitably to obtain valuable results, those results may not be useful for drawing conclusions about the presence of rather different types of compounds, such as the alkaloids.

This limitation is well illustrated by the failure of those methods to uncover the presence of another important group, the flavanoid, coumarin and cinnamic acid phenols (**85** - **117**). On the other hand, some 32 of these compounds were identified when isolation procedures specific for these types of compounds were employed. Using isolation and identification techniques which are particularly useful for alkaloids, it would be possible to determine whether any representatives of this class are present and, if so, to conduct subsequent studies for structure determination.

Finally, some comments regarding examination of physiological activity may be made. Using bioassay methods appropriate for detection of possible byssinotic activity, it appears reasonable that the phenolic compounds (**85** - **117**) and the cadinane sesquiterpenoids (**170** - **192**, **239** - **246**) should be especially scrutinized for causative agent behavior. As well, any alkaloids found must be carefully examined, in recognition of the fact that these compounds generally have potent physiological effects.

Acknowledgment

Financial support by Cotton Incorporated- the research and marketing company representing America's cotton producers- is gratefully acknowledged.

Literature Cited

1. Lynn, W.S.; Munoz, S.; Campbell, J.A.; Jeffs, P.W. Ann. N.Y. Acad. Sci. 1974, 221, 163-73.
2. Northup, S.; Presant, L.; Kilburn, K.H.; McCormick, J.P.; Pachlatko, J.P. Fed. Proc. 1976, 35, 632.
3. Kilburn, K.H. J. Environ. Pathol. Toxicol. 1979, 2, 350-1.
4. Morey, P.R. Am. Ind. Hyg. Assoc. J. 1979, 40, 702-708.
5. Morey, P.R.; Sasser, P.E.; Beathea, R.M.; Kopetzky, M.T. Am. Ind. Hyg. Assoc. J. 1976, 37, 407-12.
6. Talipova, M.; Glushenkova, A.I.; Umarov, A.U. Khim. Prir. Soedin 1981, 44-7; Chem. Abstr. 1981, 94, 205400t.
7. Ganieva, M.; Badalova, M.; Nasyrova, D. Khlopkovodstro 1981, 36-7; Chem. Abstr. 1981, 94, 153598S.
8. Hedin, P.A.; Thompson, A.C.; Gueldner, R.C. J. Agric. Food Chem. 1975, 23, 698-703.
9. Hedin, P.A.; Thompson, A.C.; Gueldner, R.C. Phytochem. 1975, 14, 2088-90.
10. Hedin, P.A.; Thompson, A.C.; Gueldner, R.C. Ann. N.Y. Acad. Sci. 1974, 221, 174-82.
11. Kajimoto, G.; Tsutsui, Y.; Yoshida, H. Nippon Nogei Kagaku Kaishi 1981, 55, 31-6; Chem. Abstr. 1981, 94, 153532r.
12. Hedin, P.A.; Thompson, A.C.; Gueldner, R.C. Phytochem. 1975, 14, 2087-88.
13. Hedin, P.A.; Thompson, A.C.; Gueldner, R.C.; Minyard, J.P. Phytochem. 1971, 10, 3316-18.
14. Hedin, P.A.; Thompson, A.C.; Gueldner, R.C.; Rizk, A.M.; Salama, H.S. Phytochem. 1972, 11, 2356-57.
15. Brzozowska, J.; Hanower, P.; Tanguy, J. Phytochem. 1973, 12, 1253-7.
16. Wakelyn, P.J.; Greenblatt, G.A.; Brown, D.F.; Tripp, V.W. Am. Ind. Hygiene Assoc. J. 1976, 37, 22-31.
17. Wakelyn, P.J.; Stipanovic, R.D.; Bell, A.A. J. Agric. Food Chem. 1974, 22, 567-8.
18. Gilbert, R.D.; Fornes, R.E.; Wang, A.; Lee, K.S. Textile Res. J.. 1980, 50, 29-33.
19. Robinson, T. "The Organic Constituents of Higher Plants", 2nd ed.; Burgess Pub. Co.: Minneapolis, Minnesota, 1967, p. 72.
20. Minyard, J.P.; Tumlinson, J.H.; Hedin, P.A.; Thompson, A.C. J. Agric. Food Chem. 1965, 13, 599-602.
21. Stipanovic, R.D.; Greenblatt, G.A.; Beier, R.C.; Bell, A.A. Phytochem. 1981, 20, 729-30.
22. Stipanovic, R.D.; Wakelyn, P.J.; Bell, A.A. Phytochem. 1975, 14, 1041-3.
23. Stipanovic, R.D.; Bell, A.A.; Mace, M.E.; Howell, C.R. Phytochem. 1975, 14, 1077-81.
24. Bell, A.A.; Stipanovic, R.D.; Howell, C.R.; Fryxell, P.A. Phytochem. 1975, 14, 225-31.
25. Stipanovic, R.D.; Bell, A.A.; Howell, C.R. Phytochem. 1975, 14, 1809-11.

26. Stipanovic, R.D.; Bell, A.A.; O'Brien, D.H. Phytochem. 1980, 19, 1735-38.
27. Bell, A.A.; Stipanovic, R.D.; O'Brien, D.H.; Fryxell, P.A. Phytochem. 1978, 17, 1297-1305.
28. Bell, A.A. Phytopathology 1967, 57, 760-64.
29. Adams, R.; Geissman, T.A.; Edwards, J.D. Chem. Rev. 1960, 60, 555-631.
30. Haas, R.H.; Shirley, P.A. J. Org. Chem. 1965, 30, 4111-13.
31. Stipanovic, R.D.; Bell, A.A.; Lukefahr, M.J. "Host Plant Resistance to Pests": Hedin, P.A., Ed.; American Chemical Society: Washington, D.C., 1977; p 197-214.
32. Davenport, A.; Paton, W.D.M. Brit. J. Ind. Med. 1961, 18, 19-32.
33. Loewenschuss, H.; Wakelyn, P.J. J. Agric. Food Chem. 1973, 21, 319-21.
34. Lloyd, G.R.; Nicholls, P.J. J. Physiol. (London) 1964, 172, 56P-57P.
35. Mohammed, Y.S.; El-Gazzar, R.M.; Adamyova, K. Carbohyd. Res. 1971, 20, 431-5.
36. Wakelyn, P.J.; O'Brien, C.A.; Loewenschuss, H. Southwest Vet. 1972, 25, 293.
37. Kilburn, K.H.; Lynn, W.S.; Tres, L.L.; McKenzie, W.N. Lab. Invest. 1973, 28, 55.
38. Hergert, H.L. "The Chemistry of Flavanoid Compounds": Geissman, T.A., Ed.; MacMillan: New York, N.Y., 1962: p 584.
39. Windholz, M. (Ed.) "The Merck Index"; Merck & Co., Inc: Rahway, New Jersey, 1976; p. 588.
40. Maugh, T.H., III Science 1981, 212, 314.
41. Battigelli, M.C.; Craven, P.L.; Fischer, J.J.; Morey, P.R.; Sasser, P.E. J. Environ. Sci. Health A 1977, 12, 327-39.
42. Cooke, T.F. "Chemical Composition of Cotton Dust and Its Relation to Byssinosis; A Review of the Literature"; Textile Research Institute; Princeton, New Jersey, 1978.
43. Hanny, B.W.; Thompson, A.C.; Gueldner, R.C.; Hedin, P.A. J. Agric. Food Chem. 1973, 21, 1004-6.
44. Ohkuma, K.; Addicott, F.T.; Smith, O.E.; Thiessen, W.E. Tetrahedron Lett. 1965, 2529-35.
45. Thompson, A.C.; Hedin, P.A. Crop Sci. 1965, 5, 133-5.
46. Shenstone, F.S.; Vickery, J.R. Nature 1961, 190, 168-9.
47. Hedin, P.A.; Thompson, A.C.; Gueldner, R.C. "Recent Advances in Phytochemistry. Vol. 10. Biochemical Interaction Between Plants and Insects": Wallace, J.W.; Mansell, R.L., Eds.; Plenum Press: New York, N.Y., 1976, p. 271-350.
48. Struck, R.F.; Frye, J.L.; Shealy, Y.F. J. Agric. Food Chem. 1968, 16, 1028-30.
49. Sadykov, A.S.; Isaer, K.I.; Ishmailov, H.I. Uzbeksk. Khim. Zh. 1963, 7, 53-6; Chem. Abstr. 1963, 59, 10473C.
50. Fargher, R.G.; Probert, M.E. J. Textile Institute 1924, 15, T337-46.
51. Guinn, G. Plant Physiol. 1976, 57, 403-5.

52. Sadykov, A.S.; Pakudina, Z.P.; Buzitskova, E.P.; Guli-Kevkhyan, A. Sh.; Karimdzhanov, A.; Isaev, Kh. Uzbek. Khim. Zhur. Akad. Nauk. Uzbek. S.S.R. 1958, 41-8; Chem. Abstr. 1959, 53, 22292b.
53. Hedin, P.A.; Miles, L.R.; Thompson, A.C.; Minyard, J.P. J. Agric. Food Chem. 1968, 16, 505-13.
54. Parks, C.R. Am. J. Batony 1965, 52, 849-56.
55. Grupenberg, J. "The Chemistry of Flavanoid Compounds": Geissman, T.A., Ed.; MacMillan: New York, N.Y., 1962: p. 423.
56. Hattorv, S. "The Chemistry of Flavanoid Compounds": Geissman, T.A., Ed.; MacMillan: New York, 1962: p. 343.
57. Sadykov, A.S.; Karimdzhauov, A.K. Uzbek. Khim. Zhur. 1960, 53-6; Chem. Abstr. 1960, 54, 25083e.
58. Hedin, P.A.; Minyard, J.P.; Thompson, A.C.; Struck, R.F.; Frye, J. Phytochem. 1967, 6, 1165-67.
59. Thompson, A.C.; Henson, R.A.; Gueldner, R.C.; Hedin, P.A. Lipids 1970, 5, 283-4.
60. Thompson, A.C.; Henson, R.D.; Hedin, P.A.; Minyard, J.P. Lipids 1968, 3, 495-7.
61. Temple, C., Jr.; Roberts, E.C.; Frye, J.; Struck, R.F.; Shealy, Y.F.; Thompson, A.C.; Minyard, J.P.; Hedin, P.A. J. Econ. Entomol. 1968, 61, 1388-93.
62. Minyard, J.P.; Tumlinson, J.H.; Thompson, A.C.; Hedin, P.A. J. Agric. Food Chem. 1967, 15, 517-524.
63. Cook, C.E.; Whichard, L.P.; Wall, M.E.; Egley, G.H.; Coggen, P.; Luhan, P.A.; McPhail, A.T. J. Am. Chem. Soc. 1972, 94, 6198-99.
64. Cook, C.E.; Whichard, L.P.; Turner, B.; Wall, M.E.; Egley, G.H. Science 1966, 154, 1189.
65. Hendricks, J.D.; Sinnhuber, R.O.; Loveland, P.M.; Pawlowski, N.E.; Nixon, J.E. Science 1980, 208, 311.

RECEIVED December 15, 1981.

Histamine in Cotton Plant and Dust Determined by High Performance Liquid Chromatography

J. H. WALL, L. L. MULLER, and R. J. BERNI

U.S. Department of Agriculture, Agricultural Research Service
Southern Regional Research Center, New Orleans, LA 70179

Histamine is quantified in cotton dust and frost-killed cotton plants. Direct determination of histamine in aqueous extracts is achieved by an ion-pairing separation mechanism on a CN bonded phase column and using H_2SO_4 as both buffer and the counter-ion in a water: acetonitrile mobile phase. Fluorescent detection of histamine is performed by a post-column derivatization with o-phthaldehyde. Histamine was found primarily associated with the $\leq$ 20 µm fraction of cotton dust and highly concentrated in the leaves of the plant. Inhalation of histamine can cause a bronchoconstriction, confusing the diagnosis of byssinosis. Earlier workers concluded that histamine's concentration in cotton dust was not great enough to elicit this reaction. Their conclusions were based on data generated from biological analytical testing. These instrumental results agree with their findings.

Scientific knowledge concerning histamine has developed in stages since it was first synthesized in 1907 (1). It was isolated from an ergot preparation by Barger and Dale in 1910 (2) and its dramatic pharmacological effects demonstrated. Dale then established that histamine was a normal constitutent of mammalian tissue and widely distributed throughout the human body (3). Next was the observation that histamine is liberated in tissues by an antigen-antibody reaction and is responsible for a large share of the symptoms of anaphylaxis and the allergic state. Histamine plays an important role in physiological functions of animals and man; for example, histamine levels change in certain pathological conditions. Histamine levels or its formation are affected also by various stress situations, such as exposure to chemical compounds, endotoxins, hyper- or hypothermic conditions.

Histamine is a potent vasodilator and a stimulator of smooth muscle contraction.

Histamine also occurs naturally in plant tissues. It arises from the decomposition of histidine, but its function has not been elucidated. Histamine levels in some plants are surprisingly high - 1,340 μg/g in the blossoms of the spinach plant (4). It is the exposure of man and animal to this botanical histamine with a possible physiological action that makes histamine of agricultural importance. The inhalation of cotton dust, for instance, has been related to byssinosis, a respiratory disease involving a lung dysfunction.

Histamine, a naturally occurring constituent of the cotton plant, is, therefore, present in cotton dust. In 1932 Maitland and coworkers (5) identified a histamine-like substance in total cotton dust collected by a high-volume filter. They found the levels ranged from 4 to 20 μg/g using biological methods for histamine measurements. They also found indications that the histamine was associated with the finer particles which would be inhaled into the lower airways. MacDonald (6) continued this work and in 1934 concluded that the histamine-like compound was a constant constituent of cotton dust, but its level varied considerably in samples measured and was almost entirely associated with the $\leq$ 20 μm fraction. MacDonald (7) isolated crystalline histamine from cotton dust. Bouhuys (8) in 1960 discovered that normal or previously unexposed individuals displayed a lung dysfunction upon inhalation of an aqueous extract of cotton dust. He also established that this dust contained 17 μg/g of histamine and concluded that this was not enough to elicit the lung dysfunction he observed. The histamine liberator or constrictor agent in cotton dust believed responsible for byssinosis is still unknown.

The evaluation of this physiological reaction to cotton dust has been hampered to various degrees, by the lack of easy and reliable methodology for the determination of histamine. Biological methods are very selective but they are time consuming and expensive. The general chemical method (9,10), based on total fluorescence, is not selective enough because of the many fluorescent compounds ubiquitous to the cotton plant (11). High performance liquid chromatography (HPLC) would appear to offer a superior and unique analytical method because of its range of separation possibilities and assays can be performed without isolation of histamine from the aqueous extract of the sample. Other HPLC determinations of histamine have been on the separation of the *o*-phthaldehyde (OPT) derivative of histamine (12,13), limiting their use to a specific matrix. The work presented here is designed to offer a more general method that separates histamine itself and have a wide application.

Experimental

Apparatus. The HPLC instrument used was a Water's Associates model 6000A pump for the solvent supply, a U6K septumless injector and a radial compression module with standard Radial Pak columns. Immediately after the column a low dead volume tee was inserted and another 6000A pump was used to deliver a solution of OPT for the post-column derivatization of histamine. Twenty feet of 9 thousandths (id) coiled stainless steel tubing was used as a mixing chamber and held at 60°C in a water bath. The reaction mixture then passed through a Water's 420 fluorescence detector which was connected to a recorder. The detector was equipped with a 340-nm excitation filter and a 440-nm emmission filter. The gain was set at 16 with the span adjusted to the maximum for all samples.

Materials. All samples and solvents were filtered through 0.2 µm Millipore filters to remove fine particulate matter. Solvents were HPLC grade and the mobile phase was prepared using a volume concentration of H_2SO_4 instead of a pH adjustment. Histamine dihydrochloride, commercially obtained from Calbiochem-Behring Corp., was used as a standard. Calculations were made on the free base. The derivatizing reagent was prepared by adding 1.6 g of OPT to one liter of 0.4 M boric acid and then adjusting the pH to 8 with potassium hydroxide. Mercaptoethanol (2.0 ml/l) was added to this solution to retard oxidation (coloration) and prolong the useful life to the reagent. We found this OPT solution useful for 12 hr with an increase in the lower limit of histamine detection after this period.

Methods. Total cotton dust was collected in a mill processing 100% cotton from the V-cell of the vacuum air-cleaning system. This dust had a wide particle size distribution. The $\leq$ 20 µm, or respirable, fraction was separated by sonic sifter methods previously described (14). Cotton plants surveyed for histamine content were Stoneville 213 variety. Frost-killed plants were used to simulate conditions found in dust generated from a cotton bale. Plants were divided, by hand, into bracts, leaves, stems, roots, and fiber. The total of each part was combined and ground in a Wiley-Mill (20 mesh screen) with an equal weight of dry ice. A three-gram portion of each sample was placed in a 100 ml tube and extracted serially three times with 30 ml of deionized water. A Tissuemizer was used to homogenize the sample for 5 min with careful filtering between extractions. The three filtrates were combined to yield approximately 90 ml with the exact volume recorded.

Plant extracts were analyzed directly and after passing through a C_{18} Waters Assoc. Sep-Pak as a clean-up procedure. Each Sep-Pak was activated by washing with 2 ml of acetonitrile.

Two ml of aqueous extract followed and the eluent discarded. Two additional ml of the plant extract were then passed through the Sep-Pak and retained for HPLC analysis. Histamine is not retained on the C_{18} packing and will always remain in the liquid fraction.

HPLC analysis was performed on 20-50 µl of these extracts with the volume of injection dependent upon the concentration of histamine. Each histamine value represents the mean of three trials to obtain a determination with a 95% confidence level. The flow rate for all determinations was 6 ml/min and peak height was used for quantification.

Results and Discussions

Detection of Histamine. Histamine has a fairly strong absorption band at 209 nm and a number of detectors are commercially available to monitor in this region, problems exist with this approach. First, solvent purity must be monitored closely for contaminants which absorb in this region. Second, some natural occurrences of histamine in cotton dust (5,6) have been reported as low as 4 µg/g. This is approaching the lower edge of of uv sensitivity when this amount is dissolved in the extraction solvent. Third, most plant extracts have many compounds that absorb in this region making resolution of the histamine impossible.

Fluorescence detection was selected to increase sensitivity and selectivity. Histamine has no natural fluorescence and a post-column derivatization with OPT was found to be facile. The OPT reaction with histamine or any primary amine will only occur in an alkaline medium. The derivatization reagent, pumped into the system after the mixture has been separated on the column, must be strongly basic to neutralize the acid in the mobile phase. The structure of the OPT adduct has been found to be dependent upon the pH at which the reaction is carried out as well as the solvent system (15).

The response of the fluorescence generated by the post-column derivatization of histamine with OPT as a function of the peak height is shown in Figure 1. The curve is linear between 0.01 and 0.1 µg of histamine, correlation coefficient = .9986. The volume of injections were adjusted so the concentration of histamine would fall within the linear range of this curve.

HPLC Separation of Histamine. There are three possibilities for separation of histamine by HPLC; normal phase on silica, reversed phase on a bonded silica column, or an ion-exchange separation. Perini (16) demonstrated that a cation-exchange separation is possible, but the analysis time was lengthy for examination of histamine in animal biofluids (70 min). Histamine is freely soluble in water, is slightly soluble in hot chloroform, and is insoluble in less polar solvents, making a

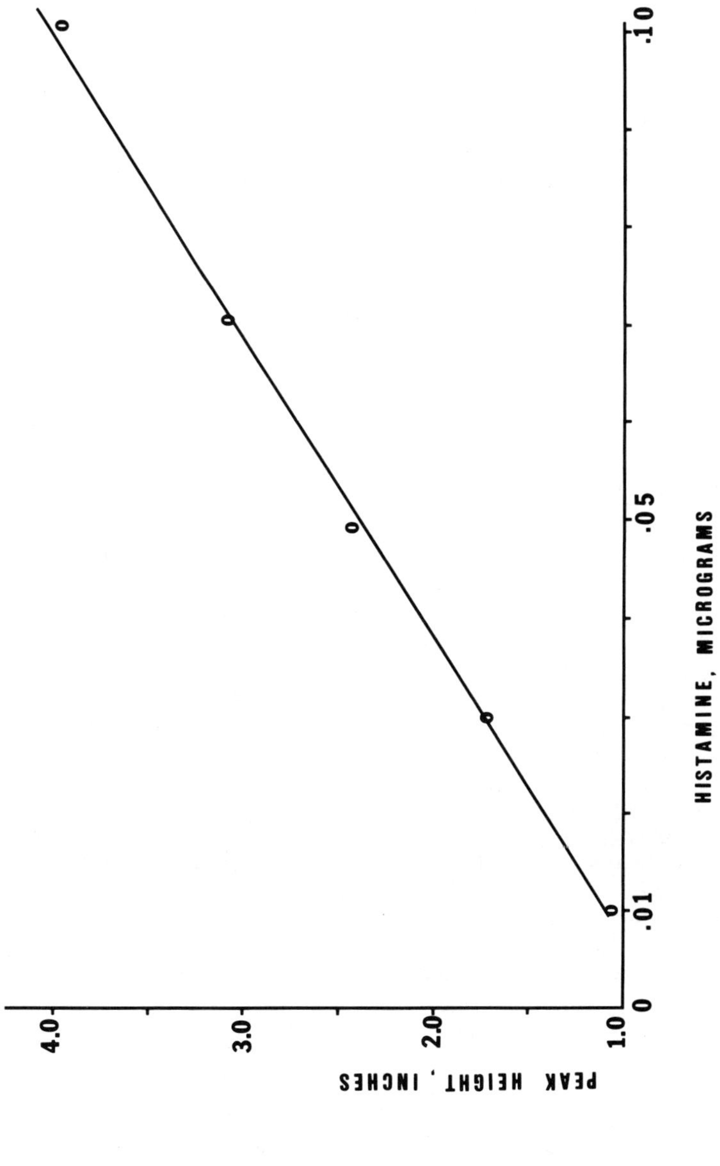

Figure 1. Histamine response, post-column derivatization with OPT.

normal phase separation on silica unlikely. A reversed phase separation is most plausible and water mobile phases would simplify the clean-up procedure for aqueous extracts before anaylsis.

Examination of histamine's structure (Figure 2) reveals its multiple ionization possibilities. The approach to separating ionizable compounds in water mobile phases is to operate with the compound completely in the ionic form, completely in the molecular form, or at some fixed degree of ionization. Ionization is controlled through buffering the mobile phase. Generally, phosphate buffers are used to achieve the desired degree of ionization. However, phosphates can cause deterioration of the stainless steel in the instrument upon prolonged use. Forcing the histamine completely into the ionic form by the addition of a strong mineral acid, H_2SO_4, to the mobile phase was the alternate approach selected.

The pH of a buffered mobile phase is significant not only because retention of ionizable compounds is dependent upon pH but because bonded phase columns are made via an acid catalyzed reaction. Manufacturers' recommendations are to avoid any system with a pH lower than 2 or accept the risk of reversing the bonding reaction. However, the effective pH experienced by a column in a water:organic mixture is difficult to predict. We have operated at a pH of 1.5 in this laboratory with no adverse effects to the column, but exercise the simple precaution of not allowing the acidic mobile phase to remain on the column overnight or static for long periods of time (1 hr). We have particularly noticed that the CN column is stable at low pH's. The upper limit of acid strength to avoid column damage is about 0.1% by volume (17).

The pKa of the imidazole ring is near 6 (16) so histamine would only exist as an ion in the acidic (pH = 2-3) mobile phase. One would predict no retention on a bonded phase column under this condition; however, it does occur. Figure 3 is the simplest way to account for this retention. Here, the mineral acid acts as the counter-ion, as well as the buffer. All of the histamine in the mobile phase is in the ionic form and is in equilibrium with the ion-pair which is only soluble in the stationary phase chemically bonded to silica. Histamine only elutes in the ionic form and is then derivatized for detection. A sharp peak in the chromatogram with good shape and no change in retention time with variation in sample concentration indicates a working system. However, if the paired ion has some solubility in the mobile phase, peak tailing occurs.

This ion-pair system was still hydrophylic in nature and with a C_8 or C_{18} column peak tailing was extremely severe (Figure 4). Generally, adjustments in the water organic ratios will not improve this condition. It can be corrected by increasing the concentration of the counter-ion in the mobile phase, but, in this case, adding more counter-ion would increase the acid

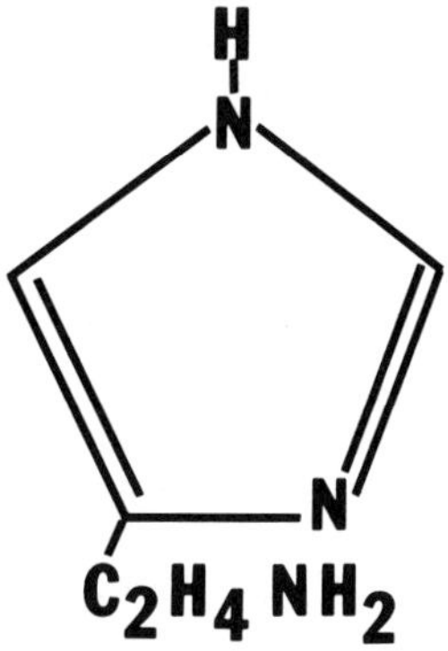

Figure 2. Histamine, UV max, 209 nm.

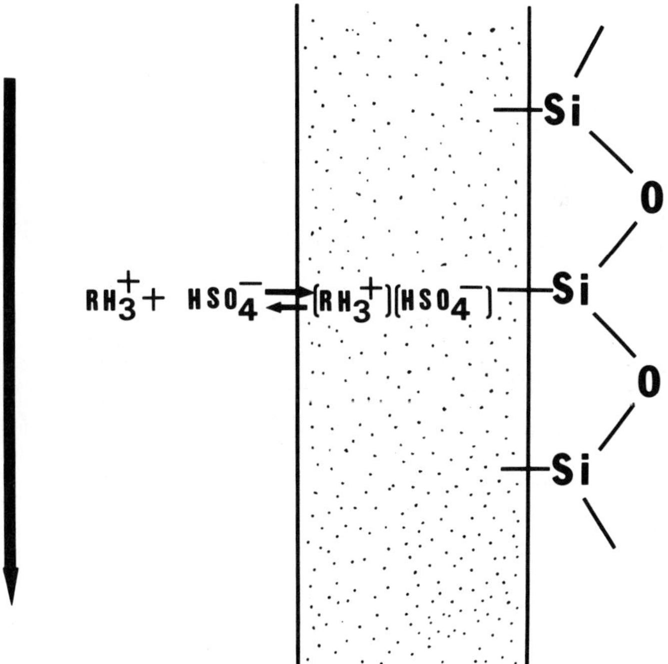

Figure 3. Ion-pairing retention mechanism.

strength. The only other possibility was to change the polarity of the bonded phase; therefore, a CN column with equivalent polarity as silica itself was chosen and tailing eliminated as demonstrated by the peak shapes in Figure 4. Using the CN column and an eluent of 25:75 acetonitrile:water with 0.035% sulfuric acid (v:v:v), good peak shapes were obtained with no change in retention time with variation in sample concentration.

Figure 5 represents a typical chromatogram with histamine eluting as the last major peak. The flow rate was 6 ml/min with t_0 at 0.5 minutes. Histamine has a k' of 4.4. Some of the initial peaks are fluorescent compounds as well as some other amines. UV detection at various wavelengths showed no compounds eluting past 6 min. UV detection was unsuitable for histamine due to interfering compounds absorbing from 200 to 240 nm.

Histamine Extraction. Some secondary plant metabolites are very difficult to extract from their natural matrix and require lengthly soxhlet extractions. Complete histamine extraction was relatively simple. The HPLC separation was used to design a technique to confirm a complete extraction. The histamine peaks from three serial extractions on the same 3 grams of cotton plant leaves are shown in Figure 6. Post-column fluorescence detection of the fourth extraction showed only the slightest response even at the highest detector amplitude. Three extractions accounted for from 95% to 99% of the histamine content. The plant residues from these extractions yielded no additional histamine after standing at ambient conditions for two weeks.

Histamine Content. Values for histamine in cotton dust and some related material are given in Table I and the 14.7 μg/g for

TABLE I
Histamine Content

Sample	μg/g
Bracts	56.3
Gin Trash	23.2
Total Dust	14.7
$\leq$ 20 μm Dust	108.9

total dust agrees with earlier work (5,8). This dust contained about a 10% $\leq$ 20 μm fraction, so 108.9 μg/g is accurate since histamine is associated with the finer particles. The bract samples examined contained only about half as much histamine as the fine dust which is surprising because it has been established that bract and leaves are the principle contributors to the $\leq$ 20 μm fraction of cotton dust (18). Data shown in Table II explains this anomaly. The leaves of the cotton plant have 3 to 4 times

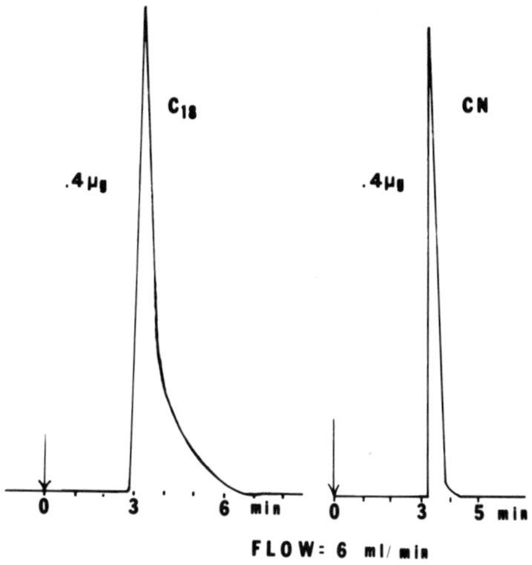

Figure 4. Histamine with OPT derivatization. H_2O/CH_3CN(75:25); .035% H_2SO_4(v); 6 mL/min.

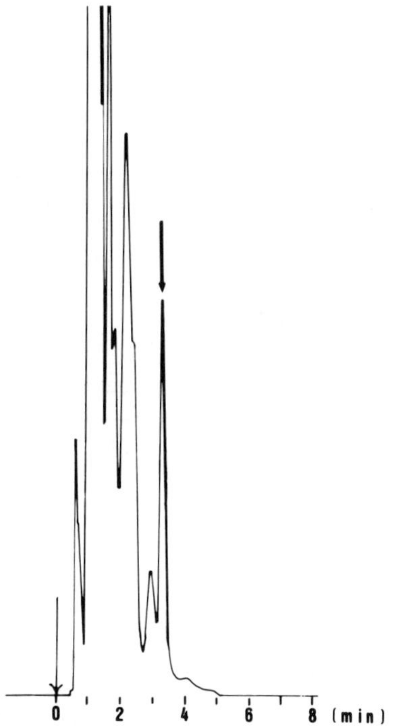

Figure 5. Histamine in cotton plant leaves, peak caused by histamine is indicated by the arrow. Key: column, radial-PAK CN; eluent, CH_3CN/H_2O(25:75);.035% H_2SO_4(v); detection, fluor., post-column with OPT; flow, 6 mL/min.

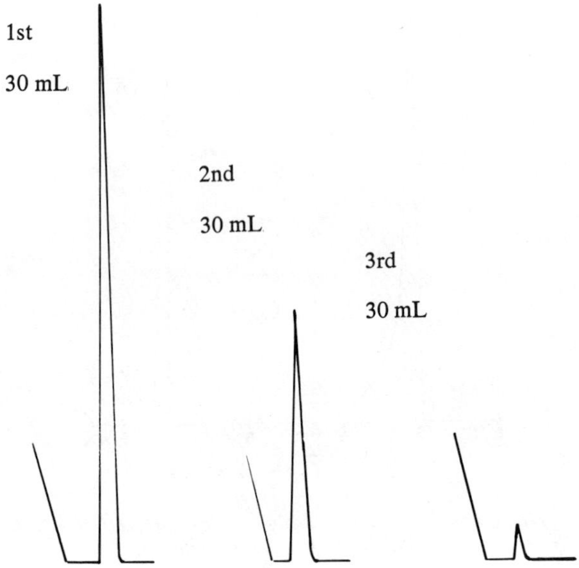

Figure 6. Water extraction efficiency. Histamine from 3g cotton plant leaves.

as much histamine as the bracts. Such difference might result from the fact that the bract is a modified leaf and provides protection for the young boll and perhaps a limited photosynthesis function. These results show that histamine is distributed

TABLE II
Histamine Distribution in the Cotton Plant

Sample	Plant No. 1 μg/g	Plant No. 2 μg/g
Bracts	48.4	74.2
Leaves	191.7	229.5
Stems	50.4	33.0
Roots	12.8	42.5
Fiber	0	0

throughout the cotton plant, except for the fiber, with a high concentration in the leaves. There should be more bracts than leaves contributing to the fine dust so around 100 μg/g in the $\leq$ 20 μm fraction is reasonable.

Conclusions

The HPLC method presented is based upon the separation of histamine itself and not a derivative of unknown structure. An ion-pair model is proposed to control retention of histamine on bonded phase columns. This method and model should be applicable to a wide range of biosystems, as well as other aqueous plant extracts. Our results determined by HPLC analysis agree closely with those obtained previously using biological methods but provide geater reproducibility and simplicity.

Disclaimer

Names of companies or commercial products are given solely for the purpose of providing specific information; their mention does not imply recommendation or endorsement by the U.S. Department of Agriculture over others not mentioned.

LITERATURE CITED

1. Windaus, A.; Vogt, W. Ber. 1907, 40, 3691-5.
2. Barger, G.; Dale, H. J. Chem. Soc. 1910, 97, 2592-5.
3. Best, C. H.; Dale, H.; Dudley, H.; Thorpe, W. J. Physiol. (London) 1927, 62, 397-417.
4. Werle, E.; Raub, A. Biochem. Z. 1948, 318, 538-53.
5. Heap, H.; Maitland, H.; MacDonald, A. "Agriculture Economics, Appendix VI"; H. M. Stationary Office: London, 1932, pp 1-96.
6. MacDonald, A.; Maitland, H. J. of Hygiene 1934, 34, 317-21.
7. Haworth, E.; MacDonald, H. J. of Hygiene 1937, 37, 234-42.
8. Bouhuys, A.; Lindell, S.; Lundin, G. Brit. Med. J. 1960, i, 324-6.
9. Shore, P. A.; Burkhalter, A.; Cohn, Jr., N. H. J. Pharmacol. Exp. Ther. 1959, 125, 182-6.
10. May, D. D.; Lyman, M.; Alberto, P.; Cheng, J. J. Allergy 1970, 46, 12-20.
11. Fornes, R. E.; Gilbert, R. D.; Battigelli, M. C. J. Environ. Sci. Health 1981, A 16 (3), 289-96.
12. Mell, Jr., L. D.; Hawkins, R. N.; Thompson, R. S. J. Liq. Chromatogr. 1979, 2(9), 1393-1406.
13. Tsuruta, Y.; Kohashi, K.; Ohkura, Y. J. Chromatogr. 1978, 146, 490-3.
14. Brown, D. F.; Berni, R. J. Tex. Res. J. 1977, 47, 152-4.
15. Bateau, C.; Duitschaver, C. L.; Ashton, G. C. J. Chromatogr. 1981, 212, 23-7.
16. Perini, F.; Sadow, J. D.; Hixson, C. V. Anal. Biochem. 1979, 94, 431-9.
17. Knox, J. H.; Jurand, J. J. Chromatogr. 1976, 125, 89-101.
18. Morey, P. R.; Am. Ind. Hyg. Assoc. J. 1979, 40, 702-8.

RECEIVED February 11, 1982.

20

Analyses of the Inorganic Content of Cotton Dust: A Review

R. E. FORNES, S. P. HERSH, and P. A. TUCKER

North Carolina State University, School of Textiles, Department of Textile Materials and Management, Raleigh, NC 27650

R. D. GILBERT

North Carolina State University, School of Textiles, Department of Textile Chemistry, Raleigh, NC 27650

Inorganics constitute a significant portion of cotton plant parts, soils and humidifier particulates which are known contaminants of dust generated by the processing of cotton. The inorganics are more easily extracted in a water medium than the organics. The lung disease byssinosis is widely considered to be induced by response to aqueous extractable components of cotton dusts which have penetrated the lower airways. Thus, complete characterization of cotton dusts is highly important in order to understand the relationship between cotton dusts and byssinosis. Samples of cotton dusts, trash, plant parts and other cotton dust contaminants and extracts of all of these have been studied by a number of investigators. A current review of these results is presented here.

Cotton dust is defined in the Federal Register (1) as "dust present during the handling or processing of cotton which may contain a mixture of substances including ground-up plant matter, fiber, bacteria, fungi, soil, pesticides, non-cotton plant matter and other contaminants which may have accumulated during the growing, harvesting and subsequent processing or storage periods." Although the inorganic fraction of cotton dust is considered by many (2-8) to contribute negligibly to the problem of byssinosis, it has been suggested by some to have possible biological significance (9-16) and it does constitute a major portion of the total dust found in a cotton processing environment (11, 15,17-21).

The OSHA standard establishes a permissible exposure limit of 200 $\mu g/m^3$ for yarn manufacturing, 750 $\mu g/m^3$ for slashing and weaving, and 500 $\mu g/m^3$ for all other processes in the cotton industry and for nontextile industries where there is exposure to cotton dust (1). The standard specifies that concentration is

0097-6156/82/0189-0313$6.00/0

to be measured with a vertical elutriator cotton dust sampler (1), or its equivalent. This instrument, which samples gravimetrically the amount of dust below approximately 15-μm aerodynamic diameter, was used in the extensive epidemiologic studies of Merchant, et al. (22), in which correlations of dust concentration with prevalence of byssinosis were made. Dusts collected by this instrument include not only particulates associated with cotton but also particulates from background air or from other sources such as solids from humidifier water. This latter source which is mostly inorganic has been noted in recent reports (23,24,25) to be the major component of cotton dust in some cases. Inorganics also constitute a portion of the plant cell components and show up as contaminants of plant parts and cotton lint. It is therefore important that the inorganic composition of cotton dust be well characterized.

Studies of the inorganics in cotton dust have incorporated the use of a wide variety of techniques. These include X-ray fluorescence spectroscopy, atomic absorption spectroscopy, electron microscopy, energy dispersive analysis of X-rays, X-ray diffraction, atomic absorption spectroscopy, neutron activation analysis and petrographic microscopy. It is necessary to use a wide array of techniques since no single technique will permit the measurement of all trace elements. Standard chemical techniques to determine the ash content of samples and of various extracts have also been used. In most of these studies the ash fraction has been considered to be a reasonably accurate measure of the inorganic content.

A major problem encountered by researchers who have attempted to characterize cotton dusts using chemical, physical or biological tests has been the choice of suitable source material. Many of the biological and chemical tests require gram quantities (sometimes kg quantities) of a sample in order to carry experiments to completion. Since a vertical elutriator sampler will collect only a few mg of dust per operating day in typical cotton processing environments (15,26), it is not practical to collect large quantities of dust samples with this instrument. Much of the work to date has been done on samples which have been relatively easy to obtain in large quantity. These include investigations of cotton plant parts, especially the bract and leaves since these are known to be major vegetable contaminants in cotton lint (27,28,29). Some workers have resorted to use of coarse trash materials collected at various stages in processing (8,15,30,31). Others have used dusts from electrostatic precipitators (11,15,26,31,32), dusts collected on filters (8,20,31,32,33) and dust collected by bubbling card room air through water (34). Brown and Berni (26) developed a novel method to separate fine dusts (in the respirable range) from cotton trash material. The dust is separated on sieves by mechanical agitation. The trash typically consists of condenser filter cake material collected by an air filtration system attached to a processing unit such as a cotton card. Samples collected by this method have been investigated extensively in recent years (17,18,19,26,30,31,35).

Analysis of Cotton Plant Dusts

Several investigations have been made of the ash contents of cotton bracts and other plant parts. Wakelyn, et al., (36) reported ash contents of seven samples of bracts ranging from 10.6% to 22.0%. One of these was a glandless variety which had a relatively low ash content (13.7%). Another of the samples was a low glanded variety and it also showed a low ash content (10.6%.). With the exception of a sample grown in Arkansas, all samples were grown in Texas. These samples were analyzed for inorganic elemental composition using X-ray fluorescence spectroscopy. For the glanded varieties (4 samples) the elements analyzed and their concentration in the sample are shown in Table I.

TABLE I

Elemental Analyses of Cotton Bracts (36)
(X-ray fluorescence)

Element	Percentage of Sample[a]	(Range)
Ti	0.001	(trace - 0.001)
Fe	0.014	(0.007 - 0.025)
Zn	0.002[b]	(0.001 - 0.004)
Cu	0.008	(0.005 - 0.015)
Si	0.55	(0.42 - 0.77)
S	1.26	(0.85 - 1.64)
Cl	1.63	(0.006 - 2.91)
K	1.88	(1.28 - 2.17)
Ca	4.22	(3.89 - 4.48)
Mg	1.34	(1.16 - 1.55)
P	1.17	(1.04 - 1.31)
Total %	12.25	(10.37 - 13.74)

[a]average of 4 samples
[b]average of 3 samples

Part of the silicon is most likely a soil contaminant on the surface of the bracts while most of the other major elements detected are known to be plant nutrients. Silicon and silicates have been detected in a number of other plant materials (37,38). The plant nutrients nitrogen, phosphorous and potassium have been reported as a function of the maturity of cotton plants (39).

Bract samples from 14 locations were investigated by others over a three year period (15,21). The average ash content of these samples was 18.0% (see Table II). Results were reported also for cotton leaf, stem and bur. The ash content of leaf material was slightly lower than bract while the ash contents of stem and bur were substantially lower. The bract and leaf materials have a much higher surface to volume ratio and it follows that surface soil contamination would likely be higher for bracts and leaves than for stem or bur. Ash contents were reported for dried aqueous extracts of these materials. The plant parts were first ground to 40 mesh in a Wiley Mill, mixed in a ratio of 1 g sample/10 ml distilled H_2O, extracted at room temperature for 1 hour, filtered through a coarse filter followed by filtration using a 0.45 µm pore filter and then dried in a vacuum desiccator. For all samples investigated, the ash contents of the dried extracts were significantly higher than that in the raw sample. As shown in Table II, the ash contents increased by approximately 2-fold for bract and leaf and about 5-fold for stem and bur. The authors argued that if the mechanism by which cotton dust interacts with the pulmonary function is through an aqueous extraction of material deposited in the airways, the inorganic fraction should not be ignored since it is the most readily extractable.

TABLE II

Ash Contents of Cotton Bract, Leaf, Stem, Bur, and Gin Trash Samples; and Ash Contents of the Dried Aqueous Extracts of these Samples[a] (21)

Sample Type	No.	Average ash content (range), %	No.	Average ash content of dried aqueous extracts (range), %
Bract[b]	38	18.0 (8.6-27.7)	38	36.5 (26.1-43.7)
Leaf[c]	26	16.6 (9.3-26.6)	26	35.2 (14.6-63.0)
Stem	28	7.2 (2.2-12.5)	28	33.6 (19.1-50.4)
Bur	27	7.5 (4.1-12.0)	26	37.1 (22.4-49.0)

[a]Samples were collected over 1974 and 1975 crop years. Values are the average of all samples of a given type.
[b]Includes samples collected from the 1973 crop season.
[c]A sample with ash value of 57% was omitted from average.

It was noted in the work of Mittal, et al. (21) that bract samples taken from cottons grown under arid conditions tend to have higher ash contents than those grown in regions with relatively high rainfall. It was also noted that the variation in ash contents of bracts as a function of year of harvest was about the same as the variation of ash contents between the fourteen locations in their study.

Berni and coworkers (40) used energy dispersive X-ray

techniques and X-ray fluorescence spectroscopy to investigate the elemental profiles of cotton bract, leaf, stem and bur (pericarp) materials. The objective of this work was to establish a means to identify the amount of cotton plant parts contained in bulk cotton dust samples. Results of the X-ray fluorescence analysis are shown in Table III.

TABLE III

Elemental Percentages of Cotton Plant Parts[a] (40)

Element	Leaf		Bract		Stem		Pericarp	
	Mean	S.D.[b]	Mean	S.D.	Mean	S.D.	Mean	S.D.
Ca	3.91	1.47	3.34	1.08	0.81	0.40	0.29	0.13
Mg	1.42	0.44	1.05	0.75	0.26	0.11	0.31	0.55
K	1.07	0.77	2.06	1.17	1.35	0.91	2.86	0.94
Cl	1.26	1.33	1.08	0.77	0.64	0.60	0.68	0.49
S	1.12	0.50	0.98	0.38	0.20	0.11	0.30	0.07
Si	0.75	1.05	1.24	1.32	0.06	0.08	0.45	0.57
Al	0.11	0.18	0.16	0.17	0.13	0.11	0.32	0.39

[a]Determined on bulk cotton dust samples from plant parts by X-ray fluorescence, averaged over eleven samples.
[b]S.D. - Standard Deviation using all eleven parts.

Using a statistical discriminant analysis, Berni and coworkers (40) were able to use the ratio of elements to distinguish leaf and bract from stem and pericarp. However, they were unable to distinguish leaf from bract or stem from pericarp. They also noted that cotton seed hull particles had characteristics similar to stem and pericarp. Calcium was the major inorganic element detected in leaf and bract while potassium was highest in stem and pericarp. Their results were averages of plant parts from eleven fields and five geographic locations. The variations were high with coefficients of variation surpassing 100% in some cases. The fraction of the total mass accounted for by the elements analyzed was 9.5% and 9.9% for leaf and bract, respectively.

Fornes and coworkers (15) used X-ray diffraction to identify potassium chloride and potassium sulfate, both of which had been precipitated from concentrated solutions of aqueous extracts of bracts. Potassium chloride was estimated to be about 1-2% of the solids in the aqueous extracts.

Hersh and coworkers (16,41) used energy dispersive X-ray spectroscopy to identify potassium chloride precipitates from water extracts of bracts. They also identified sodium, magnesium, aluminum, silicon, iron and copper in dried aqueous extracts of bracts. No quantitative analyses were made.

Analyses of Card Room and Other Textile Mill Dusts

A number of investigators have reported proximate analyses and elemental composition of textile mill dusts and trash. Only two of these involve studies of dusts collected with an elutriator sampler (20,31). Samples from both of these studies were collected in a model card room at North Carolina State University (42). In one of these, glass fiber filters were used and the dusts were analyzed for average ash contents (see Table IV). The total ash content was about 20%. The average ash content of area samples also collected on glass filters was found to be slightly lower.

TABLE IV

Ash contents of dusts collected on fiber-glass filters[a] (31)

Sample No.	Days collected	Elutriator samples Dust collected mg	Elutriator samples Ash content %	Area samples Dust collected mg	Area samples Ash content %
1	4	2.64	27.6	1.07	30.4
2	7	4.33	26.3	3.23	22.9
3	4	1.85	23.8	1.49	19.5
4	6	2.83	12.7	2.34	18.0
5	8	3.69	10.3	3.19	7.2
	Avg.	3.07	20.1	2.26	17.6

[a]One set of samples gave a negative ash value for both the elutriator and area samples and is not included.

In the other study, X-ray fluorescence spectroscopy was used to analyze trace element concentrations by observing dusts on 37 mm diameter cellulose acetate filters (20). Twenty-three elutriator and twenty-three area samples from 10 different bales of cotton were analyzed. The average fraction of total dust accounted for by the elements analyzed was 14.4% and 7.6% for vertical elutriator and area samples, respectively. Although the variation in absolute quantity of an element was high, the relative abundance of an element was consistent for measurements within a bale. Averaged over all the samples analyzed, calcium was the most abundant element detected (3.6%), followed by silicon (2.9%), potassium (2.7%), iron (1.1%), aluminum (1.1%), sulfur (1.0%), chlorine (0.8%) and phosphorous (0.6%). Other elements detected in smaller amounts included titanium, manganese, nickel, copper, zinc, bromine, rubidium, strontium, barium, mercury and lead.

Much of the variation in absolute quantity of an element was shown to be due to variation in dust concentration. The correlation coefficients of linear regression models predicting the concentration of calcium and silicon from the vertical elutriator dust concentration were 0.89 and 0.79, respectively.

Recent reports suggest that a significant portion of the dust measured by a vertical elutriator in a card room may be due to solids in humidifier water (23,25,43). Undoubtedly, much of the inorganic matter found in the model card room dusts arises from this source.

Table V shows a typical profile of elements in dust on a vertical elutriator sample.

Brown and Berni (26) analyzed the elemental composition of four card room dusts using X-ray fluorescence spectroscopy. Two of these were from filter cake material collected in two textile mills from which fine dusts (<20 μm) were separated by mechanical agitation (sonic sifting). The third sample was from filter cake material collected in a textile mill from which dust was removed by hexane washing followed by sonification of the bath, filtration and further sonification. The fourth sample came from dust collected on an electrostatic precipitator in a model card room. Results are shown in Table VI.

Most elements present in high concentrations were present also in the elutriator filter dusts discussed above (20). The hexane and sonically separated dusts which were collected from the same mill have essentially the same elemental composition and particle size distribution.

Fornes and Gilbert (19) used neutron activation analysis (NAA) and atomic absorption spectroscopy (AA) to measure the elemental composition of sonically separated dusts from a series of washed cottons. The agreement between the two methods was rather poor. Further, the copper content of these dusts was exceptionally high indicating that the cotton or dust was probably contaminated with brass or some other agent in the washing line. However, the actual source of copper was not determined. Twenty-three elements were detected by NAA. Fourteen elements were detected by AA, ten of which were common to the NAA results. The most abundant elements detected were copper, calcium, potassium, iron, zinc, aluminum, magnesium, manganese and sodium. Arsenic was as high as 90 ppm in some cases. Other elements detected included chronium, vanadium, nickel, titanium, cerium, rhubidium, strontium, lanthanum, cobalt and cadmium. In general, the sonic dusts separated from the washed cottons had much lower contents of potassium, aluminum and calcium than the control sample (unwashed).

An interesting feature noted in the washed cotton studies was that cottons from each of the washed treatments were divided into two parts. One part was processed using an electrostatic eliminator bar on the doffer of the card and the other part without. In general, much more fine dust was separated from the

TABLE V

A Typical Profile of Elements Measured by X-Ray Fluorescence in Cotton Dust Collected by a Vertical Elutriator on a Cellulose-Ester Filter[a] (20)

Element	Concentration ± standard deviations ng/m^3	ng/cm^2	Element content expressed as the % of the total elutriator dust
Al	2317 ± 342	461 ± 68	0.72%
Si	8579 ± 469	1708 ± 93	2.65%
P	2051 ± 149	408 ± 30	0.64%
S	5411 ± 287	1077 ± 57	1.68%
Cl	11369 ± 578	2263 ± 115	3.52%
K	9897 ± 498	1970 ± 99	3.06%
Ca	17235 ± 864	3431 ± 172	5.33%
Ti	237 ± 89	45 ± 18	0.07%
V[b]	-43 ± 46	-9 ± 9	-
Cr[b]	-70 ± 28	-14 ± 6	-
Mn	117 ± 25	23 ± 5	0.04%
Fe	3067 ± 161	611 ± 32	0.95%
Co[b]	4 ± 17	1 ± 3	-
Ni	42 ± 11	8 ± 2	0.01%
Cu	949 ± 53	189 ± 11	0.29%
Zn	249 ± 20	50 ± 4	0.08%
Ga[b]	-5 ± 6	-1 ± 1	-
Ge[b]	3 ± 9	1 ± 2	-
As[b]	13 ± 9	3 ± 2	-
Se[b]	-8 ± 4	-2 ± 1	-
Br	21 ± 8	4 ± 2	0.01%
Rb	17 ± 5	3 ± 1	0.01%
Sr	125 ± 16	25 ± 3	0.04%
Cd[b]	-29 ± 14	-6 ± 3	-
Sn[b]	- 7 ± 20	-1 ± 4	-
Sb[b]	39 ± 21	8 ± 4	-
Ba	569 ± 112	113 ± 22	0.18%
W[b]	39 ± 22	8 ± 4	-
Hg	69 ± 16	14 ± 3	0.02%
Pb	36 ± 14	7 ± 3	0.01%

[a]The sample is collected on an elutriator filter. The dust was collected for 230 min. at a rate of 7.4 l/min. The mass collected was 550 μg on 8.5 cm^2 of filter surface.

[b]Indicates that the concentration is below the decision limit based on a 95% confidence level.

TABLE VI

Inorganic Composition of Particulates in Carding Dusts (by X-Ray Fluorescence) (26)

Element	Mill A (Sieving)	Mill B (Sieving)	Mill B (Hexane Bath)	Model Card Room (Electrostatic Precipitator)
Ti	0.04	0.06	0.05	0.06
Fe	0.50	0.33	0.33	0.28
Zn	0.0017	0.0005	0.0006	0.01
Cu	0.0011	-	-	0.03
Al	0.50	0.57	0.66	0.73
Si	2.48	5.81	5.14	6.72
S	0.44	0.33	0.32	0.48
Cl	0.47	0.04	0.06	0.12
K	1.55	1.38	1.41	1.59
Ca	1.85	1.72	1.53	2.23
Mg	0.72	0.74	0.78	1.00
P	1.46	1.25	1.29	1.22
Total Detected%	10.01	12.23	11.58	14.47
Total Sample Ash(%)	20.1	26.8	25.6	21.5

condenser trash when the eliminator bar was used. Further, this dust was much lower in ash content than samples used without the eliminator bar. The authors suggested that the eliminator bar reduced static charge on fine particles adhering to the cotton. These were released into the air stream and entrapped in the condenser trash. The eliminator bar probably affected plant parts and short lint fiber (linters) preferentially compared with other dust components containing high inorganic concentrations. This effect would reduce the ash content of the sonically separated trash.

Mittal, et al. reported the proximate chemical composition of a number of different samples collected in the model card room at North Carolina State University (31). Samples in this study included a coarse trash which was comprised of relatively large, mostly lint-free particulate matter that fell to the floor of the condenser filter chamber in a Pneumafil filter system (Model FCV8-3MTRK) (31). The second sample set was separated by the sonic sifting procedure from the condenser trash. Another set of samples was collected from an electrostatic precipitator located in the air conditioning return of the model card room. Results of ash analyses are shown in Table VII.

TABLE VII

Analysis of materials from the Model Card Room at North Carolina State University (31)

Component	No. of Samples	Mean Value Ash %	(Range) %	σ %
Coarse Condenser Trash				
Sample Ash	138	12.5	(6.5-34.4)	4.2
Dried H_2O Extract Ash	134	36.9	(17.2-64.9)	10.3
Sonically Separated Samples				
<20 µm, raw sample	30	37.1	(23.0-65.8)	9.3
<20 µm dried H_2O extract	4	43.5	(23.4-55.1)	14.3
20-38 µm, raw sample	30	28.9	(16.8-52.0)	8.7
20-38 µm, dried H_2O extract	5	34.4	(25.4-44.9)	7.6
Electrostatic Precipitator Dust				
Raw sample	8	41.3	(31.0-45.6)	4.9
Dried H_2O extract ash	5	58.1	(53.8-62.0)	3.8

These data show that the ash content of the dried aqueous extracts tend to be higher than the original for all three types of samples. The increase is especially high for the condenser trash samples and is quite similar to the behavior of plant parts (21). There is also a trend that as the particle size becomes smaller, the ash content increases. The ash content of the electrostatic precipitator dust was particularly high (41.3%). The authors also note that the inorganic fraction of dusts is relatively high for cottons grown under dry, arid conditions.

Hersh and coworkers (16) examined electrostatic precipitator samples using petrographic microscopy. The minerals along with their chemical formula and mode of occurrence are given in Table VIII. Kaolinite and limonite were by far the most abundant minerals detected.

Batra, Fornes and Hersh (23) recently demonstrated that a significant amount of the material captured by vertical elutriators in the model card room at North Carolina State University arises from solids generated by the evaporation of humidifier water. Table IX shows variation in dust concentrations in the card room with and without the contribution of humidifier particulates (23).

Even more dramatic changes in dust concentrations were observed in a textile mill by Roberts and coworkers (25) when regular water was replaced by distilled water in their humidifiers (see Table X).

TABLE VIII

Minerals Identified in Electrostatic Precipitator Dusts Collected in a Model Card Room (16)

Mineral	Chemical Formula	Modes of Occurrence
Kaolinite	$Al_2Si_2O_5(OH)_4$	Chiefly in impure aggregates
Limonite	$Fe_2O_3 \cdot nH_2O$	Stains, inclusions, free particles
Quartz	SiO_2	Free and locked particles
K-feldspar	$KAlSi_3O_8$	Free in kaolinite aggregates
Muscovite	$KAl_2(AlSi_3)(O_{10}(OH)_2$	Free in kaolinite aggregates
Calcite	$CaCO_3$	Free in kaolinite aggregates
Plagioclase	$(Na,Ca)Al(Al,Si)Si_2O_8$	Rare
Olivine	$(Mg,Fe)_2SiO_4$	Rare
Barite	$BaSO_4$	Rare
Biotite	$(K,H)_2(Mg,Fe)_2(Al,$-$Fe)_2(SiO_4)_3$	Rare

TABLE IX

Humidifier Effects on Dust Concentrations Measured in a Model Card Room Without Feeding Cotton to the Opening-Carding System (23)

Conditions			Sampler (concentrations in $\mu g/m^3$)					
Humidifier Operating	Lint Capture System Operating	No. of Runs	VE	[a]Area	High Volume	Cyclone <10 μm	Cyclone Total	Andersen
Yes	No	2	284	219	247	214	260	239
No	No	2	40	45	78	93	130	56
Yes	Yes	3	171	161	204	156	256	174
No	Yes	3	60	71	115	77	166	85

[a]Vertical Elutriator Cotton Dust Sampler

Similar phenomena has been observed by others (43). Thus, much of the dust measured in total or elutriated samples of cotton dusts arises from the spray drying of the humidifier water.

Fisher and coworkers (24) have investigated the solids in the card room water supply. Solids content data is given in Table XI. Water samples were taken from the card room at random intervals and 1000 ml samples were evaporated to dryness in a crucible on a hot plate. The weight of the dried solids was obtained. The sample was ignited at 550°C for 5 hr and ash

TABLE X

Dust Concentrations Measured in a Textile Mill with Vertical Elutriator Samplers as a Function of Variation in Water in Humidifier System. (25)

Test #	Operating conditions	Observed mean dust conc. mg/m^3
Test 1	Air circulation ON; Atomizers, machines OFF	71
Test 2	Air circulation, machines ON; Distilled water atomized	144
Test 3	Air circulation, machines ON; Distilled water atomized	206
Test 4	Air circulation, machines ON; Distilled water atomized	212
Test 5	Air circulation, machines ON; Regular water atomized	903
Test 6	Air circulation, machines ON; Regular water atomized	1055
Test 7	Air circulation, machines ON; Regular water atomized	1120

TABLE XI

Solids Content of Model Card Room Humidifier Water Samples (24)

Sample	(PPM)		
No.	Solids	Ash	Organic
1	111	91	20
2	139	117	22
3	107	90	17
4	103	96	7
5	133	92	41
6	91	72	19
7	99	86	13
8	103	90	13
9	139	114	25
10	132	107	25
Distilled H_2O	14	9	5

contents obtained. Most of the solids went into solution when immersed in concentrated HCl although a portion of the sample did not. Examination by scanning electron microscopy revealed that the insoluble portion was highly crystalline and energy dispersive X-ray spectroscopy (EDS) showed high concentrations of silicon and aluminum elements. These were also present in high concentration in several of the minerals identified by Hersh et al. (16).

Brown and coworkers (11) examined the effects of variety and growing location on card room dust composition. Electrostatic precipitator dust in which the bulk of the weight was based on particles less than 15 µm in diameter was investigated. Six major U.S. varieties and growing areas were analyzed. The ash content and elemental analysis by X-ray fluorescence spectroscopy of these dusts are summarized in Table XII. The samples showed high variation in ash content as a function of growing location. Those grown in arid climates tend to have high ash contents. The inorganic composition reflected soil type and minerals present in soil. The major elements detected were silicon, calcium, potassium, phosphorous, magnesium and aluminum. Those samples with very high ash contents showed correspondingly high silicon content (11.9% of the sample from Texas was silicon). Since all the samples were processed in the same card room (model card room at the USDA Cotton Quality Research Station in Clemson, SC) and since silicon is not commonly found in plant tissue, the differences are largely attributable to differences in soil contamination. All the dusts were reported to be biologically active with little difference in the activity. The authors suggest that silica and other minerals might serve as synergists in byssinosis. They further conclude that growing location affects composition more than variety.

Brown, Berni and Mitcham (17) report ash, aluminum, silicon and silica contents of four samples taken from an electrostatic precipitator in a model card room. The silica determinations were made using X-ray diffraction and IR spectroscopy. The results are shown in Table XIII. Based on these data, only a small fraction of the silicon can be attributed to silica.

Weave Room Dusts

Samples of total dust were collected at four weave room sites in each of twelve U.S. cotton textile mills (44). A high volume sampler (24 cfm) with glass fiber filters was used to collect the dusts. The loose dust was removed from the surface of the filter with a fine brush and adhering dust was removed by immersing in a sonic bath. The dusts were shown to have a high sizing content (average of 39% over the 11 samples). Surprisingly, the average ash content (13.1%) was higher than the average ash content measured in dusts collected from the card rooms of the same textile mills. The card room dusts were collected

TABLE XII

Elemental Composition of Dusts from Different Varieties and Locations (X-Ray Fluorescence Analysis) (11)

Variety and Location	Percent Element in Sample													
	Al	Si	S	Cl	K	Ca	Mg	P	Ti	Fe	Zn	Cu	Total Detected	Ash Content
SJ-1, Bakersfield, CA	0.77	8.50	0.64	0.23	2.12	2.04	1.12	1.22	0.06	0.38	0.01	0.02	17.1	24.9
Coker 310 Elloree, SC	0.44	4.25	0.44	0.16	1.36	1.66	0.77	1.25	0.12	0.24	0.02	0.04	10.7	18.4
Stoneville 7A Harlingen, TX	1.35	11.9	0.38	0.06	1.59	3.12	1.25	1.10	0.06	0.32	ND	ND	21.1	27.6
Acala 1517-70, Chamberino, NM	0.50	7.94	0.45	0.14	1.30	2.27	0.97	0.69	0.06	0.31	0.01	0.06	14.7	24.6
DPL-16, Scott, MS	0.89	4.22	0.49	0.06	1.75	1.67	0.75	1.61	0.04	0.23	0.01	0.02	11.7	15.8
Stoneville 213 Stoneville, MS	0.42	3.48	0.47	0.07	1.44	2.64	1.12	1.46	0.04	0.18	0.02	0.06	11.4	17.6

TABLE XIII

Dust Levels and Ash, Aluminum Silicon, and Silica Contents of Dusts from Model Rooms (17)

Type card room	Variety and growing area	Dust level (mg/m^3)	Percentage of sample			
			Ash	Aluminum	Silicon	Silica
Model	Pima S-4, AZ	4.32[a]	18.5	0.46	3.99	0.24
Model	Stoneville 213, MS	2.59[a]	13.6	0.14	2.59	0.49
Model	SJ-1 CA	1.99[a]	24.0	0.77	8.50	0.38
Model	Coker 310 SC	2.47[a]	16.7	0.44	4.25	0.98

[a]Vertical elutriator determinations, no dust suppression system on model card room machine.

differently from the weave room dusts, however. The authors note that the amount of ash-forming materials generally decreases during yarn preparation and that the higher average ash content in the weave room dust apparently arises from trace inorganics in some of the sizing mixes. Hatcher (45) showed that the ash content of electrostatic precipitator dusts collected in in different work areas is highest in opening and decreases successively from picking to carding and to spinning. Based on the recent reports of the contributions made by humidifier particulates to the cotton dust concentration (23,25), the presence of particles from this source may partially account for the results.

Cotton Gin Dusts

Wesley and Wall (46) and Brown and coworkers (18) collected dust samples at five cotton gins with high volume air samplers at three locations in the gin. The dust was removed from the filters in the same manner as the weave room dusts discussed above. The average ash content was 32.9%. X-ray fluorescence analyses showed that silicon was the most abundant element detected (7.69%), followed by potassium (1.82%), aluminum (1.46%), calcium (1.15%), magnesium (1.05%), phosphorous (0.52%), iron (0.45%), sulphur (0.33%) and chlorine (0.16%). The total dust was separated into a "respirable fraction" (28) by the sonic sifting procedure and analyzed as above. The ash content of the respirable fraction of gin dusts increased to 46.0%. Only the element silicon increased dramatically (from 7.69% to 22.6% of the sample weight).

Brown and coworkers (17) determined the silica content of gin dusts from Mississippi. The ratio of silica content to silicon was much higher than the corresponding ratio for cotton textile mills.

Oil Mill Dusts

Brown and coworkers (18,35) used X-ray fluorescence to analyze the elemental composition of total dusts from five cottonseed oil mills. The dusts were removed from high volume samplers by forceps followed by brushing. Samples from cleaning, delintering, hulling and baling areas were taken. A summary of the data is shown in Table XIV. Silicon is the most abundant element detected in all areas except hulling.

TABLE XIV

Elemental Composition of Dust from Cottonseed Oil Mills (18,35)

	Concentration in Total Dust, %			
Element	Cleaning Area	Delinting	Hulling	Baling
Silicon	11.9	4.99	1.37	2.96
Calcium	1.53	1.27	0.85	1.02
Potassium	0.99	1.21	1.55	1.38
Magnesium	0.97	0.85	0.75	0.81
Phosphorus	0.72	0.71	0.93	0.62
Aluminum	0.46	0.09	0.23	0.09
Avg. Ash Content	30.3	14.8	7.3	1.03

The determination of silica in samples from two of the oil mills was made by Brown, et al. (17). The silica content was much higher in the cleaning area than in any other.

Brown and coworkers (17-18,47) reported compositions of dusts from cotton compresses and warehouses. Samples were removed with the aid of a sonic bath in hexane. The compresses were in Mississippi, Southeastern and Western Texas, and New Mexico. The samples in the bale press area were high in ash content with silicon the most abundant element (up to 18.7% in one New Mexico compress sample). Compared with card room dusts, samples from compresses were high in aluminum, silicon, chlorine, iron and magnesium and relatively low in potassium, phosphorus and zinc. The ratio of silica to silicon was high also for these samples compared with textile mill dusts.

Summary

Investigations reported in the literature of the inorganic content of cotton plant parts, textile mill dusts, cotton gin dusts, oil mill dusts, and solids from card room humidifier water have been reviewed.

The cotton plant parts investigated include bract, leaf, stem and bur. The ash fraction was taken as a reasonably accurate measure of the inorganic fraction. Bract has the highest ash fraction (ca. 18%), followed by leaf (ca. 16.5%), bur (ca. 7.5%) and stem (ca. 7.2%). The ash fraction of dried aqueous extracts of each of these plant parts was ca. 35% which is considerably higher than the ash fraction of the raw samples. It was noted that high variations occur in the ash fraction of samples as a function of growing location and year of harvest. The elemental composition of these plant parts measured by X-ray fluorescence spectroscopy showed the major elements to be Ca, Mg, K, Cl, S, Si, and Al. The concentration of each of these elements is very similar for bract and leaf materials with Ca being the most abundant (3-4%). Stem and bur have similar elemental profiles but they differ considerably from bract and leaf.

Textile mill dusts investigated include samples collected using a vertical elutriator cotton dust sampler, samples of fine dust separated mechanically from carding filter cake material, samples collected on electrostatic precipitators in a card room, coarse condenser trash from a card room, and weave room dusts. The vertical elutriator samples were analyzed for ash content and with X-ray fluorescence for elemental composition. The average ash content reported was ca. 20%. The major elements detected were Ca (3.6%), Si (2.9%), K (2.7%), Fe (1.1%), Al (1.1%), S (1.0%), Cl (0.8%), and P (0.6%). Elements such as Na and Cr were also present. The ash fractions of dusts collected in the same room tend to increase as the particle size of the material collected decreases. Fine dusts separated mechanically from the condenser trash had a considerably higher ash fraction than cotton plant parts. Silicon was also appreciably higher in these dusts. Elemental analyses of electrostatic precipitator dusts were made using X-ray fluorescence and one study identified a number of minerals present using petrographic microscopy with kaolinite and limonite being present in highest concentrations.

It has been demonstrated that solids from humidifier water contribute a significant fraction of total dust in cotton processing environments. These solids are mostly inorganic. Silicon is present in high concentration in many water supplies and is also present in high concentration in many of the fine cotton dusts investigated in the literature. The active component(s) of cotton dusts which gives rise to the byssinotic response of exposed persons is generally thought to be aqueously extractable.

Although the causal agent(s) has not been determined, it is considered by most medical researchers to originate from the organic fraction of cotton dust and is probably associated with the plant part bract. If these assumptions are correct, then control of the amount of bract (or other organics) is the key to the control of byssinosis. Further, it has been shown that fine dusts and especially solids from humidifier water are especially high in organics and fine dusts are deposited into the lungs of exposed persons with high efficiency. Therefore, much of the dust reaching the lower airways are from sources that may have little to do with the problem of byssinosis. Thus, it is important to characterize cotton dust as fully as possible, to determine the levels and origins of various contributions and to remove or deactivate those components causing reaction in exposed persons.

On the other hand, the inorganic fraction has been shown to be much more readily extractable than the organic fraction in cotton plant parts and in various dusts collected in cotton processing environments. Several of these elements such as silicon and nickel have been suggested as possibly causing part of the lung problems associated with byssinosis. In any case, the inorganic composition should be fully investigated in order to determine if sufficient concentrations of these elements are present in cotton processing environments to cause any reaction or harm to exposed persons.

While much work has been done establishing a data base showing expected ranges and profiles of the inorganic compositions of a number of cotton plant parts and dusts collected in cotton textile plants, much more work is needed to establish if any of these are at concentrations which could cause health problems. Establishment of methods to predict the origins and levels of the various components of cotton dust is also important.

Literature Cited

1. Federal Register 1978, 43, 27350-418.
2. Anderson, D. P.; Anglin, M. C.; Ayer, H. E.; Carson, G. A. J. Occup. Med. 1973, 15, 302-5 .
3. Ayer, H. E. CRC Crit. Rev. Environ. Control 1971, 2, 207-41.
4. Caminita, B. H.; Baum, W. F.; Neal, P. A.; Schneiter, R., Public Health Bull. No. 297, 1947, U.S. Public Health Service, Washington, DC.
5. Harris, T. R.; Merchant, J. A.; Kilburn, K. H.; Hamilton, J. D. J. Occup. Med. 1972, 14, 199-206.
6. U.S. Dept. Health Educ. Welfare, Pub. Health Serv., Pub. No. (NIOSH) 75-18, 1974, Washington, DC.

7. Prausnitz, C., London: Medical Research Council, HMSO, 1936.
8. Roach, S. A; Schilling, R. S. F. Brit. J. Ind. Med. 1960, 17, 1-9.
9. Anonymous, "Research Advances," Natl. Inst. of Health DHEW Publication No. (NIH) 1975, 75-3, p 64.
10. Beliles, R. P. "Toxicology," Casarett, L. J.; Doull, J., Eds.; MacMillan, New York, 1975, p 459-502.
11. Brown, D. F.; McCall, E. R.; Piccolo, B.; Tripp, V. W. Am. Ind. Hyg. Assoc. J. 1977, 38, 107-15.
12. Cadle, R. D., Ed.: "Particle Size, Theory and Industrial Application;" Reinhold: New York, 1965, p 180-93.
13. Charles, J. M.; Menzel, D. B. Arch. Environ. Health 1975, 30, 314-16.
14. Dulka, J. J.; Risby, T. H. Anal. Chem. 1976, 48, 640A-53A.
15. Fornes, R. E.; Gilbert, R. D.; Sasser, P. Textile Res. J. 1976, 46, 738-42.
16. Hersh, S. P.; Rochow, T. G.; Tucker, P. A.; Farwell, F. W. Textile Res. J. 1976, 46, 743-7.
17. Brown, D. F.; Berni, R. J.; Mitcham, D. Proc. Fourth Special Session on Cotton Dust 1980, p 45-49.
18. Brown, D. F.; Wall, J. H.; Berni, R. J.; Tripp, V. W. Textile Res. J. 1978, 48, 355-61.
19. Fornes, R. E.; Gilbert, R. D. Textile Res. J. 1980, 50, 84-9.
20. Fornes, R. E.; Gilbert, R. D.; Hersh, S. P.; Dzubay, T. E. Textile Res. J. 1980, 50, 297-304.
21. Mittal, D. K.; Fornes, R. E.; Gilbert, R. D.; Sasser, P. E. Textile Res. J. 1979, 49, 364-8.
22. Merchant, J. A.; Lumsden, J. C.; Kilburn, K. H.; O'Fallon, W. M.; Ujda, J. R.; Germino, V. H.; Hamilton, J. D. J. Occup. Med. 1973, 15, 222.
23. Batra, S. K.; Fornes, R. E.; Hersh, S. P. Textile Res. J. 1980, 50, 454-5.
24. Fisher, C.; Gilbert, R. D.; Hersh, S. P.; Fornes, R. E. Proc. Fifth Special Session on Cotton Dust 1981, p 30-1.
25. Roberts, E. C.; Ross, A. J.; McKay, D. L. Textile Res. J. 1980, 50, 699-700.
26. Brown, D. F.; Berni, R. J. Textile Res. J. 1977, 47, 152-4.
27. Morey, P. R. Fourth Special Session on Cotton Dust 1980, p 67-9.
28. Morey, P. R. Am. Ind. Hyg. Assoc. J. 1979, 40, 702-8.
29. Morey, P. R.; Sasser, P. E.; Bethea, R. M.; Kopetzky, M. T. Am. Ind. Hyg. Assoc. J. 1976, 37, 407-12.
30. Fornes, R. E.; Gilbert, R. D.; Hersh, S. P. Textile Res. J. 1980, 50, 617-23.
31. Mittal, D. K.; Gilbert, R. D.; Fornes, R. E.; Hersh, S. P. Textile Res. J. 1979, 49, 389-94.

32. Fornes, R. E.; Gilbert, R. D.; Hersh, S. P. Proc. Special Session on Cotton Dust 1977, p 58-61.
33. Silverman, L.; Viles, F. J. Jr. Textile Res. J. 1950, 20, 109-22.
34. Pickard, R. H. J. Textile Institute 1930, 21, T595-T604.
35. Brown, D. F.; Piccolo, B.; Tripp, V. W.; Parnell, C. B. J. Am. Oil Chem. Soc. 1977, 54, 225-58.
36. Wakelyn, P. J.; Brown, D. F.; Greenblatt, G. A. Proc. Special Session on Cotton Dust 1977, p 52-5.
37. Gauch, H. E. Inorganic Plant Nutrition Dowden, Hutchison and Ross, Inc. Stroudsburg, PA, 1972, p 227, 294-5.
38. Jones, F. T. Microscope 1975, 23, 37-46.
39. Sabbe, W. E.; MacKenzie, A. J. "Soil Testing and Plant Analysis" Walsh, L. M., and Beaton, J. D., Eds.; Soil Society of America, Inc.: Madison, Wisconsin 1973, p 299-314.
40. Berni, R. J.; Goynes, W. R.; Pittman, R. A. Proc. Fourth Special Session on Cotton Dust 1980, p 50-3.
41. Fleming, E.; Tucker, P.; Hersh, S. 34th Ann. Proc. Electron Micros. Soc. Am., 1976, p 422-3.
42. Hersh S. P.; Fornes, R. E.; Caruolo, E. V. Cotton Dust 1975, p 376-94.
43. Schofner, F. M.; Miller, A. C. Jr.; Kreikebaum, G. "Symposium on Cotton Dust Sampling, Monitoring and Control," ASME, 1980, p 33-7.
44. Brown, D. F.; Wall, J. H.; Berni, R. J. Textile Res. J. 1979, 49, 19-25.
45. Hatcher, J. D. Cotton Dust: Proc. of a Topical Symposium 1975, p 271-83.
46. Wesley, R. A.; Wall, J. H. Am. Ind. Hyg. Assoc. J. 1978, 39, 962-9.
47. Brown, D. F.; Berni, R. J.; Cocke, J. B. Proc. Third Special Session on Cotton Dust 1979, p 40-4.

RECEIVED December 15, 1981.

INDEX

INDEX

Jacket design by Martha Sewall.
Production by Florence H. Edwards and Cynthia Hale.

Elements typeset by Service Composition Co., Baltimore, Md.
Printed and bound by Maple Press Co., York, Pa.